BATTLING THE

INNER DUMMY

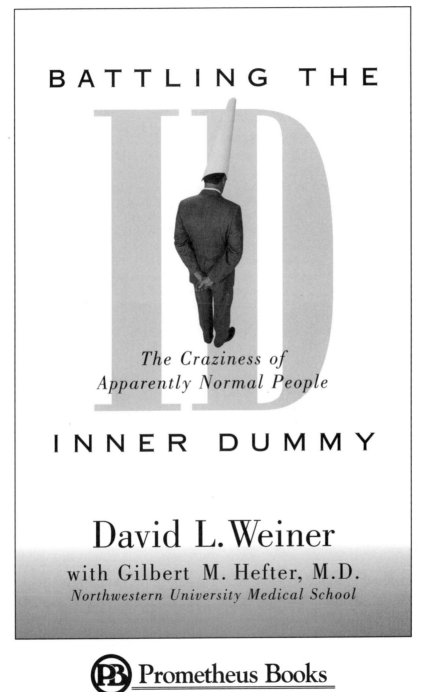

BATTLING THE

The Craziness of
Apparently Normal People

INNER DUMMY

David L. Weiner

with Gilbert M. Hefter, M.D.
Northwestern University Medical School

Prometheus Books

59 John Glenn Drive
Amherst, New York 14228-2197

Published 1999 by Prometheus Books

Inquiries should be addressed to
Prometheus Books, 59 John Glenn Drive, Amherst, New York 14228–2197.
VOICE: 716–691–0133, ext. 207. FAX: 716–564–2711.
WWW.PROMETHEUSBOOKS.COM

03 02 01 00 99   5 4 3 2 1

Library of Congress Cataloging-in-Publication Data

Weiner, David L.
    Battling the inner dummy : the craziness of apparently normal people / David L.
Weiner with Gilbert M. Hefter.
        p.   cm.
    Includes bibliographical references and index.
    ISBN 1–57392–747–3 (pbk. : alk. paper)
    1. Id (Psychology) I. Hefter, Gilbert M. II. Title.
BF175.5.I4W45   1999
154.2'2—dc21
                                                        99–34893
                                                        CIP

Printed in the United States of America on acid-free paper

To the memory of Robert M. Cox

CONTENTS

7

CONTENTS

ACKNOWLEDGMENTS

I have a lot of people to thank for assisting me in the writing of this book, in particular Dr. Gilbert M. Hefter, my professional collaborator, who offered invaluable insights as I tried to relate difficult aspects of the reference material to the drives of the id, as they are understood by professionals, who confront them on a daily basis with patients and clients.

Nanmathi Manion, who at the time of her assistance to me was studying for her doctorate in psychology at the University of Wisconsin, my alma mater, spent days and evenings at the library searching databases for materials pertinent to this book and then patiently interpreted them for me. By the time you read this, Nanmathi will probably have a "Dr." prefix before her name. Her specialized field of study was in developmental psychology.

David Amodio, another student at Wisconsin, who was also nearing completion of his doctorate, searched simultaneously in other directions and helped relate current reference texts to the concept of the id, the *Inner Dummy*. David's specialty was social neuroscience, research that examines the neurological substrates of cognition and emotion involved in social behavior, a perfect background for this book.

Professor Irwin Goldman, a specialist in genetics in Wisconsin's

Department of Horticulture, is the son of one of my oldest friends, Ted Goldman. Irwin was instrumental in referring Nanmathi and David to me.

My thanks also to Kurt Kleininger and Eva Winer of the PsycINFO User Service of the American Psychological Association, who studiously searched the vast databases covered by this service and helped direct me to key terminology that unlocked the doors. My thanks as well to Shirley Paolinelli who supervised the database searches of FIND/Svp and to Marie Dwyer who spent hours in libraries to confirm statistical and other data.

I am also grateful to Dr. Ava Carn-Watkins, assistant director of the Masters Program in Counseling Psychology at Northwestern University School of Education and Social Policy, who read the manuscript as I was completing it and thought that the structure we were creating and describing relating to the nature of the Inner Dummy might be a remindful benefit to professionals as well as to the average person curious about thoughts or actions they couldn't explain.

I would also like to thank the following who reviewed early stages of the manuscript and offered invaluable feedback: Ron Rattner; John Heilstedt; Heather McCune; Lynn Becker; Maritza Rivera; Bonnie Borgstrom; my sister Muriel Levie and her husband, Harold; and my uncle Phil Garb. My thanks as well to Lois Martyn, who is an unqualified Number Nine on the nurturance scale, kind to one and all, who read the manuscript as it progressed and told me what she didn't understand.

Then there was Larry Dore, a close friend who had retired from the corporate wars of business, who read the manuscript as I was writing and rewriting it, and gave me invaluable support.

It took a while for another friend of mine, Barry Berish, retired CEO of the Jim Beam Brands Co., and an officer of Fortune Brands, to get into the book, because as I pointed out in one of the chapters, Barry became clinically depressed only weeks following his retirement for no apparent reason. He became involved with the book in the closing days of my writing of the manuscript and relayed important information about how the book was affecting him and what more he thought I needed to do, including adding an epilogue.

Greg Schutz, who is president of a large tool company and another good friend, helped me alter the balance between the academic references and my interpretations of them.

Then there are the people who inspired me to write this book, who are admittedly candidates for the Inner Dummy Hall of Fame and admit it. They include among others, John McDonald III; Bob Schwartz; Sid Cohen, whom I write about in the book; and people like Howie Campbell, president of one of the largest distribution companies in Canada who climbed a ladder as he was moving from an old home to a gorgeous new home on a lake, to retrieve a lighting fixture with a value of less than $50, fell off the ladder, and broke his wrist. On a business ski trip with one of my oldest clients, In-Sink-Erator, Howie told me that the story wasn't quite true. But his protests came as he was arguing with a man behind the grill as to whether the french fries, costing $1.25, shouldn't come free with his grilled chicken sandwich. I told Howie I wouldn't put the story in any of the chapters, but I never mentioned the acknowledgments.

My thanks also to Donna Czukla, my long-suffering secretary of more than thirty years, who filled in whenever necessary during the writing and processing of the book and who knows the characteristics of my Inner Dummy as well as anyone.

My thanks as well to Steve Herkes, who worked long and hard to assist me with footnoting, references, and confirming other citations. My thanks also to Rick Asta, who coordinated legal matters for this book; to Dave Olsson and Frank Vallejo for helping me find a visual focus; to Mark Drespling, for helping alter the newest Web site (innerdummy.com); to Suzy Chudzik for the indexing; and to Stacy Gelman, Jennifer Jeffries, Sue Ortner, Molly Kunz, Judy Hubbard, Bud Drago, Ryan Tully, Denise Naquin, Nicole Harberts, Kenton Barello, Irene Bedzis, Melissa Levie, and others who were helpful with specific aspects of the writing, research, and the positioning. To my son, Andy, who works for Microsoft, I am grateful for some of the T-shirt ideas used in the Freud chapters, and to my other son, Barry, who in his work with the police department of a high-income Chicago suburb, understood at once the concept of an Inner Dummy.

Finally, my deepest gratitude goes to Jonathan Kurtz of Prometheus Books for his encouragement in the writing of this book. And to Steven L. Mitchell and Mary A. Read for their help in its editing.

FOREWORD

David Weiner is a talented, thoughtful, and creative man who has utilized those characteristics in the development of this unusual book. He has incorporated some of his own personal experiences from the domestic, business, and entertainment worlds into the intellectual explorations he has undertaken to produce an interesting and novel perspective on the complexities of being human. Although a "nonprofessional," David's observational skills and sensitive appreciation of the psychology of our species have allowed him to see things that professionals do not always notice. His writing offers an entertaining yet thought-provoking way of considering the problems of irrationality and how we might attempt to cope with them. The relevance of his presentation should be self-evident. We are immersed in a sea of seemingly senseless events, and repeatedly ask ourselves: "How could such and such happen?" "Why in the world did so and so do that?" "Did he or she really mean to do that?"

Although many of the manifestations of these kinds of questions are not necessarily answered in the chapters that follow, they are addressed in a cogent and often amusing manner. A broad cross-section of readers will find themselves attracted to the main theme, which is universal—there is an *Inner Dummy* in all of us.

The concept of the id formulated by Dr. Sigmund Freud was not something that Freud created out of the blue. The idea that there is something in us of which we are not fully aware is at least implicit in ancient healing rituals, philosophical systems, and theological constructs. We humans have probably been attempting to understand and master our passions and actions at least as long as we have had an inkling that other people had some relationship to ourselves. What Freud and other students of the subject in the eighteenth and particularly late nineteenth and the first half of the twentieth century did was to attempt, among many other things, to systematize the concept and ramifications of what in this book is called the *Inner Dummy*. I believe Weiner has done a fine job of articulating these qualities in a very accessible way.

He has also tried to present a range of often differing beliefs on a variety of topics related to his central subject, and has done so, I think, in a fair, reasonable, and comprehensive manner given that this is not intended as an academic textbook. When he first showed me the draft of this work, I found it to be a refreshing approach to what I had been used to reading in more formalized tomes. In the process I found myself revisiting a subject in a novel way, a subject that I had probably been taking for granted for a number of years.

As a practicing psychiatrist, I have been addressing the clinical problems associated with the behavioral consequences of limbic activity for a generation. I learned early in my education that irrational factors were important parts of the meat and potatoes of psychiatric difficulties. Mental health professionals in general direct their therapeutic efforts at enhancing the rational scope of their patients' functioning, and they often aid these efforts greatly when they help clients to understand the existence of the irrational in themselves. In a sense the task of the patient and therapist is to strive to assert (or reassert) what I call productive control by the rational self over the consequences in behavior of the emotions generated by the limbic apparatus—the goal is not to stifle the emotions themselves but to integrate them into the rational actions of the individual. At times medications are prescribed in order to further this process, but this is not always so. However, Weiner points out that the underlying factors of behavioral disturbances are at least reflected in the neuronal circuits that comprise the human brain, including its limbic components.

It is important to understand, however, that this is not a pathology text.

The phenomena that Weiner describes are everyday occurrences for all of us, and are not necessarily associated with mental illness. These brain activities are inherent, although life experiences obviously mold and modify them.

There have been numerous criticisms of Freud's psychiatric hypotheses from the moment they were originally presented. Some of them have been criticized on political, some on religious, and some on scientific grounds. The works of Freud, in general, are not the focus of this book. His development of the psychological existence of the unconscious, is however, almost embedded in much of modern psychological assumptions about human behavior. Weiner's utilization of the persona of Freud is of course a literary device—I think a rather charming one. But it also permits him to show in an uncomplicated fashion a central fact, namely, that we humans are not only what we think we are, but also what we are not always aware we are. The more we diminish what we don't know, the better off we are all likely to be.

Gilbert M. Hefter, M.D.
May 1999

[I]t assumes that a man's ego is psychologically capable of anything that is required of it, that his ego has unlimited mastery over his id. That is a mistake; and even in what are known as normal people the id cannot be controlled beyond certain limits.

Dr. Sigmund Freud, *Civilization and Its Discontents* (1930)

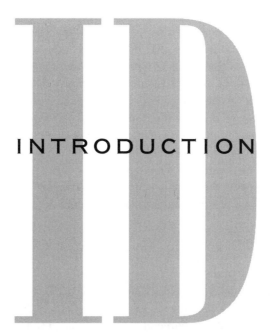

INTRODUCTION

In her 1998 book, *Reporting Live*, Lesley Stahl, a correspondent for the CBS network's *60 Minutes*, wrote about a conversation she had with retired *New York Times* journalist James Reston about the idiosyncrasies of some of the nation's presidents:

> I remarked about those presidents who, in spite of their success, hadn't felt they'd "arrived" and sat in the White House still trying "to prove something to themselves and to the world."
>
> "All these guys are beyond journalism," said Reston. "They're all psychological novels. How do you explain a guy like Nixon? He lived a life of pretense; tried to be a tough guy when he wasn't tough, tried to be vulgar when he wasn't really vulgar. The real Nixon was better than the phony Nixon, you see?"[1]

For centuries, we have observed people in all stations of life who appear apparently normal in casual conversation, but become totally irrational in outlook or actions in specific segments of their lives, and we wonder what drives them to it.

We'll wonder about a Slobodan Milosevic of Yugoslavia, who in suit and tie gazes devotedly at his wife, but believes in "ethnic cleansing," a concept that has caused the killing of tens of millions of men, women, and children in the twentieth century alone. Or we'll wonder about mothers or fathers who might be charming and delightful in their work and social lives, but behind the closed doors of their homes are incapable of giving credit to their own children for anything, belittling them instead at every opportunity and scarring for years the more vulnerable of them. Or we'll wonder about the boss, who is captivating in meetings with his or her peers and superiors, but who transforms in the presence of subordinates, acting like Godzilla on the hunt. Or the high school student who is quiet and withdrawn and kind to his parents, but one day walks into his school with a machine gun and starts blasting away.

What drives them to it? We'll wonder. We'll stare at them as we might a beautifully maintained used car we are thinking of buying, wondering what's under the hood.

Thousands of novels, plays, and motion pictures have been written around apparently normal characters who are placed in situations and settings that trigger puzzling acts of irrationality, leaving us to ponder the mysteries of human nature. To heighten the wonderment, the story lines usually offer hints about life experiences that might have driven these characters to their illogical outlooks, while reminding us of others who underwent similar experiences and came out whole.

We have yet to be presented with a completely cogent, comprehensible explanation of the side of our minds that causes these outlooks, motivating us to say and do stupid things or worse. And yet this is probably the greatest problem we have as humans occupying the planet Earth. If we could find a workable way to adjust the more serious of our irrational outlooks and modify the hatreds, jealousies, greed, paranoia, and vengeance that are among the punishing emotions triggered by them, more of us would have the opportunity to live in normal families in normal communities and in a normal world.

My objective in this book is twofold. First, I explore the underlying causes and nature of irrational, neurotic outlooks in a way that would be comprehensible to most of us. Second, I examine and describe the basic remedies that are available currently to deal with the damaging irrationalities we observe in ourselves or others.

The research for this book actually began with a previous book called *Brain Tricks*, which focused on the peculiar self-effacement qualities of the brain. It pointed out that neuroscientists have discovered that everything we remember, know, and think as humans is determined by complex, computerlike connections of neuron cells in our brains. However, while we might be told about this and all its implications and actually come to believe it, the thought doesn't get absorbed at a deeper level. Within a moment or two, most of us will begin thinking about something closer to reality, like feeding the kids.

"Okay, I agree, it's the neuron connections in my brain that make me think, not some ethereal soul source," we might say. "But where did I put the oatmeal?"

Even more puzzling is the human reaction to the fact that neuroscientists don't really know as yet how much of the mental side of our brain works, what the precise processes are. As Dr. Francis Crick, the Nobel laureate points out, one of the major problems hindering this research is that scientists can't ethically experiment with exposed, living, human brains.[2] They can experiment with animals—not a pleasant thought—but animals can't tell us how their thoughts are being affected as the process is taking place. New electronic imaging techniques are helpful in tracking such things as the coursing of blood flow in the brain as we think, but the technique is still young. As a result, as I pointed out in *Brain Tricks*, if we don't know how we think, if we don't know what the process is, then how can we be absolutely certain of anything we think we know?

"We don't know how we think? We can't be certain of anything? Well, that is surprising. Now I could swear I left the oatmeal sitting on top of the microwave."

In the second section of *Brain Tricks*, I suggested that there was a deeper level of our minds with a screen that filtered out such information. This limbic mind, I suggested, might have wired programs that work to keep us grounded to our everyday needs, and make it exceedingly difficult to reach a perspective that we are basically lost in space, time, and the mysteries of genetics, and are probably insignificant.

"Insignificant? Well, I don't think so. Amy, do you remember where the oatmeal is?"

Thus, among the characteristics of the drives of the limbic mind that I want to explore in greater detail with this book are those that could turn our minds from higher thoughts to thinking about the oatmeal in an instant. Or to cleaning out the ethnics from a neighboring province. Or to abusing our kids when we know they need support. Or to having sex with the married neighbor next door. Or to fighting to save a relationship we know is destructive for us. Surely among the thousands of books and articles relating to psychology and psychiatry, finding the documented answers would be easy. I have found, however, that the search for this documentation is extremely difficult. I have learned, as the famed evolutionary biologist Edward O. Wilson pointed out, that people know more about their automobiles than their minds.[3] What I thought would be four months of preparatory research stretched to more than a year.

In the first chapters of this book I describe the first stages of this research that works to link Dr. Sigmund Freud's metaphoric id to the limbic organs of our brain. It turns out that Dr. Freud and Dr. Joseph LeDoux, a leading authority in the field of neural science, were both seeking many of the same answers. I then describe the search for documentation of the primitive drives apparently contained in the metaphor of the limbic system and some of the interesting frustrations I encountered while dealing with the vast array of academic writings in the fields of psychology and psychiatry, even with two university psychology doctorate students, Nanmathi Manian and David Amodio, assisting me and the help of skilled specialists employed by the database search service offered by the American Psychological Association. I then point out how, with their help, I was finally able to locate the information I needed by identifying specific academic terminology that appeared to unlock the doors.

The second section of the book dissects each of the major limbic drives that are most obvious to us: power, sexuality, survival, territory, and nurturance. These drives, which are apparently instinctive, appear to be shaped by our genetics and our life experiences in combination and form a critical underpinning of our personalities. They also appear to be holdovers from a limbic brain design that was intended for primitive life in the wilderness. They apparently have never gone away. As the cerebral or thinking side of our brain evolved, it simply grew over our limbic brain. And so while these limbic, instinctive drives might have made perfect sense when we were living in caves, many of their characteristics have become totally out of place in the modern world of high technology and the arts, as useful to us today as the remaining vestiges of our tail bones. Academics now call the field of study dealing with this subject matter evolutionary psychology. There is also a field of practice called *evolutionary psychiatry*.

In subsequent chapters, I focus on how these drives appear to have their own sets of expectations and that we appear to be driven to meet them through a system of emotional rewards and punishments that, to make matters worse, has its own set of flaws. Dr. Freud originally called this system his *pleasure-unpleasure principle*. In a nutshell, we win the issue and we are rewarded with feelings of happiness and joy. We lose the issue and we are punished with feelings of depression and frustration. However, if we lose badly when our expectations are intense, the system may go awry and we might be punished with troublesome psychiatric conditions. At the opposite side of the system, if an experience gives us intense feelings of reward, we might become addicted to the experience even though it might kill us, as the repetitive use of cocaine is apt to do.

This limbic brain—the *id*—doesn't fool around and, unfortunately, it doesn't always have our real-world interests at heart. It wants its own way with primitive settings, needs, and outlooks that in some of us are more imbalanced than in others. And as Dr. Freud observed, the id is frequently impervious to reason. If you are in an elevator accident at age ten, you might still be fearful fifty years later, despite every argument and demonstration presented to you, and with which you might rationally agree.

Next, I explore what creates the intense levels of these limbic drives, which can color and even "capture" our rational outlooks. Is it genetic (nature)? Is it nurture? I quote from some of the more recent studies, particularly those dealing with twins separated at birth and reared apart. I also explore studies of trauma, which appears to be the primary device for changing the intensity of these stubborn drives when we are adults. For example, recall the stereotyped rancher most of us have seen in old western motion pictures, who has intense territorial and power drives and is obsessed with grabbing all the land around him at the expense of his neighbors, until his only son dies and he can see at last the futility of his obsession where nothing he acquires is ever going to be enough.

The last chapters deal with the remedies that currently are available to us, the "controlled traumas," or therapies that we can choose for ourselves, which might involve working with a professional. Someone doesn't always have to die, we don't always have to be involved with a serious accident, to bring us to our senses. I discovered that there are hundreds of possible remedies to protect us from punishing emotions or that work to change our outlooks or do both.

Then there is the intrusion of Dr. Freud himself. In reading popular psychology books over the years, I found that I would at times get bogged down, unable to pick up a book a day or so later, to continue reading it, as compelling as the subject matter might be. And so to offer relief and to further simplify and reinforce the subject matter, I intermittently interject chapters of a fictional plot involving Dr. Sigmund Freud brought back in time to assist a mythical advertising agency in communicating to the general public the nature of the id.

It is this agency's CEO who tells Dr. Freud that the id as a brand name for an advertising campaign "will never fly. No one will relate to it." He subsequently suggests the term "Inner Dummy" as a phrase or "sound bite the public will buy." In addition to reading books written by Dr. Freud, I read a number of his biographies, watched video of old film clips, and heard one of the only recordings ever made of his voice. I had hoped to catch his character, including his sense of humor and dry wit, as he challenges the agency's efforts to simplify his work and exploit it with such merchandising products as the Dr. Freud Inner Dummy Bathroom Scale, that always weighs eight pounds less. Of course, when this product is presented to him for his reaction, he is appalled.

When I first began to include the Dr. Freud chapters, I held my breath as I watched Dr. Gilbert M. Hefter, my professional collaborator on this book and an associate professor of clinical psychiatry, read them. I was sure he would throw the manuscript down in disgust. Instead, he began chuckling and told me it was an excellent idea. Dr. Hefter, whom I've known for many years, and whom I've admired for devoting much of his career to helping those in need, regardless of station, is an admirer of Dr. Freud, knows a lot about his career and writings, and holds a perspective of Dr. Freud's concept of the id that was of immense help in the writing of this book. He would invariably offer insights that were invaluable.

He kept saying to me, jokingly, I think, but I was never sure, "You know, my involvement with this book and my implied endorsement of your concept of the id as an Inner Dummy can cause me a lot of trouble in the professional world." And I would invariably reply, "On the other hand, look how brave this will make you appear, a professional willing to condone a bit of simplicity so the rest of us can better understand what you and your contemporaries are dealing with."

Dr. Hefter's commentary appears after many of the chapters.

NOTES

1. Lesley Stahl, *Reporting Live* (New York: Simon & Schuster, 1999), p. 385.

2. Francis H. C. Crick, *The Astonishing Hypothesis: The Scientific Search for the Soul* (New York: Macmillan, 1994), pp. 107–11.

3. Edward O. Wilson, *Consilience: The Unity of Knowledge* (New York: Knopf, 1998), p. 97.

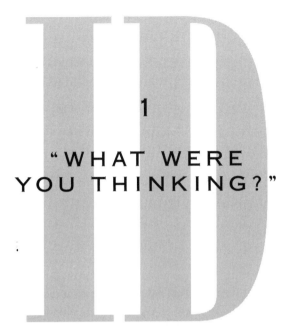

1

"WHAT WERE YOU THINKING?"

Vice officers Ernie Caldera and Terry Bennyworth of the Los Angeles Police Department followed the white BMW top-of-the-line 8 Series Sports Coupe at 1:30 A.M. as it drove along a section of Sunset Boulevard known as "Bargain Basement City" and pulled up on the comer of Courtney Avenue.

"Why is a BMW model like that stopping around here?" Caldera asked.

"Probably for the usual," Bennyworth replied.

A woman emerged from the shadows and entered the car. The vice officers followed the car as it pulled away and headed to a quiet residential street, where it stopped again. Caldera glided up and stopped behind the BMW, grabbed his flashlight, got out of the car, and waited for his partner to emerge.

As Caldera approached the rear of the BMW he thought he saw some slight motion in the backseat. He turned to Bennyworth, who with a nod indicated that he saw it as well. Caldera crouched and slowly advanced toward the car. When he reached the rear window on the driver's side, he carefully elevated his upper body and turned on his flashlight, shining it through the window. His eyes widened and he stood erect. Then with a wide grin, he turned back to Bennyworth.

"You've got to see this for yourself," he said, motioning Bennyworth over. Now they both peered through the window. What they saw was a slight, thin white man slouched down in the rear seat, looking up in shock. He had obviously been getting oral sex from an attractive, black female.

The man and woman were asked to step out of the car. They were hand-cuffed and taken to Hollywood's police headquarters, where the man was recognized as the movie star Hugh Grant. The woman was identified as a known prostitute named Devine Brown, age twenty-three. The story of the car sex and subsequent arrest quickly turned into a media frenzy.[1]

Professional and amateur psychiatrists and psychologists appearing on television had a field day. This was not only a shocker, it was a first-class puzzler. In the first place, why would Hugh Grant, with his obvious sexual charisma, even need to hire a prostitute? And second, why did he have the sexual act performed in the backseat of his car on a public street?

Grant's first television interview after the incident was with Jay Leno, host of the *Tonight* show. Leno's first question was: "Hugh, what were you thinking?" It was a question that many of us would have asked. Here, after all, was a wealthy movie star, clearly handsome, clean cut, intelligent, ener-getic, witty, and articulate, who was in a serious relationship with Elizabeth Hurley, a very attractive and erudite woman.

Grant answered the question with directness and grace, stating, in essence, that the incident was an unfortunate example of stupidity. And so our lives went on.

But the "Hugh Grant Incident" did resurrect for many of us the age-old question, "What makes apparently normal people suddenly do or say things that are obviously irrational?" We observe this kind of irrationality almost every day in news reports and in our daily lives and some of us question it almost every time.

"Why would he do some stupid thing like that?"

"What makes her behave that way?"

"I can't figure it out."

"Impossible to believe."

On the other hand, when the media report irrational acts of apparently very disturbed people, the incidents might really bother us, but we don't question why they happened. We know that deranged people can do terrible things.

This book is not about the psychotics among us, although we touch on the subject. It is about apparently normal people who display irrationalities, why they do it, and what the remedies are.

Take President Bill Clinton, for example. Here is the leader of the most powerful nation in the world; generally respected by foreign governments; and, despite a Republican-dominated Congress, apparently on his way to finishing out his second term with a flourish. He presented his intelligent wife; young, charismatic daughter; and himself to the nation as a family struggling for normalcy in the midst of an intense media spotlight. They went to church on Sundays, had Chelsea's friends over for dinner, and watched television together—in this sense Bill Clinton was apparently normal.

And then came the Monica Lewinksy affair, with the special prosecutor revealing to the general public the most intimate of sexual details, embarrassing the nation, and undoubtedly humiliating Clinton's wife and daughter. The president became the butt of crude, mean jokes, and faced the process of impeachment.

Jay Leno, who, along with David Letterman led the parade of crude humor, might have appropriately asked Clinton, "Mr. President, now with regard to Monica, just exactly what were you thinking?"

Or what are we to think of Harry Helmsley, the New York real-estate magnate, who built an empire worth billions? In his eighties he was accused of conspiring with his wife, Leona, to evade a relatively paltry sum in income taxes by deducting as business expenses the cost of furnishings and other personal items for their country estate. Purchases of products and services for personal use must be paid for with the after-tax dollars that most of us deposit in our banks. Caught by the Internal Revenue Service, Leona Helmsley was tried and sent to prison. Her husband, now deceased, and whose business reputation was previously considered impeccable, would have joined her in prison, but was let off because of poor health.

How many times have we seen apparently normal individuals and families like the Helmsleys, who have enormous wealth, go to great lengths to save a few dollars either legally or illegally and for no good reason? What drives them to it? What are they thinking?

And how many times have we read about wealthy family businesses dominated by aging patriarchs who are apparently normal but who refuse to share power, causing lawsuits that tear their families apart, pitting husbands against wives, fathers against children, brothers against sisters? Does this make sense? Isn't there enough money for all? Isn't a rational solution possible? What are they all thinking?

Or what about cult groups, like Heaven's Gate, who commit group suicide so that they can reach a new home behind a comet that is traveling by? What drives their otherwise apparently normal leaders to this kind of thinking? And what drives their adherents to follow them to the bitter end?

Or what about Charles Kuralt, the former CBS broadcaster, who appeared to be among the most apparently normal of us, as we watched him on his last series, *On the Road*? It turned out he had plenty of company on the road in the form of Patricia Shannon, who traveled with him, unknown to his wife, "Petie." Shortly after Mr. Kuralt died, Ms. Shannon surfaced, seeking 130 acres and a home Kuralt owned near Twin Bridges, Montana, which she claimed Kuralt had left her in a modification of his will.[2] How could he lead such a double life, one so different from the persona he created for public consumption? What was he thinking?

Or what about college graduates drafted by the National Basketball Association or the National Football League who demand contracts worth tens of millions of dollars and then hold out if they don't get their price? "What's going on here?" we ask ourselves. How have our athletes, entertainers, CEOs, and the like who are otherwise apparently normal people become so warped that they measure themselves by the stratospheric compensation they can command rather than on the relative importance of their jobs? Why do they become so angered if they learn a contemporary is being paid more? They know they don't really need the extra money when they are already earning millions. How many more homes can they buy? How many jets? How many dress shirts? What are they all thinking?

Or take an accountant I'm acquainted with, we'll call him Norman Stone, a placid and quiet individual, who is hard to draw out in conversation, who prefers to sit alone at business and social functions and whose role model is probably "Mr. Chips." Stone is definitely an apparently normal person. But then why does he go to violent movies, the gorier the better, and sit there mesmerized, chomping through buckets of popcorn, often staying through two or three showings of the films? Why isn't he immersed in church activities instead? What draws him to this violence, which is so out of character? And why, when he attends an occasional Chicago Bears football game, does he wear a Bears football sweatshirt and hat, paint his face, and shout profanities during tense moments? What is going through his mind? What changes him?

Don't we all know individuals who lead relatively quiet lives like Stone, but who become transformed in their cars on crowded expressways, screaming and gesturing at innocent drivers who cut into their lanes? For example, one North Carolina driver education teacher had his student driver chase down a motorist who had cut them off, and then the teacher began punching the man.

What are all of these people thinking?

Or take Adolf Hitler, who in the 1930s was considered by most Germans as a father figure, a "führer," apparently normal by most standards for politicians who fight their way into power. Today we see cable channel documentaries about his life that include film clips showing him dressed in a sport coat and tie on the sunny veranda of his country home high on a Bavarian hilltop, chatting pleasantly and politely with his guests, showing humor, nuzzling children and pets, and in other ways acting like an apparently normal person.

We can almost visualize Jay Leno with a remote television crew transported back through time, cornering the nattily dressed Hitler in his library, telling him that his actions have been causing the deaths of millions of innocent people, and asking "Adolf, you must know this is madness. Please, what are you thinking?" and then high-tailing it out before Hitler buzzed for the nearest machine gun squad.

Or what about Hitler's henchman Adolf Eichmann, who planned and carried out the extermination of millions of Jews, Gypsies, and Slavs, among others, but according to legal scholar Hannah Arendt, had been certified as normal by half a dozen psychiatrists? How could an otherwise apparently normal person do what he did? What drove him to it?

Or what about DeNeen L. Brown, a reporter for the *Washington Post*, who wrote a column about how she came home one day to find her six-month-old son in the arms of a baby-sitter, who was just doing her job? Mrs. Brown described how she flew into a rage of jealousy and subsequently sought out minuscule faults in the sitter that she could use as grounds to fire her, despite her husband's frantic efforts to bring her to her senses. Mrs. Brown described this episode as baby-sitter jealousy and pointed out that it is a relatively common affliction.[3]

What drives Mrs. Brown and others like her to it?

Or what about the British-born daughter of Pakistani immigrants, who went into hiding because her own father vowed to find her, with the help of her brother, and murder her because she left home at sixteen rather than give up her studies and accept an arranged marriage?[4] What drives an apparently normal father to turn so savagely against his own daughter?

What about mothers or fathers, who can never say anything encouraging to their children? At work or in their social lives they can be engaging or witty or display other characteristics that mark them as apparently normal, but they display another face to their children. No matter what those children attempt in their lives to make their parents proud, they are met with criticism. The torment the children feel can last through adulthood. What are these parents thinking?

It is apparent that even the most civilized among us have an inner craziness, a potential for irrationality with which we must contend. Some of us can wear a cloak of civility easily and naturally for years, but in one tense moment, we can lose control and become totally irrational. Others of us may wear the cloak of civility, but can feel drives lurking beneath the surface, ready to push us into irrational fits of anger or jealousy or envy, or into making unreasonable demands or tormenting someone in our charge. And so we work hard to control them, to keep them in check. We may question these drives. What are they? Where did we get them? But we can't find the answers or understand those we are given.

Still others of us may wear a cloak of civility with a very loose fit. Rarely a day passes when our inner craziness doesn't escape, creating agonies and anxieties among those whose actions fail to meet our expectations. In one moment we can be sweet, reasonable, comforting, and full of humor. But in an instant we can become despotic, display volcanic rages of temper, and spew out poisonous remarks. We are aware of the drives that impel our irrationality as well as our weakness in controlling them. Is there any hope for us? We are puzzled by what is going on in our minds.

Finally, there are those of us who wear a cloak of civility only as an act. The drives that propel our inner craziness are so intense they have actually captured our rationality. We view life from distorted perspectives. While we may act rationally at appropriate times, we apparently do so because these inner drives, which appear to have a warped intelligence of their own, lead us to appear rational if this helps meet their unreasoning expectations. Hitler in his early years in power would fall into this category. So would Joseph Stalin, Saddam Hussein, and to a lesser extent the Leona Helmsleys of the world. And so would millions of others who lead otherwise apparently normal lives but whose names are unknown to us.

We cannot walk up to these people, clap them on the back, and say, "Hey, you're hurting a lot of people out there. Let's go have a beer and talk about it." Their craziness has captured them. They would have no idea of what we're talking about.

Strangely enough, we appear to understand and accept people who have a severe personality disorder or who are psychotic and obviously afflicted with a serious mental illness. We also appear to understand criminals and thugs who commit violent acts. We don't like them, we try to capture and incarcerate them, but we're not puzzled by them. There have always been criminals around.

However, we are puzzled by the irrational acts of apparently normal people. If we read about the capture of a career burglar, we don't give it a second thought. But if our next door neighbor, an apparently normal person with a job and family, is caught burglarizing a home, we are puzzled. Why did he do it? What was he thinking? With a wife and family, how could he be so stupid?

Others of us will neutralize the puzzlement with authoritative statements: "It's human nature. We're not perfect, so what can you do?" Or, "It's our instincts. Some of them are good, some bad. It's the luck of the draw." Or, "There's an evil side to all of us. We all have it and we have to control it. We have to keep it in check." Or, "It's the devil. The devil got into her." Or, "It's our dark side. We all have a dark side, you know."

Some put a label on the craziness, the irrationality, to help cope with it. The Hindus call the craziness of apparently normal people *vasanass*. The Italians call it *stunad*, and the Germans *verklopfte*. The Yiddish language, spoken by Jews for centuries, contains a word for it that describes the less harmful aspects of our craziness: *mishigoss*. "Would you believe it? Allen won't come over for dinner unless he can sit at the head of the table and he's not even a relative. Such *mishigoss*." Or, "Emily is such a neatnik that early one morning her husband got up to go to the bathroom and when he got back, his side of the bed was made. Who could live with that kind of *mishigoss*?"

The inner craziness, the irrationalities we see and deal with every day have intensity levels that range from Allen's quirk about sitting at the head of the table, to Hitler's irrational penchant for power and for "cleansing" the human race according to his specifications. And yet, all of these irrational drives of otherwise apparently normal persons, regardless of their nature or intensity, appear to derive from the same basic operating system of our brains, one that most psychiatrists and psychologists have long been familiar with but which is unknown to or is beyond the understanding of most of the rest of us.

"What they were thinking," what drives apparently normal people to do strangely irrational things, becomes apparent in the following chapters.

NOTES

1. The story about Hugh Grant was recreated from varying news reports about the incident at the time it took place. Details are given in a report by Benjamin Svetkey in the July 21, 1995 issue of *Entertainment Weekly* as well as by Allan Hall and Richard Wallace in the June 28, 1995 issue of the *London Daily Mirror*, pages 1–2. The dialogue between the vice officers is fictitious.

2. Associated Press, Domestic News, January 11, 1998.

3. DeNeen L. Brown, "Monday Life," *Ottawa Citizen*, March 15, 1999, p. D10.

4. Warren Hoge, New York Times Service, "News," *International Herald Tribune*, October 20, 1997, p. 1.

2

OUR UPSTAIRS COMPUTER WAS DELIVERED TO US WITHOUT A MANUAL

In 1997, Henry and Edith Everett took back a $3 million gift they had given to the city's Children's Zoo, because they thought the plaque acknowledging the gift was too small.[1]

Did you know your brain was computerized? I didn't. About fifteen years ago I came across that fact in *The Dragons of Eden: Speculations on the Evolution of Human Intelligence* by Carl Sagan. It's been well publicized in hundreds of articles and books and on television documentaries about the mind and brain, but for the most part, this critical fact remains ignored. It is as if our brains themselves, in a peculiar phenomenon, don't want this recently found knowledge to be absorbed.

The next time you have dinner with friends, you can observe this phenomenon simply by bringing up the computerized nature of the brain as a topic of conversation. During a lull after the appetizers, say something like: "I was reading a book about the brain and I was amazed to learn that it works very similar to a computer. It turns out that even our emotions are programmed—love, guilt, hatred, trust, and all those things. Basically, as we sit here, it is our computerlike brains that are talking to one another. What do you think about this?"

The typical retort would be something like: "And how many cocktails did you have before dinner, Louise?"

In an instant, you'll note that the conversation will turn to the usual topics—restaurants, vacations, movies, politics, sports, the children, and such. Our brain/minds appear intent on keeping us focused on our own little realities.

However, gaining perspective into the inner craziness of apparently normal people requires that we know something about the computerlike nature of the brain and how it apparently evolved. So grit your teeth for two minutes of scientific detail about the brain and note for future reference that your eyes may glaze over, even for this short simplified description.

The brain uses a nerve cell called a "neuron" to perform the same task as a computer's transistor. Through the magic of chemically generated electricity, neuron cells in the course of directing our physical and mental lives are being turned "on" or "off."

The average adult brain contains somewhere between 100 billion and 300 billion neuron cells, maybe more. Until recently, most published works about the brain put the number at 100 billion, but Dr. Richard Restak, a noted neurologist and author who has written many understandable and fine books about the brain, mentioned the number 300 billion in his latest work, *The Receptors*, and who am I to argue?[2] I have difficulty keeping count for twenty-five sit-ups.

What is really mind-boggling about the brain when compared to the average personal computer is that most basic computer transistor switches are turned "on" or "off" by a single line running to them, much like the light switch on your wall. So while a computer's microprocessor might contain hundreds of millions of microscopic transistors, each of them usually receives its switching signal from only one microscopic line, coming in one side and going out another. Each neuron in our brain, on the other hand, is connected to somewhere between 10,000 and 20,000 other neurons. Instead of one line running into a neuron like a computer transistor, there are some 10,000 lines that are part of the switching mechanism, each generating electrical impulses that the individual neuron must weigh and measure to determine if it should be "on" or "off." This would be akin to turning on your computer and finding 10,000 e-mail messages, which you must pore through to determine if you should stand up or sit down. One of your little neurons has to do that instantaneously. To add two and two in your head, probably hundreds of millions of neurons are receiving hundreds of trillions of inputs to help you instantaneously come up with the answer of five. Excuse me . . . four.

In addition, each neuron cell itself is a vastly complicated piece of machinery. It took me almost a day of painstaking reading, technical dictionaries at hand, to understand a relatively short *Scientific American* article about the inner workings of a typical neuron. There are about 12,000 molecules in each microscopic neuron which together create the machinery that makes it work, almost as many parts as you'll find in an automobile. Each of these 12,000 parts and pieces must work almost perfectly to determine when to trigger an "on" or "off" response and do so within the context of at least 100 billion other neuron cells, each the working equivalent of an automobile.

I will spare you further mind-boggling brain detail, which can go on for thousands of pages, fact after eye-glazing fact. But there is one embarrassment. While science has done a remarkable job in uncovering the physical workings of our brain so that, among other things, surgeons can operate to remove tumors and such, scientists still haven't figured out how the brain's software works, primarily its mental software. In other words, we don't know much of what is going on in our heads that allows us to do such things as think, hate, love, and make judgments.

Dr. Gerald M. Edelman, a widely known and highly publicized neurobiologist, stated in an interview in the *New Yorker* magazine that it is "not even wrong to call a brain a computer." It is beyond a computer, he contends. "It is something more akin to a complex ecology like a jungle."[3] My understanding of his point is that while a personal computer will create the letter "A" on your screen every time in the same way, with the same transistors being "on" or "off," the brain might do it differently each time.

He points out that even in a relatively simple command "like seeing a spoon, not a fork—there are more than 20 major locations in the brain that have to do with that field." In other words, we have an organism in our head that in the process of allowing us to recognize a spoon, or adding two and two, is creating flashing, electrical connections that might enervate whole segments of the brain, maybe even all of it, in a way that is far different than the relatively simple connective process a personal computer would use to calculate the same sum.

And while the brain is working to add two and two, it is simultaneously allowing us to see, hear, smell, and feel what is about us; focus all of it into a seamless, aware consciousness; and at the same time control our heartbeat, liver function, blood pressure, and physical coordination that allows us to run and jump. All of this is contained in an organ that is barely three pounds.

The upshot of all this is that while most of the authority figures in the world have read something about the brain/mind and its makeup, very little really sinks in for them. Like most of the rest of us, they have been apparently misled by the unassuming nature of the brain/mind.

It is rare that you find anyone who has found great success giving the credit to his or her brain. "It's a gift," the humblest among us might say. The point is our brains are not up there sending a message to the arrogant among us to the effect: "Hey, get off of it, you didn't have much to do with anything. I'm the one working my tail off up here, writing, directing, producing, researching, creating, hitting baseballs, managing. All you're doing is acting out my script."

Just visualize the hundreds of millions of volumes of books in the world's libraries written by or describing authoritative figures who lived before 1950 and never knew that our mental faculties, including our powers of reasoning, observation, and memory are shaped by the genetic coding that creates the brain's computerlike structure. This incalculably valuable information was not handed automatically to us by a higher being as we evolved into thinking creatures. Rather, humans, with an aptitude for science, had to dig the information out through years of painstaking research, which needed to widen with exponential leaps before we even had our first clues.

Unbelievably, this enormously complex computer in our skulls, which science has described as the most complicated object yet found in the known universe, came delivered to us without an operating manual. In a nutshell, neuroscience has been trying to create such a manual. The mental section might require thousands of pages, and from what I can gather, we've probably only learned enough to fill the first few chapters, even though most of us think we are much farther along.

As one result, we are not easily convinced that our emotions, drives, and feelings, whether rational or not, are the result of something physical, the computerlike operating systems of our brains. Many of us believe that our mental consciousness and faculties are the result of a soul force that we inherit at birth and which determines who and what we are, including how we think and the level of our intelligence.

My oldest friend, Ron Rattner, whom I've known since we were both five (our birthdays are a week apart), became a student of spirituality and a self-declared, born-again Hindu, after many mystical experiences at the time of a painful divorce about twenty years ago. Eventually he gave up a prolific corporate law practice to devote full time to meditation and a life of spirituality. During the writing of my first book, which had to do with the trickery of the brain, I recall vividly a conversation we had about the view of neuroscience that our brains are the all-encompassing force and in full control of our mental faculties.

Ron, or Rosik, which is his Hindu name, argued on behalf of the spiritual belief of reincarnation, which in a nutshell means that a soul force, which has already been through endless lives, enters our bodies at birth and takes over. When we die, this soul force leaves our human remains and reenters a spiritual habitation to await its next assignment.

I pointed out to Rosik that I had read a number of books about physical diseases and maladies of the brain such as strokes, and that these will affect dramatically how we think and act. "We have all seen some of the strongest people we've known reduced to mental vegetables after a severe stroke," I said. "We have seen those who are significantly retarded because of a brain malady unable to get beyond a first-grade level of education." And then I went on naming brain-related disorders of people who lost all their short-term memory, or all memory, or who say or see everything backwards, or have other distortions. Rosik listened patiently.

"How can you disagree with this?" I continued. "You've seen examples of it. We all have."

"I didn't say I disagreed," he replied.

"So then, how can you resolve the issue of the computerized brain with the theory of spirituality and the soul force?"

"It's simple," he said. "The soul force is in there. It is the same as it was at birth. It just has to contend with a brain that is impaired or injured in some way. This was one of its challenges for this specific life cycle. There was something that had to be learned to make it better for future lives and an impaired brain was a teacher."

Rosik's point is not rationally arguable. While spiritualists claim to have answers to the secrets of life, pure rationalists, those whose minds are wide open to any form of evidence, understand and appreciate their own limited knowledge. They know that basically anything is possible. And so if you believe in a soul force and it gives you comfort, then you should know that there can be no enlightened argument against it.

Whether a soul is occupying our bodies or not, we still have to contend with the brain we were given and which the soul presumably occupies.

While we are only just starting to understand how the mental software of our brains work, neuroscientists have a pretty good idea of how our sensory mechanisms of sight, sound, smell, taste, and touch work even though they don't know how and where these mechanisms come together to contribute to our total consciousness. As Francis Crick and other scientists have pointed out, they aren't allowed to tinker seriously with living human brains. You can't ask a dead brain how its consciousness is being altered when you are probing around in it. Nobody is home.

But one thing that science appears convinced of is that the brain/mind, with its ability to create consciousness, is an organism that had humble beginnings and *evolved* into what it has become today and will probably continue to evolve. In other words, it has been growing in our heads like a cauliflower, but over thousands of centuries.

Some academics like Dr. Paul McLean, who has been director of the Laboratory of Brain Evolution and Behavior of the National Institute of Mental Health, claim that the human brain has been evolving for approximately three million years, growing in size and complexity. This growth, Dr. McLean contends, has dramatically intensified during the past 250,000 years, but it was not proportional. The growth occurred predominantly in new layers of cells that form our cerebral cortex, the brain area which processes our ability to think, reason, create, communicate through language, and be rationally aware of ourselves. These are the attributes of intelligence that moved us far beyond other higher animals such as chimpanzees, which live in close-knit families as we do, cuddle and care for their young, exhibit frustrations and jealousies, enjoy playing and romping, but which are apparently unaware of the nature of their existence and can't write an opera.

In his book, *A Triune Concept of the Brain and Behavior*, Dr. McLean describes how the structure of the brain is divided into three areas called *reptilian*, *limbic*, and *cerebral*.[4] He describes the reptilian area of the brain as being located at the very base of the brain, near the stem. Our reptilian brain is basically all we had when we were still slithering around in the wilds. It provided us with only the most basic of instinctive reactions. The limbic system was a later evolvement of the brain, which Dr. McLean contends *grew right over* the reptilian brain. The limbic system appeared to create most of the drives and emotions we share with the higher animals. If you've ever had a dog as a pet or have one now, you are basically observing in its actions and personality the limbic system you share with it. You love your dog and you can see it love you back. If you brought a new baby home you might have observed that the dog exhibited traits of jealousy. You scolded it and you saw it slink off, tail between its hind legs, displaying guilt and remorse. If the dog lived with a single neighbor and he or she died, you could see traits of grief. In sexual matters you could observe a mating dance. If there were puppies, you could see nurturing, caring, and fierce protectiveness. As the puppies grew you could observe the power struggles and an eventual pecking order. The emotional characteristics of dogs have been chronicled beautifully in Jeffrey Moussaieff Masson's 1997 book, *Dogs Never Lie about Love.*

We also see such emotions displayed in documentaries about gorillas, chimpanzees, orangutans, baboons, tigers, wolves, and elephants, the favorites of educational cable-channel program producers. In effect we are witnessing the drives of the limbic system in a state where it is unfettered by the much more evolved human cerebral cortex, which elevates us over the higher animals in total brainpower.

Chimpanzees and humans, in fact, share 98.5 percent of DNA. Chimpanzees are the closest animal to humans with a highly social and emotionally complex nature, although gorillas and orangutans are also very close. There is even an academic movement to link chimpanzees to humans on the same genus *Homo*, making them part of the family of *Homo sapiens*.[5]

Apparently, what Jane Goodall, Dian Fossey, Birute Galdikas, and other primatologists were doing, as they spent many years observing higher animals in their natural environments and social units, was observing and reporting on the behaviors created primarily by the limbic system, unfettered, as previously stated, by the higher thinking power of a human cortex. When we read books written by these primatologists or watch documentaries about the higher animals, we become captivated, apparently because we are seeing something human in them, something of ourselves that most of us are loath to admit. We have been taught that we are really not part of this higher animal family, that we are a world apart from them, that as humans we have been given a "divinity" that firmly separates us. And so our fascination, this captivation, appears to devolve from a higher plane where we inwardly suspect our kinship. This may relate to our morbid curiosity about dead humans. We'll stare and gawk at the remains in an open casket, apparently wondering how a divine human can lie lifeless like a dead animal on the road.

The point is, however, that the higher animals are very much like us when it comes to instinctive drives and emotions. And according to Dr. McLean, this is because as our enlarged cerebral cortex developed, *it also grew over* our limbic and reptilian systems. In other words, he contends, the limbic and reptilian sections of our brain, which contained the drives and emotions we needed as humans to thrive and survive in the cruel wilderness along with other higher animals, haven't gone away. They are only hidden behind the mantle of civility, which the reasoning power and creativity of our new outer, cerebral brain allowed us to develop. Neurologist Richard Restak, in one of his first books called *The Brain ... The Last Frontier* (1979), pointed out this layered evolution of the brain and candidly summarized its consequences as manifested in human irrationality. But he quickly left the subject of irrationality to delve into other information about the brain.

If the theory of the layered brain is correct, and there are some arguments against it, as the next chapter will attest, then it is shameful that we weren't informed of this design aberration by the revelations of higher being messengers, who might have been better able to communicate the reasons for good and evil or just tell us that we still had these primitive, instinctive drives programmed in our brains.

No modern design engineer worth his or her salt would create a remarkably new computer capability and simply overlay the old operating system. Rather, the engineer would either scrap or redesign the old operating system so that it would meld with the new in a seamless computer model in which all functions are coordinated.

But whether the brain evolved in layers or not, it is apparent to science, including mental-health practitioners, that we basically have two mental operating systems in our brain, one primarily cerebral, the other primarily limbic and primitive. In a civilized world the two frequently oppose each other. The sorry part is that we haven't been told by our parents or other authority figures that as we pursue our lives, we will be contending with these sometimes conflicting brain/mind operating systems.

So it is not surprising that people like Hugh Grant who find themselves caught doing something irrational and are asked "What were you thinking?" can't even begin to explain what happened. We are now about to give him an explanation he could have used to answer Jay Leno.

NOTES

1. "Notes & News," *Ethnic News Watch* 22, no. 4: 94.
2. Richard M. Restak, *Receptors* (New York: Bantam Books, 1993), p. 91.
3. Steven Levy, "Dr. Edelman's Brain," *New Yorker*, May 2, 1994, pp. 66–68.

4. Paul MacLean, *A Triune Concept of the Brain and Behavior* (Toronto: University of Toronto Press, 1973), pp. 8–12.

5. Jim Ritter, *Chicago Sun-Times*, October 12, 1998, p. 9.

3

PRIORITY MAIL
TO THE LATE DR. FREUD

```
Memo to:      Dr. Sigmund Freud
Galaxy No.:   21,455,962.980
Galaxy Star:  64,328.920.174
Planet No.:   7
Subject:      PREPARATION FOR TRAVEL
```

Pursuant to our prior note, you are to report to Station 12 for time reinstatement and transposition. You will be synthesized molecularly upon your arrival at Earth at which time you are to comply with the instructions enclosed. Upon completion of your assignment you will be retransposed back to your current location and molecular condition.

D r. Freud stared in disbelief at the message. Of all things, he was being ordered back to earth, "for just a few days," the message said, to help some American advertising agency named Croft to communicate his concept of the id to the planet at large.

This is ridiculous, he said to himself. What good would it do? Even if the people on earth understood the concept they would probably still make no real effort to control the incendiary emotions and drives that can be unleashed by the id—hatreds, jealousies, aggressions, violence, and arrogance, just to name a few. Let them go on with their selfish, primitive games. In the end, it doesn't really matter.

And then there was the unpleasant thought of his mind being crammed back into a brain, where he himself would be exposed to all the baser emotions and drives of the id that he escaped upon death, one of the true benefits of leaving the physical domain of the human race.

The Croft Advertising Agency, he thought. Who are they? How will they twist my beloved concept of the id? And what about Chicago? I have never visited there. Will it be cold? If it is, I will undoubtedly feel it.

Ach, I have no choice, he thought. A direct order is a direct order. He headed over to the retransformation center hoping to get the entire experience over with quickly.

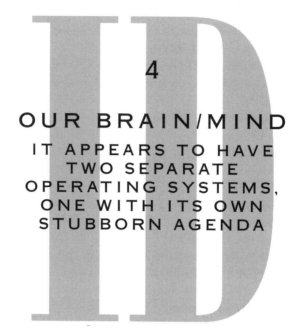

4

OUR BRAIN/MIND

IT APPEARS TO HAVE TWO SEPARATE OPERATING SYSTEMS, ONE WITH ITS OWN STUBBORN AGENDA

When Britain became involved in World War II, in 1939, the duke and duchess of Windsor were virtually living in exile, in homes in France, Spain, and Portugal. Edward VIII had been king of England, but was forced to renounce the throne when he announced his intention to marry a divorced American woman who was unacceptable to the royal establishment at the time. When war broke out, the British government asked the duke to become governor of the Bahamas. He accepted, but refused to get on the ship awaiting him until he and the duchess had their full assortment of "bed linen," which was at their home in France, behind Nazi lines. As bombs were falling on London, the duchess also requested her favorite bathing costume, which she said a courier would have no trouble recognizing since it was Nile Green.[1]

Not everyone in academia agrees with Paul McLean's concept of the triune brain. I recall watching Stephen Jay Gould, the Harvard paleontologist, in a panel discussion on a PBS television program ridicule the theory of McLean's triune concept of the brain. "Of course, the brain didn't develop in this way," he said. "Of course, there was modulation of our primitive, limbic behavior as the brain evolved." Neural science professor Joseph LeDoux, in his 1996 book, *The Emotional Brain*, called McLean's concept of the limbic system inaccurate in the sense that it appears that other parts of our brain are participants in the emotional process. He said: "Though imprecise, the limbic system term is a useful anatomical shorthand for areas located in the no-man's-land between the hypothalamus and the neocortex, the lowest and highest (in structural terms) regions of the forebrain respectively. But scientists should be precise."[2] LeDoux used most of his book to point out that the *amygdala*, an almond-sized brain member that is part of the limbic system, is the predominant controller of our emotional drives, particularly those that create fear.

Research professor Candice Pert, in her 1997 book, *Molecules of Emotion*, noted that McLean's problem was describing how much of his work was real science and "how much was metaphor."[3] By this, she apparently meant that the complexities and unknowns of the brain systems involved with emotions, including connections to the forebrain, were apparent to Dr. McLean who could simply include them in his theories of the limbic system as a metaphor, or as Le Doux put it, a "useful anatomical shorthand."

Cognitive scientist Steven Pinker's 1997 book, *How the Mind Works*, appears to agree with Stephen Jay Gould. "One problem for the triune theory," he writes "is that the forces of evolution do not just heap layers on an unchanged foundation. Natural selection has to work with what is already around, but it can *modify* what it finds." He then raises this question: "Might the software for the emotions be burned so deeply into the brain that organisms are condemned to feel as their remote ancestors did?" He answered in the negative: "The evidence says no: the emotions are easy to reprogram."[4] I read that last sentence over and over, deciding that Steven Pinker had never met my first ex-wife, Phyllis.

Daniel Goleman, author of the 1995 book *Emotional Intelligence*, agrees with LeDoux that it is the amygdala which is the primary seat of all baser emotions.[5] Then there is Susan A. Greenfield, Oxford professor of pharmacology, who in her 1997 book, *The Human Brain*, concedes that McLean's theory "might help us understand the literally mindless and uniform behavior of masses at political rallies. . . ."[6]

So it obviously isn't cut and dried that you can take McLean's theory to the bank, but I have yet to find any reference work in which the basis of our emotional system isn't attributed to the limbic area in general. And in deference to Dr. McLean, even where there is some disagreement with portions of his concept, his work is frequently described as "classical limbic theory," implying that it is at the very least a foundation for further research and thought.

As a nonacademic trying to make sense of what academics write about the mental side of the brain, I often feel like I'm observing a spectator sport. For one thing, it appears that many scientists are driven to ferocious attacks on each other, particularly when papers are published propounding some new theory. The power games and jealousies can be dumbfounding. It is the inner craziness of apparently normal people at a glorified level.

Candice Pert in her *Molecules of Emotion* alludes to the fact that her jealousies might have hurt the aspirations toward a Nobel Prize by two of her research laboratory associates, whom she thought were using too many of her ideas about opiate receptors in the brain without including her name on the application. Imagine the competition that exists when it comes to new theories and pronouncements about the mental operating systems of the brain. As previously stated, the design and operating processes of our mental software remains, for the most part, unknown to science. As a result, science still does not know the biological structure of the entity that we call consciousness or the biological process of how we think or how our memory works, although some significant strides have been made in recent years. However, those strides, in the context of all that remains unknown, only manage to get us just below the tip of the iceberg.

Every author of note I've quoted in this book or read while doing my research, admits to vast gaps of information about the brain. Scientists who inhabit the world of neural science have utilized primarily the brains of animals for their impressive studies. As a result, they, including Dr. LeDoux, admit that much of what they propound about the biological processes of the mental software of the *human* brain is hypothetical.[7]

And so, for the purposes of this book, it appears perfectly permissible to use the phrase "limbic system" as the "metaphor" or "anatomical shorthand" for the collection of brain parts in the subneocortex that harbor and control our cauldron of emotional drives and feelings, accepting that some limbic parts are more influential than others and that there are connections to other parts of the brain. And, it appears permissible to use other metaphors as well, which we will do.

We can now put the limbic system issue to rest. Let's move on to a key observation that underscores a primary reason for the inner craziness of apparently normal people: *The limbic system appears to have an agenda of its own that under certain circumstances can blind the reasoning power gen-*

erated by the neocortex and cause us to do irrational things or have irrational beliefs and attitudes.

Most of us know that our minds have separate rational and instinctive/emotional sides. But I think we all suspected that as civilized humans, not just higher animals, we have been blessed with a "divine" fusion that has created one single mind. We haven't been relating the instinctive urges we feel to any separate entity. Our mind is our mind. It is one.

For example, some of us might have felt instinctive, sexual urges at times in our lives when it made no rational sense to pursue. Perhaps we were very happily married, but met someone at a party to whom we were intensely sexually attracted and who appeared to be attracted to us. Despite the strength of the urge, we rationalized, resisted, and went home with our spouse. In this instance, it might have been beneficial for us to know that the sexual urge we felt at the party came from a separate, sexual agenda of our brain/mind's limbic system, but it would not have been crucial.

This knowledge does become crucial, however, when the intensity of our sexual or other limbic programs is so high that when they are triggered they are capable of blocking our rationality, blinding us to reason, so to speak, so that we obey the urges, even though we are still capable of "knowing" rationally that what results may be destructive to us and to others in our lives. At the time of the party, if it was our fate to have an intense, limbic sexual setting, we would have exchanged telephone numbers with the person we were attracted to and the complications would have begun, even as we might have wondered just what in the hell were we doing with our lives.

In the car one day, I heard a PBS radio report that said John F. Kennedy was allegedly asked in a private interview by a journalist why he was endangering his presidency with his frequent womanizing. His alleged reply was, "I can't help it." Whether this report was true or not, what he might have said in more literal terms was that his sexual limbic drive was so intense that his reasoning power was unable to control it.

Sigmund Freud, who died in 1939, was not privy to Dr. McLean's triune concept of a sectionalized brain, but he appeared to get close to the heart of the matter with his theory about the *id*, which is the name he gave to the brain's center of instinctual action and which he visualized as being a separate, unconscious force in the structure of our minds. Freud believed that the id has no concept of *time, awareness,* or *logic.* In other words, it can be impervious to the persuasions of what he called the *ego,* or our rational, "external conduit" (his phrase) that science believes has its basis in the brain's neocortex. And so Freud, in recognizing this separation of the rational and instinctive sides of our minds, concluded, in effect, that the instinctive or id side has its own agenda. In his book *The Ego and the Id*, Freud called the id "unyielding and obstinate."[8]

He also added the concept of the *super ego*, which he theorized as a third part of our mind that houses our morals and ideals. The ego might thus at times become the referee between the ideals of the *super ego* and the primitive drives of the *id*.

But it is Freud's concept of the id as having no sense of time, awareness, or logic, that appears to cut to the heart of why apparently normal people can harbor some type of inner craziness that can remain unchanged for years, despite changes in their lives or in the world at large that make their irrationality appear increasingly bizarre.

Someone of my acquaintance, we'll call her Sarah Reinwald, at the age of eighteen was in a terrible elevator accident. The elevator she was exiting began to slip and somehow she got caught between the door and the front wall of the shaft, which crushed her arm and leg. After almost a dozen operations, Sarah was able to resume her life. But from then on and up through today at the age of sixty, she goes to extraordinary lengths to avoid riding in an elevator. When she has no other choice but to use an elevator, she experiences intense pangs of fear.

This, then, is what Freud meant when he said the id, which apparently harbors an instinctive drive that reacts to keep us alive in emergencies, among other drives, has no sense of time, awareness, or logic. No one at all, including family, friends, and a string of therapists early on, were able to talk with Sarah rationally to resolve her fear of elevators: "Look, Sarah," we might say to her today, standing with her in the lobby of a high-rise office building and facing a bank of elevators, one of which she must take to visit her dentist on the twenty-third floor, "that accident happened to you over forty-two years ago. It is time to get over it."

"I know it is time to get over it," she will reply.

"Do you know what the odds are of that accident happening again? It is one in one billion at the least. Not only that, the elevator manufacturers have since installed safety devices that completely prevent that same type of accident from happening again. Do you understand what I'm saying?"

"Yes, I do."

"Then you must understand that what happened to you at the time of your accident was simply a matter of terrible luck. You were in the wrong place at the wrong time. You realize that, don't you?"

"Yes, I do."

"You realize that the odds of this ever happening to you again are infinite. You realize that, don't you?"

"Yes, I realize that."

"You realize that completely?"

"Yes, I do."

"So you know that if you step in an elevator car today, it is practically impossible that any harm can come to you."

"Yes, I know that."

"You definitely know that?"

"Yes, definitely."

"Well then, good. Let's get on the elevator and leave all this nonsense behind once and for all."

"Not on your life. I'm going home."

Sarah's last comment doesn't really surprise us. Most of us have observed strange fears or quirky drives—phobias and compulsions within ourselves and others that are impervious to rational dialogue. We just don't relate this illogic to a separate compartment of our minds.

We also know we have survival instincts. Let's assume that these instincts are part of what we might metaphorically call our *survival program*. Let's also visualize this survival program as being based in our limbic system, or subneocortex, or Freud's id. From this location, we can deduce that one of its primary purposes is to sense impending danger and respond instinctively with actions designed to cope with the situation and keep us alive.

As part of the sensing process, we appear to have what Daniel Goleman in *Emotional Intelligence* metaphorically called an "emotional sentinel,"[9] a *survival antenna* of sorts, that is imbedded in the vision of our consciousness. There it is, constantly on the alert for signals of impending danger, without any rational effort on our part.

Before Sarah had her elevator accident when she was eighteen, her *limbic survival program*, according to friends who knew her then, appeared to have relatively normal *settings*, to use another metaphor. She was even said to be a bit on the daredevilish side, once doing a handspring off a high-diving board as a young teenager, one friend reported, with no apparent fear at all. As the elevator from which Sarah was about to exit began to slip, we can visualize her *survival program antenna* or *sentinel* sensing an impending calamity and causing an instinctive marshaling of the forces of her entire body to cope with it.

We have all experienced the terror of an impending calamity. It is impossible for most of us to duplicate all of the feelings generated by these experiences utilizing our reasoning power alone. Try to imagine yourself plummeting downward in an elevator or being in the middle of another life-threatening situation, one you haven't experienced before. You can create the vision of the experience in your consciousness, but your survival antenna or sentinel obviously knows that it is artificial and fakery because the feelings of terror, which can permeate our entire body, aren't recreated.

Joseph LeDoux points out in *The Emotional Brain* that the instant our mind (with its sentinel on alert) senses the threat or experience of life-imperiling danger, the neural networks of the brain involved in the process of the instinctive reaction bypass the rationality of our neocortex and go directly to our limbic system, specifically our amygdala, which triggers the release of "emotional chemicals," neurotransmitters and other peptides that induce appropriate limbic responses throughout our entire body.

In Sarah's mishap, as the elevator began to slip, we can assume that her amygdala triggered the release of adrenaline and other "emotional chemicals" that caused a surge of blood to flow to her head to bring her thought processes to full alert, increased the energy and strength of her arms and legs as she began to struggle upward, and de-energized organs unneeded in the emergency, such as her stomach. The brain obviously knows instinctively when lunch can wait.

LeDoux and other neurobiologists have theorized that brain transmissions involved in life-threatening experiences are designed to bypass our rationality to save time, which makes a lot of sense. The limbic brain, the processes of which are basically identical in all higher animals, including chimpanzees, gorillas, and humans, was obviously designed for the isolation of primitive, tribal, wilderness life. If we were walking along a wilderness path and a dangerous snake slithered out, it would make sense that our limbic brain be designed for instinctive, instantaneous reaction. Even a second's delay for rational thought might be fatal.

The experiencing of an emotional trauma, such as our encounter with the snake or Sarah's elevator accident, is also the triggering point for another instinctive phenomenon that takes place in our brain, if we survive the ordeal. The experience creates what LeDoux calls an "emotional memory," or what others have called a "limbic memory." These memories also follow neural networks that bypass our rationality and base themselves in the limbic system, becoming one of those searing memories of traumatic events we don't forget. In the process, it also appears that such a memory can cause a change in the settings of the limbic program involved (there is more than one, as we'll describe later), which in the examples of the snake and Sarah's elevator accident, would be our metaphoric survival program.

Because our rationality is bypassed throughout this process, the change in the settings takes place without any conscious resolve on our part. In a sense, we have absolutely nothing to do with the result. We wake up the next morning and we are more fearful of the objects involved in the trauma than we were when we woke up the morning before.

We can also deduce that the intensity of the trauma we experience determines the intensity of the limbic memory, which then affects the level of change in the program's settings. If the snake turned out to be some harmless creature looking for food, we wouldn't be as fearful of future encounters as we would if the snake were poisonous, had actually bitten us, and we survived.

Because these settings are obviously instinctive in nature, we can apply Freud's id rule that they are *impervious to time, logic, or awareness*, and so may trigger emotional responses in the future that can be way out of proportion to any danger that may have existed because of changes in our lives or in the conditions that caused the original trauma. This would explain why Sarah remains fearful of elevators forty-two years after her accident, despite all the rational evidence that has been presented to her about new safety devices and the infinite odds of future accidents.

She sees a bank of elevators before her today and presumably her emotional sentinel triggers the limbic memory of the accident harbored by her survival program. An intense fear is then generated that has no rational basis, and which Sarah knows has no rational basis, but is helpless to do anything about. Or to put it another way, she gets it, but her id doesn't.

The settings of Sarah's survival program appear almost as mechanical as the software that creates the letter "B" in your word-processing program. Press that letter on your keyboard and the letter "B" will appear each and every time. Put Sarah in front of an elevator and even after forty-two years, a limbic fear will emerge each and every time. The difference between the letter "B" and Sarah's fear is that the fear may feel a little different each time it is triggered. Emotional feelings are not entirely robotic.

And, in accordance with Freud's rule that these instinctive drives and reactive emotions are impervious to logic, awareness, or time, there is frequently nothing that reason and persuasion alone can do to change them. Sarah has this irrational fear, and unless she can be treated successfully by a therapist, as described in chapter 32, or suffers a counterbalancing trauma, she may suffer from the fear until the day she dies.

For example, Sarah may make a rational decision, even at the age of sixty, to make an attempt to rid herself of this fear of elevators. (Frequently, according to some psychotherapists, people like Sarah are frightened of having such fears removed, thinking that the lack of fear will make them less cautious when exposed to the danger.) But if Sarah does decide to seek a remedy through cognitive therapy,* the practitioner would take her through a series of sessions, utilizing strategic, rational approaches that are designed to penetrate her limbic mind and prove to it that its fear of elevators is unfounded.

However, the human brain is not like the hard drives of computers that emanate from automated production lines. Each human brain is different. Therapists must work first to gather as much information about the individual as they can, before deciding on a strategic course of action. Sometimes the course of action they take works and sometimes it doesn't. It depends on, among many other things, Sarah's real willingness to get rid of the fear, the skills of and her relationship with the therapist, the techniques that are employed, and the intensity of the limbic memories creating the fear. Dr. Hefter points out that there are situations where therapy may not be enough to eradicate some highly intense phobias, whoever the therapist is and whatever techniques he or she might use.

Or, Sarah's fear might be cured without any conscious effort on her part, by a happenstance, counterbalancing trauma, that might go something like this: Sarah is in the lobby of the downtown office building again, on the way to see her dentist. She is waiting in a state of near terror when an elevator door opens and she sees a little girl all alone, about to emerge. Then, in horror, Sarah watches as the elevator begins to slip downward. The little girl tries to jump up and out, but all she manages to do is grasp the floor ledge with her elbows. Then the elevator doors begin to close threatening to loosen the girl's grip when Sarah jumps in, pulls the girl away from danger, and saves her as the elevator's safety devices switch in and the car comes to a safe halt. In the process of living through this *trauma*, Sarah's limbic brain (or id) somehow got the "insight" that she could deal with elevators again and so the irrational fear that she had experienced for dozens of years was neutralized, just like that. Or, without seeing a therapist or experiencing any counterbalancing trauma, or experiencing any memorable event of any sort, Sarah could wake up one day and find that her fear of elevators has mysteriously vanished. Such is the complexity and mystery of our id.

---

*The process used is usually "systematic desensitization" (see page 379).

The exploits of the traumatization, retraumatization, and untraumatization of the id or limbic brain is really the stuff of Hollywood movies. Most of us can remember movies where the lead characters needed to fight their irrational fears to fulfill some heroic act, and were then rewarded when the fears were banished. The movie *Vertigo* with James Stewart is one that comes immediately to mind. Stewart plays a character with a fear of heights, but in the end fights through it in a climb up a tall, narrow church steeple for a confrontation with a character played by Kim Novak, his costar, with whom he thought he was in love. There must be thousands of story plot lines with the same basic theme.

As we shall see, this subconscious limbic brain of ours, with its own stubborn agenda that is separate from our rationality, goes far beyond its instinctive survival role. Its plethora of programs, drives, and emotions, which can conflict with each other, literally shape the way each of us behaves. It is monumental in our lives and it is crucial that we understand it.

COMMENTARY BY DR. HEFTER

The issues presented here are fundamental ones in attempting to understand better what underlies human behavior. Although the concepts of "id," "inner force," "*élan vital*," "drives," "impulses," "urges," "desire," etc., have emerged over centuries, it is only in the twentieth century that increasingly precise connections have been made between these concepts and the anatomy and physiology of the brain itself (in earlier times, other parts of the human organism, e.g., the heart, were believed to be the locations of whatever it was that gave rise to particular feelings or behavior). The emphasis given here to the anatomic area of the brain known as the limbic region is appropriate, as long as it's kept in mind that much current thinking in the neurosciences reflects the belief that the brain as a whole, including the neocortex, has a significant role in the experiencing of emotions and the behavior that may follow from that experiencing. The association of the limbic area with the *id* is an interesting hypothesis, made particularly curious by the fact that the *id* is itself hypothetical, whatever clinical usefulness may be made of it.

NOTES

1. I saw the story about bed linen on a 1999 PBS documentary about the duke of Windsor, written by Prince Edward. The duke was Prince Edward's great-uncle. The story of the Nile Green bathing costume was in, J. Bryan III and Charles J. W. Murphy, *The Windsor Story* (New York: Morrow, 1979).

2. Joseph E. LeDoux, *The Emotional Brain: The Mysterious Underpinnings of Emotional Life* (New York: Simon & Schuster, 1996), p. 101.

3. Candice B. Pert, *Molecules of Emotion: Why You Feel the Way You Feel* (New York: Scribner, 1997), p. 134.

4. Steven Pinker, *How the Mind Works* (New York: Norton, 1997), p. 371.

5. Daniel Goleman, *Emotional Intelligence* (New York: Bantam, 1995), pp. 15–18.

6. Susan A. Greenfield, *The Human Brain* (New York: BasicBooks, 1997), p. 13.

7. LeDoux, *The Emotional Brain*, pp. 82–83.

8. Sigmund Freud, *The Ego and the Id* (New York: Norton, 1960), p. 59.

9. Goleman, *Emotional Intelligence*, p. 17.

5

IF DR. FREUD
HAD BEEN A BETTER
COMMUNICATOR . . .
WE MIGHT HAVE BEEN WAY AHEAD
OF THE GAME TODAY

The CEO of a major lawn and garden manufacturer (we'll call him Joe) was playing golf with two of his sales managers and Brian, a buyer for a huge chain retailer. Brian was responsible for purchasing more than $20 million of the company's lawn and garden power blowers and weed trimmers. After putting out on the fifth green, Joe asked Brian his score. "Five," Brian said. "I don't think so, Brian," Joe responded in a ministerial tone. "I saw you take eight strokes," and he proceeded to detail each shot, as Brian turned beet red and the two sales managers began visualizing the disappearance of the chain's business.[1]

"Dr. Freud? Please . . . Dr. Freud, we have to continue."

Freud woke from his slumber. He was sitting across the desk from a man he had never seen before.

"Continue with what, sir?" Freud asked in confusion.

"We were talking about your theories of the mind's basic structures; you told me you were assigned to return to life on earth so that you could help our advertising agency communicate your concept of the mind to the mass audience of American consumers."

"Ah, yes, excuse me. This has all been puzzling to me, to say the least.

My memory obviously slipped. Please tell me who you are and what we have been talking about. You'll have to excuse my lapses."

"No problem, doctor. I fully understand. My name is Ted Croft and I am the CEO of the Croft Advertising Agency, one of the largest independent ad agencies remaining in the United States. We received what I can only describe as a surreal communication that you would be returning to life, to work with our agency to communicate your concept of the instinctive side of the mind in all its facets."

Croft paused, smiling widely, then continued. "And you know what is really great about this? For an assignment this large we are usually in competition with many other agencies. But this was just handed to us. It's a good sign for our relationship, Dr. Freud."

"I see," Freud replied, obviously still puzzled. "And where were we in our discussion? I assume this is the first of our discussions."

"Yes it is, sir, and you were describing how the mind is basically split into three parts."

"Oh yes, of course."

"You were saying that first we have the rational part of our brain that harbors our reasoning power and intelligence."

"That is correct. It is also our conduit to the external world."

"I see . . . then you mentioned we have an inner part of the brain that contains all of our instinctive drives and reactive emotions that color our behavior, attitudes, and beliefs, and which is what our campaign is to focus on."

"Yes, and this side of our minds is basically unconscious in the sense that it is out of our conscious awareness. It is also impervious to logic, awareness, or time."

"And you said that this is the part of the mind that can cause us to act or think irrationally."

"That is essentially correct when it is strong enough to drive reason away. Pure, uncolored reasoning power would normally not cause irrationality."

"Now you also mentioned that there is a third part of our mind that acts as our moral center, being the recipient of the training, beliefs, and ideals passed along to us by our parents and other influences in our lives."

"That is also essentially correct."

"And how do you know this, Dr. Freud? What proof do you have that we have three separate parts to our mind?"

"There isn't any confirmed medical proof, of course," Freud said, now more alert and sitting up in his chair. "These are theoretical structures based on my many years of treating patients with neurotic tendencies and writing about them. You can observe for yourself the common sense logic of these three structures."

"Yes, I believe I can. And I'm sure we can get around the fact that you don't have actual proof. And for that we can thank the American public, who are more interested in a sound bite summarizing a benefit than long detail. With your concept, I imagine the benefit will be something like . . . ," Croft paused momentarily and thought, ". . . understanding and learning to shape our inner minds to further our careers and make us happier in our family and social lives."

"I don't think it's possible to summarize the benefits of this concept in one sentence," Freud replied abruptly.

"Well, let's just say that we'll work hard to create a series of benefit statements you can agree with, okay?"

"We shall see."

"Now I assume, Dr. Freud—and I apologize for not having read your books, I was a history major—that you have given names to these three parts of our mind, although the marketing hook will be on the instinctive side of your theory."

"Yes, they have names, metaphors, if you will."

"So what name have you given to this instinctive side?"

"I call it the 'id.' "

"The 'id'?" Ted Croft looked stunned. "For god's sake, what kind of name is that? What does it mean?" he asked.

"It means nothing. It is a name that was suggested to me by a Swiss doctor named Georg Groddeck, whom I met in 1917, and I thought it quite appropriate."

"Well, 'the id' is just not going to fly, I can tell you that, right now. How are we going to create a believable brand called the id? Who is going to understand it? How are consumers going to relate it to? Come on, we need to get real." Freud looked unsettled as Croft sat back and thought a moment before continuing. "Do you know what your id reminds me of?"

"Please enlighten me."

"It reminds me of OS/2."

"I'm afraid I've never heard of that."

"That's exactly my point. The OS/2 is a brand name someone at IBM, probably an engineer and not a marketer, came up with to describe the operating system for its own line of personal computers, a product you'll soon learn about. And let me tell you, IBM hammered away at that OS/2 brand name for years, spending hundreds of millions of dollars in all forms of advertising to sell it to the American public, and yet it was a marketing failure. And that's because IBM's competitor in this field, a company called Microsoft, came up with a better, more understandable branding for its product called 'Windows.' "

"Windows?"

"Yes, Windows, a name every segment of the market could relate to. The concept of Windows and its simple branding completely devastated OS/2. The point is, we don't want your id to turn into another OS/2."

"I see," Freud replied tentatively.

"It's also important because we are already thinking beyond the advertising of your brand to the merchandising."

"Merchandising? I'm afraid I don't understand."

"Videos, audiotapes, books, T-shirts, and the like. There is real opportunity there. Take the university market, for example. We could make a solid communications impact just selling T-shirts to university students. But not with this 'id' idea of yours. How many T-shirts do you think we would sell if the headline said: 'Repair our ids. Don't make war.' The students would look at that and scratch their heads. Do you get it, Dr. Freud? This name doesn't ring, it's not going to sell. The only solution is for us to give your id idea to our creative people and have them come up with something that will take off and really fly."

"Like what, if I might ask?"

"Oh, I don't know, the creatives will come up with a number of brand alternatives for us to review and then maybe we'll show the best of them to a panel of consumers to get their reactions. But let me think for a moment. Maybe we can come up with the nub of an idea right here, right now." Croft paused. "You say this id side of our mind is impervious to logic, awareness, or time?"

"Yes."

"And so it can make us do or believe in stupid things and we may not even be rationally aware of the stupidity?"

"That is correct. It senses reality, but warps it to its own vision, which may be good or bad."

"And nothing anybody can say will make any difference."

"Yes, it is impervious to logic. For example, I'm sure you have people working for your agency who believe they are much more talented than they really are and who have become arrogant and blinded to reality. In psychotherapy, we might call them narcissistic. They feel themselves to be the alphas of their worlds to whom all others should be submissive. And when they fail they blame everyone but themselves."

Croft sat back and stared at the ceiling. "Wow, you got through to me on that one," he said, sitting upright and staring intently at Freud. "This place has plenty of people like that, many of whom are absolutely brilliant, but who haven't got a clue that their power plays and arrogance are holding them back. When we talk to them about these specific issues in job reviews, they look at us like they're deaf and dumb." The ad executive stood up and began pacing around the office. "You heard me when I said 'deaf and dumb,' Dr. Freud?"

"Yes, I heard it."

"Well the instant I said it, an idea came to me like a bolt out of the blue. And it should make you happy. Here it is: Visualize this phrase like it was written on an outdoor billboard. We call your id . . . the 'Inner Dummy.' Get it? Your id is now in capital letters . . . the ID—which is now short for 'Inner Dummy.' That part of our mind which is instinctive in nature and impervious to logic. Yes . . . yes. It is our Inner Dummy, okay, and our hope is that its settings are such that it does more good for us than harm because you can't get through to it. It acts dumb because it is dumb. It doesn't get anything you say directly to it."

Croft walked to a window and began looking out. Freud looked to be in a state of shock.

"You know, the more I think of that name," Croft continued, turning back to Freud, "the more I like it. I think I can sell it to our creatives, too. And if I do, that will save us a lot of money in creative hourly charges, by the way. Just think of those university T-shirts now. Visualize them. 'Would somebody please fix my Inner Dummy before I fall in love with another idiot?' Or here's another idea, 'Would someone please tell my Inner Dummy to knock it off?' Or, 'My Inner Dummy is not the real me.' "

Croft paused, then continued. "I don't know, the headlines will take some work, but I can feel it, we're on the right track."

"I'm not quite certain that I can agree with your diminution of the concept," Freud said in a huff. "As a matter of fact, I find it totally unacceptable. It insults me and all my contemporaries."

"Please, get it out of your head for now, Dr. Freud. Don't worry about it. Let's think about it for a while. Let it stew. We'll talk about it again, tomorrow. Okay, now tell me the name you came up with for the part of our mind that is our rationality, our intelligence, and our reasoning power."

"The name I developed describes far more than that, it is our external conduit to the world, as I explained before."

"But it contains our rationality, our reasoning power."

"Yes, it does."

"Well, that's good enough. Just like your id, it's simply a matter of focusing the benefit statement. So what is the name you came up with?"

"The 'ego.' "

"The 'ego,' for god's sake."

"Yes, the 'ego,' " Freud repeated, looking hurt.

"My god, that is almost as bad as the id."

"Pardon me," Freud harrumphed, "but I thought the id was quite good, far more serious and powerful than your demeaning phrase 'Inner Dummy.' "

"Okay, okay, let's calm down here. Look, Dr. Freud, I don't know what people thought the word 'ego' meant back in the 1920s and 1930s. But today, the word implies that someone has a big head, is in love with himself or herself—'narcissistic' was the word you used, I believe. No, we have to come up with a new word and we'll have the creatives take a crack at it."

"I'm afraid your world is a bit strange to me," Freud replied, relenting. "But I have been directed to help you and I'm sure you know what you're doing."

"Thank you, sir. And now my Inner Dummy is signaling to me that I am hungry even though I had an enormous breakfast." Croft paused. "By the way, do you like Chinese? There is a place right down the street . . ."

Freud began staring vacantly out the window of Croft's office.

NOTE

1. One of my colleagues was present at the event and told this story to me.

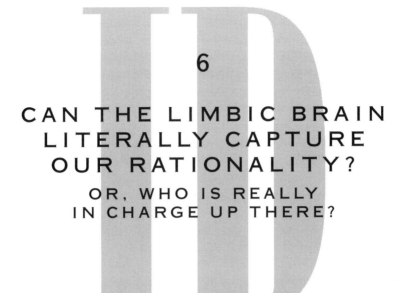

6

CAN THE LIMBIC BRAIN LITERALLY CAPTURE OUR RATIONALITY?

OR, WHO IS REALLY IN CHARGE UP THERE?

Former Labor Secretary Robert Reich wrote in his published memoir of his time in Washington that there were several incidents in which he was besieged by "the forces of evil—hostile reporters, bullying congressional Republicans and corporate fat cats." But reporters reviewing transcripts and videotapes of the incidents learned that there were never any such confrontations.[1]

I recall having dinner one night with a friend, who told me while wiping grease from his chin left by the corned-beef sandwich he was munching, that I appeared to be distracted. I admitted I was, that in the few moments before I got in my car to meet him, I was thumbing through a book titled *The Psychoanalytic Theory of Neurosis*, written by Otto Fenichel. One paragraph caught my eye, in which he described how the ego, Dr. Freud's metaphor for our rationality, can become insufficient and be literally "overthrown."[2] He alluded to the fact that neuroses are capable of capturing our rationality. This was another moment of insight.

Here was a comprehensible answer to what happened to Sarah, after her elevator accident. Her rationality was metaphorically "captured" by her limbic brain, her id, her *Inner Dummy* to the point where she was helpless

61

to enter an elevator without experiencing intense pangs of fear. She was literally being held captive by a separate operating system of her brain/mind that no one ever told her about.

Her mother or teachers never told her: "Sarah, as you grow up, you'll find that you actually have to manage two operating systems in your mind, both of which are manipulated by your brain. Your rational operating system is the one that is obvious to you. However, you have a second, primitive, limbic operating system that is always lurking behind the scenes, has no sense of logic, and is capable of 'capturing' your rational system and making you believe in or do irrational things."

Few of us are ever given this simple insight into our minds. I have been studying what academics have been saying about the brain and mind for almost twenty years and this only recently became clear to me. I am now becoming hopeful that I can learn to program a VCR.

In early 1998, President Bill Clinton was seen losing his temper on all the television news shows after his arrival on an African trip, when a huge crowd of an estimated 500,000 began surging forward and the president was afraid that those in front of him would be trampled. "Get back, get back," he screamed, with eyes popping, face tense, and neck veins bulging. In *Emotional Intelligence*, Daniel Goleman metaphorically calls this type of anger display an "emotional hijacking."[3] He also used the metaphors "neural hijacking" and "limbic hijacking."

Joseph LeDoux, author of *The Emotional Brain*, theorizes that it's the hippocampus, a limbic component, which is the headquarters for our past emotional memories.[4] It also theoretically harbors our "emotional sentinel," which is constantly checking to see if whatever we are experiencing rationally matches emotional memories that have upset us. If so, it presumably signals the amygdala, which then theoretically decides whether brain chemicals should be released that will create anger, fear, anxieties, or other such emotions.

In the simplest of terms, it was apparently President Clinton's hippocampus that theoretically remembered the potential dangers of a large, surging crowd and signaled his amygdala, which agreed and caused the release of brain chemicals that created his anger. In the micro instant that the anger was created, the neural pathways involved in the process completely bypassed his neocortex containing his power of reason and so the entire event was a "limbic happening." President Clinton was not given an opportunity by his brain to make a rational decision on whether to become angry or not.

Most of us can readily understand the concept of an "emotional hijacking" when it is related to anger. Think back to your most recent fit of anger and recall, if you can, how you felt and acted at the time. The one thing you'll probably remember is that the instant sensation of the anger not only seized your mind with almost an intrusive violence, but created tense feelings in other parts of your body. You might also have said or done something that you later regretted. "I just wasn't myself," you might have said later, in apology.

What you might have said more accurately in the apology is, "Hey, I'm as susceptible as the next person to being captured by a primitive limbic system that may not always be comfortable in a modern world and so may not always act in my best, practical interests. I intend to have several serious talks with my amygdala."

If you were riding on a train while you muttered this to yourself, the person next to you would probably start looking for the nearest vacant seat. We aren't used to communicating our mental frailties in this context.

A few years ago I was riding in a car with a university professor who was suddenly cut off by an elderly woman whose car bore an out-of-state license and was obviously lost. The professor immediately turned beet red, swerved the car, and accelerated until he was parallel to the woman's car. He lowered the window on the passenger's side where I was sitting and shouted past me to this obviously confused woman, who appeared to be in her seventies: "You no good bitch. Where the fuck did you learn to drive?"

"Steven," I remember saying, "for pete's sake, calm down, we're going to get into an accident."

Paying no attention to me, he continued: "Goddamn it, why don't you go back to where you came from? You need driving lessons, you pinhead . . ."

I remember rolling up the window and commanding him to "Drive."

Steven was ordinarily a quiet and calm man, an outstanding biochemist, with academic credentials, and the author of several books. Yet, he was just as susceptible as some of us who are less intellectually gifted, to what is commonly called "road rage," another example of a "limbic hijacking" that can cause the most outwardly rational of us to act irrationally.

The next day I reminded Steven of the incident. "It was a real shock to hear you say such vulgar things to an obviously refined elderly woman who was clearly lost and by mistake cut you off."

"Ah, it's a problem I have," he admitted. "I rarely lose my temper and when I do it's usually in my car when somebody does something stupid, like that woman did."

And then he took off on her again, only stopping when I changed the subject. A week later when I asked him about the incident again, he could hardly remember it.

Anger is apparently a "hijacking" by our limbic system that remains unaware that we are now living in a civilized world. It thus continues to react to events as if we were still living as primitive cavemen without police forces and courts of law, and, with its accompanying ferocious outburst, was probably designed to confer fear and retribution on the perpetrator, deeming it a useful tool for survival.

Fortunately, much of our anger, like Steven's "road rage," doesn't last very long. For instance, I recall boarding a crowded shuttle plane and struggling to get my briefcase into an overhead rack. Suddenly a matronly woman behind me said sharply: "You're in the way. Step aside immediately so I can get through." Her manner and tone of voice caused a sudden anger to overwhelm me. I managed to keep it under control, saying nothing, although I would have liked to shout at her with a full array of primitive facial contortions: "I had to wait to get this far, what's your problem, you ignorant big bag of wind?" I would thus have conferred upon her fear and retribution, as my limbic system was driving me to do.

The following day this little incident still bothered me, even though I knew it was all irrational, that I was being literally "hijacked" by my limbic brain, just as Steven was in the car. The woman didn't club me, she didn't cause me any real harm. Two days later, I could think about the incident and feel nothing at all. The anger was obviously superficial and gone, the "hijacking" was over.

But there is also anger that many of us feel that doesn't ever quite recede. When I think about attending the junior high school graduation of one of my sons and being relegated by my first ex-wife to sitting in back of the auditorium, I still feel a simmering anger. For the short instant I think about it, my mind is mildly "hijacked." And then there is the bottomless anger of O. J. Simpson's father-in-law, which probably won't ever recede.

The upshot is that with the brain research that has been done by LeDoux and others and from the observations most of us can make about our own minds, it is safe to assume that our emotional brain chemicals can literally "capture" our rationality to varying depths. The metaphor "capture" seems more appropriate than the term "hijacking," which conjures a more temporary situation, such as President Clinton's fit of anger in Africa. "Limbic capturing" is a metaphor that can apply to a temporary fit of anger as well as to longer term conditions, such as Sarah Reinwald's fear of elevators and other serious phobias, compulsions, anxieties, and obsessions, during which, as psychiatrist Karen Horney points out throughout her book *Neurosis and Human Growth*, people can become estranged from large parts of their worlds. "Under inner stress . . . a person may become alienated from his real self."[5]

Ellen, for example, was a fifteen-year-old, who was featured in early 1998 on the CBS television program *48 Hours*. This little waif of a person who weighed eighty-two pounds, thought that she was fat. So either she refused to eat, or after she did would "purge" herself, losing whatever food found its way into her stomach. The conversation with the CBS correspondent who interviewed her in the hospital, went something like this:

"The doctors say that if you don't eat, you may die."

"I don't care."

"Why don't you eat?"

"Because I think I'm fat."

"Let's look in the mirror together."

He slowly guided her out of bed to stand before a large mirror in the room.

"Do you see how you look?" he asked. "You are gaunt and shriveled."

"I think I look fat."

"But you now weigh only eighty-two pounds. Do you think that is a person who is fat?"

"No."

"But you think you are fat?"

"Yes, and I will grow fatter if I eat."

The correspondent then went on to describe how Ellen was fed intravenously when she intermittently fell close to death, but had to be watched because she pulled the needles out.

In attempting to trace the cause of this irrationality, the only evidence was a photo of Ellen at a slightly younger age with a much fuller face, when she admitted she was accosted in her schoolyard by a schoolmate who told her: "You look fat." Could such a simple statement create a limbic capturing among those of us who are susceptible to such slights?

I had a personal encounter with a similar situation when a few years ago one of my tennis partners said to me, "Boy, are you putting on weight." Within hours, "captured" by an irrational fear of looking fat, I was on a crash diet. The scale showed I had put on only three pounds, but it was the perception of looking fat rather than the reality that obviously created the fear.

Today, when somebody tells me something like that, I go into the bathroom, close the door, and scream at my id, my *Inner Dummy*: "Don't pay attention to that insensitive remark. Don't get upset. Do you hear me, inside there? So okay, tonight we'll lay off the mashed potatoes and gravy, but that's it."

Then there is a woman I know, we'll call her Myranda, who weighs ninety-eight pounds. If she gets on the scale in the morning and she weighs ninety-nine pounds, she will diet for the day. If she weighs one hundred pounds, she will proceed on a crash diet. If she weighs one hundred one pounds, she will starve herself until the scale reverts to ninety-eight pounds.

Another vivid example of a limbic capturing happened to a girl named Jennifer whom I came across while scanning the TV channels one night, and stopped to watch on a rerun of the *Jenny Jones* show, if you'll excuse this indiscretion. Jennifer was a beautiful model in her early twenties, who said that she was unable to have a satisfying relationship with any man because she couldn't trust men as a whole. She traced this anxiety to an experience she had in the eighth grade, when she said she was tall, ungainly, and unattractive. A plot was hatched by her schoolmates who told her that the most attractive boy in the class, the idol of most of the girls, was asking questions about her and wanted to take her out. Jennifer said she could still remember the thrill of the experience and the even greater feeling of exaltation when, as she was surrounded by her schoolmates, the boy did walk up to her during a recess, as if he were going to ask her out. Then the boy said something mildly insulting and walked away, as her schoolmates doubled over in laughter. It was a schoolyard prank, but for Jennifer the "traumatic moment" was a total limbic capturing in her perception of men, as was Sarah Reinwald's in her perception of elevators or Ellen in her perception of the shape of her body. In most other respects they were all apparently normal.

In clinical and theoretical terms, those that might be used by neuroscientist Dr. Joseph LeDoux, despite the fact that years later Jennifer turned into a beautiful model, her hippocampus or amygdala or both or in combination with other organs continued to hold the "limbic memory" of the insult complete with the experience of being perceived as unattractive. At the first opportunity in a new relationship with a man, her emotional sentinel would seek out any words or actions that would match the traumatic memory. Without any intelligence or "logic" of its own, it might mistakenly perceive an experience in the relationship as matching up with the schoolyard prank. It would then signal her amygdala, which would then cause the release of those brain chemicals that create fear and anxiety, awakening anew the limbic capturing, and the relationship would eventually terminate.

On the television show, the producers had tracked down the boy who had caused the schoolyard trauma and was now an adult with a family. He couldn't remember the prank, and seemed to only vaguely remember Jennifer. Whether confronting the perpetrator who caused her limbic capturing will allow her anxieties about men to dissipate remains to be seen.

Then there is the case of Mike Wallace, the commentator on the television news magazine *60 Minutes*, who allowed a two-hour documentary to be produced on a period of depression he endured, after being sued for libel by General William Westmoreland because of a report Wallace did that was highly critical of Westmoreland, who Wallace claimed on the air falsified data to justify the use of additional U.S. military resources in Vietnam. Wallace recounted that it was sometime during the trial when he began to feel overwhelmed by the classical symptoms of depression, which he described as hopelessness, lack of motivation, restricted social activity and interests, withdrawal, and despondency. He talked about how this was his first serious bout with depression (there are many causes of depression as Dr. Hefter will testify) and had to "drag himself to work," often reciting from his scripts by rote, having no cogent idea of what he was talking about.

With this form of depression, classical admonitions such as "pull yourself together," or "snap out of it," don't make the slightest dent. Mike Wallace was thus limbically captured in the best metaphorical use of the term. In the documentary, he allowed us to view footage of himself taken while he was in the depressive state. He described how he looked apparently normal and that he was totally aware of the depression and the irrationality of the symptoms as they pertained to his otherwise agreeable life, but he couldn't will them away. Therapy and medication were only partially successful in giving him some relief. It was only after the lawsuit brought by General Westmoreland was settled that the captive feelings of depression finally began to dissipate.

Then there is the possible application of the concept of limbic capturing to addictions of varying kinds.

Bill Moyers, in a 1997 television special on PBS entitled "Addiction Close to Home," which told the story of his son's addiction to drugs, made the statement: "The addict's brain is 'hijacked by drugs.' "

Most of us could agree without much argument. We have all witnessed cases where friends and acquaintances have been rationally "captured" by a plethora of substances that may be abusive to their health, from cigarettes to alcohol to drugs to imbalanced intakes of foods such as chocolates and ice cream. They know that what they are doing may be potentially injurious to their health, but they are unable to stop. It takes a gigantic surge of rational will to begin taking the first steps. I recall my own bout with cigarette smoking at an earlier age. My lungs, eventually, began to erupt in pain each time I smoked, but I couldn't stop. It was only when this pain became overwhelming that I stopped cold turkey, suffering the pangs of withdrawal with which my limbic brain was punishing me. But more about "limbic punishment" later in chapter 22.

Then there are obsessive compulsions, another form of "limbic capturing." Stephanie was a realtor I used when I sold my condominium to move into another. I remarked to her many times how pleasant she was to deal with, always smiling, energetic, and bubbly. After several visits together, I said, "Stephanie, this is unusual for me, but I have to tell you I haven't discovered any of your irrationalities, your craziness."

"Oh, I have them," she replied, "I just don't display them."

"Hard for me to believe," I said.

Then one day I was talking to her at my kitchen counter when I stuck my finger through the cellophane covering a cardboard tray of grapes fresh from the supermarket, took out a grape and started putting it in my mouth.

A look of sheer terror came across Stephanie's face as she lunged at me, grabbed my wrist, pulled it away from my mouth, and screamed: *"Germs!"*

I laughed as I said, "So, we finally found something."

It turned out that Stephanie had a fear of germs, which led to a compulsion that among other things, drove her to wash her hands ten or more times a day.

I'm sure you can add to these stories of the "limbically captured," including those of you who are golfers and freeze up or become "captured," when you need to make a three-foot putt in a pressure situation, a subject we'll explore later. One of the threads in the examples I used in this chapter is that all of the men and women were *aware* of their problems. Sarah admitted to her fear of elevators. Steven was embarrassed by his bouts of road rage. Ellen knew intellectually that she wasn't fat. Jennifer could see the absurdity of her anxiety based on a schoolyard incident. Mike Wallace was aware of his depression and fought hard to dispel it. Bill Moyers's son knew the hopelessness of being addicted to drugs. Stephanie was aware of her fear of germs.

In searching for remedies to dissipate limbic capturings that have imprisoned us or others in our lives, whose irrational quirks and eccentricities are driving us up a wall, the hope is usually greater when we or they have an awareness of the capturing. Those whose awareness is also part of the capturing, who are thus unaware that anything is wrong, are the most difficult to deal with.

In this sense, there appear to be two forms in a capturing. One is an "aware capturing," such as Steven's problem with road rage, or Sarah's elevator phobia. Both are aware of the capturing, just as others might be aware that they are addicted to nicotine, but feel helpless to do anything about it.

An "unaware capturing" would include the arrogant and power-driven people we know, who think nothing is wrong with them. They have behavioral traits that are hurting them and/or others, but you can't talk to them about it, because they won't admit to anything. An unaware capturing might also include alcoholics who won't admit to their problem. You can talk to them day and night, pointing out the evidence, but they look at you as if you are the one with a problem, not them. A psychotherapic term for this condition is "denial." But it is apparent that many who are the victim of an unaware capturing have no idea of their condition and so believe there is nothing to deny.

In business, when someone who has the intelligence and drive for a job, but is too power-driven or paranoid or insensitive or whatever to fulfill the job adequately, you often hear the phrase, "If we could only get inside this guy's head and make a few adjustments." However, we all seem to know instinctively how tough it really is to get someone like this to "make those few adjustments."

On the other hand, we also appear to instinctively know that there is considerably more hope in getting "adjustments" made, if a person is "aware" of his or her "capturing," who will admit, "Yes, I tend to put down people, I demean them in front of others," or "Yes, I am totally paranoid about trusting other people," or "Yes, I am an alcoholic, now let's try to do something about it. "

COMMENTARY BY DR. HEFTER

The interactions between the "limbic brain"; the "rational" part of one's personality; one's history, family, and other environmental influences; the general culture; and the expectations of oneself, are complex and variable. The last few decades have been marked by significant findings by scientists about the infrastructure and the actual elements of the brain, which are very likely to be involved in the behavior so well described in this chapter. The identification of neurotransmitters (substances apparently responsible for the transmission of communication between brain parts); the increased understanding of the specific brain parts, which may be the sources of the kinds of behavior, which are "irrational"; the ability to measure more precisely the anatomy and the physico-chemical reactions conducive to different kinds of behavior; and the impact of different kinds of treatment (e.g., medication, various interactive psychotherapies, behavioral modification techniques, etc.) have all combined to produce important leaps in comprehension of how the brain functions, and the intricate ways in which emotions are affected by these discoveries.

One area alluded to in which our understanding has increased, is the clinical entity called depression, which constitutes one element in a more general category known as mood disorders, which includes manic behavior as well as depressive experiences. In some individuals, the genetic contribution to the condition seems to be quite strong. In others, early familial experiences appear to be primary. In still others, environmental factors (medications, alcohol, and other drug abuse, and trauma, for example) present major contributing factors. And the likelihood is that no one factor is the sole source of the mood disorder. The fact that some antidepressant medications work with some individuals and not others, who may have very similar symptoms, is intriguing in this regard.

The part played by the limbic brain probably varies in the several clinical conditions described here. Future research will hopefully elucidate this function and in the process point the way to even more effective means of treating the difficulties resulting.

NOTES

1. Editorial section, *Chicago Tribune*, June 14, 1997, p. 22.

2. Otto Fenichel, *The Psychoanalytic Theory of Neurosis* (New York: Norton, 1972), p. 268.

3. Daniel Goleman, *Emotional Intelligence* (New York: Bantam, 1995), pp. 13–14.

4. Joseph E. LeDoux, *The Emotional Brain: The Mysterious Underpinnings of Emotional Life* (New York: Simon & Schuster, 1996), pp. 186–89.

5. Karen Horney, *Neurosis and Human Growth: The Struggle Toward Self-Realization* (New York: Norton, 1950), p. 13.

7

DR. FREUD
AND THE THEORY OF
"LIMBIC CAPTURING"

Slobodan Milosevic, president of Yugoslavia, who was ultimately responsible for the killing and raping of thousands and displacing millions of people from their homes, calls his wife, Mira, "dumpling."[1]

"**G**ood morning, Dr. Freud," Wendy Smith said brightly as she walked into the ad agency conference room, where Sigmund Freud was waiting patiently, hands clasped across his vest. "My name is Wendy Smith, from our public relations department. We all know your time with us is limited, but I hope you can spare a few minutes to answer some questions I have."

Wendy was probably in her mid-twenties, Freud noticed, and looked bright, energetic, and shapely.

"I can assure you that I am wholly at your disposal," he replied.

"Oh, thank you, sir. I'll try to make this as brief as possible," she said gushingly as she removed a number of documents from a file folder and began shuffling through them. "First of all," she continued, "I am pleased to tell you that the branding of your id as the *Inner Dummy* has been approved by the agency's Executive Creative Committee. They asked me to give you this good news right away."

"I am afraid I cannot share your enthusiasm."

"Oh, and why not?" She appeared surprised.

"As I told your Mr. Croft, I believe that this euphemism for my concept of the id is degrading to a pivotal segment of the work I assembled during my lifetime, and which while it has had its detractors, I assume is still supported by a sizable segment of the academic community concerned with psychiatry and psychology. I am certain that very few of them will find this branding, as you call it, reinforcing."

"I'm sorry sir, but I was told our campaign is to be directed toward ordinary consumers and not the academic community."

"Yes, that was the mission for which I was returned to earth."

"Well, then, I must tell you that regardless of what the academic community thinks of the branding, I think it will make for wonderful consumer positioning. And in just the short time I was given to study it before our meeting this afternoon, I have already put it to good use."

"How so?"

"I'm sure you'll find this story interesting, Dr. Freud. Just this morning I was sitting at my desk, when one of my co-workers, Alfred Kennerman, who is obnoxiously condescending to everyone in the department, walked into my office and asked me to run down to the cafeteria and get him a toasted bagel and some coffee. Can you imagine that? I don't even work for him, but if I did, I would still find the request condescending. Frequently he'll make demeaning utterances that really infuriate me, including some carefully crafted sexual remarks he knows falls just short of the legal interpretations of sexual harassment.

"As usual, I became rude to him, an attitude that invariably sails right over his head, and said, 'Alfred, I am not your errand girl. If you want a toasted bagel and coffee, get them yourself.'

"He replied, 'I am very busy and you don't look busy.'

"I said, 'I am very busy and getting you food is not part of my job description, so please don't bother me.'

"Then he started running off at the mouth about how his career would eventually go much farther than mine, that someday he would be my boss, and that if I didn't start recognizing this inevitable result now, I would ultimately wind up as a dismal failure."

"Alfred sounds a bit arrogant."

"A bit arrogant? He is beyond arrogant. Anyway, do you want to know what I said to him?"

"Please tell me."

"I said to him, 'Alfred, your whole problem is with your Inner Dummy, which will shortly become a pseudonym for Dr. Sigmund Freud's concept of the id, which he contended was the center of our primitive, biological instincts and has no concept of awareness, logic, or time. Your Inner Dummy is driving you to believe that you are the dominant, alpha male of our department, despite the fact that in the real world you come off as a lightheaded, squirrelly little jerk.' "

A deep laugh began to rumble out of Freud's throat. "And how did he respond?" he asked, getting himself under control.

"He grew all flustered. He seemed to understand exactly what I was saying, even though he told me I had no idea what I was talking about, that I was the one with problems, that everyone in our department had problems, and that someday he would get even. But I could see that what I said made a real impression on him, the first time I recall that happening. And you know what? Just saying what I did made me feel a lot better, and so please, Dr. Freud, don't underrate this new branding."

Freud replied amusedly, "In deference to you, Wendy, today I will attempt to tolerate it. Now what questions do you have for me?"

"First of all, Dr. Freud, what would you think of the term '*Dummy Snatched?*'"

A bewildered look crossed Freud's face as he said, "I really haven't the vaguest idea what you mean."

"Oh, I'm sorry. Our creative department, I guess, has been working overtime to develop a fuller characterization of the Inner Dummy and they developed the term *Dummy Snatched* to describe how, when it has been threatened or strained or put under trauma, it may literally 'capture' or 'snatch' away our rationality, or to use your term, 'ego.' Anger, for example. The Inner Dummy 'snatches' our rationality to the point where we may say or do stupid things. Things like that."

"I understand what you mean, of course, but I don't recall using the term 'captured,' let alone 'snatch,' even when describing drives created by the id that can be overwhelming."

"You don't know this, sir, but I have been a great fan of your work," Wendy said, looking shyly down at her notes. "As a matter of fact, I have read many of your books, trying to get an understanding of your work."

Freud looked pleased. "It is very gracious of you to tell me that."

"Yes, sir, at least I've read all the ones they sell in bookstores today. They are in paperback now."

"Paperback you say?" he responded with interest.

"Yes, sir. But anyway, in your book, *The Ego and the Id*, which I brushed up on last night, you made this statement." She pulled a copy of the thin book out of her pile of papers. "By the way, here is how all your books are being stylized by this publisher." She handed the book to Freud, who examined it with interest, before handing it back with a bemused look.

"You should be happy with this paperback treatment, sir. Your books are much more inexpensively priced than they would be if they were only available in hard cover. And so many more people are capable of purchasing them."

"Well, I suppose that part is good."

"Anyway, I marked this page. The statement reads: 'Thus, in its relation to the id, the ego* is like a man on horseback who has to hold in check the superior strength of the horse; with this difference; that the rider tries to do so with his own strength while the ego uses borrowed forces. The analogy may be carried a little further. Often a rider if he is not to be parted from his horse, is obliged to guide it where it wants to go; so in the same way the ego is in the habit of transforming the id's will into action as if it were its own.' "[2]

Wendy closed the book and placed it on the table in front of her.

"I think what you are saying there sir, is that the Inner Dummy is the horse, which wants to go its own way, even though from all appearances, the rider still appears to be in control. In other words, the horse is now being ridden by a rider who has been Dummy Snatched."

A series of slowly emerging chuckles began to pass through Freud's lips, as he looked away, one hand on the table, fingers thumping against it.

"This is unbelievable," he finally managed to say.

"You mean you don't like it?" Wendy asked with real concern.

"I haven't gotten that far, yet," Freud replied, shaking his head as if in wonderment.

"But don't you see, Dr. Freud? I couldn't have talked to Alfred when he insulted my intelligence this morning about how he was 'limbically captured,' or overwhelmed by the drives of his id. That would have gone right over this head, just as being rude to him does. But I do believe I saw a light go on after I described the concept of the Inner Dummy to him. Now, the point is, if I had told him that he was prideful and arrogant and unable to see reality, because his mind had been Dummy Snatched, he might not have been turned off immediately by the comment. It has a bit of humor, it is a light concept, rather than a heavy one. And then I could have told him that his biggest problem was working to understand that he had a problem.

---

*The actual passage substitutes the word "it" for "the ego."

And that once he did, there was a lot he could do to help himself. And in the meantime, it would be helpful to others in his life if he would wear a badge pinned to his shirt that doesn't sound so bad. It would say: 'Please cut me some slack. I have been Dummy Snatched, but I'm working on it.' "

Freud doubled over in laughter.

"No, sir, I'm serious. I think we have a solid concept here—a fuller characterization of the Inner Dummy and all its ramifications that ordinary people like myself can understand. I hope we have your approval to continue on this course. There is more creative work to be done in the very short time you've been allowed to stay with us."

Freud pulled a long, white handkerchief out of his pocket and began wiping his eyes and blowing his nose.

"To be quite frank, Wendy, I am rather in a state of shock. I vaguely recall the advertising agencies of the 1930s, but I never thought that anything I would ever do would need their services. You have now managed to arouse my curiosity, so of course please tell your colleagues to continue. I cannot agree to your concepts at this point, but I assure you I will await each subsequent meeting with great anticipation."

"Thank you, sir," Wendy said as she began gathering her things. "I'll get to work at once on a position paper for the Dummy Snatched concept for your approval. I am thrilled that you are allowing us to proceed."

After she left the room and closed the door, Freud began to howl with laughter. It wasn't always well known, but as was noted in Peter Gay's biography, *Freud . . . A Life for Our Time*, Freud had a fine wit and a keen sense of humor.[3]

NOTES

1. Michael Sneed, *Chicago Sun-Times*, May 27, 1999, p. 4.

2. Sigmund Freud, *The Ego and the Id* (New York: Norton, 1960), p. 19.

3. Peter Gay, *Freud . . . A Life for Our Time* (New York: W. W. Norton, 1988), p. 159.

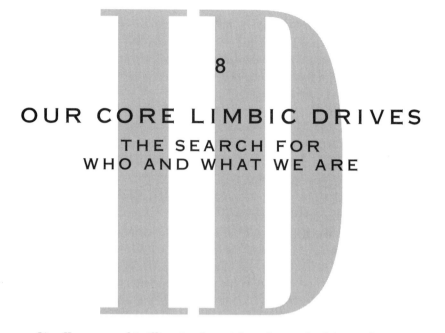

8

OUR CORE LIMBIC DRIVES

THE SEARCH FOR
WHO AND WHAT WE ARE

Lisa Henry, a multimillionaire financial analyst and adviser, refuses to make long-distance telephone calls from hotel rooms because most hotels add a surcharge to their bills, which are over and above the costs of the actual long-distance call charges. The surcharge is normally between 50 and 75 cents per call. Ms. Henry views this charge as unwarranted and so no matter what time of day or night or the inconvenience, she'll go down to the hotel lobby and use a pay phone, even if she has to wait in line.[1]

For more than four years, I searched textbooks and databases in an unsuccessful attempt to find academic studies or reports that would summarize our most basic instinctive, or limbic drives as a group. Then in early 1997, I thought I saw an article in the *New York Times* that quoted the American Psychological Association as stating that we had five basic "psychological drives," that included power, sexual, territorial, nurturance, and survival. Relieved, I dutifully cut the article out and placed it in my pile of reference data. However, when I began this project, I sifted through the pile time and again and the article wasn't there. I then searched through other massive piles of reference data, all to no avail. And so I went to the association's Web site where they offer a "PsycINFO User Service" that utilizes experts to search its database of papers and books. Two experts, both psychologists, were unable to find any information at all about these "psychological drives," as the article described them. "It had to come from somewhere else," they said. Most of the abstracts that they did send me were wide of the mark.

Next, I subscribed to the *New York Times* online service, the week it made its archives available on the Web, thinking that I certainly couldn't have dreamed up this article. And so with bated breath, I put the key words into the search engine. No luck. Then I tried other keywords. No luck. Then I tried a myriad of keywords. No luck. Then thinking I might have read the article in the *Chicago Tribune*, I went to Lexis-Nexis, which maintains an enormous database of articles from thousands of publications and newspapers. I keyed in on the *Tribune* and again found nothing. Then I went into the database's file of "All English Language Newspapers" and again, nothing.

How could I have been dreaming when this information was so important to me and was to form the basis of this book? In my previous book, *Brain Tricks*, I delineated in its second section what I thought were our basic limbic drives: *power, sexual, territorial, social, security*, and *purpose*.[2]

During interviews about the book on media tours, I would invariably be asked how I came up with the designations for these drives. I usually replied that they were empirical, the result of my own observations and experience. "But what are your credentials for making empirical observations?" I would be asked. "Well," I would answer, "I'm a curious human being. Doesn't that count?" It didn't.

Further, I could never bring myself to tell these inquiring reporters how I really came up with those designations, which was while I was riding in a cab coming home from a dinner that included a few drinks. They just came to me. So I stopped at a nearby bar and wrote the designations down on a bar napkin. How would that have sounded during interviews?

And so I began a search for academic reference endorsement thinking that if I could support the designations with other data, it would make my communications in this book about them sound more credible.

When a friend asked me how I knew I didn't dream up that article, I replied, "Then how would I know that 'power,' 'sexual,' and 'territorial' were the same labels I used, when I metaphorically called them *programs*, such as the *power program* and *sexual program*?" I also pointed out that the article in effect labeled the limbic programs I called *social* as "nurturing" and *security* as "survival." I thought immediately that these were better descriptors and so decided to use those names for this book. In addition, I recall the article labeling as drives what I called programs, the *power drive*, the *nurturing drive*, and the *sexual drive*, for example. "Since all of the labels are metaphoric anyway," I recall saying to my friend, "the small changes in terminology were immaterial."

To make a long story short, I then began an intensive search with the help of two psychology doctoral students at the University of Wisconsin, to seek out the nature of these instinctive drives individually. What follows is a quick summary of what later chapters spell out in some detail.

LIMBIC SEXUAL

Let's start with the sexual drive, since it's the most obvious. We don't need to read a lot of academic information to know that we have a sexual drive.

Science writers Jo Durden-Smith and Diane Desimone said the following in their book *Sex and the Brain*, "The sex hormones are among the most subtle and powerful chemicals in nature."[3] No kidding. As I pointed out in chapter 1, even Charles Kuralt, the CBS correspondent and one of the most seemingly benign and gentle of men, appeared to have a sex drive strong enough to carry him into an extramarital affair.

The origin of sexual arousal is thought by many neuroscientists to be in the limbic organ called the hypothalamus, about the size of a thumb tip, believe it or not. Writer Nigel Calder made this illuminating statement about the organ: "Had its functions been known in medieval times, the hypothalamus would no doubt have been designated the Devil's playground."

Evolutionist Richard Dawkins, in one of his legendary books, *The Selfish Gene*, makes the contention that the entire apparatus of our genetic structure has as its ultimate design a propensity to cause us to reproduce. And the last I heard, in order to reproduce, some form of sexual activity must take place, even if it's an ejaculation into a test tube.

And if you take into consideration all of the basic brain mechanics having to do with sex, including the sexual mating dance, jealousy, preference, attraction, arousal, permissiveness, coupling or lack of it, possessiveness, and so forth, using the metaphor *sexual program*, from time to time, to cover all of it would seem permissible, with apologies to Dr. Gerald Edelman, the neurobiologist who contends, as pointed out in chapter 2, that the brain's software is so complicated that it's "not even wrong to call it a computer."

LIMBIC SURVIVAL

A second drive which is as easy to identify as the *sexual program* is our survival instinct. In their book, *Shadows of Forgotten Ancestors*, Carl Sagan and his wife, Ann Druyan, made the following statements: "Passions for life and sex are built into us, hardwired, preprogrammed. . . . Most people would rather be alive than dead. . . . Except in the most hopeless of circumstances, hardly anyone is willing to give it (life) up voluntarily, at least until very old age is reached. . . . Every one of us can recognize these two modes coexisting within us. A moment of introspection is all it takes."[4] The two authors are basically describing both our sex drive and our survival instinct. Richard Dawkins talks about humans and the other higher animals who have survived the evolutionary process as *survival machines* apparently because their primary responsibility is to survive long enough to pass on their genes.

I recall many years ago traveling in one of the earlier jets, about to make a landing at Salt Lake City. Everything appeared to be proceeding toward a normal landing when the pilot applied full thrust and after gaining a higher altitude, began circling the field. The pilot explained that while the landing gear was down, the instrument panel light that was supposed to indicate that the gear was locked in place was not working. The pilot said that it was probably a malfunction. But if it wasn't, the landing gear might buckle on impact. In any event, the pilot and the airport officials didn't want to take any chances. The plane would stay in the air until foam was placed on the runway and fire trucks were positioned.

As we circled the field, we could see all of this taking place. Then a man stood up near the front of the coach section and clearly heard above the din of the jet's engines, shouted, "I know in my heart we are all going to die. If you have sinned, repent now," and then he started crying and screaming. Up till then, the passengers were relatively calm. But after this man's performance, hysteria slowly began to spread throughout the cabin.

Fortunately, I was working on a speech I was to give the next day, and was preoccupied with that, until the man next to me, who looked like a champion wrestler, started bawling and telling me that he would never see his kids again. I asked him, "How old are they?" He replied, "They're not even born yet, but they would be if I lived."

"Look at it this way," I remember replying. "At least they're not going to feel bad if you die."

That was obviously the wrong thing to say because he looked up and his howling became even more intense.

Watching the evolving state of terror on the plane did begin to give me a few qualms. I don't know what it is, but despite some of the worst rides one could have through lightning and storms, I have always felt safe on passenger planes. However, I would frequently feel terrorized by my two ex-wives.

Finally, the pilot announced that the runway was foamed, everything was in readiness, and we were about to land. Cries went up throughout the cabin. We landed safely. It was indeed the instrument light that had malfunctioned, but I had witnessed the survival instinct in all its glory. Had we crashed, I'm sure that many of the people would have clawed their way out, over children and the elderly, if necessary, to find their way to safety.

Our survival instinct has been the most clearly delineated drive in Dr. Joseph LeDoux's research. Theoretically, our emotional sentinel senses a danger that matches an "imprint" on the limbic memories of our amygdala, which causes the release of brain chemicals that will "capture" some of us to the point that we might trample over others in our efforts to elude a foreboding danger.

However, in others of us the brain chemicals might create fright or terror, but not "capture" us. And so we would still have the rational sense to try and help others who are also in danger. No two human brains are alike, fortunately.

As you'll note later, the survival instinct is a highly complicated limbic program that includes irrational fears, anxieties, and phobias, among other things.

LIMBIC POWER

English zoologist Desmond Morris, in his book *The Human Zoo*, makes these points: "In any organized group of mammals (humans included), no matter how cooperative, there is always a struggle for social dominance. As he pursues this struggle, each adult individual acquires a particular social rank, giving him his position, or status, in the group hierarchy. . . . The general result is a constant condition of status tension."[5] To paraphrase Carl Sagan and Ann Druyan, every one of us can recognize this mode existing within us. A moment of introspection is all it takes.

Many families represent the modern-day equivalent of the primitive tribe and are truly reflective of the instinctive power drive. The movie *Avalon* had a scene in which an older brother arrives late at the family's

Thanksgiving dinner, held at the home of a younger, but much wealthier brother. When he sees the family already seated at the table and that the turkey has already been sliced, he becomes angry, makes some hurtful comments, and stomps out, pulling his wife with him. This older brother apparently perceived that in the eyes of his family he was now lower on the family *pecking order* than his younger brother, who had more money. Otherwise the family would have waited for him before they sat down to dinner.

Most of us have seen fathers with strong drives for social dominance or power actually become jealous of their successful offspring. The kids, expecting love and approval, get a smack in the face. It's the stuff of movies. I know a father of six adult children who cannot give them credit for anything. A typical conversation at a family gathering might go something like this:

"Dad, I finally got a promotion at work."

"So, you work hard, you get a promotion."

"But it was a real struggle. I was competing with others for this position."

"Look, it was my money that put you through school. If it wasn't for me, you'd be digging ditches for a living."

"But it takes brains to get ahead today."

"Brains, I got plenty of brains. But I never got the breaks. You kids get all the breaks. Remember one thing, in this family I'm the one with the brains. I decide things. Now just shut your mouth and pass the peas."

In an A&E *Biography* program of comedian and artist Jonathan Winters I happened to watch, his wife said it was her opinion that some of Winters's mental problems—for a while, he had been in and out of mental institutions—could be attributed to his parents. No matter how successful he became, they never gave him any credit for it. "I think it was jealousy," she said. "They were actually jealous of his success, when they should have been praising him and giving him their approval. I can't imagine what was going through their minds."[6]

Well, for one thing, they probably had a high power drive, that as we will soon see, may cause anger, jealousy, and envy when its hierarchal expectations aren't met, even if those who challenge the expectations are loved ones. As the noted Norwegian biologist Thorlief Schjelerup-Ebbe put it in the 1920s, "Despotism is the basic idea of the world, indissolubly bound up with all life and existence. . . . There is nothing that does not have a despot." Even the occasional family. And as Carl Sagan and Ann Druyan put it more hopefully in *Shadows of Forgotten Ancestors*: "Dominance hierarchies requiring debasing submission and obedience to the alpha male, as well as hereditary alpha-hood, were once the global standard of human political structure, justified as right and proper and divinely ordained by our greatest philosophers and religious leaders. These institutions have now almost vanished from the Earth."[7]

I'm not sure I would agree with that last sentence, but it is true that general human behavior can change for the better as we realize that we have the inherent brain power to recognize these limbic, instinctive drives within us, and seek out strategies for sidestepping them.

In any event, it should be permissible to use the metaphor *power program* or *drive* when including all its trappings, some of which are neatly documented in Desmond Morris's book on what it takes to maintain leadership status, including: ". . . aggressive use of threats, displaying postures and gestures of dominance, forcibly overpowering subordinates, suppressing squabbles between subordinates, and rewarding immediate subordinates by permitting them to enjoy the benefits of their higher rank."[8]

Michael Hutchison, author of *The Anatomy of Sex and Power,* links the power and sex drives together. "There's no question but that a high level of testosterone is associated with aggressiveness and also associated with the sex drive," he writes.[9]

Or as Henry Kissinger echoed, "Power is a great aphrodisiac." A female correspondent on a Sunday morning television news show parroted this statement by reflecting that Jack Kennedy and Bill Clinton might have been the victims of aggressive women who approached them, not the other way around.

The brain chemicals testosterone and serotonin have frequently been credited as the hormones behind our power drive, since for one thing, they have been found in greater abundance among business and government leaders. Since the metaphoric *power drive* is found in the lowest forms of the animal kingdom, including ant colonies, which pay homage to their queens and are grouped by ranking, but whose members have no discernible neocortex, it is safe to assume that the origins of the power drive or *program* are limbic in nature.

LIMBIC TERRITORIAL

Most of us are aware of the territorial instinct in higher animals. Wolves, we are told, urinate on their borders to mark them. In his landmark book, *The Territorial Imperative,* anthropologist Robert Ardrey states: "We deal here with an open instinct in which final behavior is regulated by a genetically determined pattern filled out by social tradition and individual experience."[10]

I came across an article written by a Los Angeles freelance writer for the real-estate section of the *Los Angeles Times*, that I thought aptly "brought home" the limbic drive that regulates our territorialism:

> Two neighbors are locked in heated discussion over a hedge that separates their homes. They disagree over how to trim it. In theory, they share the hedge. But in reality, each believes it is his alone. Each wants to mark it as exclusive territory. . . .
>
> Their faces flame red, voices sharpen, gestures become truculent. As emotions rise, each one steps closer and closer to the hedge, so that finally, their faces are only inches apart. Both stand tall, chests out, jaws thrust forward. . . .
>
> Dogs, cats, birds—and people. Like animals, people often respond instinctively in matters of territory.[11]

She then went on to describe scenes many of us are familiar with: the rage we might feel when a neighbor's pickup truck is parked in front of our house, or when his dog howls during the day or they have a loud party, penetrating our territorial environment, or they have a large tree that casts too much shade in our yard.

I have a close friend with a tree in his backyard that is planted next to a hedge on a line that borders his neighbor's yard. The instant the neighbor notices that the leaves of the tree are beginning to spread over his land, he runs in the house, fetches a chain saw, and uses it, preferably in full view of my friend, to lop off the errant branches.

In his book *The Third Chimpanzee*, UCLA professor Jared Diamond tells the following story to illustrate the concept of territorialism: "Whenever I go bird watching in New Guinea, I take pains to stop at the nearest village to request permission to bird-watch on that village's land or rivers. On two occasions when I neglected that precaution (or asked permission at the wrong village) and proceeded to boat up a river, I found the river barred on my return by canoes of stone-throwing villagers, furious that I had violated their territory."[12]

Like the power program, the territorial instinct is present in the lowest of animal forms, which show no evidence of a neocortex and so can be considered metaphorically limbic in nature. And like the combination of power and sex, the combination of power and territorialism also appear to work frequently in combination. I have seen business people become enraged when forced to move from a window office, to a smaller, interior office. Not only did they lose the territory they instinctively came to "own," but they lost status with the smaller office and the loss of a view.

LIMBIC NURTURANCE

Finally, we come to the last of the "obviously" limbic programs. Our innate drive to nurture, to form attachments, was probably designed for evolutionary purposes to keep us in nuclear tribal and family units, which in the wilderness were absolutely essential for survival, sustenance, reproduction, and guardianship.

In their compendium book, *Origins of Nurturance*, Alan Fogel and Gail Melson, professors of child development and family studies, contend that there is a biological basis for nurturing, that while differing in form, it is consistently present in all higher animals in which the offspring need to be raised and cared for, unlike newly born minnows, which simply swim away on their own as soon as they are hatched.

An interesting paper on the Web site of the Virginia Commonwealth University noted the following: "Aristotle proclaimed that humans are social animals by nature. We seek solitude from time to time, but we spend much of our lives in the company of other people." William McDougall in his *An Introduction to Social Psychology*, published in 1908, contended that it's a "herd instinct" that drives us to join others. He also wrote of "The Gregarious Instinct, which leads men to seek to share their emotions with the largest possible number of their fellows."

If you've ever felt a deep abiding love for a son, daughter, parent, sibling, spouse, or friend, then you understand how the feeling can be easily characterized as instinctive or limbic in nature. You cannot will yourself to love someone this afternoon whom you didn't instinctively love this morning. Our rationality can't do this kind of job on its own, although we might try to fool ourselves that it can.

The *Oxford Companion to the Mind* points out that "Many behavioral scientists now believe that affectional bonds, such as love, are better understood in terms of what has come to be known as the attachment theory."[13] It turns out that "attachment behavior" is indeed the underlying foundation of the nurturance program or drive as described in detail in chapter 16. Parents become "attached" to their offspring at birth. We become attached to family, friends, and co-workers. And we can regrettably become attached to people who are not in our rational self-interest. For evidence, just look at the divorce rate or the number of business partnerships that disintegrate because of the differences in outlooks between the partners that should have been obvious at the beginning.

And so to conclude this chapter, it would appear permissible to use the metaphor *nurturance program* to describe our apparently instinctive propensity to nurture, and attach, faulty as it might sometimes be, and to describe the emotions and drives that were apparently designed to keep our wilderness families and tribal units in harmonious units and which include in its arsenal love, guilt, trust, shame, loneliness, and compassion, among many other emotions.

By packaging our behavioral drives into a handful of metaphoric *limbic programs* that are embodied in our id or Inner Dummy, where they can be impervious to logic, awareness, or time, we might more readily develop insights into the causes of the irrationalities of apparently normal people, and the choices we have for dealing with our own, if we are predisposed to doing so, or dealing with those in others.

COMMENTARY BY DR. HEFTER

The "limbic drives" described in this chapter are probably inherent in people (as perhaps the "highest" of the higher animals), regardless of what particular nomenclature one uses, e.g., needs, motivations, forces, instincts, etc. The classification used here is as reasonable as any, since what is described probably leads people to act, whether or not they are conscious of the process. (In the absence of the conscious experience of the "limbic drive" the behavior of the individual or group can be seen as a manifestation of the drives.)

An interesting question related to the subject described is how "deep-seated" these drives are. I am not referring to the anatomic location in the limbic area of the brain—rather, I'm talking about the chronological period when these drives are first apparent. Thus, there are some drives, e.g., attachment behavior of the infant and mother, which are evident within the first year of life, and other drives which do not become more apparent until later in life, e.g., those of power and sexuality.

Another aspect of the limbic drive hypothesis has to do with the satisfactions or rewards associated with the goal-seeking behavior. Do those satisfactions and rewards have to be tangible, or can they be appreciated in fantasy? There are many examples in our daily lives, e.g. art, literature, movies, wishes, etc., in which it is evident that the satisfactions and rewards are quite attainable in fantasy. This chapter emphasizes the "blurring" of limbic drives in actual behavior so that any one of them may join with or conflict with any other. This is important to keep in mind—it is a reminder of the complexity of human behavior.

NOTES

1. Lisa is a friend and she freely admits to the story.

2. David L. Weiner, *Brain Tricks: How to Cope with the Dark Side of Your Brain and Win the Ultimate Mind Game* (Amherst, N.Y.: Prometheus Books, 1993), p. 312.

3. Jo Durden-Smith and Diane deSimone, *Sex and the Brain* (New York: Arbor House, 1983), p. 91.

4. Carl Sagan and Ann Druyan, *Shadows of Forgotten Ancestors* (New York: Ballantine, 1992), p. 159.

5. Desmond Morris, *The Human Zoo: A Zoologist's Classic Study of the Urban Animal* (New York: Kodansha International, 1996), pp. 41, 59.

6. The program aired on Thursday, June 17, 1999.

7. Sagan and Druyan, *Shadows of Forgotten Ancestors*, p. 414.

8. Morris, *The Human Zoo*, p. 69.

9. Michael Hutchison, *The Anatomy of Sex and Power: An Investigation of Mind-body Politics* (New York: W. Morrow, 1990), n.p.

10. Robert Ardrey, *The Territorial Imperative: A Personal Inquiry into the Animal Origins of Property and Nations* (New York: Kodansha International, 1996), p. 45.

11. Teresa Yunker, *Los Angeles Times*, March 1, 1998, p. K-1.

12. Jared Diamond, *The Third Chimpanzee: The Evolution and Future of the Human Animal* (New York: HarperPerennial, 1992), p. 228.

13. Richard L. Gregory (ed.), *The Oxford Companion to the Mind* (Oxford: Oxford University Press, 1987), p. 57.

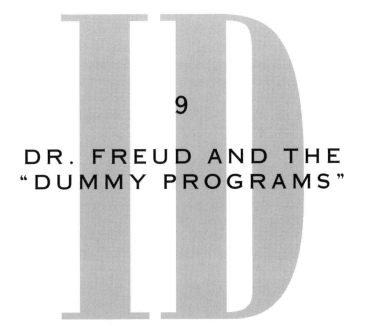

9

DR. FREUD AND THE "DUMMY PROGRAMS"

A team of British researchers reported they are finding an increasing number of men who pretend to talk on cellular telephones. The findings included men in night clubs who wheel and deal on fake cellular phones and those who speak into cellular telephones in locations where it is impossible to get a signal. The researchers documented one instance where a man was in the middle of a heated business discussion on his cellular phone when it rang.[1]

D r. Freud was sitting in the ad agency conference room the day after his meeting with Wendy Smith, waiting for his next appointment. He was reading Joseph LeDoux's book *The Emotional Brain*, and had a stack of other recently published books about the brain and mind scattered about the conference table in front of him.

The door opened and a tall, thin man, with wire-framed glasses and wearing a starched white shirt and tie, entered the room. He had a gaunt, academic look, which Freud observed to himself looked out of place in the outwardly casual ambience of the agency. But there was a softness about him.

"Dr. Freud?" the man asked inquiringly.

"Yes," Freud replied.

"Of course I recognized you," the man continued. "But it is very unusual to talk to a dead person and so I hope you don't mind my verifying your identity by asking that question."

"I don't mind at all. I know this must be unusual for you."

"Yes, I have only talked with live persons, although I once felt I had come in contact with my dead mother while kneeling beside her grave at the cemetery. But of course that was a spiritual happening and here you are in the flesh, in a manner of speaking. Do you mind if I shake your hand?"

"Not at all," Freud said as he stretched out his hand.

"My name is Samuel Ollander," he said as he shook Freud's hand. "I am the director of research at the agency."

"Pleased to meet you."

"This won't take very long," Ollander said as he took a seat opposite Freud at the conference table. "I just need to ask a few questions."

"Go right ahead," Freud replied pleasantly.

Ollander stared at the pile of books in front of Freud. "I see you are brushing up on your field of study."

"Yes, and I find it quite interesting, particularly the biochemical work that has been done regarding the brain and the limbic system in particular. I was in neurology research before I began my career in psychiatry."

"I didn't know that."

"Yes, I dissected many brains and we were quite familiar with the organs of what has become known as the limbic system. As a matter of fact, LeDoux's book here reminds me of one I read two years before my death, in 1937, written by J. W. Papez and titled *Archives of Neurology and Psychiatry*. As I recall, Papez didn't put much emphasis on the amygdala, which appears to be LeDoux's primary area of focus, but instead centered on the thalamus, hypothalamus, and hippocampus."

Freud began poking through some of the books in front of him, then said, "It is amazing that in this state I can remember such details. And now, what can I do for you, Mr. Ollander?"

"Well, sir," Ollander began hesitantly, "I have been assigned the project of preparing the consumer-focus groups that will allow us to assess the accessibility of the branding of the Inner Dummy and the word and phrase designations that will make up its fuller characterization."

"Please clarify what you mean by focus groups and accessibility."

"Oh, of course. Please excuse me. It is easy to assume, Dr. Freud, that in your transposed state, you know everything."

"I assure you, I do not," Freud replied, amused. "That is one reason why I am going through all of these books." He pointed to the stack in front of him.

"Well, then, let me explain. Focus groups are small groups of eight to ten people that we bring into one room to determine their reactions to the concepts we present. Of course, the people we select, the 'screening,' as we call it, are critical to the process. If we were doing a focus group to determine potential customer reaction to a new hand tool, we would select hand-tool users. Or if it were on cuisine cookware, we would select consumers who like to cook.

"However, since the concept of the Inner Dummy is targeted at the general public, we will select the focus-group participants at random, making sure, however, that in doing so, we cover various educational levels, which brings us to accessibility. Are you following me so far?"

"Yes, I am."

"We want to learn how accessible, how understandable this concept will be to people with varying levels of education. At what level does the concept become incomprehensible? This will help us select the most demographically suitable television programs and other media for our TV spots and print ads. We will even be testing the concept among academics."

"Why would you do that?" Freud asked in surprise. "Surely they would have no problem comprehending concepts that are so simplistic."

"But that's the point, exactly," Ollander said, holding back a chuckle. "Is the concept so simple that many academics will reject it out of hand? And even if they do, will they allow the concept to emerge without being heatedly critical and creating negative publicity in the media?"

"Yes, yes, I see," Freud said as he stroked his beard. "While my work was considered anything but simplistic, I still understand quite clearly what you mean. In 1886, I gave a lecture on male hysteria to the Vienna Society of Physicians, and they were actually hostile to me. It was a humiliating moment. It was only later that my concepts began to generate some respect, but I always had my detractors among the academic community."

Freud leaned back in his chair and stared at the ceiling, obviously irritated as he remembered the event. Then he composed himself and addressed Samuel Ollander.

"And the Inner Dummy," Freud grimaced as he uttered the expression, "is, I imagine, one of the concepts you will test."

"Oh, that's the main one, actually. We will also be testing alternatives to the expression *Dummy Snatched*, for example. *Dummy Swiped*, I believe, is one of them. We won't hold these focus groups until most of the word and expression designations have been developed by our creative department."

"I see," Freud replied glumly.

"This morning, for example, I was given the designation *Dummy Drives* to test."

"Did you say *Dummy Drives?*" Freud asked with obvious distress.

"Yes, doctor, we will test the accessibility and acceptance of five Dummy Drives: power, sex, territorial, nurturance, and survival. We will also be testing the expressions *Dummy Programs* and *Limbic Programs*. And probably one or two others as well."

"This is unbelievable."

Mistaking Freud's distress for enthusiasm, Ollander continued ebulliently, "Of course, we will also be testing the designations in relation to the five individual programs. For instance, is *Power Dummy Drive* more acceptable than *Power Limbic Program?*

"Or as was suggested by one of our writers last night in a meeting, can we characterize someone with a very intense power thrust as someone with a *Dummy Power Program in Overdrive*. Or, someone who has an intense sexual force as having a *Dummy Sexual Program in Overdrive*."

"Unbelievable," Freud moaned again.

"Actually, in my position as director of research, I theoretically should have no opinion. My job is to listen to consumers and feed back their opinions, without any filtering of my own. But I do like the characterization *Dummy Power Program in Overdrive*. That would certainly describe my older brother, who is in theatrical work and is a control freak of the first order."

"Your older brother, you say?" Freud began stroking his beard.

"Yes, he is a director who does off-Broadway plays. He has never directed a mainstream Broadway play and this has made him not only a control freak, but a frustrated one. I recall one of his power plays quite vividly. His former wife was an actress and she agreed to be in a play he was directing. But then the play she was currently appearing in was held over. She asked him to find another actress, but he wouldn't hear of it. She agreed to be in his play, he told her, and that was it.

"When she didn't show up at my brother's theater on the first day of rehearsals, he threw a fit in front of the entire cast, who he had made stand around all day, doing nothing. Then three days later he had divorce papers served on her. And he made his lawyer do it personally, directing him to serve the papers during the intermission of her play. Can you believe that?

When she came home that night, he refused to discuss the matter. A week later, she moved out. Now he could easily have gotten another actress to take his wife's place and let her enjoy her success, but he wouldn't do it."

"An interesting case."

"When I was reviewing these new concepts from our creative people, I could visualize asking our art department to make up a framed wall certificate that would say: 'Beware of Christopher Ollander. He has a Dummy Power Program in Overdrive. Attested to by his brother, Samuel Ollander.' "

Freud chuckled. "I'm not certain he would hang it on his wall."

"Oh, I think he would. He would hang anything on his wall that had his name inscribed on it."

Ollander had worked himself up while telling the story. Now he was attempting to calm himself down as Freud continued to manage a small grin.

"You know, Mr. Ollander," Freud said, turning serious, "to be quite frank, I'm still not sure myself whether to laugh or cry at this whole process being undertaken by your agency."

"Was it something I said?"

"No, this has nothing to do with you. Despite the cleverness that your agency has displayed, I cannot transcend the feeling that of all these modern communication forms are highly demeaning to my work."

"Demeaning? But I thought your mission in coming back to life was to make your concept of the id understandable to the ordinary person. And that our assignment is to develop a communications platform that will get the job done."

"Yes, you are right. And perhaps I am one of those academics you will indeed encounter who will raise barriers because what you are developing is so simplistic."

"You mean you don't like the idea of the Inner Dummy and the Dummy Drives?"

"I thought that was obvious. It is just hard for me to accept." Freud thought for a moment. "You know," he continued, "if you are simply offering alternative concepts for reactions in these consumer groups, why not include my libido metaphor?"

"The libido?" Ollander looked surprised. "Sir, if you'll forgive me, the libido is a designation that is certainly associated with your work, but it is a word, like the id, that is foreign to the great majority of the American public. I don't need a research study to tell me that. In addition, those who are familiar with your concept of the libido, would, I'm quite certain, associate it only with sexuality."

Freud stood up abruptly and banged his fist hard on the table. "Ah ha," he practically shouted. "I have already perused many of these books," he pointed to the stack in front of him, "and I will tell you, most of those that denigrate my work make me out to be obsessed with sex; they contend I attribute almost all neurotic behavior to early sexual patterns."

Freud began pacing back and forth, hands behind his back, spouting the words in angry professorial tones.

"But they neglected many of my later writings in which I refined my earlier thoughts. And to that point, I redefined libido as the psychic energy associated with all the instinctive biological drives: sex, aggression, hunger, thirst, and so forth. The libido, it could be said, was ultimately my descriptor for the biology that drives the instincts of the id. Do you follow me, Mr. Ollander?"

Ollander shuffled in his chair, uncertainly. "I believe I do, sir."

"And so I will give into your agency's bent toward consumerism to this extent." Freud placed both hands on the table, leaned forward, and stared directly at Ollander.

"The id is the id and not your Inner Dummy. That is final. But to compromise, I will allow you to describe the core instinctive, biological drives of the id that underlie human behavior as *power libido*, *territorial libido*, *survival libido*, *nurturance libido*, and, of course, *sexual libido*. There," Freud said smugly, "*that* is my compromise."

Ollander looked confused. "I'm afraid, Dr. Freud, that what you are proposing is beyond my authority. You are the client, of course, but you will have to take this up with our CEO, Ted Croft, whom you met previously. And if I may offer an opinion, sir, I hope he talks you out of your idea for compromise."

"We shall see."

Ollander gathered up his papers and prepared to leave. "I will make another appointment with you, Dr. Freud, when all this has been straightened out and there are additional concepts to discuss with you, if you don't mind."

"Not at all, it has been a pleasure meeting you, Mr. Ollander." Freud resumed his pacing, hands behind his back, deep in thought, as Ollander quietly opened the door and left the room.

NOTE

1. Zay N. Smith, *Chicago Sun-Times*, September 12, 1997. Mr. Smith has a column, "Quick Takes," which includes short stories about human irrationalities, which he garners from the Associated Press and other sources. Many of the items he has selected for his column make perfect anecdotes for this book.

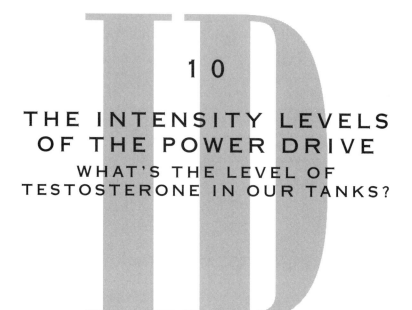

1 0

THE INTENSITY LEVELS
OF THE POWER DRIVE
WHAT'S THE LEVEL OF
TESTOSTERONE IN OUR TANKS?

Kanwar Abson, a Pakistani, was handcuffed and taken to jail after marrying a woman against her father's wishes who belonged to a rival ethnic group. The bride was sentenced to death by her father and a council of Pathan tribal elders, who declared that Pathan honor had been violated, making it impossible to do anything else but either shoot or stone the young girl to death. This incident took place in 1997.[1]

I t is apparent in looking at the organized social structures of past and present primitive human societies living in isolation from one another, that an instinctive, innate system in our brains creates a pressure for ascendancy, for power, that causes the struggles that ultimately determine who will lead the societies and who will follow.

In his book *Sociobiology*, Harvard University scientist Edward O. Wilson quoted Robin Fox, who made a career of studying past and present primitive societies, and spoke in his 1971 book, *Man and Beast: Comparative Social Behaviors*, about man's capacity to develop a culture which includes a system of social status, seemingly from ground zero, in isolated tribal environments. He spoke hypothetically as follows:

If our new Adam and Eve could survive and breed—still in total isolation from any cultural influences—they eventually would produce a society which would have laws about property, rules about incest and marriage, customs of taboo and avoidance, methods of settling disputes with a minimum of bloodshed, beliefs about the supernatural and practices relating to it, *a system of social status and methods of indicating it,* initiation ceremonies for young men, courtship practices including the adornment of females, systems of symbolic body adornment generally, certain activities and associations set aside from which women were excluded, gambling of some kind, a tool- and weapon-making industry, myths and legends, dancing, adultery and various doses of homicide, suicide, homosexuality, schizophrenia, psychosis and neurosis and various practitioners to take advantage of or cure these, depending on how they are viewed.[2] (Emphasis mine)

Many of these cultural developments in primitive isolation are probably manifestations of the five metaphoric limbic drives: *power, sexual, territorial, nurturance,* and *survival* (plus the drive for *purpose,* which we haven't touched upon yet). However, they appear to become more submerged as our civilizations become more advanced. We work on computers in our skyscrapers, travel on jets, have indoor plumbing, read great literature, listen to exalted music, and take advantage of the myriad of living and work conveniences available to us, while rarely giving a second thought to the fact that these limbic, instinctive drives continue to reside within us, propelled into action when they sense that events or our actions are not in accordance with their expectations.

Edward O. Wilson, as I quoted him in the introduction, put it this way in his 1998 book, *Concilience,* "People know more about their automobiles than they do their minds."[3]

It practically takes a decline into primitive living conditions such as the gangsterism of the ghettos and underdeveloped countries, where power ranking and territorialism, with graffiti-marked turf, among the manifestations of other instinctive drives, emerge in their *crudest* of forms, for us to become aware of and question them.

In his 1994 book *Prisoners of the Japanese,* historian Gavan Daws reported on the subprimitive conditions of the Japanese prison camps, in which British and American prisoners of war were being held, during World War II. He wrote:

Early on in the camps, a higher sort of unity was talked about, a brotherhood of man among POWs . . . but [it] had two strikes against it from the start. First, prisoners of one nationality could never bring themselves to agree that all prisoners of all other nationalities were truly their brothers. Second, within any given nationality, the officers as a high caste could never bring themselves to concede that the low caste of enlisted men deserved to be equal in brotherhood.[4]

That our innate, instinctive drives reemerge in their crudest of forms when conditions reduce us to primitive living has been the stuff of many Hollywood movies.

But while in our civilized state they are less obvious to us, presumably because we confuse them with faulty reasoning power, the drives or *programs*, to use this metaphor, continue to apply their pressures, as a daily reading of the newspapers will attest. The *limbic power program*, for example, might be described as the metaphor for the drive or pressure that motivates us to organize by social rank or status. Primatologists report that when a herd of chimpanzees moves from one place to another, it usually does so in a formation that reflects the social rank of its members within the group. The weaker members are frequently out on the flanks where they are more vulnerable. Attacks on them will warn the others.

In 1997, while I was on vacation in Maui, Hawaii, the annual Lahaina invitational basketball tournament was taking place, featuring some of the top college teams in the nation. Each morning I would watch from my patio as two powerful and well-known coaches with their large families following—sons, daughters, spouses—would jog down the very narrow beach sidewalk in the exact same line of order each day, with the power-driven coaches naturally in the lead. The questions arise: What makes a power-driven coach always want to be in the lead even if the group is his own family out for a casual morning jog? What is it in his mind that allows others to be submissive to him and comfortable in that role? We see the same scenario of power ranking played out in business, government, institutions, our social lives, and in our own families.

To learn the answers I once more turned to the American Psychological Association's PsycSEARCH service, this time asking for information on research undertaken with regard to the *intensity pressures* of the instinctive power drive. What is it precisely, that causes one person to be more power-driven than another? I asked in the research project request. What combination of brain chemicals and connections create specific longer-term intensity levels? And is there a formal ranking, a scale of the characteristics that has been developed from studies of this pressure?

Once again, the results were sparse, until the psychologist researcher assigned to the project, Kurt Kleininger, called to discuss the problem and asked me, finally, to e-mail him a synopsis of this book, which I did. A day later he called me with an incisive answer. "In psychology," he reminded me, "we don't call these innate forces instinctive drives, but motives."

"Motives?" I asked. "Even for a harsh drive that is obvious soon after birth? And isn't that descriptor a little weak, a tad euphemistic for the havoc that the drive for power can sometimes play in our lives and in the world at large? Would we say that Adolf Hitler had bad *power motives?*"

"Motives," he repeated.

"Okay," I said, "run the search." The next morning he e-mailed me a stack of abstracts of articles that contained information about power motives. Most of the articles, however, described experiments that had been undertaken among various groupings of people, including CEOs, reporting on how they responded to specific stimuli; for instance, how they would react to controlled forms of success or failure. The research material, in other words, focused on the practical manifestations of the power motives, not on the innate stuff that creates and characterizes the drive itself.

The use of the more "enlightened" term *motives*, however, prompted me to reread a 1996 introduction by Irven DeVore, professor of anthropology at Harvard University, to Robert Ardrey's 1967 book, *The Territorial Imperative*. In the introduction he said:

> Ardrey's attacks on behaviorism and the 'humans-have-no-instincts' school of cultural anthropology (together with his assertion that important human behaviors were the result of evolutionary based drives, instincts, and motives), did not sit well with a great many scholars in the social sciences. . . . Despite his lack of formal training in the sciences, Ardrey was an amazingly prescient harbinger of the ways we now seek to understand behavior. . . . More interesting still is the most recent trend in psychology, evolutionary psychology. A blend of psychology and natural selection theory, its precepts are based on human adaptations in our evolutionary past, our "environments of evolutionary adaptiveness." In important ways, this mode of analysis brings us full circle back to Robert Ardrey.[5]

Ardrey, by the way, was a successful playwright, who in his later years returned to school to attain enough background to do the research for his book . . . a person I can relate to.

In a nutshell, it appears that the school of behaviorism believes that all behavior is learned from infancy and can thus be shaped. The school of instincts appears to believe that we share genetic drives with the higher animals and that these are innate, part of our human nature, and which presumably would include the limbic power drive. It appears that the truth lies in a combination of taught behavior and genetics, which we'll get to in chapter 26.

Returning to the search for a power-drive scale, Kurt Kleininger of the APA did one more database search using the key words "power and motive and scale." It unearthed only one additional abstract among APA's enormous database, but it wasn't pertinent.

And so I turned to a more detailed look at studies about "dominance hierarchy," the term used for social status and the trappings of primacy among species of animals and insects that live in social groups, including gorillas, baboons, orangutans, and chimpanzees. This bore considerable fruit and also taught me to look for key phrases in the search for the innate stuff of the other limbic drives. For nurturance, it was "attachments," as I previously pointed out.

Dominance hierarchies and their resultant *status*, have been detailed quite clearly by the studies of the primatologists and others. In a herd of chimpanzees, which Jane Goodall, in her book *Through a Window*, said have "brains more like those of humans than any other living being," there is usually a dominant male leader, who anthropologists have labeled the "alpha male." Below him is the beta male and then the ranking follows down to the omegas, who are at the very bottom, the buck privates of these animal societies. It is apparently from the alpha designation that we have developed our concept of the power-driven, frenetic *Type-A* person.

Chimpanzee females have an alpha-omega ranking of their own, but the females of this species are all ranked below the dominant alpha male, which may be why power and sexuality are so often linked together, not only in the world of the higher social animals, but among humans as well. It was only recently in many Western countries that the concept of women's rights was developed, to free females from the domination of males, which it turns out, might have been a genetic predisposition we picked up in the DNA we share with chimpanzees.

However, as a quick aside, many societies throughout the world haven't as yet used their reasoning power to catch up to the limbic nature of this male drive to dominate females. In Iran, for example, a 1998 *New York Times* article stated, "[W]omen cannot work or get a passport without a husband's permission, they must have a father's written consent to marry, they can be divorced for no reason and with few exceptions, they automatically lose custody of their children when a marriage dissolves." They also cannot attend public athletic events, such as soccer games, and in many societies may legally end up in a harem as one of four wives, who by the way are also ranked, usually by seniority.

Under the customary rules of higher social animal life, the alpha male of the herd literally has to fight his way to the top. Most of us have seen this scenario acted out in dozens of animal documentaries on television; the physical combat between the leader of an animal herd and the challenger, locking horns (a familiar human term), if they have them, with the loser dazedly walking off into the sunset, an outcast living on the edges of the herd.

We can conjecture that the animals that ultimately rise to challenge their herd's alpha male for leadership have the stronger instinctive power drives and physical strength, which work to propel them through other members of the herd. When the challenge is made to the alpha male, the final decision is determined in the same way; by which one has the greatest resolve, physical strength, and endurance in battle. There can be only one alpha. Nature is apparently not big on committees.

This challenge to power was characterized by Edward O. Wilson, who wrote in his book *Sociobiology* (also the name given to the field he pioneered before it became better known as *Evolutionary Psychology*) about biology-based social behavior:

> The social behavior of chickens is relatively simple and is based to a large extent on the dominance order. . . . The hierarchy that quickly forms is in a literal sense a peck order; the chickens maintain their status by pecking or by a threatening movement toward an opponent with the evident intention of attacking in this manner. High-ranking birds are clearly rewarded with *superior genetic fitness* . . . the fitness of dominant hens is probably greater because of the more than compensating advantages gained in access to food and nests.[6] (Emphasis mine)

In his book *Chimpanzee Politics: Power and Sex Among Apes*, primatologist Frans de Waal said: "This habit of making the body look deceptively large (the animal's hair was constantly slightly on end) and heavy is characteristic of the alpha male. . . . The fact of being in a position of power makes a male physically impressive, hence the assumption that he occupies the position which fits his appearance."[7]

Just as an aside, could this be why human society is afflicted with so many large and/or powerful males who are compelled to serve subservient roles in corporations, on the factory floor, in the military and on police forces, who will bully subordinates and even their equals every chance they get? Are they frustrated and angry because their limbic power program, their Inner Dummy, is telling them that they should be leading the pack but they are not, because in the reality of the modern world, thinking power has become part of the equation and these bullies don't have enough? Thought or reason—the major difference between the higher social animals and humans in the manifestations of the limbic power program, which we apparently share—is presumably how the battles for ranking and dominance are won today.

In a familiar and memorable scene from the motion picture *Butch Cassidy and the Sundance Kid*, Butch (played by Paul Newman) returns after a long absence, with his sidekick, the Sundance Kid (played by Robert Redford) to their mountain hideout, where Butch rules over a gang of outlaws. He had been the alpha male of the gang. Upon their return, Butch is confronted by Harvey, who has assumed the gang's alpha role in Butch's absence and invites Butch to accept that Harvey is the new leader. Harvey is tall, muscular, and fierce, while Butch is shorter and more wiry than muscular. If these were two chimpanzees confronting each other, the battle would doubtless go to the chimp equivalent of the stronger Harvey. Butch's challenger pulled out a knife. Chimpanzees may have brains that are close to humans, but they can't manufacture knives.

Butch utilized strategic thinking, a gift provided by a level of human intelligence and creativity not available to chimpanzees. As he unbuttoned his shirt, with Harvey circling about him brandishing the knife, Butch talked to Robert Redford's Sundance Kid in a way that reflected his pessimism about the impending confrontation and intended to build a false confidence in Harvey. Then, with his shirt off and Harvey taunting Butch to begin the fight, Butch said something like, "Hold on, Harvey, we have to discuss the rules." Harvey replied, "There are no rules in knife fights." Butch, however, kept up the dialogue, arguing the need for rules even in a knife fight, as he casually walked up to the puzzled Harvey. When he was close enough, Butch kicked him ferociously in the crotch, dropping Harvey to the ground like a rock and ending the challenge.

Thus, the smaller, weaker guy won, which dramatically illustrates the major divergence in how humans versus the higher animals can get to the top. Most of us have witnessed during our lives figurative "surprise kicks to the crotch," subtle or not, physical or vocal, in power battles that we were part of or observed among others.

What is it, however, that creates the pressure for power in the minds of the Harveys and Butches and the other alphas and alpha hopefuls of the world?

Once again, Sigmund Freud appeared to be on the money in this area when in a paper he delivered in 1915, titled *Instincts and Their Vicissitudes*, he stated:

> We are now in a position to discuss certain terms which are used in reference to the concept of an instinct—for example, its 'pressure', its 'aim', its 'object' and its 'source.' By the pressure of an instinct we understand its motor factor, the amount of force or the measure of the demand for work which it represents. . . .[8]

Freud thus recognized that there are instinctive "pressures" which create the intensity of our drives. I found another interesting quote from Dr. Freud on how these pressures need to be discharged, in an *Encyclopaedia Brittannica* section titled "Emotion and Motivation, Humans." ". . . instinctual energy [is noted] as requiring discharge and accumulating, if not vented. It seems obvious that there was a limit to the amount of energy that could be accumulated before discharge was necessary. This formulation has been interpreted as following a *hydraulic mode*" (emphasis mine).

Most of us can more readily recognize the "hydraulic" nature of Freud's primal instincts through the observation and remembrance of our instinctive sexual drive. It is probably easier to quantify the intensity levels of our sexual drive than it is our power drive, which may be more subtle. At one time or another, we were impelled toward having sex by what we believe to be irresistible "hydraulic" forces and we either gave in or we didn't, depending on the nature of the circumstances or the strength of our resolve, if the sex was to be illicit.

For the hydraulic-like pressure of our metaphoric *limbic sexual program* to be sensed the *emotional sentinel*, as described by Daniel Goleman, that prompts it, needs a stimulus—either the direct sight of an attractive, potential sexual partner or the visualization of one. In the same way, our emotional sentinel also apparently needs a stimulus for our limbic power program to manifest its hydraulic-like drives. We don't feel these drives sitting on a beach alone reading a tame novel. One of the most common of such stimuli is a challenge to our *status*. People with more intense limbic power programs will respond dramatically to a challenge to authority, with the hydraulic pressure to react building quickly inside. For example, Paul

Newman's Butch Cassidy to the challenge made by Harvey. Or the brother in the movie *Avalon* who walked out in a huff because the Thanksgiving turkey was cut before he arrived. Or ourselves when someone rudely cuts in front of us in a line at the supermarket checkout counter. In fact, most of us are commonly placed in situations where we perceive a challenge being made to our authority, even by a child of three in front of family gatherings.

But someone with an obviously less intense, metaphoric limbic power program, a St. Francis of Assisi, for example, who, born in the twelfth century, gave up the life of an aristocrat to become a humble servant of God, and carrying no money and wearing only a rough frock, would react to most challenges to the perceptions of his status by turning the other cheek.

Most of us can sense that there is such a phenomenon as a limbic power scale, ranging from an Adolf Hitler at the top to a St. Francis at the bottom, that we share with the higher animals. But for humans its manifestations differ from that of other animals because of our ability to think and to strategize against those persons or circumstances within our lives we perceive as a challenge to our status.

If we think back for a moment, we can observe how some of the greatest problems in our lives and in the world have been caused by people with more intense power drives. At one level there is the likes of Fidel Castro, for example, who gave up a life of wealth to fight the corruption of the existing government in Cuba, to establish a rule of communism with the ideal of creating equality for all, but once in power he became despotic, jailing those who opposed him and threatened his status.

At another level, there is the despotic parent who wants everyone in the family to do precisely what he or she dictates. I recall an incident involving a large family on a vacation weekend in upper Michigan. The mother, who apparently had an intense power drive, had the entire weekend planned. If any member of the family wanted to do anything on their own, she apparently perceived this as a threat to her status and became incensed. She actually had a raging argument with her daughter because she stayed behind from an excursion so that her two-year-old child could take a nap.

The irrationalities, the inner craziness generated by the limbic power program appears to emerge from those higher on a metaphoric power scale. They lose sight of reality in their quixotic quest to maintain or advance their status in life, for it is *status that is apparently the ultimate aim of the power drive.*

In the world of the higher social animals as in the primitive human world, dominance or power is achieved, as previously pointed out, by resolve, endurance, and physical strength. Once the hierarchy of a herd or tribe is established, harmony is maintained by the discipline enforced by the alpha male. Those who challenge the authority of the alpha and lose in battle were usually made outcasts of the tribe or herd, presumably because alphas instinctively felt that such challengers, if left in their midst, might try again.

In the modern world where humans have considerable reasoning power, the challenge to authority is no longer always in the realm of the physical, although mafia and gang leaders and the like still make good use of it. More often, if a challenger perceives himself or herself as being deprived of power or status, he or she might use intelligence and creativity to avoid frontal assaults and instead, lie, cheat, exaggerate, demean, betray, defraud, slander, falsely flatter, or connive, among other things, to reinforce or advance their perceived status.

Thus, the head of the family previously mentioned, who couldn't give his children any credit for their accomplishments might have acted in this way because his id, his Inner Dummy, perceived these accomplishments as being challenges to his own authority and status. And so, instead of complimenting and encouraging his children, he was apparently driven instinctively to demean them. If compelling rational persuasion, or a trauma or the use of therapy could somehow get through to his impervious id that what he was doing was irrational—if they could get his id to "see the light"—there would be hope for him to change, as we'll describe in chapter 26.

The intelligence and creativity possessed by humans may also lead them, unlike chimpanzees, to use dress or other objects in an effort to advance or maintain their perceived status. We idiomatically call them *status symbols*, but they are probably manifestations of a strong power drive.

Those who feel themselves frustrated in their drive for power or status might dress in a manner that matches the level of dominance they perceive themselves as having or surround themselves with symbols of status—a Rolex watch, an expensive car, Nike shoes, pin-striped suits—and they might associate with people who they perceive as bolstering their status.

Reflecting themselves in this way to others makes them feel better because what they are doing apparently eases the frustrations of their metaphoric limbic power program, which is making them unhappy because its drive for real and higher status is not being fulfilled. We'll point out beginning in chapter 22 how the limbic drives can literally punish us with a flood of depressive feelings when their expectations are not being fulfilled.

And so the television commercials for Nike shoes and other status brands don't feature an engineer with a pointer describing why the products are better than others. They don't describe the thickness of the soles or the support they give to the ankles. Rather, they show the shoes on the feet of the Michael Jordans of the world, the people whose status others want to emulate. This attracts as customers those people with higher power drives who have not achieved the status their drives expect. When they wear these products or do something like drive a big, black Harley motorcycle without a muffler through quiet neighborhoods, they are working to reflect the higher level of status at which they want to be perceived.

Status symbols, however, are not only for those whose power drives are frustrated. They are also used by those who have achieved status, who have achieved power, to reflect that they indeed do have the power.

I have known chief executive officers of big businesses whose offices and furnishings reminded me of the Taj Mahal, complete with private bathroom, steam room, exercise room, and shower. Usually these people put a strut in their walk and use a display of arrogance to reflect their level of achievement and power. They can also become envious and jealous of others whose achievements they perceive as threatening their status. As we shall see in chapter 18 describing our limbic survival program, achieving great power and status doesn't always raise our self-esteem, our sense of self-assuredness, and security. We can lead an enormous business or even an army and still have low self-esteem. The lower the esteem of someone in power—e.g., a CEO, the head of a governmental agency, anyone in a position of authority—the more the trappings of power, including arrogance, need to be displayed.

The November 12, 1998, edition of the *New York Times* reported that in Brazil, where there was at the time fear that the economy would default, the minister of communications spent $4,000 on Turkish rugs and the Supreme Court ordered $38,000 in Persian rugs.[9]

On the other hand, I recall one CEO, the head of a large family manufacturing and distribution business, whose office was smaller than the other officers and who always rode coach on the airplanes, even though he could afford charters, let alone first-class tickets. He was self-assured enough that he didn't feel the need to reflect the trappings of power, and in my experience, it has usually been executives like this one who commanded the greatest respect from those who worked for and with them.

Most of us recognize innately that the drive for power and status can be a great barrier to achieving harmony. Even on a factory floor, the foreman with an intense power program usually cannot be approached as a chum with an idea that will improve productivity. He must be approached in a way that will make the idea look like his, or else he will reject it out of hand because he perceives that any subordinate getting credit for a good idea will be a threat to his status . . . the craziness of apparently normal people.

In her book *After the Fall*, the actress Suzanne Somers describes the power-crazed world of network television where there is an incessant fight to maintain or advance status: "Over the last twenty-five years that I've been part of show business, I've come to realize that the one thing that keeps getting in the way of great business ventures is the 'out-of-whack' egos. It's about control. It's about loss of power." She described how she was fired from her popular 1980s television series *Three's Company* because of the power-laden characteristics of the show's producer.

> I think Mickey [the producer] believed that the success of the show was about him. It was as though in his mind, the world had finally recognized him for the creative genius that he knew himself to be. So everything I did that did not involve his show (outside nightclub engagements, posing for magazine covers, etc.) was an unnecessary distraction. He was unable to see all the parts of the puzzle. He was king of his little fiefdom, with no one questioning his judgement.[10]

Without Ms. Somers, the show soon collapsed.

In his book called *Jolson*, about the life of Al Jolson, probably the most powerful entertainer of the 1920s and early 1930s, author Michael Freedland described how Jolson, who apparently had an intense power drive, combined with low self-esteem, practically forced his second wife, Ruby Keeler, to divorce him because he was extremely jealous of her success in the movies and constantly demeaned her, in public and private, and because, as his career declined, he was compelled to relate to her day and night how great an entertainer he once was.[11]

I personally witnessed a CEO of a successful company turn down an acquisition that was priced right and made perfect sense because it was suggested by an executive vice president he had inherited when he was named to the CEO position, a person he saw as a threat to his status because this skilled manager always stated his positions honestly and without a separate agenda in staff and board meetings, and which frequently were in disagreement with the positions of the CEO. "I won't take action on anything that SOB suggests," the CEO told me in private. "He'll only use it to try to get my job."

We all could probably write our own books listing the irrationalities of power-driven people who have passed through our lives or are still in them.

But let's step back for a moment and return to the search for an articulation of the intensities of a metaphoric *power scale*. As of this writing, nothing could be found among the vast databases available to the American Psychological Association or in reference libraries, which were searched. I decided to turn to a limbic power scale which I developed after the publication of *Brain Tricks*, and which was posted in quiz form on a Web site, www.braintricks.com. Because I've received an access report every day for the three years the quiz has been posted, along with quizzes relating to the *sexual* and *territorial programs*, I know that at least 175,000 people have taken it. More than 150,000 have taken the *limbic sexual quiz*. Through a feedback form on the site, I requested input from visitors who took the quiz, but thought the results weren't consistent with their own perceptions. And so for more than a year I refined the quizzes. For the past twenty-four months, the only feedback has been from participants who related that the results appeared to be in the ballpark. Several months ago, for the purposes of this book, we put monitoring software on the quizzes that allowed us to determine how many people scored at which level, without revealing who they were, so that confidences would not be breached.

I claim no scientific validation to the metaphoric *limbic power scale* that follows. It is a start and perhaps those in the academic world can find ways to improve on it. Following the scale is the percentage breakdown of the more than 50,000 participants who were monitored for each level. According to my friends in market research, this sampling would have an accuracy of ±1 percent, against the more than 175,000 persons who took the quiz since it was posted.

Here is the scale:

NUMBER ONE:

You probably could be happy sitting in a room by yourself all day or simply roaming about, without much of a care in the world. You may be kind and considerate to a fault, would gladly give away everything you owned. There is nothing wrong with you. Make sure you get enough to eat.

NUMBER TWO:

You are probably frightened much of the time. You find it hard to hold your own with anyone. You may feel you are being pushed around, but it really doesn't seem to matter. Being part of a group in which you are a quiet member is comforting.

NUMBER THREE:

You are a good worker and diligent in other ways, but you probably don't like to supervise. You are happy to defer to work leaders and stronger family members and keep out of the limelight.

NUMBER FOUR:

You are not preoccupied with gaining power. It's okay if it happens, but you don't plan or work very hard for it. At home or in the office you are content with being in a subordinate role, if that's the way it is. Fours are usually pleasant company.

NUMBER FIVE:

You understand the concept of power and may try to gain it. You might be disappointed in having less than a high leadership rank, but you accept it and get on with your life.

NUMBER SIX:

You like the feeling of power. You work hard at gaining it, even though it doesn't consume you. You are very disappointed when you are stymied. You accept it, but only grudgingly. It rankles.

NUMBER SEVEN:

You strive for power. You enjoy the feeling of it. You like to dominate, to be in charge of others. You could be a prime candidate for some form of bigotry (explained in chapters 22 and 24, an intense power program can create and lead bigotry). You find it really rankles when you find yourself in situations where you are perceived as being in a lower rank.

NUMBER EIGHT:

You are absolutely intent on moving upward in your family, business, and avocations. You like the fight of moving upward as much as the result. You are constantly thinking about how to get ahead and will probably blame others for the problems you encounter that keep you from progressing the way you want to. If you find yourself perceived as being in a lower rank, you may lie or in other ways deceive to build your status.

NUMBER NINE:

You will do practically anything to claw your way to the top. You will probably be willing to sacrifice family, friends, whatever it takes. Once you reach a position of power, you will absolutely dominate it. You are fearful of delegating authority lest your power base be undermined. Further, you will continue to claw upward. You are never satisfied.

NUMBER TEN:

Time to check yourself in for treatment. You are probably a megalomaniac who may even *kill for power*, if that's what it takes and you believe you won't get caught or punished. You are merciless, eliminating whoever or whatever gets in your way. There is a messianic aura about you that frightens people and at the same time attracts and molds them to your will. If you ran a government, you would imprison, exile, or kill subordinates you perceive as threatening to your dominant rank. Joseph Stalin would have understood you.

It has been my experience that the Number Eights, Nines, and Tens are frequently "limbically captured," to the point that they cannot admit to the nature of their power program. They may even attempt to display airs of humility. On the other hand, the CEO I referred to previously was quite aware of his power program, even though "captured" by it. "I know I am power hungry and paranoid, but I don't know what to do about it," he once told me, an example of an "aware capturing."

If you are unsure of your power ranking, take the quiz on the site. It will give you a rough idea and you might not like it. But since there is no scientific validation to the limbic power scale as I've outlined it, or to the related quiz, then there is nothing for you to worry about.

The following table indicates how the power rankings broke down from the responses that were monitored as of June 1999. I arbitrarily adjusted the "Number Ones," down from 3.3 to 2.5 percent and the "Number Tens" down from 1.8 to 1.3 percent, because a number of visitors entered the number "one" or "ten," all across the board, maybe to impress someone. Other than that, the percentages are shown as monitored:

	Percent	**No. of responses**
NUMBER ONE	2.5 (see above)	2,116
NUMBER TWO	3.1	1,906
NUMBER THREE	9.0	5,919
NUMBER FOUR	19.0	12,647
NUMBER FIVE	26.0	16,944
NUMBER SIX	23.0	14,081
NUMBER SEVEN	10.0	6,853
NUMBER EIGHT	4.0	2,521
NUMBER NINE	1.4	894
NUMBER TEN	1.3 (see above)	1,145

How might we have ended up with whatever our ranking is on this metaphoric limbic power scale? The short answer is that it is probably the result of some combination of our genetic predispositions when we emerged from the womb and the traumatic events we later endured as infants, children, and adults. We'll explore this in chapter 26.

COMMENTARY BY DR. HEFTER

The intensities of the drives of humans is a subject of more than casual importance, since it largely determines the when, where, why, and how of much of behavior. In this chapter on the power drive, and which touches briefly on the sex drive, there are rather clear extensions of the limbic drives in higher animals to humans, i.e., the similarities are evident. However, the possibilities for the "blurring" of what is "innate" and what is learned are increased. Thus, although there are individuals for whom the leadership role is evident at an early age, there are also many instances in which the leadership role emerges later in life when the opportunity arises. In the family constellation, the youngest child may defer to older siblings, but may become a leader in later environments. In fact there are mechanisms in place in business and government in which leadership, which may be regarded as the exercise of power, is taught and developed. In the realm of sexuality, it is not at all unusual that what on the surface appears to be a strong sexual inclination is in reality an intense drive for power (or nurturance, etc.). And as women assume more leadership roles outside the immediate family, how will this affect the "innate" power and sexual drives of both women and men?

Regarding St. Francis of Assisi, this chapter assumes that he was low on the "limbic power scale." One might challenge that assumption by thinking of St. Francis as a very powerful person as a consequence of his seemingly "powerless" behavior. The same could be said about Jesus Christ, Martin Luther King Jr., Florence Nightingale, and other individuals with a "peace agenda." It is an interesting speculation.

The focus on the intensities of the power and sex limbic drives is important, too, because it calls attention to the role of intensity in other drives, which may serve as modifiers of the power and sex drives, and in the process minimize the likelihood of destructive consequences of the power and sexual forces.

NOTES

1. Various news reports, including the Associated Press and the *Birmingham Post*, March 5, 1998, p. 12. The man was later shot by Pathan tribesmen, including the bride's father and mother, and critically wounded while on his way into a courtroom. He later recovered.

2. Edward O. Wilson, *Sociobiology* (Cambridge, Mass.: Belknap Press of Harvard University Press, 1980), p. 284.

3. Edward O. Wilson, *Concilience: The Unity of Knowledge* (New York: Knopf, 1998), p. 97.

4. Gavan Daws, *Prisoners of the Japanese: POWs of World War II in the Pacific* (New York: William Morrow, 1994), p. 134.

5. Irven DeVore, " Introduction," in Robert Ardrey, *The Territorial Imperative: A Personal Inquiry into the Animal Origins of Property and Nations* (New York: Kodansha International, 1996), p. 10.

6. Wilson, *Sociobiology*, p. 138.

7. Frans de Waal, *Chimpanzee Politics: Power and Sex Among Apes* (Baltimore: Johns Hopkins University Press, 1989), p. 87.

8. Peter Gay (ed.), *The Freud Reader* (New York: Norton, 1989), p. 566.

9. Diana Jean Schemo, *New York Times*, November 12, 1998, p. A3.

10. Suzanne Somers, *After the Fall* (New York: Crown Publishers, 1998), p. 177.

11. Michael Freedland, *Jolson: The Story of Al Jolson* (London: Virgin Books, 1995), n.p.

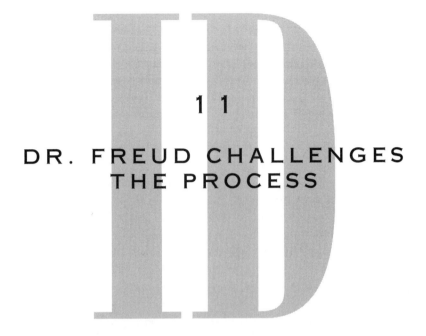

11

DR. FREUD CHALLENGES
THE PROCESS

A judge in Santa Ana, California, sentenced a man in 1998 who stole four chocolate chip cookies to twenty-six years to life in prison under a strict interpretation of the state's "three strikes" law.[1]*

Dr. Freud was back in the office of Ted Croft, the head of the agency, sitting across the desk from him and looking visibly upset.

"To be quite frank with you, Mr. Croft, I am thinking of appealing this whole nonsense of the Inner Dummy to my Regional Higher Authority."

"Please be reasonable, sir," Croft replied irritably. "I have already been contacted by our accounting department and told that the hours we are putting into this effort are already exceeding our standard allotment for pro bono assignments and we've hardly begun."

He leaned back in his chair, putting his hands behind his head.

---

*After a person's third conviction for a criminal offense, the judge is required to issue a stiff sentence, usually mandatory life imprisonment. The idea is that three strikes, or convictions for criminal offense, and you're out of society. I'm not sure that the sponsors of this law imagined that stealing four chocolate chip cookies would count as a "strike."

"But money aside, for the moment," he continued in a calmer voice, "Samuel Ollander, our director of research, whom you've met, did an initial test study last night on a small group of consumers we had gathered for another purpose and his report here," Croft held up a single sheet of paper, "indicates that the Inner Dummy concept and the characterizations of it that we have developed to date show every indication of being a winner. It would appear that the general public will understand this concept and respond very positively to it and *that*, Dr. Freud, is what our business is all about. We try to persuade consumers to buy, whether it is selling the mind-shaping benefits of the concept of the Inner Dummy or the weight reduction benefits of a hearty-tasting, low-fat breakfast cereal."

"That is not the point at all," Freud responded anxiously. "I have an academic reputation to protect. What my academic detractors have said in their criticisms of my theories and methods during my lifetime and since my death will be nothing compared to what they will say about me with this so-called Inner Dummy concept. It will be a massacre, plain and simple."

Ted Croft stared at Freud and was surprised at the flash of real sympathy he felt. He got up from behind his desk and began pacing the room.

"Just give us a little time to work further on this," Croft said as gently as he could. Maybe when you see the whole thing—"

"I can't conceive of what will change my attitude, sir," Freud replied quietly but emphatically.

Croft moved close to Freud, put his hands on the table, and leaned toward him.

"All we're asking is that you give us just a little time to develop a formal presentation," he said persuasively. "We'll make this presentation to you when all the alternative concepts, characterizations, and merchandising ideas have been tested among additional groups of consumers and adjusted as needed. I will guarantee you that I will be sitting right next to you in our conference room and will view the materials with dispassion and your interests at heart. Then, if you still have objections, we'll discuss what compromises we can make that will make you happy."

"I don't know . . ."

"Look, Dr. Freud, just last night I was going over the limbic power scale that our creatives have been working on and which they now suggest we develop into a small handbook."

"A handbook?"

"Yes, a small pocket, reference guide that will make it easier to peg the power characteristics of people and, depending on how things turn out, may also include some of the other basic limbic drives, if they appear pertinent and can be scaled."

"I'm afraid I'm not following you."

Croft thought briefly as he walked to one of his office windows and stared out at his view of the city.

"Okay, take my brother-in-law, Lester, my wife's brother. Until yesterday, I didn't know how to describe this craziness he has to be in charge of everything."

"In charge of what, specifically?" Freud looked interested.

"In charge of everything, period. He's an accountant. As a young man he worked night and day, because he wanted to become a junior partner at the age of thirty. He became one. Then he worked even harder so he could be named a full partner by the age of thirty-five. He succeeded in that, as well. Then he politicked with every influential partner in his firm, until he was named managing partner of the firm. This meant adding to his already full docket of client work, the job of managing the accounting firm as a whole, establishing budgets, developing management strategies, going after new business, recruiting key graduate students, and so on. Then last month he told me that he was working on a merger with an even bigger accounting firm than his, but with the proviso that he would be the managing partner of the merged and larger firm."

Freud was now stroking his beard, lost in Croft's story.

"But that's just the start of it," Croft continued. "In the suburb where he lives, he served three terms as president of the school board. Then later he became president of the PTA. He also ran for president of his congregation, he's Jewish, and he won. When his son become active in Little League baseball, he volunteered to coach his son's team. Then he volunteered to become coach of his son's hockey team."

"This man sounds obsessed," Freud said.

"But there's more. He has been president of two local charities and this year he tells me he is running for president of the trade association that is composed of accounting firms throughout the nation, a position of great importance. And then there is the poker club we both belong to—"

"Poker?" Freud exclaimed, breaking into a small grin for the first time during the meeting. "He has time for poker?"

"One night a week and he hardly ever misses. The man is incredibly organized. But get this, he insisted early on that we take a formal vote, there are only six of us, to name a chairman of our little club. We all went along in good nature and of course named him the chairman. It was obvious he wanted it and the rest of us couldn't care less."

"Chairman, you say. What are the chairman's duties, if I might ask?" Freud asked, amused.

"He actually developed a list of duties, which he presented to us one night for approval, which we gave him. One of the main duties is that if someone is unable to be present on a poker night, he's in charge of getting a substitute. He also handles the money. We always take a few dollars out of two or three large pots for sundries and when we have a surplus, he invests the money in interest-bearing accounts, even though it's rarely more than a hundred dollars. But he insists on giving us a written report on the interest income earned.

"His duties also include developing a chart every six months, that shows at whose house the club will meet. I used to tell my wife that I thought he was obsessed with himself, just as you suspected, and she agreed. But yet the guy is really sort of pleasant and even a bit modest. But now I know what to call him."

"What?"

"He's a Number Eight on the Inner Dummy power scale."

"Oh, no," Freud's expression once again turned glum.

"But don't you see, that's a perfect designation. If somebody would ask me now what's wrong with my brother-in-law, who wants to be in charge of everything, I could simply say, 'Oh, Lester, he's just a Number Eight on the power program. Perfectly normal, otherwise.' The other person might reply, 'So that's it?' And I would say, 'That's it.' End of story. Do you see the point, Dr. Freud?"

"I'm afraid I don't."

"Well, if we are successful in getting this concept across to the general public, most people would know that a Number Eight on the limbic power scale has, in a sense, been captured by the power drive of his Inner Dummy. Or, if the term works out, they would know that he has been Dummy Snatched."

Freud winced noticeably.

"They would know," Croft continued, "that the Inner Dummy is a pseudonym for your concept of the id, a second operating system in our minds that has no concept of awareness, logic, or time. They will know that it would be useless simply to walk up to Lester and say, 'Let's get real here, Lester. You are compelled with being in charge. No matter what organization or group you become associated with, you automatically want to lead it. You want to be in charge of everything. This would be okay if you didn't have a family, considering that you are a pleasant fellow, all in all, and you do a good job.

"'But your children are feeling ignored. They think they are your last priority. And look at you. You look tired and worn out. There are rings around your eyes. It is hard to get a laugh out of you. This is all craziness on your part so get off of it.'

"Now his wife has tried this calm, rational approach with Lester several times, one time with my wife and I assisting her. And all Lester could tell us was that he could see his compulsion, but he couldn't help it."

"Did you suggest therapy?"

"We only hinted at it."

"But therapy could be very useful."

"Yes, it could. But don't you see, even in this day and age, a lot of people are ashamed of submitting to it, or don't think their problems are serious enough. However, if we could get them to understand that they have this Inner Dummy operating in their heads that are composed of Dummy Drives that are deaf, dumb, and blind to reality, then that would be the first step.

"Then if we could show them that they are an Eight or Nine or God forbid, a Ten on the dummy power scale or one of the other scales and that they are ruining their lives and those of their families, or co-workers or whatever, the light-hearted nature of the terminology would make the use of therapy appear to be a more natural solution."

"I'm not certain about that."

"But look at how Lester could now frame his problems to his family and friends. He could say, 'It dawned on me that I am a Number Eight on the power program scale. This is just something that happened to me, for whatever the reasons. I did not walk into a brain store and buy it. It exists within me and it is tiring me. It is ruining my marriage. It is alienating me from my children. I frequently become abrasive. So I am going to a therapist, or he might even say, an Inner Dummy specialist, to get some treatment, just the way I get treatment for my arthritis."

"Oh, no," Freud responded, again cradling his head between his hands.

"All right, forget the Inner Dummy specialist. It was a thought that occurred to me at the moment. But the point is, Dr. Freud, what if Lester had to tell people he had an imbalanced power libido, which Ollander told me was your concession to the program. It doesn't sound the same. It sounds too serious, it sounds like there is something really wrong with him."

"The concept of the libido as a biological force is serious," Freud replied, "and there is indeed something wrong with this man."

"Yes, and being designated as having a Number Eight, Nine, or Ten power program is serious as well. But we want to help the world by lightening the concept and offering acceptance to these people in the sense that yes, we know you are an Eight, Nine, or Ten, but either you try to do something about it, whether it's therapy or something else, or we're going to do everything possible to avoid being around you, even if you are a valued coworker, a brother, or even a mother. Don't you see the possibilities? We're saying, 'Hey, we accept you, we know you didn't walk into a store and buy your dummy program, but you have it and you are responsible for doing something about it, because it's out of whack."

"Oh my," Freud moaned.

"And we've only just begun," Croft went on. "There is hardly an hour that goes by in this place where someone isn't coming up with a new idea. You have energized the entire agency, Dr. Freud, and all I am asking is that you bear with us until we are finished. And in the meantime, cooperate with the people who need to talk to you."

Freud remained looking glum.

"Come on, Dr. Freud, what do you say?"

Freud once again cradled his head in his hands as he thought. Then he slowly looked up and said, "Okay, I will go along with this process, as you call it, but I reserve the right to make a final judgment when your concepts are completed."

"That's a deal and I love you for it," Croft said excitedly as he walked over to Freud and kissed him on the top of his head.

"My God." Freud looked stunned.

"Just a little affection, doctor. This is the advertising business you know."

"Yes, but a kiss?"

"First time I ever kissed a dead man, though. How about some lunch? We can do some Mexican down the street."

"I am afraid I have no appetite just now," Freud said, standing up stiffly. "I would like to go back to the conference room where there are some additional books I've ordered and I understand they have been delivered. I need to catch up with my critics."

"No problem. You know the way?"

"I do, Mr. Croft, and thank you for your time."

Freud got up, the office door was open, and walked out.

NOTE

1. News section, *International Herald Tribune*, March 16, 1998, p. 3.

12
THE STRENGTH
OF OUR SEX DRIVE

When Franklin Delano Roosevelt became President of the United States in 1933, and was scheduled to go to an outdoor event when it was raining, his mother would call him from her home in Hyde Park, New York, and remind him to wear his rubbers.[1]

I will start this chapter with the story of four business friends I knew in my career as a business consultant, each with a different level of *sexual libido*, to use that metaphor in a passing deference to Dr. Freud. They are all male, but I could tell you about four females I've known with similar characteristics. I have found that in the business world, you can develop many true and caring friends, if you are sincere and open to it, and you can talk about subjects as delicate as sex, just as you might with any friend in which confidences are exchanged.

One of my closest friends, Bob Cox, who was a client for many years, was getting married for the second time, some years after his first wife died. He asked me to handle the arrangements for a stag dinner and I asked him who I should invite.

"The usual," he replied.

"I know about the usual," I said, "but what about your personal friends?"

"Those are my personal friends." And they were.

Like Bob, who with his gentle and caring ways that were never impaired by his enormous success in the corporate world and who was my mentor for much of my life, I found a great deal of satisfaction in being with my business friends. And because we were on the road alone a great deal, we probably all learned more about each other than many do in traditional friendships, including, in some instances, details of our mutual sex lives. I've picked the following persons to represent four levels on a metaphoric *limbic sexual scale.*

The first—I'll call him Bryan—was in a high-level sales position and commonly on the road. I traveled with him frequently.

On a scale of *One* to *Ten,* as per the limbic power scale, *Ten* being the most intense, Bryan was at least an *Eight.* We no sooner checked into our hotel during the evening before the meeting we were scheduled to attend— we always went the evening before—then we were off to his favorite bar, where in each major city from coast to coast, he knew the precise times that would give him the greatest odds for finding a woman to have dinner with and so forth.

Bryan was tall, thin, and handsome, but had a childlike demeanor and soft, unassuming voice and manner that masked not only the Number Eight sexual program I had him pegged at, but a Number Nine power program as well. In terms of working a bar looking for new conquests, he took on the determined demeanor of a hunter in the woods.

One night, he found a woman within ten minutes and before I knew it, I was having dinner alone. Another night, I remember the city was Dallas, I was waiting for him in the crowded bar he had designated, before he arrived; he was taking a separate plane. I remember him walking in precisely at the appointed time of 5:30 P.M. and striking the pose of a hound dog . . . head high, nose in the air, one foot behind the other, almost raised. It was a picture I will never forget. Within the hour he had found a wonderfully loquacious woman and they were acting as if they had known each other for years. I headed back to the hotel for room service.

Bryan was actually married with a family and I would question him about this obsession for conquest. Even when he established semipermanent girlfriends in two or three cities, he would cheat on them as well as his wife. His reply to me was that while he was content in his marriage, he couldn't help himself. He would spend hours dreaming about the forthcoming trip and the strategies he would utilize. His descriptions reminded me of those told to me by Mike Keenan, a professional hockey coach. Keenan said he would sit in a dark room before a game for hours and strategize about how he would react to possible moves of opponents.

When Bryan and Keenan told me about how they thought about impending strategies, one for winning sex, the other for winning a hockey match, they both had a dreamlike quality in their faces as they spoke.

No matter how much sex Bryan had, no matter how many women he was with, it was never enough. This is apparently a characteristic of anyone with a highly intense limbic drive, whether power, sex, or territorial. No matter how much you acquire, it is never enough. After some momentary satisfaction, the need for more renews. It was also important to Bryan that others were witnessing his sexual prowess, apparently another characteristic of combined, intense sexual and power programs.

The second friend—I'll call him Mark—was also in sales and had a wife and children. However, he rarely talked about his sex life and I thought he was true-blue, until one day I was buying a newspaper in a downtown Chicago building and saw Mark walk by with his wife. I was just about to hail him, when on closer inspection, I saw that it was not his wife at all, but someone who looked just like her.

At dinner about two weeks later, I mentioned the encounter to him and he looked embarrassed. He told me that his infidelities were only occasional and that he had a relationship with this one woman for a few months. New sexual conquests weren't a pressing issue for him, he said to me, but if it happened it happened. At the time of this occurrence, he was in his fifties.

He told me that at a younger age he had to travel frequently and would do the bar scene depending on his mood and energy at the time. He wasn't obsessed with the thought like Bryan. Now that he was in his fifties and still on the road a good deal of the time, he rarely visited bars, preferring room service at his hotel and a good book. So for some of us things can change, but not for all of us, I might add. My second ex-father-in-law, when he died a widower at the age of eighty-four, was still making passes at every woman he found attractive and at one time, I actually passed an open door at his home in Wisconsin and there he was, doing it. He waved at me.

But getting back to Mark, I would peg him at perhaps a Number Seven on the sexual program. The power program didn't appear to reinforce Mark's sexual program as it did Bryan's. Mark appeared to be sexually active simply because of the gratification that sex alone might give you. He didn't need the stimulation of conquest.

One odd thing is that I've known many men like Mark and if they were happily married, as Mark was, the women who were part of their infidelities usually looked very much like their wives. The same was true about women I've known who participated in infidelities. With both sexes, if they were unhappy in their marriages, however, then the illicit partner usually bore little similarity to the marital partner. Nothing scientific about this, just an observation.

The third friend—I'll call him Eric—was president of a large corporation. Each time we had lunch or dinner on the road, he would practically twist his head off looking at attractive women. Eric was very happily married with a family. I would kid him by saying something like, "For God's sake, you're really happily married. You talk incessantly about how wonderful your wife is, but you're practically falling off your chair looking at all these women. What is the matter with you?"

And he would reply, "I may be married, but I'm not dead."

Each night we were on the road, Eric would dutifully go to bed. He swore to me that in twenty-five years of marriage, he never cheated on his wife, and I believed him. "But I think about it a lot," he said.

And so I pegged Eric to be a Number Five on the sexual scale, maybe just under former President Jimmy Carter who came right out and said that he had "lusted in his heart," but, because of the nature of his character and strong religious beliefs, I think most of us assumed he never acted on the lust he felt.

The fourth friend—I'll call him Allen—was the director of research of a large corporation, who I befriended while attending many of the consumer-research focus groups he conducted throughout the country. When we were having lunch or dinner, no matter how attractive or sexy any woman who passed by, he never noticed.

I recall having dinner with him one night at a very fancy Manhattan restaurant. A voluptuous model walked by, causing my hand in the process of delivering a slice of bread to my mouth, to freeze in midair. She paused for a moment to look at Allen as if she knew him, shook her head, and went on. Allen at the time was talking to me nonstop about some new statistical formulation he was working on to create a new deviation standard, I think that was the subject. He hardly gave the woman a glance, continuing his discourse as if nothing had happened.

And so I interrupted him and said, "Allen, didn't you see that?"

"See what?" he replied.

"That gorgeous woman."

"What gorgeous woman?"

"The woman who just went by and stopped to look at you."

"I didn't notice," he said.

"Is there something wrong with you? You have a family, don't you?"

"What are your implying?"

"I'm just inquiring in a roundabout way, if you are heterosexual, not that it would matter in the slightest if you were not. I mean, how could you not have noticed that woman stopping and staring at you? I've seen you do this before."

"Of course I am heterosexual, I have children, and no, I really didn't notice her."

"But you never seem to notice the most beautiful of women."

Allen thought for a moment, then went on to tell me in the confiding, secretive manner of researchers and accountants, that sex was never important to him. He did it with his wife to be a dutiful husband, but if he never had to do it again, that would be fine with him. He told me he wasn't attracted to other men, he wasn't bisexual, he just didn't care very much about sex, period.

"It feels all right, but you know, whenever I have to do it with my wife, I am usually thinking about work and how I am going to determine the proper statistical values."

And so I pegged Allen at a Number Two on the limbic sexual scale.

Of course, like the limbic power scale, the limbic sexual scale, which follows in this chapter, is of my own making. And once again for the writing of this book, I was determined to learn if such a scale existed in the world of academia to give it credibility.

At this point in time, I retained Nanmathi Manion, who was studying for her Ph.D. in Developmental Psychology at the University of Wisconsin, my alma mater, and had some hours available to do research work for me over the summer. The first thing she did was revisit the *Power Scale*, using the databases with which she was most familiar. She could find nothing more than the PyschSEARCH service of the American Psychological Association, described previously.

She then turned to a search for a limbic sexual scale, reminding me that in psychology the sex drive was referred to as the *sexual motive*. Not motives again, I thought. Nanmathi did come close in turning up questionnaires and data that included *The Sexual Desire Inventory* (Spector, Carey, and Steinberg, 1996) and *The Sex Inventory* (Thorne, 1996).

At the same time, on my own, I examined some published books offering psychological tests, including one authored by Louis Janda entitled *The Psychologist's Book of Self-Tests* and found tests for sex that included: "How Much Do You Know About Sex?" "What Do You Think About Sex?" "How Anxious Are You About Your Sexuality?" "How Sensual Are You?" "How Satisfying Is Your Relationship?"[2] The measurements for these tests were excellent and enlightening, but not what I was looking for.

I did, however, find a book, *The Sexual Desires Disorder* by Helen Kaplan, M.D., a sexual therapist, in which she developed what she called a "Continuum of Sexual Desires," which reflected six levels of sexual desire at the top of which was *Hyperactive Sexual Desire*, which she described as "Intense, spontaneous sexual desire and fantasy; compulsive sexual behavior; high frequency; inadequate control of sexual impulses; distress."

Next down the scale was *High Normal Sexual Desire*, which she described as "Spontaneous sexual desire and fantasy, proactive sexual behavior; normal sexual functioning; high frequency," followed by *Low Sexual Desire*, described as "No spontaneous sexual desire or fantasy."

Farther down the scale was *Severe Hypoactive Sexual Desire*, described as ". . . poor sexual functioning; sexual avoidance; very low-frequency or celibacy; distress." At the bottom she had *Sexual Aversion Disorder*, described as "Active aversion to and/or phobic avoidance of sex; very low frequency or celibacy; distress."[3]

It was quite a relief to find such a scale even though it focused on disorders, as she defined them, and not on a limbic scale, which might be more readily recognized as a measurement of the inner craziness of some otherwise apparently normal people. Bryan never felt distress. I think we recognize innately that there is a definite scale to the intensities of the sexual drive and to the other drives as well. To depart from the sex drive for a moment, I recall in the mid-1990s being interviewed for my book *Brain Tricks* on a Chicago radio show hosted by Danny Bonaduce, an apparently normal person, who as a child was one of the red-headed children on the network television show *The Partridge Family*, which also starred Shirley Jones.

I had given Danny an early draft of the limbic power quiz before the show and he suggested that I read the questions to his listening audience and after giving them time to calculate the numbers, he would read the answers, which comprised the Number One to Ten scale, as shown, with some modifications, in the previous chapter. And so I read the questions, I still have the tape of the show, and when Danny finished reading the description of the Number Tens who may be willing to kill to fulfill their desires, he said, "That's me. I admit it, I'm a Number Ten. If I could get away with it, I would kill to become a star in Hollywood again."

While he said this in his usual fun, joking way, I was looking into his eyes at the time, and I suspected there was more to it, but who's to say?

Then I recall John McLaughlin, host of his own roundtable program, *The McLaughlin Group*, on PBS, mentioning on a show in June 1998 that Monica Lewinsky's mother had voluntarily agreed to visit the special prosecutor, Kenneth Starr. McLaughlin made the point, to the effect, "Here is a Jewish mother, who has to be near *primal* in her nurturance of her daughter." There was no disagreement of this assessment among the panelists.

So it's obvious that many of us do recognize the *primal* tendencies we might exhibit as a normal part of our own natures, even though we will raise the question "What were they thinking?" It may be that we have become so engulfed in our intellectualism and civilities that we find it difficult to grasp the concept of a wild, instinctive id—an *Inner Dummy*—operating independently inside our heads that only becomes obvious when out of balance or when severely jolted by disappointment.

Yet there is little doubt that ultimately these programs are chemical in nature, controlled by hormones and other brain chemicals, and it is the combination of how these substances are produced in our bodies and directed by the organs involved that create the drives themselves, the levels of their intensities, and the experiential circumstances under which they'll emerge to influence or take charge of our minds.

In their book *Sex and the Brain*, science writers Jo Durden-Smith and Diane Desimone say the following:

> Scientists have found the beginnings of a connection . . . between sexual drive and testosterone, not only in men, but also in women. If a female-to-male transsexual is given large doses of testosterone, then her libido increases. And so does the libido of women who for one reason for another—because of disease, medical treatment of persistent and grueling exercise, perhaps—are exposed to higher levels of testosterone than usual.[4]

In *Brain Tricks*, one of my characters talked about how the sex drive was actually a brain trick in itself, because the design of nature made it feel so good and that we as humans are drawn to rewarding feelings. And so, unwittingly or not, we follow nature's basic desire to pass our genes along from one generation to the next, without realizing that this is what sex, as well as the other core limbic drives—nurturance, power, territorialism, and survival—are really designed to achieve.

This thought was echoed in molecular geneticist Dean Hamer and writer Peter Copeland's book *Living with Our Genes*, in which they said:

> To guarantee their survival, the genes found a clever trick. Instead of appealing to our higher sense of calling, or our duty to continue the human race, the genes made sex feel good, real good. Genes code for millions of touch receptors in the genitals and for the nerves that connect them to the brain, the most important sex organ. The somatosensory cortex, the part of the brain linked to the genital area, is larger than any other, which is why the genitals are so delightfully, exquisitely sensitive to the touch. . . . Still other genes, presumably in the primitive limbic part of the brain, help make us receptive to the social interactions and signs of mutual attraction that we feel instinctively and now call love.[5]

That last paragraph, by the way, was the thumbnail, technical version of our sexual biochemistry, the knowledge of which would have made no difference to Bryan during his bar visits.

"So, it's my brain chemistry that's the villain?" he might ask.

"That is correct," we would respond.

"Well, great. I see a girl sitting by herself in the corner. Let's see if the chemistry does any good with her."

And so it goes with human nature.

The real complications of the sex drive in our everyday lives get caught up in the metaphoric *sexual program*, which combines the other mechanisms that drive us to sex and its ultimate objective of reproduction. These mechanisms would include the mating dance or courtship, the soap opera scenario that ultimately leads to sex; how we dress ourselves to attract sex; sexual jealousy and the pain of separation, the thought of which may help us to stay together.

As background for the evolutionary need for a mating dance or courtship, the following passage from my book *Brain Tricks* indicates why females on the average are fussier about who they have sex with than males and who obviously find real value in the mating dance for selecting the most appropriate mate:

> Nature did not treat females and males equally. The female possesses the capacity of between 400 and 600 eggs at birth . . . each containing 23 chromosomes. Each ejaculation of the male produces from 100 to 500

million sperm cells, each of which is equivalent to the female egg with 23 chromosomes.

The result is that the average female is obviously driven by nature to be more fussy about whom she chooses as a sex partner. The male can spray away. The contradiction . . . is that our children need the guardianship of a mother and father, and so while males may be driven to spray away, they are also compelled by nature into the formation of a family unit.

Against this background, the mating dance continues and fools with our rationality, whether it be a chaperoned walk in an old Spanish village or a singles bar in Greenwich Village.[7]

In her book *The Alchemy of Love and Lust*, sex therapist and researcher Theresa L. Crenshaw, M.D., made the following observation: "Clearly, our mating dance, the desires that drive us and frustrate us, the bonds we make, the love we give and take—the hearts we break, the differences that might delight and infuriate us, the mystery of attraction, 'sexual chemistry,' and the agonies and ecstasies of intimacy—all this and more is influenced by the ever-changing bouillabaisse of chemicals in our bodies that I think of as 'sex soup.' "[8]

According to some theorists, females are attracted primarily to those males who their instinctive programs sense will create the strongest possible baby. This could be why so many males and females end up in the wrong relationships. The ultimate baby, if it is produced, may be strong, but in the meantime, if the couple has very different interests, combined with intense limbic power programs, with both spouses attempting to be in control, the marriage could be one long shoot-out. After two divorces from fine women, I, for one, understand this concept very well.

Another part of the sexual program is the way we dress ourselves. If we are high up on the sexual scale, we might wear revealing clothes, heavy makeup, and jewelry, tailored power suits, whatever it takes to make us appear more attractive and sensual, no matter what our age. Of course, this need to attract could also be part of our limbic power program, one more reason why the two drives are often associated.

We might consider a third part of the program to be sexual jealousy, which can be far more intense than the envies and jealousies created by other core limbic programs when they are disappointed or crossed in some way.

Jealousy, when we fear or know a spouse is having sex with someone else, creates such a negative, depressive feeling that it works to punish the victim as well as the guilty partner. Jealousy thus may be a design of nature intended to help keep couples together. Or, as Dean Hamer and Peter Copeland put it in their book, *Living with Our Genes*: "When a man and woman mate, the genes have a vested interest in their staying together long enough to produce and raise a child. . . . A man is furious when a woman strays because she could become pregnant by another male, which means the first male would spend all his energy raising someone else's genes. If a man strays, the woman is jealous because she needs help nurturing the child."[9]

As an aside, this primal male need to be obsessed with assuring that the female is carrying his genes and not some interloper's is reflected in the higher animal world, where the first thing a new dominant, alpha male does in some species is kill the current offspring of his harem so that he can start all over again. Isn't this a wonderful world we live in?

We might consider a fourth part of the sexual program to be the pain of separation. It is currently thought by many neurobiologists that humans are not only genetically designed to have sex to produce children so that our genes are passed onto the next generation, but that in the process of natural selection, strong adults acting as mother and father are required to properly nurture offspring during infancy and childhood.

If we consider this to be true, then it makes perfect sense that nature would include in the design of our metaphoric limbic brains a punishment for human couples with children who separate. This punishment, as I personally can attest, having gone through my first divorce with children, is a lingering, intense, depressive pain. However, I have seen both men and women with children fresh out of divorces looking happy and relieved. So the intensity of the pain may be a result of the combination of both our *sexual* and *nurturance programs*. The pain would probably be less intense if we were lower on the nurturance scale than it would if we were higher.

I don't know Monica Lewinsky's mother, to use one example, but if I did and could agree with John McLaughlin that she might be *primal* in her nurturance, then I am sure she felt plenty of pain during the process of her divorce from Monica's father.

Where children are not involved, where it is a broken relationship of a childless couple, the intensities of our sexual program may be more involved than our nurturance program, but then if we begin to speculate on all the possible combinations of the programs in producing a specific punishment or reward, our eyes would become quickly glazed. At least mine would.

We now come to the sexual limbic scale that I devised. As pointed out previously, this limbic sexual quiz has been on the *Brain Tricks* Web site (www.braintricks. com) since 1996. Early on, the site as a whole, after being placed on the main search directories, averaged about sixty to eighty visitors a day.

Then in mid-1997, a direct link to the sex quiz alone was made from some higher traffic sites, one of which was a self-improvement site on American Online; another was an electronic magazine called "Hot Rod Your Head." But there were other direct links made as well. The result was that on average, between 200 and 400 persons daily have been taking the sex quiz for more than a year, with a monthly average of about 9,000 visitors. Adding this average to those who visited the quiz before the high traffic links were made, a minimum of 150,000 persons have taken the quiz as of this writing.

Further, the visitors have come from all over the world. In particular, the quiz has had thousands of visitors from Australia, Singapore, Japan, South Africa, India, and most of the countries of Europe, including those which were once part of the former Soviet Union.

As with the power quiz, we added monitoring software several months ago that told us what percentage of people were ending up at which specific level on the scale. More than 51,000 have been monitored, which again gives us an accuracy level of ±1 percent against the entire sampling of more than 150,000.

However, I was concerned during this writing, that the monitoring did not differentiate between male and female. This was not a concern for the power scale because I have dealt with as many power-crazed females as I have males. Further, the dominance hierarchy, which is the underpinning of the power scale includes both females and males in the struggle for status. This *status tension* continues to exist when females as a whole are made subservient to males by the rules of the herd if we're referring to the higher animals, or the culture if we're referring to humans. And so I am simply deferring to Dr. Helen Kaplan, who in her book *The Sexual Desire Disorders*, showed no differentiation between males and females in her "Continuum," or scale of sexual levels.

Further, in her discussions about the characteristics of these levels, Kaplan tells about one female who she labeled: "Case 4.4—'Tina Jefferson,' Hypersexual Desire in a Depressed Heterosexual Female in a Good Sexual Relationship." What follows is a short excerpt about Mrs. Jefferson.*

---

*This is not the patient's real name

But when he [her husband] happened to be unavailable or too exhausted to make love, Tina would feel mounting and distressing pelvic discomfort, which was not relieved until she had intercourse.

Mrs. Jefferson's craving for sex was intrusive and interfered with her functioning at her office job. She often could not bear to sit at her desk more than two hours at a time before she would feel a compelling urge to have intercourse. She would gradually become too uncomfortable and "frustrated" to be able to continue her work.[10]

Mrs. Jefferson would probably be considered a Number Eight or Nine on the limbic sexual scale, since there was no mention that she was willing to throw everything she valued away in the process of establishing a life structure that would better satisfy the extreme and intense expectations of her sexual drive.

Once again, I claim no scientific validation for the metaphoric limbic sexual scale that follows. As with the power scale developed from the power quiz, I requested, through a feedback form on the site, input from visitors taking the quiz, who thought the results weren't consistent with their own perceptions. And so for many months I refined the quiz and the answers. The feedback, incidentally, included messages from homosexuals, both male and female, who for the most part, felt the results were appropriate, but asked me to frame the questions and answers so that they would feel better about participating, which I did.

For the past twelve months the only feedback has been from participants who related that the results appeared to be in the ballpark.

Here is the scale:

NUMBER ONE:

You are somewhere near totally asexual. You might never have had sex and don't care if you do. You might even be repelled by the thought of having sex. But this doesn't really matter. There are billions of other people having sex, so the earth will be well populated anyway.

NUMBER TWO:

You do have a sex drive, but it doesn't take any priority at all in your life. You may even dress yourself to be sexually unappealing so that you don't have to contend with sex or any of its aspects. If you have a sex partner and you discover he or she is having an affair, you might feel more relieved than jealous.

NUMBER THREE:

You have a sex drive and you might enjoy sex when you have it, but you are not going to do very much to attract it. If you're married or in a relationship, you would probably never think of cheating.

NUMBER FOUR:

You may have an active sex life, but sex is not frequently on your mind. If you need to go without it for a relatively long period of time, it probably won't be depressive. You may dress fashionably, but not intentionally to appear sensual. You are probably not a candidate for an affair, but will feel jealousy if your significant other wanders.

NUMBER FIVE:

You're where most of us are at, according to the monitoring software. You have an active sex life, or wish you did. You dress to be attractive to the opposite sex, but you don't overdo it. Sex is just a normal part of your life and you're happy with where you stand with it.

NUMBER SIX:

Sex is an important part of your life. You'll dress so that you perceive yourself as being attractive to potential sexual partners. You like the idea of sex, but the urge is not strong enough for you to have an affair, unless the attraction of the potential partner was overpowering. If your significant other wanders, you will feel jealousy.

NUMBER SEVEN:

Sex is on your mind a good part of your waking hours. If you are married or into a serious relationship, you are ripe for an affair if a discreet opportunity presents itself. On occasion, you will find yourself openly flirting with a potential sexual partner, who is very attractive to you. You like the whole idea of the mating dance. If your significant other wanders, however, you will feel very depressed and jealous.

NUMBER EIGHT:

Sex is uppermost in your mind. If you are female, you might be into such things as short skirts, tight clothing, extra bright makeup, spiked heels. If you are male, you might be into such things as tight pants, gold jewelry, open shirts, or even power suits, intended to attract. You love the whole idea of the mating dance. With both sexes, however, your clothing may also reflect your power program. Whether single or married, you are looking for sexually oriented affairs. You are out for it one way or another. But if your significant other wanders, you will feel intense jealousy.

NUMBER NINE:

You may be among the nymphomaniacs of the world, whether female or male. You may sacrifice family or friends, if you find this necessary, to live in a world of sex. You will join sex clubs if they exist where you live. You will spend vacations at resorts that imply sexual adventures. You may put your life and your well-being at risk for sex if necessary. You are capable of becoming furious with jealousy and taking revenge without qualms.

NUMBER TEN:

Time to check in somewhere. You may murder for sex. You may try rape, particularly if you also have an intense power program and can't meet your expectations any other way. You may do whatever it takes to fulfill your sexual urges and fantasies. You are dangerous. You are also capable of killing if you catch your significant other, who you think you own, having sex with someone else.

If you are unsure of your limbic sexual scale ranking, take the quiz on the Web site. As with the power quiz, it will give you a rough idea of where you stand, but you might not like it. However, since there is no scientific validation to these limbic scales as I've outlined them, or to the related quizzes, then once again, let me remind you, there is nothing for you to worry about.

Here is how the sexual rankings broke down with the responses that were monitored, rounded off to the nearest percentage, except for the Number Nines, which were only slightly more than the Number Tens, and I thought could use a decimal point.

	Percent	**No. of responses**
NUMBER ONE	2.0	1,303
NUMBER TWO	4.0	1,876
NUMBER THREE	13.0	6,585
NUMBER FOUR	23.0	11,756
NUMBER FIVE	25.0	12,855
NUMBER SIX	18.0	9,480
NUMBER SEVEN	9.0	4,893
NUMBER EIGHT	1.5	750
NUMBER NINE	1.4	734
NUMBER TEN	1.0 (see below)	889

If you have a calculator, you'll note that the numbers don't add up to 100 percent. That's because 2 percent of the visitors ended up with 0 percent, obviously not doing something right. And about half the Number Tens, marked Ten for every answer, just in it, obviously, for the fun. So I reduced the Tens from 2 to 1 percent.

It would appear that only about 4 percent of all people are "off the wall" when it comes to sex, according to these results. This is a little better than the number stated by a psychologist being interviewed on National Public Radio, whose name I didn't catch, who said he thought that 10 percent of the population was composed of dangerously sexual people.

In any event, all of us appear to occupy some level, whether defined properly or not, on the limbic sexual scale on a consistent basis, which means not taking in account periods of high passion with a new partner or periodic events or circumstances that might stimulate or turn us off sexually. This doesn't mean we are stuck with a particular positioning on the scale that we don't like. It might be changed with remedies, described in chapters 32 and 34.

Someone asked me to explain the actions of Bill Clinton with Monica Lewinsky, in terms of the concepts offered in this book. This is how our conversation went:

"How can you explain this guy, the president of the United States getting involved with a young intern?"

"It is simple," I replied. "Bill Clinton was apparently between an Eight and Nine on the limbic sexual scale. When it comes to sex, he is probably always on edge, he is after it. He will probably do everything he can to control his urges, considering his office, but when a woman he is attracted to and is coming on to him, opens her jacket, revealing her thong underwear, then it is all over. The game is up. It is off to a secluded rendezvous. The next time we elect a president who is a Number Eight or Nine on the sexual scale, we need to have guards around him at all times, and perhaps for the good of the country, ask the women who are around him to wear chadors, heavy veils that cover them head to toe. This would be a great public service, we would tell them."

"But we are talking about the president of the United States, here. Surely someone who has fought his way up to the top of the world's ultimate power structure can control his sex urges."

"Not true," I replied. "That part of Bill Clinton's id, his Inner Dummy, that controls his sex drive couldn't care less that he is president. It might even feel, 'Wow, now that I am president, I can use my power as an aphrodisiac and get even more sex, get my genes spread into a lot of women and build a stronger world. Hey, there's a nice-looking woman standing over there eating a canape. Bill . . . hey, Bill . . . move on over there. Let's do our stuff.'"

"That is one sick scenario."

"It is, isn't it? Maybe we should require candidates for president to take this sex quiz or another one like it, that would give the nation an idea of their number right from the get-go. Since strong power and sex drives do appear to combine, apparently because nature wants the strongest genes to inhabit the next generation, then we deserve to know what a candidate's sexual level is. If it's too low, we should be suspicious . . . can this man wield power? If it's normal that's okay. If it's high like Bill Clinton's and we think the man would make a good president, the press should quiz him on how he will handle his intense sex drive."

"What do you mean?"

"I mean we should ask him what precautions he intends to take. The nation can't take another Monica incident. For example, the candidate might put forth the chador idea, or pledge that, 'Whenever my wife is not with me in the office or at functions, one of my sisters will be, at all times. They will be my guardians. They will never leave my side. The Secret Service will protect my life, my wife and sisters will protect me from my sex drive and will be duly sworn in. That is my pledge to the American people.'"

"And we should be satisfied with that?"

"You don't like it? Okay, let's think of something else."

Before we leave this chapter, I thought you would be interested in a quote by Bill Clinton from a June 2, 1998, fundraising dinner, reported by Robert Woodward in his book *Shadow*, and taken from the "Public Papers of the Presidents":

> How many of us—haven't all of you been—had at least a moment of being downright dumb when you were really successful? Is there a person who is here say with a straight face you never had one moment of stupidity in the aftermath of some success you enjoy? Nobody can say that.[11]

Was he alluding to our Inner Dummies?

COMMENTARY BY DR. HEFTER

The narrative in this chapter appropriately considers the relationship of the "sex drive" to the other drives, e.g., power, nurturance, and so on. This is significant because sexual behavior is so much related to other behaviors.

Our legal system is cognizant of these relationships in specifying certain sexual activities as having significant legal ramifications. Thus rape, sexual harassment, and some pornography are not perceived as primarily sexual in nature but as actions that have far broader ramifications.

If we reflect upon our sexual behavior, an honest appraisal will recognize the interrelations of sexual activity with other interests, both those of which we are aware, and those whose existence we sometimes can only deduce. As the chapter points out, one of the aspects of sexual behavior that is apparently crucial to the frequency and intensity of its drive is the pleasure derived from it. And like most pleasurable activities, there is often difficulty in channeling this behavior appropriately.

The chapter also refers to individuals with less driven sexual behavior. To some extent, this is a relative concept—i.e., psychological, societal, and biological factors are all involved in the overt expression of sexual behavior. The "sex drive," for example, is influenced by our mood, societal norms, and our age. The use of drugs like Viagra®, for example, requires a wish to use it, a situation conducive to it, and a degree of non-Viagra® induced stimulation, in order for the biological effects of the medication to manifest themselves.

NOTES

1. I heard this story related in a radio interview by a biographer of Roosevelt's, whose name I didn't get. However, a number of Roosevelt biographies attests to his mother, Sara, and her power hold over him, long into his presidency and until she died.

2. Louis Janda, *The Psychologist's Book of Self-Tests* (New York: Perigree, 1996), pp 189–228.

3. Helen S. Kaplan, *The Sexual Desire Disorders: Dysfunctional Regulation of Sexual Motivation* (Bristol, Pa.: Brunner/Mazel, 1995), p. 15.

4. Jo Durden-Smith and Diane deSimone, *Sex and the Brain* (New York: Arbor House, 1983), p. 95.

5. Dean Hamer and Peter Copeland, *Living with Our Genes: Why They Matter More than You Think* (New York: Doubleday, 1998), p. 163.

6. Kaplan, *The Sexual Desire Disorders*, p. 58.

7. David L. Weiner, *Brain Tricks: How to Cope with the Dark Side of Your Brain and Win the Ultimate Mind Game* (Amherst, N.Y.: Prometheus Books, 1993), pp. 30, 109.

8. Theresa L. Crenshaw, "Introduction," *The Alchemy of Love and Lust: Discovering Our Sex Hormones and How They Determine Who We Love, When We Love, and How Often We Love* (New York: G. P. Putnam's Sons, 1996), p. xxi. (Introduction).

9. Hamer and Copeland, *Living with Our Genes*, p. 162.

10. Kaplan, *The Sexual Desire Disorders*, p. 58.

11. Bob Woodward, *Shadow: Five Presidents and the Legacy of Watergate 1974–1999* (New York: Simon & Schuster, 1999), p. 413.

13

DR. FREUD MEETS
AN IMAGE OF HIMSELF

U.S. Navy Commander Michael Alfonso, commander of the Trident nuclear submarine the USS Florida, was extremely competent in managing the submarine's systems and operations. On shore, his neighbors stated that he always had a greeting for everyone, and was unfailingly polite. However, he became enraged on the submarine when his fork was missing from his dinner place setting, shouting at a subordinate who had mistakenly taken it, "It's my fork don't touch it."[1]

D r. Freud was sitting in the agency's conference room, studying a note that was sent to him by Ted Croft's secretary, when the door opened and a man and woman entered, the woman pulling behind her a metallic equipment case strapped to a rolling, luggage tote.

As the woman stopped and began undoing the straps, the middle-aged man, who was large, overweight, and energetic, bounded around the table, stopped in front of Dr. Freud and said, "Doctor, this is a great privilege to meet you, a great honor indeed. My name is Peter Norton, vice president of sales of the Manchester Doll Company, and that," pointing across the table, "is Jenny Kagan, our communications director."

Kagan, who was young and shapely, looked up and said, "Very happy to meet you, doctor."

Freud, looking puzzled, said to Norton, "I'm afraid there must be some mistake. This is a note," he showed it to Norton, "from Mr. Croft's secretary saying that I was to be interviewed about my thoughts on the hydraulics of the sexual instinct."

"Oh, that's great," Norton boomed. "Hey, Jenny," he looked across the table at her, "how about giving the good doctor here a little discourse on some sex hydraulics? I know it would relieve some of that hydraulic pressure I'm feeling."

Jenny looked at him as if she had been through this before. "Get lost, Peter."

Norton's booming laughter reverberated against the wood-paneled walls of the room.

"Isn't that great, Doctor? Doesn't she have a great sense of humor? I can say things like that to her and never worry she's going to call a lawyer or something like that."

Jenny looked at Freud. "That's because I haven't found one mean enough yet."

Norton's laughter boomed out again, with Freud looking at the man as if he were dysfunctional, and moving his chair ever so slightly away.

Then Norton sat down next to Freud and moved his chair close enough so that their knees were almost touching. Freud looked annoyed and attempted to hide the discomfort he felt, not only because of the unseemly closeness, but because Norton's breath was bad.

Freud again edged his chair back and said, "I can assume then, that you are not the interviewer for the sexual instinct."

"I wish I were, doc, I wish I were. I know Jenny wishes I were; she just loves it when I talk dirty."

"Get a life, Peter," she responded.

Norton's laughter boomed out again, this time louder than before and increasing Freud's annoyance. "Isn't she great? Isn't she just great?"

"Mr. Norton, please," Freud broke in, "tell me immediately what this is about. I have a great deal of research work to do, as you can see." Freud pointed to the pile of books that were now scattered about the table, having grown in number since his last meeting with Samuel Ollander, the agency's research director.

"Well, of course, doctor," Norton responded, turning serious. "Your appointment with the copywriter handling the *Inner Dummy Sex Manual* has been postponed to later, since they wanted me in here right away to get your impressions on the prototype we intend to—"

"Did you say 'sex manual'?" Freud interrupted.

"Yes, that's my understanding."

"I know nothing about that." Freud looked annoyed again.

"I imagine it's just another part of the campaign, doctor. I'm sure you'll learn more about it when the writer talks to you." Then he looked over at Jenny. "Hey, Jenny, how about you and me being the models for that sex manual?"

Jenny, who was still busy adjusting her camera, replied, "Drop dead, Norton."

Norton's laughter boomed out again, louder than ever as he took his seat, edging closer to the annoyed Dr. Freud, who edged his chair backwards again.

"Sorry, doc, I just can't help myself when Jenny is around."

"Please, Mr. Norton, get to the point," Freud said heatedly. "What is the purpose of this meeting?"

"I'm truly sorry, doctor," Norton said, making a sincere effort to look apologetic. "I don't know what gets into me sometimes. We're here about the doll program."

"Doll program? I know nothing about a doll program."

"You mean, they didn't tell you about this?"

"Not at all."

"Ah, well, everything is moving so fast on this campaign, maybe that's why. As a matter of fact I have never seen any campaign of this magnitude move so fast. The agency creatives are coming up with one idea after another and they seem to be running with most of them, figuring the consumer research will filter out the duds. So right now, the doll idea is on a fast track and that's why we're here today, to meet you and get some photos of you so that our model shop can build a prototype for the first doll. If the idea works out, we're hoping to come out with a whole line of them."

"I would appreciate it, sir, if you would enlighten me about these so-called dolls." Freud was annoyed.

"Okay, then, the first thing is the name the agency people have given them, which I think you'll really love. It will be one more great legacy for you."

"In that case, I'm almost afraid to ask what the name is."

"Hey, I told you you'd love it. We're going to call them *Dr. Freud's Inner Dummy Dolls*."

"*What?*" Freud stood up in apparent shock, his face whitening.

"You see? I knew you'd love it," Norton said, mistaking Freud's chagrin for acceptance. "And we're putting the same design team on this business that have come up with all the giveaway dolls for McSweeney's."

"McSweeney's?" Freud could barely utter the word.

"Oh, that's right, you've been dead. McSweeney's is a big, international fast-food restaurant chain. The account is handled by this agency. The dolls are offered on television to kids to get them to entice their parents to bring them to a McSweeney's restaurant. The dolls are usually associated with a movie, or some kiddie craze; we've never done a psychological doll, but hey, we consider ourselves at the cutting edge of the doll industry. Isn't that right, Jenny?"

"If you say so, Peter."

Freud remained standing, his face now contorted with worry.

"Sit down, doc. Take a load off. Here, let me show you the working sketches we have for the first model. Hand them to me will you, Jenny dear?"

Jenny reached down into her equipment case and pulled out a large envelope, handing it across the table to Norton.

"Here they are, doc," Norton said, removing two art boards from the envelope and holding them against his chest, so that Freud, now seated, couldn't see the sides that were illustrated. "These sketches are pretty rough, but they'll give you the idea."

Then Norton slowly turned the first art board toward Freud and laid it on the table. It was a black and white sketch of Dr. Freud as a doll, in a sitting position, with his rear affixed to a wooden straight-backed chair, one leg crossed over the other, and his hands folded across his chest.

Freud looked at the sketch aghast.

"Oh, I know, it's not the greatest likeness, doc. The artist got your face off one of your book covers. Jenny brought a digital camera along to take some quick photos of you so that our model shop can create just the right likeness."

Freud was unable to speak.

"But here's the hook, my friend," Norton said to Freud as he turned the second art board around so that Freud could view the illustration. It was a back view of the doll and on it was a dial that looked like a pocket calculator, with buttons that numbered one to twelve and an additional row of buttons beneath them.

"Each of these numbered buttons," Norton continued, "triggers a short statement contained on a microchip inside the doll that repeats itself for half an hour, or until you touch this 'off' button." Norton pointed to one of the lower buttons labeled "off."

Freud was still unable to speak.

"Now, here's the idea, as I understand it," Norton went on, shifting himself in his chair. "The concept is based on a higher-consciousness theory that contends that short, pithy statements, directed repeatedly to your unconscious, which the agency, as you know, has branded the *Inner Dummy*, will give you relief from what these higher-consciousness people call unwanted, emotional addictions. Are you with me?"

Freud remained motionless, eyes expressionless.

"Okay, let me give you an example. Say you have a fat phobia. You think you look fat, but you really aren't. Well, when you get up in the morning, while you're getting ready for work, you push one of these buttons and a voice that sounds like yours, Dr. Freud, accent and all, comes on and says," Norton lowered his voice and clumsily attempted to imitate a German accent: " 'Eat, eat, eat. You never looked so thin. Eat, eat, eat. You never looked so thin. Eat, eat, eat. You never looked so thin.' "

Norton paused and looked squarely at Freud. "Do you get it? Isn't this great? This same short, precise message plays on and on and on. That's all it says until you push the 'off' button. The doll is talking to your Inner Dummy, don't you see? The thought is that by repeating one precise and pertinent point day in and day out, maybe you can get through to it. That's the idea. Isn't this just stupendous?"

Freud continued to stare at the sketches as if he had become lost in a swirl of strange madness.

"And hey," Norton went on, "here's another feature you're just going to go bonkers over."

Norton moved his chair closer to Freud and held the sketch so that it was almost touching Freud's knees, making him noticeably more uncomfortable than he already was.

"Now say you just broke up romantically with somebody you really cared about," Norton said, "and so now you are upset, depressed, and anguished. If you are a female, you press the appropriate button and the doll starts to say," Norton lowered his voice, again trying to imitate Dr. Freud's German accent:

" 'You're lucky he's gone. He was no good for you. You'll find someone better. You're lucky he's gone. He was no good for you. You'll find someone better. You're lucky he's gone. He was no good for you. You'll find someone better.' And on and on and on until you shut it off. Isn't this great? Come on, admit it, doc, you know this is the greatest idea ever."

Freud turned his head up and stared with glazed eyes at the ceiling, still unable to respond.

Then Jenny said hesitantly and softly, looking at the distraught doctor, "I don't know if this means anything, Dr. Freud, but last month I broke up with my boyfriend of five years. We loved each other very much, but our interests were so different that we were constantly arguing. And so we both agreed to part. It was an amiable parting, but I really haven't been able to get over it. So last night, after reading about the concept for the doll, I decided to record a message very similar to the one Norton just used, on my cassette tape recorder, repeating it over and over.

"This morning I played the tape. Then I rewound it and played it again, four times in all, while I was getting ready for work and packing up my things. And I have to tell you, Dr. Freud, that I did feel relief. I don't know if this is scientific or not, but I can't wait to get home tonight, to do it all over again. I'd probably be first in line to buy one of these Inner Dummy dolls."

"You see, Dr. Freud?" Norton said cheerfully. "Now, Jenny, did I tell you to relate that story to the good doctor, here?"

"Of course not," she replied.

"Well there you are, doctor. And we've hardly begun to figure out how to really utilize this idea, what the statements should be, exactly."

Freud slowly slumped forward in his chair, elbows on his knees.

"And hey, " Norton continued relentlessly, "if you loved the last two statements, you're going to fall head over heels over this one. Say you're unhappy or depressed because you've been rejected for one reason or another, at home, at work, whatever. You just put your Dr. Freud Inner Dummy Doll in your bedroom at night, set the timer, which we intend to add to the instrumentation, press the appropriate button, and it repeats this statement or something like it for forty-five minutes, hopefully by which time you'll be peaceably sleeping." Norton used his clumsy German accent to say energetically: "Deep down everyone loves you. Cheer up. Deep down everyone loves you. Cheer up. Deep down everyone loves you. Cheer up.

"See what I mean? Isn't this great? A statement like this aimed directly at your Inner Dummy can make you feel more positive, more motivated. And now we're doing more than just defining the problems and the scales of the Inner Dummy. We're beginning to find remedies for the problems they cause. This makes our company part of the agency team. This is a thrill. Don't you agree?"

Freud remained immobile.

Norton, ignoring Freud's nonreaction, continued.

"We'll have fifteen messages built into the doll's microchip, maybe more. And hey, we may even have a line of miniature diskettes that include a whole array of other messages. You just slip a diskette in that has on it the message that most directly addresses your upset. Well?" Norton paused, looking directly at Freud who now had turned his chair to the table slumping over it in a familiar pose, head between his hands, staring down. "Come on, tell us, what do you really think?"

Freud slowly raised his head and looked at Norton. "What do I think, you ask," he said, his voice husky. "I'll tell you what I think, Mr. Norton. I think the idea of this doll is beyond absurd, beyond moronic, and I will have nothing to do with it."

"But why, sir?" Norton responded, for the briefest of seconds looking chagrined.

"Because you cannot get over even mild depressions, anxieties, compulsions, and phobias with some doll looking like me mouthing pithy little statements. The id is obstinate and unyielding. It is resistant. I do not intend to lecture you. And I certainly do not want my name linked to the concept of Inner Dummy Dolls."

"Oh, Dr. Freud," Jenny broke in, "I know you've gone along with other things suggested to you by the agency that you feel are beneath you. We understand that. We have sympathy for you. So can't you just go along with us on this one additional concept?"

"I'm afraid not, my dear."

"But I'm sure no one will feel that these dolls are a cure-all. But I know how I felt after listening to the tape I made. I do feel better. Maybe later today or tomorrow I won't. But why not give this concept a chance?"

"I don't think so, Jenny," he said, softening.

"Look, sir. I know our company. And Norton here, as obnoxious as he is, is certainly no reflection on the quality of the products we produce."

"Hey, I resemble that," Norton said gleefully, obviously inured to insult.

Jenny continued, "The proof of the pudding, Dr. Freud, will be in the several working prototypes our company intends to build. We'll test those prototypes with a fair sampling of consumers. If the concept has no value, those consumers will let us know and I can assure you that the project will then be killed. So what do we have to lose?"

Freud looked softly at Jenny. "You are a bright and persuasive woman, my dear."

"Thank you, sir. I love the concept of the Inner Dummy, just the little I read about it. And anything we can do to extend its value to consumers can only be a help to people."

A slow grin broke across Freud's face.

"What are you thinking, sir?" Jenny asked.

"Ah, I was just thinking of Carl Jung, an early collaborator of mine, who turned against my theories in a way that grieved me deeply. I was thinking that if I could get him transposed in time to today, that I would gladly see him locked in a dark room with an Inner Dummy Doll that would say to him incessantly and with no relief, "Carl, you should be ashamed of yourself. You were a traitor to Dr. Freud. Carl, you should be ashamed of yourself. You were a traitor to Dr. Freud." He broke into a soft chuckle.

"You see?" Norton said. "We knew you'd like the idea."

"I never said I liked the idea, Mr. Norton. I am simply temporarily defeated and each day seems to bring a new defeat in my feeble attempts to hold the high ground against the concepts that are being developed against my wishes."

"Well, we understand that, sir. This has to be difficult for you. So why not let Jenny here snap a few photos of you and we'll be quickly out of your hair. We'll be back shortly with a working prototype and maybe an idea for two additional doll models to round out the line. The Dr. Freud Inner Dummy Dolls could be the world's next version of the Barbie Dolls."

"I'm afraid, Mr. Norton, that in the books that have been put at my disposal for bringing myself up to date with the modern world," he pointed to those in front of him, "computers and microchips have been covered, but not Barbie Dolls. I would appreciate some enlightenment."

"No problem at all, doc. You are talking to the world's greatest expert on Barbie Dolls. Jenny, why don't you start snapping your photos while I talk."

"Is that okay with you, doctor?" Jenny asked.

Freud nodded, "Yes, yes, go ahead, my dear."

As Jenny began shooting photos of Dr. Freud from varying angles, Norton talked about Barbie Dolls and their impact on children. As he did so, Freud began stroking his beard.

NOTE

1. Thomas E. Ricks, *Wall Street Journal*, as reported in the *Pittsburgh Post-Gazette*, November 23, 1997, p. A-23.

14

THE STRENGTH OF OUR TERRITORIAL DRIVE

"PLEASE, I NEED MY SPACE"

Thieves ransacked the apartment of Women's National Basketball Association star Cheryl Miller, taking four championship rings and other items while she was at practice with her team in Phoenix. The thieves also opened her refrigerator and drank three beers.[1]

I recall being on an airplane while I was writing *Brain Tricks* and glancing at the work the passenger next to me was doing. I do my best not to strike up a conversation with anyone seated next to me, being a bit low on the stranger nurturance scale. But I couldn't help noting that the person was an astronomer. He was studying some charts that appeared to be groupings of constellations. I hesitantly interrupted and asked him if he was an astronomer. He said he was. I told him I was writing a book and in one chapter dealing with the size of the universe, I was having problems comprehending some of the dimensions. This caught his interest and he courteously asked me to tell him what my problems were. I'll give you the gist of the conversation as I remember it:

"The first problem I have is with the distance to the nearest star, which I understand is about four light-years away."

"That's correct," he replied, "the star's name is Proxima Centauri and I believe the distance is 4.1 light-years."

"Okay, but let's round it off to four light-years, for the sake of our discussion. That doesn't seem like a very long distance. I think most people believe that if we could get in a fast spaceship, we could travel four light-years in maybe ten years, or twenty at the outside. In other words, the concept of light-years makes the universe appear considerably smaller than it is."

"Yes, that's quite true," he replied.

"But I think the concept helps destroy the benefits we all might enjoy from a galactic perspective, one that might help us transcend our earthly, limbic instincts that keep us grounded and in many instances fighting and hating each other."

The astronomer began to look uncomfortable. "I'm afraid I don't get what you mean."

"Okay, according to my calculations, if we were able to travel in a spaceship at the speed of 400,000 miles per hour, which is about sixteen times the speed of our current space shuttles, which travel at about 25,000 miles per hour, it would take us about 7,000 years to get to Proxima Centauri. I'm unsure of the exact number of years because my calculator couldn't handle all the zeros and I had to figure this out by hand."

"That does sound right," he said, looking intent. "Let me take a minute to check."

He pulled a highly sophisticated calculator out of his briefcase, entered some numbers, and said, "Yes, 7,000 years is definitely in the ballpark. If you'd like me to give you a definitive number, I can look up the precise distance to the star and do another quick calculation."

"No, that's close enough," I replied, and then went on. "The point is, if Jesus Christ were able to board this space shuttle during his lifetime and he was traveling all this time, he still wouldn't be even halfway to that star."

The astronomer thought a moment and said, "Yes, that is approximately correct."

"But don't you see?" I replied. "Most of the world would never be able to grasp the enormity of the distance to this nearest star from the term 'four light-years.' We probably think of that star, if we know about it, as more or less a next-door neighbor. And yet, Jesus Christ, if he were still in that spaceship would have another 5,000 years to go before he arrived there. And that is another perspective all together."

"Yes, I suppose I can see your point."

"Okay. Then maybe you can clarify just one more thing. How long would it take to get to the borders of our Milky Way, the galaxy in which the earth resides?"

The astronomer pulled a book that looked like a manual out of his briefcase, jotted down some numbers, then entered them in his calculator and said, "Yes, the Milky Way is approximately 100,000 light-years across, and assuming we had to travel that whole distance, which we wouldn't, because earth is well within the galaxy, it would take your spaceship about 100 million years to make the trip."

"But don't you see? Look how hard it is to comprehend that fact. If we're lucky, we have a lifetime of eighty or ninety or even one hundred years. We are basically trivial against 100 million years. Just to get to the borders of our own galaxy at the speed of 400,000 miles per hour, we would have had to begin traveling before humans really started to evolve from other species. Who can fathom what we would have looked like 100 million years ago, when we boarded that space shuttle in some animal cage, on the way to the far reaches of our own galaxy, only 100,000 light-years away."

"Heh, heh," he chuckled stiffly. "I guess that's right."

"And in our Milky Way galaxy alone, as I understand it," I continued, "there are approximately 100 billion stars, each of which is basically equivalent in its atomic structure to our sun and many of them could have planets orbiting about them like ours. Is that correct?"

"Yes, approximately 100 billion stars is the accepted number and I imagine that many of them could have orbiting planets that harbor life."

"And beyond our own galaxy of the Milky Way," I continued, "the nearest galaxy is 2.2 million light-years away and to get there at 400,000 miles per hour, we would probably have had to pack a piece of earth in the space shuttle, because there was probably no life on earth at all, when we might have started. We were just organisms floating around in the slime. Is that correct?"

"I'm afraid I know very little about our early Paleozoic periods," he said stiffly.

"And beyond our nearest galaxy, there are about 50 billion additional galaxies, each with approximately 100 billion stars, all with the same basic atomic structure of our sun and many of which may also have planets orbiting them, capable of sustaining human life."

"Well, there may be far more galaxies than that. That count is only a rough calculation."

"So," I said, "when you look at the earth against this incomprehensible proportion of the universe, we are basically lost within it. There is no map that exists of the entire universe with all those trillions upon trillions of stars pinpointed, on which we could circle the location of the earth in case someone was lost out there in space and needed directions to our planet."

"Well, of course, you're joking."

"No, I am not joking," I responded. "Do you agree with the statement that earth, our planet, is basically lost in space?"

He sat back in his seat, put his hands behind his head while balancing his briefcase in his lap, and said, "Well, I can't disagree with it. I can't say we are not lost in space, because for one thing, we don't know how large the universe really is, or if it's expanding and getting even bigger."

"So if we are lost in space, why haven't you told people this? Why isn't it front-page news? Why don't we see the headline: 'Flash, Earth Lost in Space.'"

"I'm sorry, sir," he sounded irritated, "but we have made no secret of the dimensions of the universe. It is probably mentioned in some way in every book written for laymen about the universe. It has been discussed on countless documentaries on television. And if the media doesn't choose to make it front-page news, that is not for me to comment. Further, it would be my judgment that most people who are educated know that the universe is enormous and within its scope we are apparently insignificant."

"If this is so," I answered, "then why do we have so many educated government leaders, some with doctorates, leading their nations into wars fighting over a relatively few square miles of land? If my memory serves me correctly, we have more than fifty wars going on right now in the 1990s, some more violent than others, and primarily regarding territorial disputes."

"I'm afraid you've lost me."

"I mean, why are we fighting wars or generating other forms of violence to settle disputes about this national border or that one? Are these borders visible from space?"

"Not at all," he said. "All borders are manmade, although they will frequently follow some topographic feature such as a river or mountain range that is visible from space."

"So humans must be territorial creatures?"

"Look, sir, you are now really out of my field of expertise. You ought to speak to some anthropologist."

"No, I'm just curious about your thoughts. If you study outer space, you undoubtedly have the best perspective to discuss issues like these. All I asked was your opinion, based on that perspective. Are we territorial? After all, we create nations on a larger scale; states, provinces, and cities, towns, and villages on a smaller scale. And on the smallest scale, we have legal deeds that indicate the precise borders of the land we might own, even if it's a tiny lot holding a small home. And the media is filled with disputes about borders, some of which involve violence. So we must have some instinct for territorialism, right? And in some of us, it must be so strong that it is capable of overriding any chance we have at achieving a galactic perspective that would help us all come to our senses."

"Excuse me, sir," he said, rising out of his seat, looking at me as if I were dysfunctional, trying not to spill his charts and other reference materials in the aisle as he transferred them back to his now empty seat. "I do have to get to the bathroom."

He didn't come back for half an hour, shortly before we started our landing approach, so I knew I probably went too far. It couldn't have been the liquor. I only had a diet cola. But it did pass the time pleasantly and I was able to confirm my own calculations of the incomprehensible scales of the universe, which were extremely difficult for me because I get lost with mathematics, even long division when there are a lot of zeros involved.

I thought this chapter opening would be another interesting change of pace, since the territorial drive doesn't have the pizzazz of the power and sexual drives and it doesn't get the press or much attention in our everyday conversations. As Robert Ardrey wrote in his book *The Territorial Imperative* in 1967, the last book he could find on the subject of human territorialism was written in 1920. Yet, our limbic territorial program can be just as lethal as the power or sex drives at their more intense levels and appears to combine with them in many emotional situations. To quote Robert Ardrey: "The territorial imperative is as blind as a cave fish, as consuming as a furnace and it commands beyond logic, opposes all reason, suborns all moralities, strives for no goal more sublime than survival."[2]

Most of us can feel our territoriality during those moments when our emotional sentinel picks up a signal that our territory is being violated in some way. And since some of us are much more sensitive than others, when our perceived territory is challenged there is apparently a limbic territorial scale that is similar in its varying intensities to the limbic power and sexual scales.

The territory we perceive as our own is what we experience as our space. It can be our place in line at the checkout counter, the hallway in front of our apartment, our space at work, the space immediately in front of us on the highway, or our seat in a theater. The limbic territorial program has to do with *space*. The limbic power program has to do with status. And the limbic sexual program has to do with *reproduction*. These are three of the attributes aside from the instincts to nurture and survive that many of us would include were we given the authority to design a limbic brain that would have the best possible chance to reproduce humans so that our genes are carried forward to future generations for whatever our ultimate purpose is, if we even have one.

Our territoriality also appears to deal with space that is both permanent and impermanent. Our space in the checkout line is impermanent, yet if we are a Number Eight on the territorial scale and someone abruptly cuts in front of us, we might lash out in anger or worse. At the time we are occupying that space, we instinctively sense that it belongs to us. Maybe this is why I've seen some people look longingly back at a theater seat they've just occupied.

The intensities of our territorialism, however, are best exemplified when the space we occupy is relatively permanent. For example, picture yourself lounging on a beach chair in a small backyard of a home you own in a subdivision, on a bright summer day, reading a book. Suddenly, a group of teenagers bursts through the bushes that divide your backyard from your neighbors, and laughing and talking loudly they amble across your backyard on their way to someone else's home. If you were a Number One or Two on the limbic territorial scale, you might simply wave at the group and ask them if they'd like some lemonade. If you were a Four or Five, you would probably become annoyed and ask them to move quickly along and please, find some other route the next time they have to get to your neighbor's home. If you were a Seven or Eight, you would probably become very angry, shouting threats and telling them they are trespassing and the next time you'll call the police or their parents. If you were a Ten and had a gun in the house, you would go inside, get it, aim it at them, and threaten to use it on them if they "didn't get the hell out of your yard right now and never come back."

Those high on the territorial scales would, in addition, presumably never be happy with the amount of land they have. I recall a story about a well-known corporate mogul who owned a 100,000-acre ranch out west and felt "a little cramped." And so he purchased an additional 100,000 acres and has since added to that with large ranch holdings in South America.

Those who are excessively high on the territorial scale can never have enough space or the possessions within that space, just as those who are excessively high on the power scale can never have enough power or the trappings that go with it. And so it should be of little surprise to us when we learn that these people, when they are wealthy, have purchased additional apartments and homes or ranches or whatever throughout the world that they will hardly use.

On the other side of the scale, I've known people who couldn't care less about owning a home, let alone two of them. Nor do they care much about possessions. And unlike those higher on the territorial scale who react with anger and rage when they lose a valued possession, those lower on the scale appear to care less. "Okay, I lost it. I'll just get another one," they might say.

Although from our own observations we can conclude that there is a scale of territoriality, we were unable to find any definitive academic information pertaining to its *primal* nature. The closest was *The Territorial-Intrusion Personal Scale* (Lane, 1986, as a part of his dissertation), which was for the nurse-patient setting. The nurse removes a chair from your room without asking if you will be using it. We also found one psychological test involving parking spaces, which hit me close to home.

When I'm in a crowded parking lot and about to back up and depart, I feel some annoyance when someone is waiting close behind me, ready to take my parking space. "Hey, back off," I'd like to say. "I'm still here."

Interestingly enough, Edward O. Wilson in his book *On Human Nature* made reference to a territorial scale that is based on what he calls a density-dependent factor that implies we become more territorial when we are crowded, such as in a crowded parking lot. He said: ". . . territoriality prevents the population from either exploding or crashing." He added: "The study of territorial behavior in human beings is in a very early stage."[3] In his book *Consilience*, written about twenty years later, Wilson said: "Humanity is decidedly a territorial species. Since the control of limiting resources has been a matter of life and death through millennia of evolutionary time, territorial aggression is widespread and reaction to it often murderous."[4]

Some zoologists, according to Wilson, have observed that the fighting between some species of animals becomes more intense as the population becomes more crowded. Thus the territorial program appears to help thin the population so that there is enough food and resources for all.

One wonders whether this instinct for territorialism, combined with power, was the primary cause of the wars fought in the twentieth century that resulted in the deaths of an estimated ninety million people. Was this *nature's primitive triggering device for causing us to thin our population?* And was our ego or reasoning power not strong enough to recognize what was taking place and move us to throw the fanatics out of power before the wars even began?

There is also a sexual hypothesis that appears to cling to the territorial program, in some situations, in combination with the power program. Edward O. Wilson made reference to it at the beginning of this quote from *Sociobiology*:

> ...*competitors may even race to outbreed each other.* Resources are sequestered. Justice and liberty decline. Increases in real and imagined threats congeal the sense of group identity and mobilize the tribal members. Xenophobia [fear or hatred of strangers] becomes a political virtue. The treatment of nonconformists grows harsher. History is replete with the existence of this process to the point that the society breaks down or goes to war. No nation has been completely immune.[5] (Emphasis mine)

Perhaps what we've seen during the twentieth century in Nazi Germany, Bosnia, Kosovo, Armenia, Ireland, Israel, Kashmir, and the like may have been apparently manifestations of our primitive ids, our Inner Dummies, which we were unable to transcend to reach equitable solutions without bloodshed, no matter how civilized or educated we thought we were.

In some of these instances there was the sexual innuendo of the need to breed to build the tribal stock. During the wars that followed the breakup of Yugoslavia, the men were killed and the women raped by the tens of thousands, in what might be construed as an instinctive effort by the new alpha males to supplant the genes of the former alpha males, now dead, imprisoned, or exiled, to assure the genetic stamp of the conquerors on their newly gained territories. Doesn't this sound like those higher animal species where the new alpha male of a herd kills all the young to assure that all new offspring are products of his genes?

In her book *The Rape of Nanking*, Iris Chang meticulously details the crushing violence unleashed by the conquering Japanese on the city of Nanking in 1937, during which, in a six-week period, they systematically raped, tortured, and murdered more than 300,000 Chinese civilians. She reported: "Certainly it was one of the greatest mass rapes in world history. . . . It is impossible to determine the exact number of women raped in Nanking. Estimates range from as low as twenty thousand to as high as eighty thousand."[6]

The Japanese on their march through China had a slogan they called the "Three Alls. Steal All. Burn All. Kill All." The same might have been said of the march of the German army through Russia, which began in 1941, and in the many territorial wars that have taken place before and into the 1990s, under the guise of "ethnic cleansing." This moronic of all causes is apparently fed by the Number Nines and Tens on the power and territorial programs, who in positions of leadership convince their clans that they are an elite and the minorities in existing or new territories are subhuman and should be removed or exterminated. And, that the women remaining should be impregnated with the clan's genes to assure the genetic stamp we spoke of. If anyone is subhuman, it would appear to be the perpetrators, many of whom are well educated, but never stop to consider that our earth is lost within the space of an incomprehensibly large universe, that all borders are made by we humans, and that all races of humans are equal in their basic ignorance of any ultimate and rational answers as to why we live or die.

Becoming a government leader apparently doesn't correct the programs of the id or Inner Dummy that are out of balance. Government leadership, it would appear, simply provides an opportunity for a power- or territorial-driven id to wreak great havoc.

Strangely enough, once the wars are over, the citizens of both the conquering nations and the conquered who survive attempt to resume their normal lives, following the basic rules of their societies that they had temporarily abandoned, almost as if the violence never happened, even though the hatreds inbred by war might linger in some. They'll watch documentaries about what they did, hardly ever giving a second thought to the idea that it was all sheer madness.

It would thus appear that the limbic nurturance program, our instinctive program that propels us to bond with each other, is more vulnerable to change or disruption than the power, sexual, *or* territorial programs, which when very intense, apparently seek out opportunities to fulfill their expectations, applying injury in proportion to the freedoms they are given.

Although we could find no academic studies relating territorialism to possessiveness and they may exist, it would appear that if a primary objective of our instinctive, territorial drive is to defend our territory and the "resources" within it, then the objects we own within the "space" of our territories could be assumed to be governed by the same instinct.

Thus, if a farmer were to lose his most valued possessions in a massive burglary while he was away, he would probably feel the same level of anger and anxiety as if he lost his land through a bank foreclosure. As we'll point out in chapter 20, the metaphoric limbic system punishes us with negative feelings when we don't meet the expectations of its drives—e.g., we allow our land or possessions to be lost for whatever the reasons, whether we were rationally at fault or not. And it rewards us with positive feelings when we do meet their expectations—e.g., we acquire a lot of new land and/or possessions we have coveted.

I had a neighbor many years ago from whom I borrowed a rake. When I finished using the rake, I saw that my neighbor's house was dark and so I left it in my garage, to return the next day. When I walked out on the lawn the next morning to get the newspaper, he was standing in front of my home, glowering at me.

"What's wrong?" I asked. "Who died?"

"That's not funny, and you know what's wrong."

"No, I don't know what's wrong."

"You have my rake."

"I know I have your rake. When I finished with it last night, your house was dark and so I thought I would return it to you this morning."

"You should have returned it last night. That is my rake."

"I know it's your rake, for god's sake."

And so the conversation went. I would peg him as probably a Number Eight on the territorial scale not only because of the rake incident, but because of similar incidents, including one that has remained a limbic memory. My young sons and I played badminton in our backyard and on very rare occasions, the shuttlecock would fall in his backyard. Whenever he was present and I quickly proceeded to retrieve the shuttlecock, he would look upset.

One day a team of contractors showed up and within the week, a brick wall six feet high, the maximum height allowed by code, was constructed, surrounding his entire backyard. We hardly ever saw him again out back, but I could hear him pulling his lounge chair over the patio, so I knew he was there. It was the wall incident that prompted me to peg him at about an Eight on the territorial scale.

Then an odd thing happened. About six months later, his wife and children left town for two weeks to visit her family while he stayed home. I bumped into him on the front lawn, which was still only separated by a sidewalk, and he looked unhappy.

"What's wrong, Ed?" I asked.

"I don't know. I don't see any of you anymore and sometimes it gets lonely."

"Lonely? For god's sake, Ed, you built the fence."

So there it was. His territorial and nurturance programs were battling each other, which, I learned later in a reference by psychoanalyst and author Karen Horney, can create more anxiety than a battle between our rationality and a limbic drive. It is apparent that the drives of our metaphoric limbic system are not all pulling together for our common good. And when they are in conflict with each other, the anxiety we feel can be multiplied.

It may appear farfetched to compare the incidents of the rake and wall with the violence and carnage that takes place in disputes between nations. However, the instincts involved are the same. They are primitive in nature and as Freud suggests, are harbored in a metaphoric id, or Inner Dummy that is unaware of time, logic, or awareness. Under this assumption, the id is incapable of knowing that our earth has grown from small tribal societies into a large, civilized world, with precisely mapped borders and mammoth engines of war. "Oh, is the atomic bomb better than a spear?" the id might say if it could talk. "Then let's use it." Or, "That person's skin is black. He and everyone like him is dangerous to our status and space. Let's start with a projection of hatred and see if that chases him away."

The blessing and hope that we have as human beings is our intelligence. It has slowly begun to see the irrationality of the hatreds, anger, and violence that can be unleashed by an unthinking, primitive id and is helping us make adjustments in our rational thought processes. The problem is that it isn't happening fast enough.

I have had a territorial quiz on my Web site for well over a year, as of this writing. It is the least popular of the three quizzes. Well over 150,000 persons have taken the sexual quiz, about 175,000 have taken the power quiz, but only about 40,000 have taken the territorial quiz.

Again, I claim no scientific validation for the metaphoric *limbic territorial scale* that follows. As with the other quizzes, I requested through a feedback form on the site, input from visitors taking the quiz, who thought the results weren't consistent with their own perceptions. And based on this feedback, I refined the quiz and the answers. Here is the scale:

NUMBER ONE:

You probably would be happy just living your life out of a sleeping bag in the countryside moving here and there as needed. The idea of owning land might even seem repulsive to you. All of your possessions would be practical ones, easily replaced, and losing all but the ones that have emotional meaning for you wouldn't bother you very much.

NUMBER TWO:

You would probably be content spending much of your life living in the homes of friends and relatives eager for your company and sharing costs, if that would become your lot in life. Having their name on the title of the home or apartment lease wouldn't bother you. You readily share whatever possessions you have with people who are close to you.

NUMBER THREE:

You would probably be quite content living in a rental apartment unit that fulfills your very basic needs. You have no compelling desire to "own" a home with your name on the title, although you are not repulsed by the idea. You would become only mildly upset if your favorite stereo headset was stolen and you could easily afford to replace it. You wouldn't be down at the police station filling out reports. You probably would only become slightly annoyed when someone sneaks in line ahead of you in the ticket line at a movie theater. You wouldn't say anything.

NUMBER FOUR:

You might dream of having a home of your own someday, you'll feel good if it happens, but it won't depress you if the opportunity never comes along. Your possessions are practical and you feel comfortable with whatever you have. You are protective of what you own, but you don't perceive of yourself as possessive.

NUMBER FIVE:

You have a desire for a home or condominium unit of your own, a living unit you have purchased individually or jointly with a spouse or friends and your name is on the title. You will work hard to achieve this. You take pride in the possessions you've acquired and will make strong efforts to protect them.

NUMBER SIX:

You are intent on having a home of our own, if you don't already. If you were (or are) living in an apartment building you've grown comfortable with, and learn it's being converted to condominiums, you would probably be first in line, if you could afford the purchase. You want your name on a title. You have a strong desire to "own." You husband your possessions and like to show them off. If you are in a relationship, you would probably be happiest if you had your own bathroom. You feel some jealousy of others you know who you perceive as having better homes.

NUMBER SEVEN:

You would probably be depressed or stressed out in some way if you were at an age where your goal was to have your own home or condominium and it hasn't happened. You crave a living space that you own. If you do own a living unit, what you have is probably not enough, you dream of ways to make it better, probably bigger or more lavish. You may find it hard to let neighbors and friends, even relatives, borrow possessions that are meaningful to you. You will feel some anxiety when these possessions are out of your control. You can become fiercely jealous.

NUMBER EIGHT:

If you are at the age when you think you should have a living unit that you own and don't, you are probably becoming irrational in many of your thoughts and actions. You are tremendously frustrated. If you have succeeded in your goal to own your living unit, you probably feel driven to own a second or third home, perhaps in the country or at resorts you favor. You are fiercely jealous of others and try not to let them one-up you. You don't like others violating your space. If someone is mistakenly sitting in your seat when you go to the symphony, you will probably become upset and possibly obnoxious. One more thing . . . depending on your income situation, it is likely that when purchasing a new home, you will spend more than you can practically afford.

NUMBER NINE:

You probably measure your life by the amount of space you have accumulated for living your lifestyle. You are driven incessantly to look for more. If you owned 10,000 acres of ranch land in Montana, you would probably look for the first opportunity or practical excuse to double the acreage or triple it or more. Absolutely nothing you possess, no matter what the scale, is ever enough. If you could afford it, you would be acquiring homes and condominiums in "important" cities and resorts around the world, even though you know you wouldn't be spending any meaningful time occupying them. You simply are driven to want them. You probably accumulate possessions with the same passion. Your feeling of euphoric satisfaction when you acquire something new, rare, and dramatic passes quickly. The relentless hunt continues.

NUMBER TEN:

Time to check in somewhere. For one thing, you may be willing to have murder committed, in the belief you won't be caught, to acquire the land or object that you covet. Or, to neutralize the feelings of jealousy you have for others. If you were cast in the role of a frontier rancher or a dictatorial government leader, the lives of others would become meaningless in your quest to conquer those whose land or material possessions are in your sights. Murder and carnage are just part of the game to you. You are probably clever, ruthless, relentless and insatiable. You will do whatever it takes. You are probably not warm and nice.

If you are unsure of your limbic territorial scale ranking, take the quiz on the site. As with the power and sex quizzes, it will give you a rough idea of where you might stand.

Here is how the territorial rankings broke down with the 3,600 responses that were monitored from January to June 1, 1999. We were late in adding monitoring software to this quiz.

	Percent	**Number of responses**
NUMBER ONE	1.6	63
NUMBER TWO	2.4	86
NUMBER THREE	8.4	304
NUMBER FOUR	15.1	545
NUMBER FIVE	24.7	880
NUMBER SIX	23.6	850
NUMBER SEVEN	14.0	524
NUMBER EIGHT	6.1	220
NUMBER NINE	2.1	77
NUMBER TEN	1.1	41

Although we haven't monitored it, it would be my suspicion that people who are high on the territorial scale are also high on the power scale. Think, for a moment, how much the world would have been better off, if nature would have eliminated the Numbers Eights, Nines, and Tens from our limbic power, territorial, and even sexual programs. The result might have been a much more peaceful and harmonious planet.

COMMENTARY BY DR. HEFTER

The territorial drive focused upon here is probably as powerful a force, when unleashed, as any of the limbic drives described. It is also evident at an early age, witness the strong reactions of young children who feel their possessions may be taken away by an older sibling, or the pride with which the three-year-old son of a friend of mine indicated the fact that "this is *my* house."

It is of course, not only in the physical arena that territoriality is played out but also in the psychological one. Thus, this chapter points out the intense feelings involved in jealousy. There is also, for example, the pride of ownership of an idea or of a way of looking at things or of a creation, be it a business enterprise or artistic—fights over who thought of it first can be quite vicious and not just for financial reasons.

The reference to competing drives, e.g., nurturance versus territorial, again indicates the complexity of what appears to be initially simple "limbic issues." Evolving from being only a "limbic" person to a mature one requires an individual to learn how to master, to a significant degree, this drive competition. In other words, the ego, as elucidated by Freud, has to get into the action of the Inner Dummy.

NOTES

1. "From the Wires," Sports section, *Chicago Sun-Times*, May 30, 1998, p. 104.

2. Robert Ardrey, *The Territorial Imperative: A Personal Inquiry into the Animal Origins of Property and Nations* (New York: Kodansha International, 1996), p. 236.

3. Edward O. Wilson, *On Human Nature* (Cambridge, Mass.: Harvard University Press, 1978), p. 107.

4. Edward O. Wilson, *Consilience: The Unity of Knowledge* (New York: Knopf, 1998), p. 171.

5. Edward O. Wilson, *Sociobiology* (Cambridge, Mass.: Belknap Press of Harvard University Press, 1980), p. 290.

6. Iris Chang, *The Rape of Nanking: The Forgotten Holocaust of World War II* (New York: BasicBooks, 1997), p. 89.

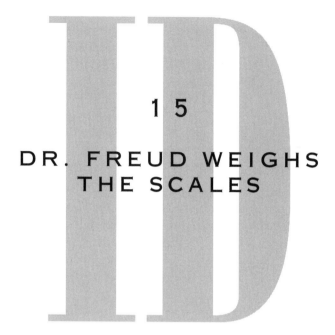

15

DR. FREUD WEIGHS THE SCALES

Conservative Jewish men and women praying in front of the Wailing Wall in Israel were accosted by Orthodox Jews, who were incensed by the sight of women praying with men. The Orthodox Jews spat on them and pelted them with feces from the windows of a yeshiva, a school of religious studies.[1]

Dr. Freud was walking down a corridor of the ad agency on his way back to the conference room when he bumped into Samuel Ollander, the agency's director of research.

"Dr. Freud," Ollander greeted him, delighted to see him. "I'm Samuel Ollander, do you remember me?"

"Of course I do," Freud replied politely.

"Oh, that's good," Ollander looked relieved. "It is hard to tell what someone in a transposed state will remember and not remember."

"Rest assured my brain is functioning almost as it was," Freud replied in amusement.

Ollander looked down at the floor in some embarrassment and after a brief moment, looked up at Freud brightly. "Well, anyway, sir, I was just on

160

my way to see Ted Croft's secretary to learn if you could spare me about five minutes this afternoon to give me some insights on the Dummy Scales. We are going to present them to a new consumer-focus group tonight."

Freud assumed his usual look of discomfort when conversing about anything having to do with the Dummy concepts. "I suppose now is as good a time as any," he said, somewhat stiffly.

"Fine, my office is just a few doors down. Why don't we just sit in there? This won't take long."

Freud assented and they walked to Ollander's office, where they both sat around a small, circular table in the corner of the office.

"Now," Dr. Freud asked, "what was it about these so-called scales that you wanted to talk to me about?"

"As you know, sir, we have so far developed scales for three of the Dummy Drives—power, territorial, and sexual. I know you have seen them and I am curious about your reaction."

Freud pondered a moment. "They are metaphoric and simplistic, of course."

"That may be, but are they useful?"

"Would you mind if I diverged for a moment?"

"Not at all."

"As I'm sure you know, I placed great emphasis on the theory of instincts. It was my belief that instincts generated pressure whose sole aim was to create satisfaction. And the term *libido* as it remains in modern definition is the energy or drive associated with instincts. Do you follow me?"

"I think so."

"In my later writings, I talked about both the sexual libido, for which the term has become most widely known, and nonerotic libidos, which could engulf your metaphors of power and territorial, or status and space. It is obvious that the pressures driving these libidos can vary and so the development of a scale of measurement is not without merit."

"So you agree with the One to Ten scales we've developed?"

"I didn't say that. On the other hand, the definitions you have developed for the highly intense libidos appears to correlate with another theory of mine."

"Excuse me, sir, when you say highly intense libidos, are you referring to our Eights, Nines, and Tens?"

"Please let me generalize by simply calling them highly intense, if you don't mind."

"That is fine, sir."

"I don't want to sound depressive and ruin your day, but these highly intense libidos appear to correlate with what I called the 'death instinct.' "

"The 'death instinct.' I believe I read something about that many years ago, when I was still in college."

"Perhaps so. It was one of two overriding instincts that I theorized. The first I called Eros, the instinct for self-preservation, the manifestations of which are conspicuous and noisy enough because we know well enough the troubles we all go to in order not to die. The 'death instinct,' I theorized, operated silently in its quest to create our dissolution."

"So what you are saying is that we are all basically suicidal."

"No, what I am saying is that the 'death instinct' creates aggressiveness and destructiveness in a manner we are not aware of, which is not the case when one is suicidal. It lies silent within us, waiting for its moment. Now I noticed in a preamble to my essay 'Civilization and Its Discontents,' Mr. Peter Gay in a compilation of my works, ascribed the development of my concept of the 'death instinct' to the encroachment of Nazism, during the last years of my life in Germany. And this may be true, to some extent. But all one needs to do is look at history to notice that Nazism was only one of thousands of propagandist causes that have driven humans to destroy each other. You can agree with that, can't you?"

"Oh, yes sir, I quite agree with that. Humans have been killing each other off all through history out of all sorts of irrational motives and it continues up to this very day."

"That is why I was much taken with Edward O. Wilson's comment in his book *On Human Nature*, that the general instinct for territoriality might have something to do with keeping the population from either exploding or crashing. This may correlate to my theory of the 'death instinct,' in that one of the awakening moments for the instinct might be when there is a perception among a given grouping of people that its population is becoming too thick for the resources contained within its territory. And so instinctually a leader emerges, who is capable of motivating the population to invade adjacent territories, with the purpose of killing the occupants and usurping their resources, which at the same time satisfies the aim of the 'death instinct' to thin the population."

"So your 'death instinct' in its aim applies to wars between population groupings to achieve satisfaction?"

"Only partially. Within groupings of humans themselves, there have always been people who are aggressive and destructive, homicidal, shall we say, who by carrying out their acts of violence help thin the population. This may also be another manifestation of our 'death instinct.' Perhaps these people have been planted within us in every generation, and within every grouping of humans as a purposeful force of nature. It would certainly explain the perpetuity of the homicidal mind."

Freud paused, looking amused and stroking his beard. Then he continued, "Of course, this is all bold speculation. I doubt that these last statements would find much acceptance among my colleagues. They are interesting points, though, are they not?"

"Oh, quite so, sir, they absolutely never crossed my mind."

"And now, let's examine one more possible correlation of my 'death instinct' involving the pressures of the libidos. If as the work on your scales assumes, the most intense libidos can cause humans to kill to create satisfaction for the instincts from which they evolve, then the assumption follows that not all humans are equal in their silent hunger for aggression and destruction. The heaviest of these passions would devolve primarily on those who have libidos that are so extreme in their intensity that they are capable of overriding the reasoning powers of the ego."

"So you are suggesting, sir, that your 'death instinct' may not affect the meeker among us, who are largely content to nurture and survive."

"Yes, well put, Ollander. That is definitely a possibility, although I have treated many meek patients, to use that word in its most generalized sense, who concealed strong urges for revenge and destruction. Perhaps the issue, then, is not so much what one thinks, but what one is actually capable of doing. There is, of course, much more work to be done on the theory."

"Then may I assume that in a roundabout way you are not contesting our examination of the intensity of the power, territorial, and sexual libidos, which we are temporarily calling Dummy Scales to determine if we can connect with the ordinary person?"

Freud smiled. "No, Ollander, I will not contest your research with ordinary people. As I told your Mr. Croft, I will allow all of this to take place with whatever insights I can provide, pending a final presentation at which time I will have my last say on the matter."

Ollander stood up and shook Dr. Freud's hand. "Thank you, sir," he said. "After listening to you, I don't think that we are that far apart in what we are attempting to communicate. May I show you the way back to the conference room from here?"

"No, no, I quite know the way. And thank you for your kindness."

Freud turned around and walked through the doorway.

NOTE

1. *Dallas Morning News*, June 13, 1997, p. 19A.

16

OUR CAPACITY TO LOVE AND NURTURE
TROUBLES ON BOTH SIDES OF THE SCALE

In the book Titan, *John D. Rockefeller Sr. comes off as a bit detached. For example, here is the letter he wrote to his son, "Junior," when he gave him money that would be worth almost ten times the amount in 1998 dollars: "Dear Son: I am this day giving you $65,000,000 par value of United States Government First Loan 3% bonds. Affectionately, Father."[1]*

W e can all recognize that each of us has the capacity for reflecting nurturance in varying intensities. But this drive appears to be more compartmentalized than our power, territorial and sexual drives. We may be extremely nurturing to our children, but low in the nurturance of relatives and friends, co-workers, or strangers. Or, vice versa. Or, we may be extremely nurturing to our dog or co-workers, but low in the nurturance of our spouse. Or, vice versa.

At first, I thought the reference materials on the nurturance drive were sparse, and so did Nanmathi Manion, who was now joined in research for this book by David Amodio, another psychology doctoral student at the University of Wisconsin.

Then David sent me a paper entitled "Love Conceptualized as an

Attachment Process," which appeared in the *Journal of Personality and Social Psychology* in 1987 and authored by attachment specialists Cindy Hazen and Phillip Shaver of the University of Denver, who I learned later did considerable work in developing measurement scales. The paper defined "attachment" as the operative word in a field of study, apparently pioneered by English psychiatrist John Bowlby, whose book *Attachment* is considered the landmark work for the drive. Dr. Bowlby made this point about the strength of adult attachments in general in his book:

> That attachment behavior in adult life is a straightforward continuation of attachment behavior in childhood is shown by the circumstances that lead an adult's attachment behavior to become more readily elicited. . . . No form of behavior is accompanied by a stronger feeling than is attachment behavior. The figures towards whom it is directed are loved and their advent is greeted with joy.[2]

Is the feeling of attachment to others stronger than with any other form of behavior as Dr. Bowlby suggests? Is it stronger than an intense power or sexual drive? I think it depends on where we stand on the intensity scales of the other drives. For example, a good friend of mine, Barry Berish, was CEO of the Jim Beam Companies, a division of Fortune Brands. At the age of sixty-five, his retirement was mandatory. And so one day Barry simply packed up and walked out of his office, to lapse into a depressive state that was probably as much of a surprise to him as it was to Mike Wallace of the CBS news program *60 Minutes* in the story we told in a previous chapter.

About three months after he retired, we had dinner and I said almost tongue in cheek, "You look worse than you did after your mother died."

"You know, I think you're right," he replied, seriously. "I know I felt terrible when my mother died, but I can't imagine that I felt a lot worse than I do right now."

Was it Barry's id-based power drive that was punishing him, because it missed the power and trappings of the CEO office of this company, or was it his nurturance program, which "attached" him to his job? Or was it a "blurring" of the programs that Dr. Hefter wrote about in a previous commentary, or something else all together? No one can say. Fortunately, as of this writing, Barry has snapped out of it and is busy pursuing a new and exciting field of endeavor.

How we react to specific disappointments appears to depend on where we stand on the various scales. If we are high on the nurturance scale and our child goes off to college, we may feel depressed. If we are low on the nurturance scale, we might feel relieved.

One of the major problems of the nurturance drive in general is that it is apparently vulnerable and weak, particularly in the mid-ranges of this scale. Recall the reports of Iris Chang in her book, *The Rape of Nanking*, about how Japanese soldiers raped, tortured, and murdered more than 300,000 civilians during a six-week period, in Nanking, China, in 1937. And these were Japanese, considered one of the most courteous and well-mannered of all the world's cultures, certainly apparently normal people.

Chang quoted a doctor in Japan named Nagatomi Hakudo, who at the time of Chang's interview was sixty years old:

> Few know that soldiers impaled babies on bayonets and tossed them still alive into pots of boiling water. They gang-raped women from the ages of twelve to eighty and then killed them when they could no longer satisfy sexual requirements. I beheaded people, starved them to death, burned them and buried them alive; over two hundred in all. It is terrible that I could turn into an animal and do these things. There are really no words to explain what I was doing. I was truly a devil.[3]

Compare what the Japanese actually did in Nanking to the section of the compendium *Origins of Nurturance*, entitled "Becoming Nuturant in Japan: Past and Present," authored by Hideo Kojima of Nagoya University, in which he said:

> But, his concept [referring to a definition put forth earlier in the book] of nurturance reminded me of a stereotyped Japanese sentiment and attitude about living things in general, and about human beings and animals in particular. Perhaps due to the Buddhist precept against killing animals, a traditional Japanese conception was that human beings and other living things were basically similar to each other, and the Japanese were led to have a sympathetic attitude toward all living things, for each of us was a member of them.[4]

I don't mean to pick on the Japanese as examples of violent behavior. There is hardly a country in the world where similar, hardened acts of violence have not taken place. However, as pointed out, the Japanese culture has always been perceived as being among the most nurturing in the world, and the fact that it could have been so easily deflated offers a stark study of contrasts. As Chang pointed out in her book, the new Japanese soldiers felt horror at what they were seeing and asked to do; they had to be "desensitized" by their officers, who convinced the soldiers that the Chinese were subhuman and could be destroyed like animals without guilt.

"Desensitized" appears to be the operative word in describing the lowering of nurturance and the fact that it is so simple to achieve is probably one of the greatest problems of the human condition. This method of "desensitization" in which the enemy is portrayed as subhuman happened in Germany during World War II; it happened in Bosnia and Kosovo, and history is replete with episodes of apparently normal people carrying out the most unimaginable of heinous acts after being suitably "desensitized."

If we could get inside our brains and change anything, it would probably be to strengthen our collective nurturance program to a firm Number Seven, invulnerable to the influences of leaders who want to massacre or in other ways violate populations they view as the enemy.

I have also seen individuals become "desensitized" because of traumatic events in their lives, further attesting to the weakness of this program. An acquaintance, we'll call him Daniel, was highly nurturing and loving as a young man. But after an ugly divorce, which involved estrangement from his children, followed immediately by the death of his mother, to whom he was fervently attached, Daniel became cold and uncaring. We had lunch one day and I asked him about what had happened to his outlook.

"I don't know," he replied. "I just don't feel the same about people."

"Do you like feeling this way?" I asked.

"No, I would rather be the loving and caring kind of guy I used to be. I liked myself better that way."

He told me that he was seeing a therapist and thought he was making some progress. I didn't see him again for five years and when I did he was beaming from ear to ear.

"I can see that the therapy helped," I said.

"I'm not sure about that. What I know did work was that I found another woman I loved, married her, and we already have two small children who I love and adore."

I asked him whether he felt as warm and nurturing to people in general, as he did when I knew him before and during his first marriage.

"No, I can't seem to get it all back. But for me this is a big improvement."

So perhaps it is possible for us to recover to some extent from "desensitizing" events in our lives. But now let's return to how to measure the intensities of our drive to nurture, to attach, wherever it is at the present moment in our lives.

The problem with the nurturance program in terms of intensity measurement is its apparent compartmentalization, as implied by John Bowlby. There are apparently four of them and we may nurture differently within each of them. They include *parent-child*; *romantic*; *relatives, friends, and co-workers*; and *strangers*.

The intensity levels of parent-child nurturance are not difficult to measure. Those of us who have had children or infant pets know the intense feeling of bonding that can take place within hours. The love I felt for my two sons, from their infancy on, was fierce. But on the other hand, we read in the newspapers of infant children being placed in dumpsters or left to die. We also read of infants and young children being abused in every conceivable way by unloving parents, the Number Ones, who have little or no feelings of empathy, altruism, compassion, or love. We can only imagine the damage caused to the ids (the Inner Dummies) of these children.

Freud once pointed out that in its earlier years, Rome was conquered and vanquished many times. Each time the city was leveled, however, it was rebuilt upon its foundations. But the human mind is never rebuilt in this sense, he said. It keeps growing on top of the "wreckage" that becomes part of the foundation and which we might presume resides in the metaphoric id (or Inner Dummy) where, impervious to time, awareness, or logic, it is exceedingly difficult to reach. Thus, one cannot simply walk up to a child who has been damaged by parental abuse, to tell him or her that when it came to having parents, he or she simply lost the lottery and now it's time to buckle up and move on. For most children, the message simply can't sink in.

The upshot is that there is apparently a scale that covers parental loving and caring, with some of us being far more loving and caring than others.

From the infant's point of view, I thought emeritus professor of social planning Peter Marris put it nicely in his book, *The Politics of Uncertainty: Attachments in Private and Public Life*:

> We evidently possess an innate predisposition to form, before the end of the first year of life, specific attachments to a few discriminated and identified figures, of whom one or two are characteristically pre-eminent. . . . Once this bond of attachment is formed, a child will not accept a substitute in the primary nurturing role and a prolonged separation will provoke

first distress, then withdrawal and quiet misery and at last detachment—and indifference to the bonds of affection, including repudiation of the attachment figure when he or she returns.

After a while, once the attachment figure is at home again, the bond will re-establish itself, probably now shadowed on the child's part, by a lingering anxiety that is never completely overcome. If the attachment figure never returns, the child's capacity for forming bonds of attachment may be lastingly inhibited.[5]

Once again, the vulnerability of the nurturance drive is shown, even at the parent-child level. Ignore the child, hurt, or "desensitize" him or her and the bonding may never reestablish.

A second compartment of the limbic nurturance drive, *adult-romantic*, is an attachment most of us have experienced at one time or another, or still do and which we can presume is as unique a compartment of nurturance as that for parent-child.

The seminal study on adult-romantic nurturance appears to be the paper I described earlier in this chapter, "Romantic Love Conceptualized as an Attachment Process," written by Cindy Hazan and Phillip Shaver of the University of Denver. They said in its preamble: "This article explores the possibility that romantic love is an attachment process—a biosocial process by which affectional bonds are formed between adult lovers, just as affectional bonds are formed earlier in life between human infants and their parents."[6] So it's my biosocial attachment process mechanism that caused my two divorces. Finally, I have something to blame.

I noted in other reports as late as 1998 that references were made to the 1987 study by Hazan and Shaver as one of the most authoritative. So we might assume that the following romantic attachment scale is as pertinent today as it was a little over ten years ago:

Secure: I find it relatively easy to get close to others and am comfortable depending on them and having them depend on me. I don't often worry about being abandoned or about someone getting too close to me. (56% in this classification.)

Avoidant: I am somewhat uncomfortable being close to others; I find it difficult to trust them completely, difficult to allow myself to depend on them. I am nervous when anyone gets too close, and often love partners want me to be more intimate than I feel comfortable being. (25% in this classification.)

Anxious/Ambivalent: I find that others are reluctant to get as close as I would like. I often worry that my partner doesn't really love me or won't want to stay with me. I want to merge completely with another person, and this desire sometimes scares people away. (19% in this classification.)[7]

The authors noted that there were only minor differences in responses between the sexes. Of course, this study and others I found like it don't get into the primal scales of the instinctive nurturance drive toward romantic attachment. I've taken a guess at what this scale is at the end of this chapter, which applies to the other compartments of the nurturance drive as well.

In *Brain Tricks*, I described romantic love as one of nature's most ingenious devices or tricks for bringing two people together to reproduce and provide a happy, loving environment for raising children. Romantic love, in this sense, is one of the greatest rewards of the metaphoric limbic system. Whether it's love at first sight or not, when it hits you, it rewards you with positive feelings of happiness and giddiness. Romantic love is the picture of Gene Kelly dancing down the street in the rain in the motion picture *Singin' in the Rain*, when he sings, "What a glorious feeling, I'm happy again." Or, the lyrics of the many famous love songs sung by Frank Sinatra, including "What Is This Thing Called Love?" (Now we can tell him, "It's a mechanical, biosocial, attachment process.")

I have long envied couples I have known, whose romantic love has endured over many years. My Aunt Tillie and Uncle Irving were still holding hands after fifty years of marriage. On the other hand, I noted a news report from India in 1998 that a bride there was so upset at the groom for showing up drunk at the ceremony that she dumped him and married someone else the same day. Facts like these apparently confirm that some of us have a propensity for becoming more romantically attached than others.

A third compartment of the limbic nurturance program is the one that drives us to attach to *relatives, friends, and co-workers*, and others who are or can become a close part of our lives. In the book *Attachment in Adults*, the authors, psychologists Michael B. Sperling and William H. Berman said:

Although some peer relationships may be considered attachment relationships, and one may feel quite comfortable and open with friends, the vast majority are based in an affiliative rather than an attachment domain. . . . Finally, when one is sick or threatened, one tends to be drawn to family members, to a spouse or partner, or perhaps to one long-term, very close friend.[8]

We might presume from this that the intensity scale of attachments we feel toward friends and kinfolk is based on the amount of grief (the academic term is "attachment distress") we would feel if someone dies.

Sperling and Berman in their book even make the point that we might not know how attached we really are to someone until they actually do die. They said, "For example, a man may show little affection toward his wife through the marriage, but at her death he may exhibit very severe emotional and physical reactions to the loss, including depression, illness or even death."

Is this why Cher looked so bereaved when her ex-husband Sonny Bono died in a skiing accident in 1998, to the point that Sonny's current wife began wondering who the real widow was? In press reports, Cher was said to have shown little affection for her ex-husband while he was alive. She divorced him twenty years before his death, and some reports state that she even belittled him. But when he died, there she was all over television, saying what a close friend he had become and even delivered a eulogy during his funeral. Was it her limbic power program enjoying the status of being the center of national attention that motivated her, or her limbic nurturance program under distress, or a little of both? We are left to wonder.

Under the theory of an attachment scale measured by one's "attachment distress," upon the death of an "attachment object," one would think that in comparing the four compartments, at the top of the hierarchy would be parent-child, followed by spouse, close relatives, close friends, close pets, and then on down the line. However, I knew one woman who was more upset when her pet cat died than when her husband died. I remember saying to her after the funeral of her husband:

"My god, you ought to show a little remorse."

"Why? He was a bastard. He slept with everything that walked."

"But when your cat, Harry, died, you were so full of grief you were inconsolable."

"Harry didn't sleep around."

"Well, can you sniffle a little, just for show?"

"Hey, get lost."

A little low on the adult-romantic nurturance scale, wouldn't you say?

Maybe worse was the president of a very large company, we'll call him Edward, whose wife, we'll call her Josie, died after an illness of about six months. After the funeral, Edward asked me to meet him at his favorite cocktail lounge, where he introduced me to his young, new fiancée, a cabaret singer. Later when were alone in the bathroom, I said to him, "For god's sake, Edward, Josie's body is hardly cold and you're already engaged."

"I know," he replied. "Isn't she beautiful?"

Edward was also obviously quite low on the adult-romantic nurturance scale.

At the other extreme, I've known husbands and wives who felt such grief at the death of their spouses that they focused the remainder of their lives dedicated to doing good things in their memories. But getting back to the third compartment of nurturance, attachment to friends, coworkers, and relatives, Sperling and Berman made the point that it would also include the concept of kinship. We do have a propensity to attach to others with whom we share common interests.

In his book *Anthropological Perspectives on Kinship*, Ladislav Holy said: "Kinship ties which people acknowledge and distinguish determine whom to marry, where to live, how to raise children, which ancestors to worship, how to solve disputes, which land to cultivate, which property to inherit, who to turn for help in pursuing common interests, and many things besides."[9] This might explain why so many of our attachments in the United States, which is a melting pot of cultural diversity, offering open avenues into interesting and different modes of attitude and thought, continue to devolve, for the most part, around our own racial, religious, country-of-origin and socially comfortable groups.

I recall listening to a conversation between a Catholic husband and wife who were very upset because their son was going to marry someone from another parish. Talk about taking kinship to an extreme.

Presumably, a scale of attachment intensity exists for kinfolk, just as it does for parent-child and romantic attachments. Some of us enjoy being around our kin; others of us when pressured to attend gatherings of kin, will be found reading books in a corner.

Finally, what about the fourth and last compartment, the nurturance of *strangers*? Some of us are obviously more predisposed to being nurturant to strangers than others. It would appear that the higher we are on the nurturance scale, the more open we would be to strangers. On the other hand, while we might be open, we might be shy and thus inhibited from association with strangers. In this sense, shyness might be viewed as a "limbic spike," part of our limbic survival program, which is apparently not only the caretaker of our physical safety, but the safety of our self-esteem as well, which is described in some detail in a following chapter.

Philip G. Zimbardo, the well-known professor of psychology at Stanford University, described shyness as follows in his book *Shyness: What It Is, What to Do About It*:

> The prevalence of shyness varies from culture to culture and with different types of people. . . . At one end of the continuum are those who feel more comfortable with books, ideas, objects or nature than with other people. . . . The middle range of shyness includes the bulk of shy people, those who feel intimidated and awkward in certain situations with certain types of people. . . . At the far end of the shyness continuum are those individuals whose fear of people knows no bounds—the chronically shy.[10]

Zimbardo pointed out that "Even San Francisco lawyer Melvin Belli, who was noted for his dramatic courtroom tactics, admitted that not only had he 'often been shy,' but that he became flamboyant to hide shyness." I think Melvin Belli, who has since passed away, exemplified a great many people who outwardly exhibit no signs of shyness, but inwardly can feel it.

Another factor that can affect our nurturance is what psychologist Kim Bartholomew called "defensive maintenance of self sufficiency" or "dismissing." In essence, "dismissing" people are those who don't want to attach to others because they think these "others" are beneath them.

If shyness is a manifestation of the survival program, then being dismissive is a manifestation of an intense power program, which seeks status. If status is not enhanced by reaching out to other people who the power-driven people believe are "beneath them," then at cocktail parties or other functions where direct contact is made, it's "Glad to meet you, but I do have to rush off." Sound familiar? In any event, one might envision that there is an intensity scale for our propensity to associate with strangers that would need to take into consideration one's shyness or tendency to be dismissive.

In general, it would appear that the limbic nurturance program, like the power, territorial, and sexual drives, is hydraulically based. One can envision a piston creating a relative, constant pressure for nurturance (factoring in times when we feel more or less nurturing) that at the more intense levels needs to find an outlet. The outlet might be children or a spouse. Or if neither are existent in our lives, it might be one or more pets or a coterie of close relatives or peers.

And like the power, territorial, and sexual drives, those who are most intense on a metaphoric nurturance scale would presumably be highly aggressive and possessive in their nurturance and react with jealousy, depressive sadness, envy, anger, grief, hatred—the full arsenal of emotions that can be unleashed by the disappointed Inner Dummy, when an attachment is broken.

A Number Ten male on a nurturance scale, whose wife leaves him for another man may attempt to kill her or have her killed by someone else. A Number Ten female whose child or spouse dies may grieve for years and might even attempt suicide.

But unlike the power, territorial, and sexual drives, it would appear that there is trouble at the low end of the nurturance scale as well. People who are Number Ones on the power, territorial, and sexual scales can be assumed to be harmless. But a Number One on the nurturance scale presumably has little or no empathy, altruism, affection, or sense of guilt. Combine this with an intense limbic power program, and he or she could be a psychopathic danger to society.

In what I thought was a brilliant book, *Inside the Criminal Mind*, criminologist Stanton E. Samerow writes:

> This is not to deny individual differences among criminals in their aesthetic tastes, sexual practices, religious observance, or favorite sports team. But all regard the world as a chessboard over which they have total control, and they perceive people as pawns to be pushed around at will. Trust, love, loyalty, and teamwork are incompatible with their way of life. They scorn and exploit most people who are kind, trusting, hardworking, and honest. Toward a few they are sentimental, but rarely considerate. Some of their most altruistic acts have a sinister motive. . . . The criminal believes that he is entitled to it [wealth] and grabs it any way he can, not caring whom he injures, and then he thirsts for more.[11]

Samerow also made the following point regarding guilt, which might be considered an ingredient of the nurturance program in that it helps us to maintain our bonding or attachment with others. Guilt, if we are high enough on the scales to feel it intensely enough, is among the most punishing of feelings, particularly if we break or betray an attachment to another:

> As I see it, criminals do experience guilt and remorse. They have a conscience, but it is not fully operational. When they commit a crime, they can shut off considerations of conscience as quickly and totally as they

can shut off an electric light. Just the fact that the criminal can feel guilt, no matter how ineffective it is as a deterrent, helps him to maintain the belief that he is decent.[12]

Of course, Samerow is probably speaking here of what he called the typical hardened criminal.

In the business world, the Number Ones, Twos, and Threes are those with whom you want to have written contracts, with every detail spelled out. They would probably feel very little remorse if they betrayed their spoken word.

Because of all the compartments within the limbic nurturance program, I found it difficult to develop any meaningful quiz for it on my *Brain Tricks* Web site. Presumably a scale of intensity would be needed for each of the four compartments.

However, the nurturance scale that follows covers the program in general in an attempt to provide an easy reference or quantification for our very basic, primal levels of nurturance. And so if you find Numbers that appear to describe you, they may be combinations of any two, or maybe three Numbers, like "Oh, yes, I'm sort of a Three and Four, with perhaps a bit of a Seven, when it comes to loving my dog." We also need to consider that on some days, we can feel more nurturing than on other days, but in general, will usually fall back to our base level. This is just one more challenge in penetrating the enormous complexities and mysteries of the human mind.

NUMBER ONE:

You are probably incapable of forming a meaningful relationship with anyone else. You have little or no sense of love, compassion, trust, guilt, or remorse. Your feelings of empathy and altruism are at rock bottom, or as Stanton Samerow said, you use them to your benefit. If you have an intense power program, you are a likely candidate for committing criminal acts.

NUMBER TWO:

You would probably rather be alone most of the time. If you have a family, its members don't hold much meaning for you. You probably don't have any close friends. At work, you prefer not to socialize with your co-workers. You actually enjoy being a recluse. You might commit criminal acts without guilt or remorse, if you thought you could get away with it. If you have a child, he or she will be in for a rough time.

NUMBER THREE:

You may find yourself attached to a spouse or to children, but you find you cannot be sincerely nurturant to all of them. You may wonder why you are deprived of the love and compassion you see in others. You won't grieve for very long if someone close to you leaves your orbit of family and friends. You don't mind being alone and can actually find it a relief. Others may call you antisocial. If you have a strong power program, you might also be called "dismissive," in which case you feel that most of the people you meet are beneath you.

NUMBER FOUR:

You probably feel strong love and compassion for your family and friends, but you may not feel comfortable in making substantial sacrifices for them. You are probably happy with your nurturing role and are not anxious to make new friends. Your close circle will do. You don't like being alone, but you don't mind it, either. You probably believe that the level of empathy and altruism you feel and demonstrate is enough. You are comfortable with yourself in this area.

NUMBER FIVE:

You probably feel a normal and healthy level of love, compassion, empathy, and altruism. You are loving to your children, if you have them, and your family and friends. You feel guilty when you know you have wronged someone. You are protective of those close to you and will grieve when someone close to you leaves you or dies. You may be somewhat outgoing to strangers if you are not inhibited by shyness.

NUMBER SIX:

You probably have strong feelings of nurturance and seek attachment. You will strongly bond with your children, if you have them, or a pet, and work hard to form a strong relationship with your spouse, if you have one. You feel a bonding with relatives, peers, and others in your life and are somewhat possessive. You don't like to be alone. You have strong feelings of guilt when you perceive that you have wronged someone close to you. You are probably active in church, club life, or charity work and enjoy it, if you are not inhibited by shyness.

NUMBER SEVEN:

You are probably very outgoing and deeply concerned about others, even strangers, who you meet and perceive as suffering hardship. You are very possessive of your children, spouse, or pets, if you have them. You have a close circle of friends or co-workers and you are probably on the telephone talking to one after the other on a frequent basis. You want to know what is going on in their lives. You don't like to be alone and you feel an overpowering sense of guilt when you perceive you have wronged someone. You may have an extremely active social life, probably belonging to clubs, charity groups, and so forth, if you have the opportunity.

NUMBER EIGHT:

You are probably gushing in your nurturance and are aggressive in pursuing it. You make efforts to find outlets for it and usually find that what you have is not enough. If you have a small family and are able to do so, you may add cats and dogs. The love and compassion you feel toward others is very intense. At social gatherings, whether with people you know or strangers, you are very happy. You may feel driven to have an extremely active social life. Being alone can be torturous. If someone close to you leaves you or dies, your grief may be enormous. You are frequently wracked with guilt over things that you've done or haven't done, but think you should have.

NUMBER NINE:

You are suffocating in your nurturance of others. Once people are in your orbit, whether child, spouse, relatives, peers, even pets, you will cling to them. You will feel anger if you suspect they are not returning your love, and jealousy and envy if you think they are becoming more attached to someone other than you. You will be inconsolable and wracked with guilt for months or years if someone close to you leaves or dies.

NUMBER TEN:

Time to check yourself in for treatment. You are probably a megalomaniac who may even *kill* to assure that your children, spouse, or others who are the object of your attachment remain within your orbit. You are overbearing, suffocating, clinging and impossible to be with for very long. Everything is your business. Nothing that anybody does to return their love is ever enough.

Since there was no quiz for nurturance on the Web site, there is no way to determine what rough percentage of people have a close match to each Number level. I find myself to be a mixture of Four and Five.

COMMENTARY BY DR. HEFTER

The process of nurturing is fundamental to the survival of all of us. When it is present between a parent and a young child, it is taken for granted— in fact, it is the absence of significant parent-child nurturance that is more striking. The lack of appropriate nurturance during the early years is a foundation for future troubled behavior. The work of Bowlby in the area of attachment, nurturance, and separation is very interesting and important, and has considerably furthered our understanding of these subjects.

As alluded to in this chapter, there are grievous consequences from "overnurturance," i.e., a situation in which the "nurturee" is not readily permitted to be autonomous. The occurrence of this action in early childhood may well influence all subsequent relationships in which an individual is involved. This may be seen as a component of the power drive of the early nurturer. The opportunities for conflicting relationships because of it are obvious, particularly when the original "nurturee" either unconsciously imitates the nurturer or overreacts in an overly independent way to the experience of "overnurturance."

Another aspect of nurturance is the effect on the nurturer of the behavior of the individual being nurtured. Thus, in the example of the parent-child relationship, a reasonably nurturing mother may have difficulty meeting the needs of a child who often requires a great deal of nurturance, and consequently a process is set in motion in which neither parent nor child feels satisfied. This situation is common in later relationships and a frequent source of interpersonal difficulty. For example, a husband may feel chronically frustrated if he requires a great deal of nurturance and his wife may be only average in her nurturance.

NOTES

1. Ron Chernow, *Titan* (New York: Random House, 1998), p. 623.

2. John Bowlby, *Attachment* (New York: BasicBooks, 1982), pp. 207–208.

3. Iris Chang, *The Rape of Nanking: The Forgotten Holocaust of World War II* (New York: BasicBooks, 1997), p. 59.

4. Alan Fogel and Gail F. Melson (eds.), *Origins of Nurturance* (Hillsdale, N.J.: Lawrence Erlbaum Associates, 1986), pp. 135–36.

5. Peter Marris, *The Politics of Uncertainty: Attachment in Private and Public Life* (London: Routledge, 1996), p. 41.

6. Cindy Hazan and Phillip Shaver, "Romantic Love Conceptualized as an Attachment Process," *Journal of Personality and Social Psychology* 52, no. 3 (1987): 511.

7. Ibid., p. 515.

8. Michael B. Sperling and William H. Berman (eds.), *Attachment in Adults: Clinical and Developmental Perspectives* (New York: Guilford Press, 1994), pp. 15–16.

9. Ladislav Holy, *Anthropological Perspectives on Kinship* (London: Pluto Press, 1996), p. 13.

10. Philip G. Zimbardo, *Shyness: What It Is, What to Do About It* (Reading, Mass.: Addison-Wesley Publishing, 1977), pp. 14–19.

11. Stanton Samerow, *Inside the Criminal Mind* (New York: Times Books, 1984), p. 20.

12. Ibid., p. 163.

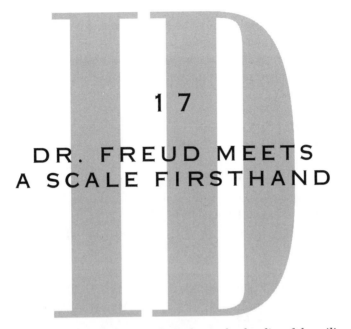

17

DR. FREUD MEETS
A SCALE FIRSTHAND

U.S. Army paratroopers consider themselves to be the elite of the military. Until recently, when the practice was eliminated, the paratroopers, when they graduated from training school, would have their new metal insignia hammered into their chests, clasps and all.[1]

Dr. Freud sat nervously in the conference room looking at his watch. He was asked by Ted Croft's secretary to meet once again with Peter Norton, vice president of sales of the Manchester Doll Company.

"Really, is this meeting necessary?" he asked the secretary. "I am really not interested in hearing any more about his dolls."

"I'm sorry, Dr. Freud, but Ted has now asked Peter to head up all the product licensing for the Inner Dummy program and I believe Peter has a new product concept to show you."

"You mean he has something besides those insidious dolls?"

"I believe so. We'd appreciate it if you would see him."

"Very well."

And now Dr. Freud was waiting nervously because he didn't like to be around pushy people and he considered Peter Norton to be pushy.

The door to the conference room burst open and Norton strode enthusiastically into the room.

"Hello, Dr. Freud," his voice boomed out, shocking Freud with its volume. "What a great pleasure to see you on this very beautiful day. Have you been out?"

"I'm afraid not."

"My goodness, Dr. Freud, you could use a little air. Why don't you take a walk? Would you like to take one with me right now? I have time."

"No, no, I am very busy catching up with the reference work."

Norton came around the table and sat in a chair next to Freud, edging it as close as he could to him and put out his hand to shake Freud's.

"Well, how have you been, sir?"

"Fine, just fine," Freud replied, trying to edge his chair away. Norton's breath was as bad as the last time they were together. "And where is Miss Kagan?"

"Oh, we don't need Jenny today. What I have to show you will only take a minute. She did send you her regards, however."

"Thank you very much."

"She's some woman, isn't she?"

"Please, Mr. Norton, I would like to get back to my studies. What is it that you have to show me?"

Norton leaned over and said in confidential tones, "I have some very good news, sir."

"And what is that?"

"Ted Croft was so impressed with the concept of the Dr. Freud Inner Dummy Dolls that he has asked me to take over the rest of the product licensing."

"So his secretary told me," Freud replied distastefully. "But what does that mean?"

"It means that there will now be other products under the franchise of the Dr. Freud Inner Dummy brand name. The dolls are just the start of it."

"Oh, no," Freud mumbled.

"Please, cheer up, Dr. Freud. People will love this stuff. Here let me show you the product idea of the day."

Norton stood up and began opening a small case he had placed on the conference room table when he walked in the door. Then he gingerly lifted out what looked like a bathroom scale.

"And what may I ask is that, sir?" Freud asked, skeptically.

"Oh, you're going to love this. This is just great."

"But what is it?"

Norton placed the product on the floor behind his chair.

"I'll tell you what it is. It's the Dr. Freud Inner Dummy Bathroom Scale."

"Oh, no." Freud felt himself becoming faint.

"Hey, I haven't even told you how it works."

"Maybe you shouldn't bother."

Norton burst out laughing, with a deep, raucous sound that was shocking to Freud. Even more shocking was Norton's hard slap to Freud's shoulders.

"You just slay me, doc, you really do. I'd give a bundle just to have you hang around here for a long time."

"Fortunately for me, I will be gone shortly."

Another raucous laugh.

"You're a card, doc, a real card. Now here, let me show you how this works. This product will be for people who have a fat phobia. No matter how much they weigh, if it's only a hundred pounds, they think they are overweight. I don't know if you have people like that up in heaven, or wherever you are living now, but we have people like this in our country alone by the millions."

Norton paused and looked at Freud for effect.

"Now . . . do you want to know what the selling hook is?"

"Not really."

Another hearty, raucous laugh, with a hard slap to the shoulders. Freud began to think of other responses he might use. It might be worth it to show a bit of enthusiasm just to stop the painful slaps to his shoulders, he thought.

"Well, let me tell you," Norton went on. "You get on the Dr. Freud Inner Dummy Bathroom Scale, just as you would any other scale. But you know what the difference is?"

"Please tell me," Freud replied, trying his best to sound positive.

"You weigh at least eight pounds less."

"What?" Freud looked shocked.

"That's it. You weigh eight pounds less, but sometimes you only weigh four pounds less. The scale keeps you guessing to some extent, but we intend to program the chip inside so that most of the time you think you are losing weight and you almost never think you are gaining weight, unless you are truly adding the pounds. Then a light flashes when you get on the scale and a sign lights up that says: 'You don't want to know. Wait until tomorrow.'"

Freud moaned.

"Don't you get it? This scale is telling your Inner Dummy with its expectations for status and attachment that your weight is just fine. You can get on this scale in the morning and we can almost guarantee that you will feel great."

Freud moaned again.

"Come on, doc. Tell me. Don't you think this is marvelous? Isn't it almost as good as the Inner Dummy dolls that we thought would be impossible to beat?"

"Ah, Mr. Norton," Freud said dazedly as he rose from his chair. "I'm sure you people know what you are doing, but I am a bit under the weather today, and I wonder if we could discuss this at some other time."

"You didn't say you were under the weather before, doc."

"Well, I am now."

Norton doubled over in raucous laughter, the sounds bouncing off the walls of the conference room.

"You are a card, doc, an absolute card. And you know what?"

"What, please?"

"You're a good sport. I know these products are hard on you, with all your books and your degrees and so forth. But people will love this and you deserve credit for going along with us."

"Thank you, Mr. Norton. But now I must return to my studies."

"Hey, no problem, doc. Ted wants me to run all the new ideas for licensed products by you, just in case you find something totally repulsive."

"I'm afraid I've found everything I've seen so far totally repulsive."

"Then let's just say that Ted wants you to note anything you find *beyond* repulsive."

Again the raucous laugh, the reverberation against the walls.

"But hey, I'm out of here," Norton said as he placed the scale back in the case and strapped it. "Don't want to take up any more time than I have to."

"Thank you, sir."

Norton headed for the door and as he got there he wheeled around and said, "See you soon, doc. And by the way, the creative team came up with two or three new product ideas last night. We're prototyping them, but I want you to be surprised."

"I'm sure I will be, Mr. Norton," Freud replied weakly as Norton left the room.

NOTE

1. James Malone, *Louisville Courier-Journal*, December 22, 1997, p. A1.

1 8

OUR DRIVE
FOR SURVIVAL
MEASURING THE LEVEL OF
OUR IRRATIONAL FEARS

A grandmother in Columbus, Ohio, thought she was doing a charitable act when she fed the parking meters of two strangers. However, it is against the law in Columbus to feed a parking meter, unless it is your own. And so the grandmother was handcuffed and fined $500.[1]

How many times have we heard about a golfer needing to make a one-foot putt to win a tournament, freeze up, and blow it as the putt spins away? An instant later the golfer puts the ball in the same position and now, under no pressure at all because the tournament is over, drills the ball into the center of the hole time and time again.

During the festivities preceding the all-star game of the National Basketball Association, there is a three-point basket shooting competition, during which it is not uncommon for the participants to make three-point baskets, from a distance of just over twenty-three feet, eight to twelve times in a row. But during a championship game when everything is on the line, those same shooters more often than not clink the basketball off the rim.

Casey Stengel, a crusty, old manager of the New York Yankees baseball team in the 1950s, while watching his hitters hit the ball into the stands during batting practice, made the statement, "Anyone can hit a home run during batting practice." He was implying that during a game, when the pressure is on, it's another story all together.

Why is it that most of us get nervous under pressure when we are about to perform in front of others, whether it's a baseball game or a piano recital? Why doesn't the mental side of our brain, which is our own flesh-and-blood organ, support us during times of pressure instead of making us nervous and anxious, which makes it difficult for us to do our best?

When *Brain Tricks* first came out, I would say in interviews that our "brain was not always our friend." The publicist who was handling the book kept telling me that "I shouldn't say that."

"Why not?" I would ask. "It's true."

"It doesn't sound professional and you can't really explain it in psychological terms."

"Oh," I would reply and continue saying it.

He was correct in saying that I couldn't explain it in psychological terms. Then, in 1993, I was reading a book titled *Anxiety Disorders and Phobias* authored by cognitive therapist Aaron T. Beck and Gary Emery with Ruth Greenberg. In it I read:

> A person's fear of making irreversible or fatal slips may be just as intense when speaking before a large audience as when walking along a high bridge. It seems that the same apparatus (inhibition, instability) that prevents a person from venturing into physical danger also deters him from exposing himself to psychological danger (say, public display of incompetence). Ironically, the inhibition, instability, and blocking in a social situation, by impeding skilled performance, increase the very danger they are designed to protect the individual against.[2]

After reading this, it struck me that the limbic survival program, which I called the *security program* in *Brain Tricks*, is responsible not only for protecting our physical safety, but our self-esteem as well. And in doing so, it can interfere and come in conflict with our other limbic programs and on occasion literally overpower them using two of the strongest weapons in the *limbic emotional arsenal*, fear and anxiety.

While we are hovering over that golf ball in a competitive tournament, we are not in any physical danger. Yet we might feel as much fear and anxiety as most of us would on our first parachute jump, when the feelings would be appropriate.

The conflict between our metaphoric *power* and *survival drives* might have started when we received the invitation to play in the golf tournament. The power drive, if it was relatively intense, probably wanted us to go for it, because if we won or did well our *status* would be enhanced.

Our *survival drive* if it was relatively intense would be intent on keeping us out of the tournament. It would sense in its way that if we lost badly, our self-esteem would take a beating and we would be punished by a disappointed power program with depressive feelings, such as anger, bitterness, and sadness. In the "emotional conflict" between the two instinctive drives, our rationality or ego would be in the middle, attempting to come to a decision. Does this quandary sound familiar?

We may decide to enter the tournament and simply play through our anxieties or fears. Or, we may decide not to play. And our survival program, in its continuing effort to protect our self-esteem, might drive us to construct an excuse that would prevent our peers from thinking poorly of us. "I've just come down with a touch of the flu," we might say. Or, "My mother called and she is coming for a visit." "A customer called and insists on a weekend meeting." "I have too much homework." This is just one more episode in the saga of the inner craziness of apparently normal people.

When you think about it, most of our feelings of nerves, worries, anxieties, and fears are triggered today more by social threats to our self-esteem than by threats to our physical safety, if we are living relatively normal lives in peaceful communities and are healthy, with jobs that entail no physical risk. I'm not sure, however, that "social phobias," which is what psychologists call these feelings, are what any ultimate designer might have had in mind when the limbic survival program was developed. The design might have been intended more for hunting and gathering in a wilderness full of predators, than for golf tournaments, piano recitals, public speaking, and other such activities, to which it apparently evolved to cover.

In attempting to find measurements that would define the core hydraulic force that creates whatever base level of survival propensity each of us has over a given period of time, the studies that made the most sense had to do with the scales of risk taking and sensation seeking. Nigel Nicholson made some interesting points about risk taking in his article "How Hardwired Is Human Behavior?" in the July–August 1998 issue of *Harvard Business Review*. In it he wrote:

> Human beings who survived the harsh elements of the Stone Age undoubtedly tried to avoid loss. After all, when you are living on the edge,

to lose even a little would mean that your very existence was in jeopardy. Thus, it follows that ancient hunter-gatherers who had just enough food and shelter to survive weren't big risk takers. That doesn't mean they never explored or acted curious about their world. Indeed, when the circumstances felt safe enough, this is very likely just what they did. . . .

But what of those Silicon Valley entrepreneurs who have made a high art form of bet-the-company behaviors? . . . Human behavior exists along a continuum. On average, people avoid risk except when threatened. But imagine a bell curve. At one end, a small minority of people avidly seek risk. At the other end, a small minority of people are so cautious that they won't take risks even when their lives depend on it. The vast majority fall in between, avoiding loss when comfortable with life and fighting furiously when survival requires them to do so.[3]

One of the major idiosyncrasies of the limbic survival program is that it is subject to "spikes" involving specific physical or social activities that do not relate to where a person might consistently be on a metaphoric survival scale. On this scale a Number One would be practically fearless, even when a gun is placed to his or her head. "Go ahead and shoot, make my day," they might say and actually not feel any fear. Number Tens might never go out of the house and may wear gloves and a mask to ward off the germs they believe are trying to get them.

It is apparently in the lower numbers on the scale where the metaphorical "spikes," which take the form of irrational phobias and anxieties, both physical and social, create idiosyncrasies. Thus, Number Twos, who are champion ski jumpers, who face risk of physical injury during endless days of practice, might have arachnophobia (a fear of spiders), or taphophobia (a fear of graves). And yet, they might otherwise be relatively fearless.

These metaphoric limbic spikes, like the base survival program from which they emerge, can be envisioned as housed in our Inner Dummy, because they are impervious to time, awareness, or logic. You can't simply walk up to a successful person like the entertainer Judy Garland, who was known to have low self-esteem, and say, "It is ridiculous that you are walking around with such low self-esteem. You are a great success in your career, you have two fine daughters. Now, get that self-esteem up, right now." Nothing will happen in that instant. If self-esteem is to rise, it will do so only after a lot of hard effort by someone who is aware of the irrationality and wants to work on it. In this sense, there is a great paradox to self-esteem in that one may be a great success in life and still have low self-esteem. It appears to have an Inner Dummy agenda of its own.

In the book *Self-Esteem, Paradoxes and Innovations in Clinical Theory and Practice*, psychology professor Richard L. Bednar and graduate school instructor Scott R. Peterson wrote:

> The (following) is a statement from a seventy-year-old man, reflecting on his lifetime effort to better the world he lived in:

> My whole life has been a succession of disappointments. I can scarcely recollect a single instance of success in anything that I ever undertook.

> The origins of this statement are not to be found in a life dominated by failure, nor was this person an object of pity and scorn to his contemporaries—nothing could be further from the truth. The writer was John Quincy Adams, who served with distinction as the sixth president of the United States, a senator, a congressman, a minister to major European countries, and a vital participant in many of the early and crucial events influencing the development of the nation.[4]

It is obvious that simply telling John Quincy Adams that he should "snap out of it and get that self-esteem up" would do no good. Nor can you walk up to someone who has a phobia of any kind—spiders, graves, heights, elevators, whatever—and say, "This is ridiculous. Get real. There is nothing to be afraid of. This is all in your mind." Neutralizing phobias may take months of cognitive therapy and may never fully go away.

In her book *Triumph Over Fear*, Jerilyn Ross characterizes what a limbic spike is like as she describes her first panic attack, at the age of twenty-five, when she and a friend, during a trip to Europe went to the Cafe Winkler in the city of Salzburg, Austria, "which was on the top floor of a mountainside building . . . with floor-to-ceiling panoramic windows." A music festival was taking place and she was dancing with a young, "handsome Austrian," when:

> Then something happened. Suddenly I felt as if a magnet was pulling me toward the edge of the room. The pull was so strong I thought I was going to jump out of the window. Everything started to spin. I felt as though I was on the verge of completely losing control of myself.
>
> "My god!" I remember thinking, "I certainly don't want to commit suicide! What is going on?"
>
> I felt I was in terrible danger. Everything in my power was fighting that magnetic pull. The feeling was so seductive—it was like being in a vacuum or the middle of a tornado, holding on for dear life. It took all my

energy to prevent myself from running across the room and jumping out
the window. It felt as if my heart was pounding out of my chest. . . .

I had to get out of there, off the dance floor, out of the building. In the
midst of my panic, much to my amazement, I heard myself speaking
calmly to my partner.

"Excuse me," I said. "I have to make a call."[5]

She then described how she left the room and that by the time she got
to the elevator, the "terror was gone." It was later that she discovered she
had a phobia, a fear of heights called *acrophobia*. Ms. Ross later studied
psychology and became a psychotherapist, specializing in anxieties and
phobias, and still later became president of the Anxiety Disorders Association of America.

No matter how low we are on the survival scale, how generally fearless
we might be, we will feel fear and anxiety when we perceive we are actually being threatened in reality. This is obviously the purpose of the program in protecting our safety, to use the prospect of the negative feelings of
anxiety and fear to keep us out of harm's way. Even Number Ones on the
survival scale would not willingly walk into a cage of wild lions, where they
would likely experience a panic attack, one of the severest manifestations
of fear, similar to the one described by Ms. Ross.

Aaron T. Beck, in his book *Anxiety Disorders and Phobias*, explained
how phobias may not have any relation to one's general vulnerability to fear:

Many people who are phobic about certain situations are completely comfortable in situations that produce severe anxiety in others. One patient,
for instance, who had a great dread of being crawled over by cockroaches
and other small insects, was always calm in public speaking, relished
meeting new people, and was fearless in various athletic events. He felt
extremely anxious when he was alone in his apartment at night because
of his fear of being attacked by insects. As a result of this phobia, he
sought professional help.[6]

Beck later pointed out that one phobia may lead to others that have some
similarities, in what are called "spreading phobias," where the fear is
linked to similar situations, "according to the type of danger that he could
encounter." He wrote:

For example, a laborer was struck by a truck while painting a white line
on a road, and subsequently developed a phobia of working on the road.

The phobia then spread to a fear of riding a motorcycle or bicycle on a road (Kraft and Al-Issa 1965a). The same authors (1965b) described the case of a girl who witnessed the removal of the charred bodies of two children from a burning house. Subsequently, she developed a fear of washing in warm water, eating hot foods or drinking hot water. The phobia spread to touching an electric hot plate in the "on" or "off" position. . . .

In other words, the phobias extended not to objects or situations present during the trauma (as one might expect on the basis of classical conditioning) but rather to situations that could produce the same type of damage.[7]

Phobias might thus be described as irrational fears, or one more manifestation of the inner craziness of apparently normal people. In describing the origins of phobias and their resultant panic attacks, Jerilyn Ross writes:

The human body evolved so that primitive people could instantaneously switch into "red alert" when physical danger threatened. Called the fight-or-flight response, this response is still part of the modern human's physiological—and psychological—makeup . . .

But nature is not perfect and for reasons not yet understood fully by scientists, sometimes the brain receives images that set off what amounts to a false alarm. Although there is controversy as to whether a panic attack is actually a response to this false alarm, in many ways the experience feels as if one's fight-or-flight response is being inappropriately activated.[8]

False alarm appears to be the operative words in describing the irrationality of phobias. The limbic memory that causes the phobia, as Beck pointed out, may have been an experience where there was only a *similarity* in danger. But once imprinted on the limbic amygdala-based brain link, it will be activated, apparently, when our emotional sentinel alerts it, whether it makes rational sense or not.

Those of us with phobias of one kind or another can take heart in Beck's observation that a phobia is a unique fear that may not have any effect at all on other aspects of our lives. The man he described as being afraid of insects at night didn't experience any other abnormal fears or anxieties. A phobia may thus be safely described as a false alarm that creates a limbic spike.

A classic case of one such spike is evident in John Madden, the television commentator who covers the most important games played in the National Football League. Madden in his youth was a football player who later worked himself up to be coach of the Oakland Raiders, at the time known as one of the toughest teams in the league. It was this experience primarily that led to Madden's reputation as a proponent for toughness on the football field. In recent years, he has even developed the annual "All-Madden Football Team," composed of the toughest players who ever played the game. And yet, when Madden boarded a commercial airplane, he suffered from severe claustrophobia. We can envision his knees becoming weak, he begins to sweat profusely, and his mind literally throws him into the kind of panic described previously by Jerilyn Ross at the Austrian dance.

As he said in his book, *One Size Doesn't Fit All*, "I wasn't afraid that the jet was going to crash, I just didn't like being cooped up in that metal tube. In the 1979 season, I switched to trains."[9]

Today, as a television commentator, instead of fighting or treating the phobia, Madden simply refuses to fly. He purchased a bus and had it custom fitted to provide all the comforts of home. During the football season, he criss-crosses the country during the week so that he can be in whatever city the league has scheduled for the Sunday game he is to cover. As a result, during the football season, he is on the road almost constantly, traveling thousands of miles, sometimes driving from coast to coast in a single week.

Other than this single phobia, Madden is an apparently normal person. He suffers from a single limbic spike.

On the other hand, it is possible to suffer from multiple phobias that are apparently unrelated to one another. In his book *Phobia Free*, Harold N. Levinson describes Susan S. as follows:

> Seeing Susan's perpetual smile, one would never guess that she was the victim of severe, paralyzing phobias. For many years she suffered from:
> - Fear of crossing streets
> - Fear of becoming lost
> - Fear of riding escalators
> - Fear of going on elevators alone
> - Fear of driving and being in cars
> - Fear of being in New York City alone
> - Fear of heights
> - Fear of water and of drowning
> - Fear of thunderstorms
> - Fear of traveling[10]

Susan was quoted as saying the following in the book, about her many phobias: "Due to all my fears, I became overprotective of my daughter. I wouldn't allow her to ride a bicycle or roller skate because I was afraid she would hurt herself. It was hard for both of us."[11]

It is apparent that the limbic survival program is more suited for primitive living, for which it was ostensibly designed, and can become lost in today's industrialized society. What makes the *survival mechanism*, as Aaron T. Beck put it, of one person more susceptible to a given phobia than another remains unknown. But there should be little doubt that a limbic brain designed to have imprinted on it for future reference, the dangers of primitive living—snakes, tigers, lonely dark forests and trails, strangers, abusive peers and authority figures, caves that might harbor predators, and so forth—can become confused, as Susan's did, in the big-city, modern world of a New York City.

Perhaps her Inner Dummy is mistaking streets for dangerous animal trails, escalators for risky natural river crossings, being in New York City alone as being lost in a foreboding forest.

In their book *Evolutionary Psychiatry*, psychiatrist Anthony Stevens and researcher and lecturer John Price actually made this point as follows:

> Anxiety and fears are adaptive responses to the kind of dangers humans have been exposed to in the course of their evolution. This is why we fear ancient dangers such as snakes, spiders, high or open spaces, and not modern dangers such as cars, guns, cigarettes, whiskey and saturated fats, which kill off our contemporaries in far greater numbers. Modern phobias such as going to school or to the dentist or of contracting AIDS are contemporary versions of adaptive fears of going off the home range, getting hurt, or getting infected.[12]

As a matter of interest, the American Psychiatric Association estimates that between 5.1 and 11.5 percent of us are afflicted with some form of phobia. My own guess would be that this number is higher than 70 percent, particularly when you include chrematophobics. These are people who have a fear of spending money, even though only a few dollars are involved. In other words, they are "cheap," and if fear of spending small amounts of money is a form of chrematophobia, then phobias abound in the world.

I recall leaving a restaurant with a close friend, John McDonald III, who is CEO of a large Midwestern company and comes from a wealthy family. The valet had left my car outside and I was about to give him a ten-dollar bill as a tip, when John grabbed my wrist and said, "For god's sake, don't give him that money." I said, "What are you talking about? This man left my car right in front of the door and he looks like he can use some extra cash."

"I don't care," John replied. "Don't give him that money. Give him five instead."

I looked in his eyes and there was a form of fear there. It was as if he was confronting a wild dog. I gave the valet the ten, anyway, and John never forgot it. I told him later, while recounting other escapades involving just a few dollars, "You've got to be the cheapest person in the whole world."

John, who is proud of his Scottish heritage, replied, "I hope so."

Another friend of mine, Sid Cohen, who is just as tight with money, and though retired, remains strong, wiry, and somewhat threatening, reminiscent of his youth when he was the Pacific boxing champ in the U.S. Army, was with a group of us a few years ago, who went to a restaurant after a movie. I had ordered spaghetti and meatballs, but before the meal was served, the waitress came to the table and told me she was sorry, but the kitchen was out of meatballs. "No problem," I said, "just bring me the spaghetti."

It was Sid's turn to the pay the bill and when he got it, he studied it as he always did, with the intensity of a biblical scholar. Then he looked up at me and said, "I can't believe this, they charged you one dollar for the meatballs and you didn't get any."

"Forget it," I said. "It's only a dollar."

"Are you kidding?"

At that point, he stood up and waved frantically at the waitress across the room beckoning her to our table. He said to her with a voice that bordered on the frantic and pointing to the incriminating item on the check, "You charged us a dollar for the meatballs and my friend here never got them."

"I'm sorry, sir, I'll take care of that right away."

She picked up the bill and started to head toward the kitchen when Sid thought for a moment, got up, and yelled after her, "And don't forget the tax."

That would have been eight cents.

Unlike John, Sid won't admit to being cheap. "It's a matter of principle," he says. In my opinion both are chrematophobics, they have a fear of spending money, particularly small amounts, even if they have enough to spend. There is an explanation in *The Encyclopedia of Phobias, Fears and Anxieties* by psychology professor Ronald M. Doctor and Ada P. Kahn about why this phobia exists, which says, "Fear of loss of money represents a fear of losing the external validation of one's worth provided by money."[13] I'm not sure this explanation applies to John or Sid. But I was happy to tell them both that their cheapness was a phobia.

Another friend, Bob Schwartz, apparently shows no fear at all when he goes to Las Vegas and literally has thousands of dollars on a crap table at one time. This is something I absolutely cannot do, ten dollars for me would be a big bet, and yet he does it with absolute aplomb. You would think he is fearless.

Yet, he has a germ phobia or mikrophobia. When he leaves a public bathroom, he uses a tissue to grasp the handle. And one time at a barbeque he wouldn't eat the food because the cooks behind the hot grills were sweating.

"Did you see the sweat drop into the food?" I asked.

"No."

"Then why didn't you eat the food?"

"Because the sweat might have dropped when I didn't see it. So I had a salad."

"At an outdoor barbeque?"

"Yes."

There are apparently a lot of people with a germ phobia. *The Encyclopedia of Phobias, Fears and Anxieties* lists more than a thousand phobias, including a fear of getting haircuts, otherwise known as the barber's chair syndrome. There is even a fear of the northern lights called auroraphobia and the color red called erythrophobia.

Then there are anxieties, a second weapon of our "survival mechanism."

While phobias are the stark fears and panic we might feel in a given situation, anxieties are the worries we experience about impending outcomes.

In the book *Anxiety, Phobias and Panic*, Reneau Z. Peurifoy, a counselor on anxiety-related problems, describes the result of anxiety and fear as follows: "Both anxiety and fear trigger unpleasant mental symptoms such as a sense of helplessness, confusion, apprehension, worry and repeated negative thoughts."[14]

I thought one of the better definitions of the differences between anxiety and fear was given in the *Encyclopedia of Phobias, Fears and Anxieties*: "Anxiety and fear have similarities and differences. Fear is sometimes defined as a response to a consciously recognized and usually external threat. In a general way, fear is a response to a clear and present danger, whereas anxiety is a response to a situation, object, or person that the individual has come to fear through learning and experiences."[15]

In other words, if we are walking along a narrow trail in the woods and a rattlesnake strikes from the brush we will feel *fear*. The next time we walk in the woods, there may not be a rattlesnake for miles around, but we will feel some level of *anxiety*.

The level we feel would appear to depend on where we stand on the metaphoric survival scale and the event we are worried about. A Number One on the survival scale, who is incapable of feeling fear, except in the most threatening of situations, and who has very high self-esteem, would probably feel less anxiety when walking in the woods again, than a Number Ten, who might need to be forced out of his or her bedroom, just to begin the day.

Friends of mine from the business world exhibited varying and relatively consistent levels of anxiety. A president of a company in Pennsylvania, let's call him Walter, never appeared to be fazed by anything. According to his wife, he slept each night like a baby no matter what turmoil he had confronted during the day. I recall being at the company's headquarters the day the company lost its biggest customer, accounting for about 15 percent of its business. "My god," I said to Walter, "you'd better take a tranquilizer. This is a catastrophe."

"Nonsense," he replied. "These things happen. You have to expect it. We'll tighten up for a while, but we'll make it, we'll come back."

In all the years I worked with him, I never saw Walter in bad spirits, never saw him mean-spirited or demeaning to others. He admitted to me that he was normal, that he wasn't some "cold fish," that he did have anxieties from time to time, but they quickly vanished.

His wife told me she thought his secret was in his extremely high self-esteem. Through high school, college, and his career years Walter was always the ultimate success: star of the football teams, class valedictorian, head of the local Boy Scouts, active in the PTA, successful in every business position he occupied with his company, which was the only one he ever worked for. Walter appeared to be the perfect example of what can result when one has a powerful, positive attitude about life. No matter what went wrong, he believed like the Michael Jordans of the athletic world, that in the end he would win.

Another business associate, let's call her Susan, was like many of the rest of us. If Walter was a Number Two or Three on the survival scale, Susan would be a Six. She usually had a positive outlook, but if a handful of things went deeply wrong during the day, she would go home feeling deep anxiety, with a sleepless night in the offing.

If a customer called and told her that an order he was expecting hadn't arrived, Susan would start running around the office, papers askew, looking for the answers. Her sense of anxiety, her mild paranoia, was actually a help to her career. She never took anything for granted.

I recall that on her bulletin board she kept a cover of a *Fortune* magazine issue, featuring Andrew Grove, then CEO of Intel, whose famous quote was set in headline type: "Only the Paranoid Survive."

As an aside, I would frequently wonder about business associates who appeared to show no anxiety or paranoia at all even though their general abilities were below par. The combination of these two characteristics are almost as bad in the business world as the combination of being in a position of power, being dumb, and being stubborn.

Finally, there was Jim, whose level of anxiety was such that psychologists might call him a *catastrophic worrier*. No matter how minor the setback, Jim worried that it would have much greater implications. If a customer didn't pay his bill on time, Jim would automatically worry that he had lost the customer. If an employee resigned, he would worry for weeks that he would lose customers because of it. If his monthly sales weren't up to forecasted projections, he would envision having to shut down the company. Jim would tell me that he would wake up early in the morning and remain in bed for an hour, reliving each experience over which he felt anxiety. If the anxiety was intense, he might have remained awake much of the night. Now he's retired and his wife tells me he still does the same thing. The rubber molding had come loose from the garage door, she told me, and he worried about it during his early morning anxiety session, thinking that maybe the house was beginning to fall apart.

Most of us, from time to time, will feel anxiety or worry at intensity levels that are far greater than the situations might warrant. These are the minor "false alarms" of the survival program that none of us, save possibly the Number Ones, are inured to. We consider these worries a normal part of our living, and never give a second thought to the fact that the mechanism that regulates our level of anxiety is a holdover from our primitive brain that can become confused in a civilized world.

In terms of classifying our everyday anxieties, Dr. Freud appeared to be closest to the mark when he classified them as "reality," "neurotic," and "moral."

Reality anxieties, he said, are those we feel when we sense a physical threat. We might imply from this such experiences as crossing a busy intersection that has no stoplight, or finding ourselves alone in a city park after midnight, or thinking we hear a burglar in our home.

A neurotic anxiety is one that emanates from our unconscious id, he said. From this we can imply the anxiety someone high up on the power scale might feel in the business world, when he suspects that his subordinates or peers are out to get him fired, when in reality they are supportive. The anxiety is thus neurotic, delusional.

Or, we might envision a spouse high on the sexual and nurturance scales, who begins to feel anxiety because she believes her husband is having an affair; he isn't attentive as he used to be, she thinks, when in reality the husband is caught up with distractions in his career.

The limbic programs all have specific levels of expectations that are determined by their levels of intensity, their positions on the varying scales. When they are threatened, whether the threat is real or perceived, they will create some level of anxiety within us, whether a false alarm or not.

A moral anxiety, according to Freud, is one we feel when there is a conflict between the id and our superego. As you'll recall, Freud used the term *superego* as the metaphor for that part of our minds that holds our standards for morality and ethics. Thus, if our id-based sexual drive is hydraulically moving us toward having an extramarital affair with someone we find sexually attractive to an extreme, and we have a very high morality level, imbued in us by our parents or religion or other influences, we will feel anxiety.

However, there is apparently a line between our normal anxieties, even those felt by catastrophic worriers such as Jim, and *anxiety disorders*, which might be so intense that they work to place us higher on the survival program scale.

In her book *Overcoming Anxiety*, Helen Kennerly describes one person whose anxiety met the definition of one quoted in *The Oxford Companion to the Mind*, as "sometimes taken to refer to feelings of apprehension which are difficult to relate to tangible sources of stimulation."[16] In other words, we can't figure out the underlying reasons for our anxiety. The person in Helen Kennerly's book described her anxiety disorder as follows:

> I always worry and I never relax nowadays. There is never a moment when I am free of aches and tension and my mind is always focused on worries. It makes me so tired and irritable and I have not been able to sleep or work properly and have not felt well in months. . . .
>
> I saw my doctor who said that I should join a yoga class and learn to unwind —I tried but I found it impossible to concentrate and I ended up getting more and more irritable. Now I try to cope by keeping busy in the shop, but this isn't easy because I am so tired that I can't seem to con-

centrate so I make silly mistakes and that stresses me and winds me up even more. I feel so hopeless that I just can't imagine when this is going to end.[17]

At least Jim, the catastrophic worrier, knew the causes of his anxieties because that is what he thought about at night or early morning in bed and could more readily attack his problem if he had the will to do it.

Joseph LeDoux in his book *The Emotional Brain* had this to say about fear:

> Escaping from danger is something that all animals have to do to survive. . . . What is important is that the brain has a mechanism for detecting the danger and responding to it appropriately and quickly. . . . The particular behavior that occurs is tailored to the species (running, flying, swimming), but the brain function underlying that response is the same—protection against the danger. This is as true of a human animal as of a slimy reptile.[18]

Of course, we need to be grateful that our limbic brains have been imbued with a "survival mechanism," which with its *arsenal* of emotions can alert us to both impending and actual danger.

However, in writing this chapter, this "survival mechanism" of ours with its limbic spikes and false alarms, reminded me of the story of the gorilla that could play golf and was said to have the ability to drive the ball 400 yards. Heavy bets were placed on him to win the tournament. On the first tee, sure enough, he hit the ball 400 yards, far enough to land the ball on the green, only two feet from the hole. Those who bet on the gorilla were ecstatic, as they walked behind him on the fairway, heading toward the green. On the green, the gorilla carefully lined up the putt, studying it front and back. Then he took a putter out of his golf bag and proceeded to hit the ball 400 yards.

Our "survival mechanism" might thus be likened to this gorilla, that can only hit the ball 400 yards, even when all that's needed is a two-foot putt. It can create fears, phobias, and anxieties even when there is only a slight threat of danger, when our common sense *knows* the threat of danger is slight. For many of us it has little sense of nuance as it subjects us to these false alarms, these limbic spikes, some of which can last for weeks, years, or a lifetime.

In my opinion, this is no way to design a brain, but then to whom might we object? Unfortunately there is no system of justice when it comes to the imperfections in the design of our brains or our bodies as a whole, for that matter. If there were, then the lawyers would have a field day.

In evaluating our basic fear level, whatever its singular "limbic spikes," we might relate to Nigel Nicholson's observation, quoted earlier about the bell curve, with people at one end avidly seeking risk and at the other end avoiding risk at all costs, with the vast majority of people falling in between. The studies of risk taking and sensation seeking appeared to be the most appropriate for developing a survival scale (see the end of this chapter) and which helps us measure our most basic vulnerability to fear.

Marvin Zuckerman of the University of Delaware Psychology Department seems to be the guru of "sensation seeking" as a field of study, just as Ardrey was for territorialism and Bowlby for attachment. In a paper entitled "Sensation Seeking and Its Biological Correlates," that appeared in a 1980 edition of *Psychological Bulletin*, Zuckerman, with Monte S. Buchsbaum and Dennis L. Murphy, discussed what they call a Sensation Seeking Scale, which I found difficult to decipher. But they did make what I consider to be one understandable observation: "Essentially the model suggests that as riskiness of situations increases, anxiety tends to increase more and sensation seeking tends to decrease more in low sensation seekers than in high sensation seekers. The tendency to enter into risky situations is a function of the interaction of anxiety and sensation-seeking states that in turn are related to the trait of sensation seeking."[19] As I understand this, our propensity toward sensation seeking or risk taking depends on how much anxiety we feel when we consider doing something that we rationally perceive as perilous. In other words, someone who is low on the scale would feel less anxiety about bungee jumping than someone higher on the scale.

As an aside, there appears to have been considerable study done with regard to the genetic basis of sensation seeking, which lends credence to the theory that we are born with a specific vulnerability level to fear, which then may be shaped by the environment. This is discussed in detail in chapter 26.

However, genetics was touched on in an article in the May 1986 edition of *Psychology Today*, by Frank Farley, titled "The Big T in Personality," with the subhead of *"Thrill-seeking often produces the best achievers, but it can also create worst criminals."* Farley said: "I suggest that the answer probably lies in a person's biological, possibly genetic makeup. Experiences around the time of birth or perhaps early nutrition may also play a role."[20]

But the more interesting part of this article was the scale that Farley created based on the letter "T." "Big Ts" were high on the thrill or sensation seeking scale and could be either "constructive" or "destructive." He said:

> Since Type T people may have physiological and personality characteristics that can lead toward either creative or destructive behavior, a key question is: What leads them to choose one path or the other? I don't have a definitive answer, but I have some clues. Biology seems to set the stage for being a Big T, but social circumstances probably determine in large measure whether a Big T person will become a creator or a destroyer.[21]

Most of the studies on sensation or thrill seeking indicate that those high on the scale are also "aggressive," a characteristic of those high on the power, sex, and territorial programs. Perhaps nature, which ostensibly designed our limbic, instinctive system with primitive life in mind, genetically instilled *those cavemen with the propensity to become leaders, with a lesser level of biological fear* so that they could dominate their tribes in all respects and control or attack others, when necessary, with a feeling of relative impunity.

While I've considered myself to have a high power program, I've gone through life feeling a lot of fear. So maybe this means that if I lived 25,000 years ago, I wouldn't have been leading the pack. Or maybe through sheer guile, I might have found a way, which illustrates the major difference between our limbic, instinctive programs and those of the higher animals. If a chimpanzee feels enough anxiety and fear when he is being driven to challenge the chimp on top of him in the hierarchal rank, he will, in all probability, do nothing.

Humans, however, have a much larger cerebral cortex and can think. If we feel fear and anxiety in the anticipation of challenging an authority figure, we can either back away, as the chimp might do, or make the challenge anyway, gritting our teeth and enduring the fear. In other words, we might simply summon the "courage," to move ahead, which, according to references I've read, is a rational manifestation of our will when it is in battle with those instinctive feelings that are driving us to run. Or, we might find a way to do an end run around the authority figure, or since we now have guns, we can shoot him. Chimps can't do that.

In essence, the survival program for humans apparently has two objectives: to prevent us from becoming physically injured and to prevent us from experiencing failures that would depress our self-esteem.

Underpinning the normal fears and anxieties we experience is our level of self-confidence, which in turn underpins our level of self-esteem. Whether genetic or learned, the Number Ones, Twos, and Threes on the survival scale exhibit high levels of self-confidence. How else could they calmly bungee jump off a high bridge heading to a rocky gorge below? Further, one's self-confidence at this level appears to be less fragile. On the physical side, I can remember the motorcyclist Evel Knievel breaking bones consistently as he crashed attempting to jump over row upon row of cars. He seemed to take pride in his ability to come back after the accidents and try the same thing all over again.

If a Number Eight on the survival scale were finally convinced by a motivational expert to make such a jump and crashed, he or she would probably walk away into the sunset, never to be seen near another motorcycle again. Whatever level of self-confidence that was generated to convince him or her to make the jump, was quickly, and probably forever, evaporated. Apparently the higher we are on the survival scale, the more fragile our self-confidence becomes.

Self-confidence is also a factor on the social side of fears and anxieties. I recall knowing a salesman for a valve manufacturer in Iowa, many years ago, who prided himself on making twenty calls a day, half of which would be cold calls on strangers, most of whom rejected him.

"How do you handle all that rejection?" I recall asking him. In all my days in business, I could never make a cold call, even on the telephone.

"It doesn't bother me at all. It's simply business," he replied.

Another salesman working for the same company found it extremely hard to make a cold call. He would tell me that he would sit in his car outside the customer's door for an hour or more, thinking of all the reasons why he shouldn't make the call.

One day he broke down and began to cry while in a customer's office making a cold call. The customer ended up giving him an order, but he never would make a cold call after that, and became a sales clerk in the factory.

The first salesman, the one who could make cold calls without hesitation each day, was probably between a Number Two and Four, while the salesman who felt high anxiety was between a Seven and Nine, and obviously in the wrong line of business.

I've felt for some time that the tapes and programs of Anthony Robbins and other motivational experts were aimed at the Numbers Sixes and up, whose survival program created a barrier of fear that was keeping them from "following their dreams." The object of these motivational programs is to boost self-confidence so that we might more easily develop the courage to quit our job and open our own car wash. If we are successful, this might raise our self-esteem a notch and give us the confidence to move to another venture. If it is unsuccessful, our self-esteem might plunge to a new low, taking our self-confidence for engaging in new ventures with it.

The interesting thing about self-confidence is that it can be compartmentalized. While as a Number Six or up, we may be hesitant to borrow money to open our own car wash, if we are successful with the venture, we might end up owning a dozen car washes, along with a new home and a sailboat. We might even take to strutting about town, reflecting arrogance, a feeling of reward triggered by the satisfied expectations of our power program.

However, we may be terrible at golf and so we avoid the game because if we do poorly at it in front of others, it makes our self-esteem, which remains fragile no matter how successful we were with the car washes, vulnerable. This is the life of a Number Six and up. Or, if we love the game so much that we are impelled to play, we'll probably find partners at our level and play at a secluded country club at tee times when the course is relatively empty.

It is ordinarily difficult for people at higher levels on the survival scale, who have become successful in specific areas, to become engaged in other activities where they stumble about and reflect lesser status, except in private, where they might eventually hone their skills enough to make public debuts. Those lower on the scales, the Ones to Threes, could care less how they look to others, whatever the field of endeavor. On a ski slope, they might continually fall down as they learn and their only reaction is to get up and try again.

In the world of athletics and entertainment, one's ability to maintain self-confidence in the face of adversity is paramount in achieving any great success. The animal body is intrinsically inconsistent. That's why the same horse doesn't win all the horse races, why Michael Jordan had nights where most of his shots clinked off the rim, why the best starting pitchers in baseball would have days when the hitters would chase them out of the park, why entertainers would have off nights, and why the best public speakers might stutter through a speech they've given dozens of times before.

It is apparently this inconsistency that gives many of the most successful athletes and entertainers, those within the normal range of the survival scale, cases of "Stage Fright." They are concerned about their next performance. Their Inner Dummies can drive them almost senseless with anxiety and thoughts about all the things that might go wrong. Most of these people tell us that no matter how long they've been doing their jobs, no matter how much success they've had, the "stage fright," the nerves before a performance, continues.

Those who are low on the survival scale, the Ones to Fours, are the ones who usually appear calm before their performances. Their general core level of fear is simply low.

I remember being a seminar speaker many years ago and pacing back and forth studying my notes, experiencing my usual "stage fright," when I saw another seminar speaker who was to speak in the room next to me, casually reading a newspaper and eating a corned-beef sandwich.

"What's the matter?" I asked him. "Aren't you human? Why aren't you nervous like the rest of us?"

"What do you mean, the rest of us? I don't see anybody else here who looks as nervous as you."

"Okay, then. Correction. Why aren't you as nervous as I am?"

"Because I'm not." He picked up his newspaper and walked away. Probably a Number Three on the nurturance scale.

But obviously this man had high self-esteem and a level of self-confidence in his public speaking to match. His fear of failure was thus very low. He was of the ilk, if he had the natural talent, to be a major-league relief pitcher. These are the people who get called into the game in the ninth inning, with a one-run lead to protect, bases loaded, the team's big slugger up to bat and he is expected to throw hard strikes around the edges of the plate.

If I was out there, I would undoubtedly throw the first ball over the catcher's head and bean the umpire. Those relief pitchers who are most successful are usually described as having "ice water in their veins." This would also be an excellent description of the Number Ones to Threes, the sensation seekers, the thrill seekers, the people who love risk, the big Ts.

Or, they might be higher up on the survival scale, have a higher core fear level, but have thrown thousands of pitches a week against their garages or in the park for years. Or hit thousands of golf balls each month. Or thousands of tennis balls. Sports psychologists stress tens of thousands of repetitive practices as a key factor in building enough confidence to compete under pressure. Sometimes this works and sometimes it doesn't.

People with very low self-esteem are usually advised to "learn to do one thing very well." The idea is that if you can learn one skill intensely enough to have self-confidence and be respected in that field of endeavor, that this can raise your general level of self-esteem a notch or two, and perhaps allow you to "come out of your shell." On the other hand, this didn't seem to work for John Quincy Adams.

As pointed out previously, it is apparent that the instinctive drives and programs of our limbic system are not always acting in our best real-word interests. However, as humans we have the power to think and create rational ego strategies that are capable of outflanking these limbic programs that still think we are living in caves.

One last underpinning of our survival program is trust. Earlier in the writing of this book, I thought trust might be an underpinning of the nurturance program, along with compassion and guilt. But it becomes apparent that our level of trust in others belongs to our survival program. The more trusting we are of others in our lives, the less fearful we are of them. The less trustful we are, the more fearful we become.

I recall working with a president of a large distribution firm many years ago who had an extremely low level of trust. If you weren't in his "inner circle," he simply didn't trust you, no matter what your past credentials were. The security system inside and outside of his network of warehouses was extreme to the point that the employees felt demeaned. The atmosphere in the corporate office area reminded me of what we've read about the White House, with different groups plotting against each other to get the ear of the president.

Another executive I knew had similar paranoia. There was no such thing as a handshake agreement in his business career. Even the smallest of agreements were covered by thick documents drawn up by his lawyers. Business paranoia is good for lawyers. In Japan, where trust is instilled in the corporate culture and one's word is his or her bond, there are far fewer lawyers than there are in the United States.

On the other hand, Bob Cox, who I mentioned before was my mentor in business, was born and bred in the United States, ran a big and dynamic operation, and always reflected considerable trust in others. Distrust had to be earned. Bob also had high levels of self-esteem and self-confidence in business and so perhaps it is all interrelated. The point is, it was much more pleasant to be around Bob's office than it was to work with the paranoid executives, who were probably between a Number Seven and Eight. Because Bob was my mentor, I have usually reflected high levels of trust in others, which makes life more pleasant all around.

Because of all the quirks and "limbic spikes," including irrational phobias and anxieties that may have no effect on one's general standing within the limbic survival program, I found it difficult to develop any meaningful quiz for it on my *Brain Tricks* Web site.

And so like the nurturance program, the scale that follows not only has no academic credence, but it is untested as well. It is merely an attempt to provide an easy reference or quantification for our levels of fear as they apply to how we might react to physical and social situations where this program may think our survival is at risk.

Here it is:

NUMBER ONE:

You are probably incapable of feeling fear, except in the most extreme circumstances. You probably love the thrill of taking risks, of seeking sensation. Your self-esteem is high and strong and won't be depressed by failing in new risks. You have probably been told that you have "ice water running in your veins." If you have an intense power program and a low nurturance program, you are a likely candidate for committing criminal acts, and if you have high intelligence, you'll likely be good at it. You would probably be a good poker player.

NUMBER TWO:

You rarely feel any real form of fear. If you are in the business world, making cold calls or entering strange situations would give you no anxiety. If you are an athlete, no matter how much you were battered the day before, you'll come out playing the following day as if nothing had happened. You have high levels of self-esteem and self-confidence and failing in tasks doesn't seem to alter those levels. You may feel phobias and anxieties, but probably won't admit to them. You are probably generally trusting of others. Someone has to cross you before you become distrustful.

NUMBER THREE:

You are probably known as "gutsy." In the business world you will take risks. You reflect a high level of self-confidence. If you are into athletics you will go all out and probably not be concerned about being injured. If you're a golfer, even on bad days you will swing away with your driver as if nothing is wrong. You may be subjected to phobias and anxieties, but you either work through them or around them. You may or may not be into seeking new experiences, but fear isn't the factor that will hold you back. For the most part, you are probably generally trusting of others.

NUMBER FOUR:

You will take risks when necessary, but you probably wouldn't do so if rationally you conclude that the risk is imprudent. If you have phobias or anxieties you treat them as wayward children and are not afraid of admitting to them. You have reasonably high levels of self-esteem and you have high self-confidence in the activities in which you engage. You are probably not afraid to fail and will readily admit to it when you do. You probably give people the advantage in terms of trusting them. However, you remain suspicious until you know them.

NUMBER FIVE:

You probably feel a normal level of fear in appropriate situations. Your level of self-esteem is reasonably strong, but you still may be nervous in some social situations such as public speaking. In athletics you are either cautious or aggressive in accordance with what you perceive the situation to be. In golf or tennis, you might be prone to choke up a bit in pressure situations. You are generally open to new situations, if you find them interesting. You are normal in your level of trust and are very trusting with people you know.

NUMBER SIX:

You probably feel significant anxiety when taking important risks. You would rather play things safe, given the choice. However, you will become involved in risky situations when necessary. Your self-confidence may be very high in activities in which you excel. However, you probably shy away from new experiences or activities where failure might dent your self-esteem. If you suffer from phobias and irrational anxieties, you probably worry that they might belittle you in the eyes of others. You are probably not very trusting of people unless you know them well.

NUMBER SEVEN:

You probably experience extreme anxieties when thinking about taking any significant risk, whether in your business or personal life. You will only enter a risky situation after much hand wringing, and you'll continue to feel a high level of anxiety. In athletics, you'll probably avoid any situation in which physical injury is possible, unless you have strong self-confidence in a given sport. You probably worry a lot on a day-to-day basis. In competitive, pressure situations you might choke up, afraid of potential failure and the blow it would strike against your self-esteem. Much of your self-esteem is based on those activities in which you've learned to excel. You are not very trusting of people in general, and a perception of the slightest impropriety might make you suspicious of those closest to you.

NUMBER EIGHT:

People probably call you paranoid. If you are a supervisor, people won't like working for you because you show them no trust and reflect that you have little faith in them. You will not enter a risky venture unless there is absolutely no other choice. If it were up to you, the status quo would always prevail. If your family pressures you into a ski trip, you'll remain on the bunny slopes. If you suffer from phobias and anxieties, your life may be caught up in them. The suffering you feel may even be a comfort to you as it permeates other areas of your life. And oddly enough, all of this could make whatever sense of humor you have left actually appealing.

NUMBER NINE:

You are suffocating in your paranoia. You probably trust no one, including members of your own family, thinking the whole world is out to do you in. You are probably delusional about plots aimed against you. You will take no risks, no chances, unless the odds are completely on your side. You will dig in your heels initially, when faced with the prospect. If you are forced to concede when you believe the situation is not in your favor, you might think your whole life is about to be reduced to shambles. You are probably fearful of being in public places and treasure your phobias and anxieties.

NUMBER TEN:

Time to check yourself in for treatment. You are probably a megalomaniac who may even *kill* if your delusions convince you that you're in dire danger. You probably never leave your home, where you prefer to be alone, except perhaps with a sibling or son or daughter, whose life you've literally captured. Any risk is out of the question, no matter what bearing it might have on your life. Athletics? Forget them, too dangerous. You are no fun at all.

Since there was no quiz for survival on the Web site, there is no way to determine what rough percentage of people have a close match to each Number level. I find myself to be a mixture of Five and Six.

COMMENTARY BY DR. HEFTER

This is a particularly interesting chapter, inasmuch as it describes a basic condition of human existence—how we feel contributes to how we survive with some basic contradictions.

The "risk-taker" may be someone who has considerable self-confidence, and may utilize that self-confidence to help himself succeed, but that self-confidence may also be a factor in the generation of tragedies because there are variables in life that are inherently unpredictable—avalanches can overwhelm the most self-confident, skillful skier.

At times this relates to the intelligence of the risk-taker—an individual with low intelligence but high self-esteem is no bargain.

The presence of anxiety and fear is often not the primary factor in accommodating to the exigencies of life. More crucial is how an individual integrates those feelings into his way of coping with the stresses of his life. A phobic person, as noted in the narrative, may be either little affected by his phobia, or in effect functionally paralyzed. What that individual brings to bear, his character strengths, on the phobic aspect of his personality is important. One can, for example, utilize a variety of therapeutic methods to neutralize or sometimes even eliminate the effects of phobias or panic reactions on his behavior as is noted in chapter 32.

The influence of other people is a significant factor in general when discussing "limbic drives." Although evolution and/or an "Ultimate Designer" may have provided us with the various limbic drives, it or they also provided us with the capacity to be responsive to less driven aspects of our world, such as the influence on us of others. Our anxieties, our fears, our self-esteem are all potentially modifiable.

NOTES

1. John Bacon, News Section, *USA Today*, p. 3A.

2. Aaron T. Beck, Gary Emory, with Ruth L. Greenberg, *Anxiety Disorders and Phobias: A Cognitive Perspective* (New York: BasicBooks, 1985), p. 76.

3. Nigel Nicholson,"How Hardwired Is Human Behavior?" *Harvard Business Review* (July–August 1998): 138.

4. Richard L. Bednar and Scott R. Peterson, *Self-Esteem: Paradoxes and Innovations in Clinical Theory and Practice*, 2d ed. (Washington, D.C.: American Psychological Association, 1995), p. 5.

5. Jerilyn Ross, *Triumph Over Fear* (New York: Bantam, 1994), pp. 5–6.

6. Beck, Emory, and Greenberg, *Anxiety Disorders and Phobias*, p. 117.

7. Ibid., p. 119.

8. Ross, *Triumph Over Fear*, p. 18.

9. John Madden, with Dave Anderson, *One Size Doesn't Fit All* (New York: Jove Books, 1988), p. 14.

10. Harold N. Levinson, with Steven Carter, *Phobia Free* (New York: M. Evans and Company, 1986), p. 26.

11. Ibid., p. 28.

12. Anthony Stevens and John Price, *Evolutionary Psychiatry: A New Beginning* (London: Routledge, 1996), p. 101.

13. Ronald M. Doctor and Ada P. Kahn, *The Encyclopedia of Phobias, Fears, and Anxieties* (New York: Facts On File, 1989), p. 274.

14. Reneau Z. Peurifoy, *Anxiety, Phobias and Panic: A Step-by Step Program for Regaining Control of Your Life* (New York: Warner Books, 1995), p. 2.

15. Doctor and Kahn, *The Encyclopedia of Phobias, Fears, and Anxieties*, p. 43.

16. S. Rachman in Richard L. Gregory (ed.), *The Oxford Companion to the Mind* (Oxford: Oxford University Press, 1987), p. 257.

17. Helen Kennerly, *Overcoming Anxiety: A Self-Help Guide Using Cognitive Behavioral Techniques* (Washington Square, N.Y.: New York University Press, 1997), p. 34.

18. Joseph E. LeDoux, *The Emotional Brain: The Mysterious Underpinnings of Emotional Life* (New York: Simon & Schuster, 1996), p. 107.

19. Marvin Zuckerman, Monte S. Buchsbaum, and Dennis L. Murphy, "Sensation Seeking and Its Biological Correlates," *Psychological Bulletin* 88, no. 1 (1980): 191.

20. Frank Farley, "The Big T in Personality," *Psychology Today* (May 1986): 47.

21. Ibid, p. 49.

19

DR. FREUD MEETS
A SCREEN SAVER

A Malaysia Airlines flight attendant had his ear surgically reattached after another flight attendant bit it off during an argument.[1]

D r. Freud was sitting at the desk of a secretary just outside the agency's conference room, tapping on a computer keyboard, with the secretary at his side giving instructions, when Wendy Smith, from the agency's public relations department and whom Dr. Freud had previously met, walked up to him carrying a laptop.

"Dr. Freud," she gushed. "Look at you, working on a computer."

Freud looked up at her shyly. "Yes, yes," he said. "This is an amazing invention. I am in the process of sending an e-mail message to Mr. Croft."

"You are?" Wendy gushed again. "That is marvelous. You are already a modern man."

"I wouldn't say that," Freud replied somewhat embarrassed and turning back to the computer. "I have only just begun tapping on the keys with one finger, of course."

He finished up the note as the secretary looked on. Then she instructed him to use the mouse to click on the "send" icon.

"And that's it?" he asked the secretary.

"That's it," she replied. "Mr. Croft, if he is in front of his computer, could be looking at his message already. And if you sent this message to someone halfway around the world, they, too, could be looking at the message this instant."

"How marvelous," Freud said. "If we had e-mail in my day, I might have been able to stay in touch with Carl Jung when he made his trip to America and began to criticize my theories, which he had previously supported and perhaps nipped his defection in the bud."

"Oh well," Wendy said, "that is all past history, Dr. Freud, no use getting into it now."

"Yes, but I can't stop thinking about it, even in my transposed state."

"Does that mean you are Dummy Snatched?" Wendy asked, a twinkle in her eye.

Freud harrumphed and stood up, thanking the secretary for her time. Then he turned to Wendy with a small grin and said, "And what can I do for you, my dear?"

"Peter Norton called and asked me to show this to you," she said enthusiastically, nodding to the laptop in her hand.

"And what, might I ask, is that?"

"It's a laptop computer, sir, one you can carry with you. But that's not the point, it has a program on it that our agency creatives developed yesterday as part of the Dr. Freud Inner Dummy series of products."

Freud's head dropped dejectedly.

"Oh, but you'll really love this, Dr. Freud," Wendy responded, seeing his dejection.

"I don't think so."

"Well, let's walk back into the conference room where I can show it to you. Peter sends his apologies for not coming personally, but he told me to tell you that he is a little clumsy when it comes to computers. As a matter of fact, he doesn't even know how to work one. So I will have to do for today."

"Wendy, my dear, I guarantee you that whatever pain I feel from seeing this latest demonstration of simplistic work will be much less being inflicted by you than by Mr. Norton, who is rather a pest."

"My, my, Dr. Freud, I wouldn't think anyone could get to you with all your years of studying the mind."

"My brain remains human, my dear. My unconscious continues with its libidinal instincts that may not be attuned to what I would rationally want.

My ego, my will, does all it can from keeping the stronger of these instincts from driving me to say things that make me appear neurotic. There is something in my unconscious that causes me to dislike Mr. Norton and my will can do nothing about it. I still think he is a pest."

Wendy burst out laughing. "Oh, Dr. Freud," she said, "you are really something. And to tell you the truth, I don't like Mr. Norton very much either. He is a bit on the obnoxious side."

Freud looked fondly at Wendy and said, "Ah, Wendy, if only I were 120 years younger."

Wendy laughed again. "I bet you were quite the ladies' man."

"Not really," Freud said smiling. "Those were different times."

Wendy thought a moment. "Say, how would you like to come with some of my friends to our favorite bar tonight? I guarantee you that you will be the hit of the evening and that my friends will be *very* interested in you." She winked.

Freud bent over with a deep, staccato laugh. Then he looked up and said, "How kind of you, Wendy, but I think not tonight. Some other night perhaps."

"I hope so."

"Now then, what were you going to show me?"

Wendy placed the laptop on the conference table, opened and powered it up, and waited while the computer booted.

"This will take just a minute to get started, Dr. Freud."

"No problem, I have all the time in the world."

"Literally, I bet."

"Yes, literally."

"Maybe sometime you'll tell me what it's like on the other side."

"You mean the experience of being dead?"

"Well, yes."

"I'm afraid not, Wendy. I am under orders from the Regional Ultimate Authorities to discuss nothing about that experience. My only task is to help this agency spread the word about my concept of the nature of the brain, particularly the id, and then I go back."

"That is too bad."

The computer beeped and Freud looked startled.

"Well, here we are, Dr. Freud," Wendy said as the screen lit up. "Now let me explain. All personal computers have a screen saver. This means that whatever is on the screen, if left alone for an hour or two, might ultimately damage the screen. It can actually create a burn in the screen."

"I think I understand."

"So what we use are screen savers. Here, let me show you one that comes standard with this laptop." A few clicks and a screen saver with a flowing image of birds came on the screen.

"You can choose from many of these flowing images, or even make one up yourself. I like this one with the birds because they are so beautiful."

"And this is the concept you want to show me today."

"Oh, no. I was only explaining to you what a screen saver was so you could better understand the idea we have."

"And what is that?"

"We intend to call them the Dr. Freud Inner Dummy Screen Savers."

Freud's head dropped.

"Oh, come on, Dr. Freud," Wendy said cheerfully. "This is actually quite good. What we've done is created a series of screen savers aimed at boosting self-esteem or giving you courage, just like the Inner Dummy Dolls. Here, let me show you my favorite. The techies made a separate program of these, so that they are not only usable as screen savers, but any time during the day, you can dial up the message you want to see and hear."

Wendy clicked on a couple of icons and the first screen saver came on the screen. It was a likeness of Elvis Presley, who talked in his own voice with his lips actually moving. As he talked, his message was actually printed out on the screen in type next to him. Elvis said:

"Wendy, you are absolutely the most beautiful girl in the world. If I were there right now, I would take you in my arms."

Freud was staring puzzled at the screen, which now was static, with Elvis smiling and his message remaining in print.

Wendy said dreamily, "Now isn't this just wonderful? And see, if I want him to say it again, I just click on this icon in the corner," which she did. The screen cleared and the video and message repeated.

"Who is that man?" Freud asked.

"Why, that's Elvis Presley, who was my favorite entertainer. He died some years ago, but he stole the hearts of millions of women."

"And that was his actual voice?"

"Yes, the consulting engineers our agency retains were able to digitize his voice and put it into computer language. All I have to do is type in the message I want Elvis to say and he will then do it on the screen in his own voice. Isn't this wonderful?"

"It is certainly interesting."

"And here is another one." Wendy clicked on the proper icons and a likeness of the motion picture star, Antonio Banderas came on the screen and said in his own voice:

"Wendy, don't be afraid of love. You are precious to me and all men who are sensitive to beautiful and intelligent women. Look for the man of your dreams. You will find him."

"Amazing," Freud said. "And who was that gentleman?"

"He is a movie star. And here's another one." She clicked and a likeness of Michael Jordan came on the screen, delivering a message in his own voice:

"Wendy, don't be afraid of failure in writing that romance novel. Go for it. Keep working at it. Eventually you will succeed. You can do it, Wendy. I know you can."

"And who was that?" Freud asked.

"That was Michael Jordan, a famous basketball star, known for making baskets that win games under intense, competitive pressure. Now here's one more."

She clicked the mouse and a likeness of Dr. Freud came on the screen. Freud quickly straightened up in his chair. The message in Dr. Freud's own voice was:

"Wendy, in my brief acquaintance with you, I can assure you that you are absolutely normal. The few quirks you worry about are just part of the human experience."

Freud bent over and began his slow, staccato laugh.

"Amazing," he said, as he took out his hankie to blow his nose.

"Isn't it?" Wendy replied. "Of course, we'd have to get permission of these people or their estates to use their likenesses and voices and that may be a problem. But our creatives felt we could find people who were in the public domain. You, for example, Dr. Freud."

"Oh, really, so my great-great-grandchildren will not benefit?" he said jokingly.

"Well, we'll see. It's all hypothetical at this point. Have you seen enough?"

"Yes, I have and this was all fantastic, the technology, I mean. Reproducing voices and such. These were things in my day, which was only sixty or eighty years ago, that we never even dreamed about."

"It is marvelous," Wendy said as she shut off the computer and closed its cover. As she got up to leave she said, "They are working on additional personalities as examples of what this Inner Dummy product can do. Would you like me to come back and show you any of the new ones?"

"I am always happy to see you, Wendy."

"Thank you, Dr. Freud, and if you change your mind about coming out with the girls tonight, please buzz me before five."

"I don't think I'll change my mind, but if I do, I will certainly call you."

"Thanks, Dr. Freud. See you later."

Freud watched her as she left the room with a bouncing walk and thought for a moment that he was no longer married and could feel guilt-free in joining Wendy and her friends.

"Ah, what is the matter with you?" he muttered to himself, as he turned to his books.

NOTE

1. Zay N. Smith, *Chicago Sun-Times*, July 20, 1998, p. 26.

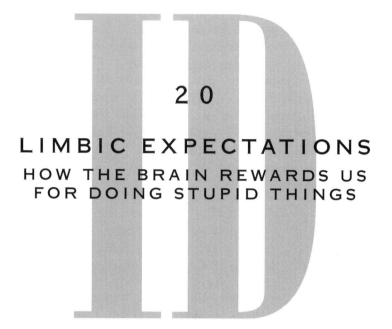

20

LIMBIC EXPECTATIONS

HOW THE BRAIN REWARDS US
FOR DOING STUPID THINGS

Jay Leno, host of the Tonight *show, thinking in January 1993 that he was going to lose the show to David Letterman, snuck into the NBC entertainment division offices late at night, intent on listening to a conference call between East Coast and West Coast executives, and sat in a cramped closet for more than two hours, taking notes.*[1]

I recall going to a small party given by a doctor I know, who insisted I come to meet his wife's cousin, who was newly divorced.

"Look, Kyle," I said to him. "Why do you want to torture me? I don't like parties and I don't want to meet your wife's cousin. I don't want to meet anyone's cousin."

"I know, I know," he said, "but do me a favor. Roslyn [his wife] wants you to come and if you don't she'll make my life miserable and then look how bad you'll feel that I was made miserable."

"I won't feel bad at all. As a matter of fact I enjoy it when I make you miserable."

"Oh, come on, for pete's sake. Stay a couple of hours and then you can leave. We're inviting some interesting people and you can talk to them."

Finally, I agreed. I dislike parties and thinking this might be a phobia I looked it up in *The Encyclopedia of Phobias, Fears and Anxieties*. It turns out that there is a phobia against parties, which they simply label a social phobia. After reading the description I decided I don't have a party phobia, I just dislike them. However, I did find an adjacent phobia listing for eating peanut butter called *arachibutyrophobia*, which I thought you might find of interest.

And so I went to the party on a Sunday afternoon and it turned out that I had a nice time after all, because a geneticist was one of the guests. After I listened with eyes glazed to my friend's wife's cousin for half an hour telling me about her problems with her mother, her kids and her ex-husband, I managed to edge over to the geneticist, who was nursing a drink and telling one joke after another to a small group. He was short, overweight, and jovial.

I introduced myself and soon managed to get him alone. I told him I was writing a book, which had a chapter on genetics written for the average person and would appreciate a few minutes of his time so that I could confirm a few facts.

"Sure, no problem," he said. "Let's go over to the corner there and talk."

We sat down and he said, "Okay, what are the questions?"

"First," I began, " I'd like to confirm that our DNA exists in every cell in our bodies, which I understand is about sixty trillion cells?"

"Sixty trillion? Is that how many cells we have?" He pointed to his ample stomach. "Hey, I bet I have more than that. But the answer to your question is a qualified 'Yes.' Almost all of our cells, with some exceptions, have the identical DNA."

"And might one visualize the forty-six chromosomes that form our DNA as separate threads?"

"Threads? Sure, why not. We've used the term 'string.' " He took a minute to inspect his sport coat and pulled a thread from the inner lining. "Yeah, this is about right and it's about two inches long, which is the length of a chromosome. Of course, they're all tightly coiled so you'd have to stretch one out to make it look like this."

"So that comes to about ninety-two inches or almost eight feet of thread if you were to connect them all in a straight line."

"Hey, you figured that faster than Trigger."

"Trigger?"

"You remember, Roy Roger's horse." He laughed uproariously. Then he stood up and said, "How much is two and two, Trigger?" He stamped his right foot four times. "One more, Trigger."

Now he was laughing so hard he was almost doubled over.

"I'm sorry," he finally said. "I don't know what gets into me."

"No problem," I said, laughing hard myself. "I enjoy your sense of humor."

"That's good, I appreciate that. Now go ahead with your questions."

I took the thread from his hand and asked, "As I understand it, if this thread was actually a DNA chromosome, it would be so thin it would actually be invisible to the naked eye."

"Quite correct. It's not only invisible to the naked eye, it's invisible to some of our strongest electron microscopes. It takes sophisticated X-ray equipment to examine these 'threads' as you call them. Today, the sequencing equipment uses lasers."

"Now the term 'gene,' as I understand it, applies to sections of this eight-foot thread of DNA, just imagining that this thread is eight-feet long," I said, dangling the thread he had given to me. "Is that correct?"

"Yes, and the commonly held lay notion that there are approximately 100,000 genes is a method for classifying sections of the thread."

"Now here's the hard part, which I find difficult to comprehend."

"Go ahead, test me."

"Well, as I understand it, there are actually twenty billion bits of information on this DNA thread, which converts to about three billion letters, of which there are only four."

"Four letters, you mean."

"Yes."

"What you said, then, is all quite true. There are approximately three billion copies of four letters encoded on our imaginary string or thread of DNA, each one representing one of four proteins, which are the building blocks of everything in our bodies. Amazing, isn't it?"

"To say the least. And I read that under the Human Genome Project, which is currently underway, scientists worldwide are literally copying the sequence of letters on this thread and when they are through, there will be the equivalent of 300,000 pages of letters, if it were set in the type of a standard encyclopedia."

"Sounds about right. I've seen the coding referred to as the equivalent of four hundred volumes of the *Encyclopaedia Britannica*."

"And all from this one eight-foot thread." I waved the little thread in the air.

"Yes, yes, quite correct."

"And these letters are the basic coding for the human body."

"Yes, in the sense that without them there would be no human body."
He laughed uproariously. "Oh, that's good, isn't it?"

"Very good," I replied smiling. I liked this man.

"Now is it true," I continued, "that as our cells divide, each of those
three billion letters are replicated?"

"Oh, yes, it is quite a process."

"Now I read this somewhere and it's sort of mind-boggling, is it true
that before the cells divide, little checkers, so to speak, go down each of the
new DNA threads to make sure the replication is accurate, and if mistakes
are spotted, these checkers can actually fix them?"

"Checkers, did you say?"

"Yes, checkers."

Again, he broke out laughing. "You know," he continued, "you do have
a way of reducing the most complex processes to embarrassing simplicity."

"Yes, but it took at lot of time poring through books to figure out that
the enzymes that do the job are really little checkers and that they can cut
out and repair mistakes on the DNA that is being replicated."

"Yes, in essence that is what the enzymes do."

"Then I learned that our cells divide at different rates, with some
dividing in under two hours. So this whole process of creating a 300,000-
page volume of human coding can be done that quickly and with checkers
making sure those sequences of letters were all copied correctly. Can you
say this isn't true?"

"No, it's true all right."

"So the Ultimate Designer has to be some kind of super-duper design
engineer."

"The Ultimate Designer?"

"You know, the fellow upstairs." I pointed to the ceiling.

"Oh, that's great," he said laughing. "Yes indeed, someone had to be an
engineer beyond all comprehension to design this system. You don't want
another drink and some peanuts, do you?"

"I could do with one more and yes, some peanuts."

I told him what I was drinking and he left me staring at the thread.
While he was gone, I went over to Roslyn and asked her if she had any
thread in the house.

"Thread? Are you crazy? I don't sew."

"You mean in this whole house, you don't have one spool of thread?"

She thought for a minute. "You know, I do have some thread in my traveling kit. Do you really want it?"

"If it wouldn't be much trouble. And if you get it, I promise I'll talk to your cousin again."

"Done." She ran off to get the thread and arrived at the time the geneticist returned with the drinks and a bowl of peanuts.

She looked at him and said, "He wanted some thread."

The geneticist smiled and said, "So the thread from my coat lining wouldn't do, eh?"

"No, it wasn't that, I just wanted to draw off eight feet of thread so that maybe it might be easier for my brain to register these facts."

"Well, go ahead. Do you want a tape measure?"

"No, I'll use my shoe, it's about twelve inches long."

I measured out about eight feet.

"There," I said. "Now the big difference between this thread and our DNA chromosomes, if they were all connected together like this, would be that it would be invisible to the human eye."

"And some of our strongest microscopes, as well."

"So the threading on a spider web would be thick by comparison."

"Of course."

"But yet every organ in our body is encoded into the three billion letters on this invisible thread?"

"That is correct."

"Including our brain, the most complex object in the known universe."

"Well, yes, including our brain, which by the way takes up in the neighborhood of a third of all those letters."

"Now in the photo reproductions I've seen of DNA, which most of the world saw in those demonstrations during the O. J. Simpson trial, the four basic letters are represented by markings that look like bar codes."

"Bar codes?"

"Yes, you know, the bar codes on boxes of cereal and cans of soup and such that they scan at check-out counters at supermarkets."

He thought a moment and then started to giggle. "You know, they do look like those bar codes."

"So it wouldn't be inaccurate to say that all of human life emanates from a series of bar codes."

He continued giggling. "You're not going to quote me, are you?"

"No."

"Well then, yes, you could say that we all come from a series of bar codes."

"All classified neatly on this eight-foot string of thread."

"Yes."

"Which in the laboratory might one day be cloned to produce a human being."

"Yes, the possibility exists for that to happen."

"Which means the possibility exists that we might one day be able to clone each of the sixty trillion cells in our body to create enough humans to suffocate the earth."

"You know," he pointed to his drink, "maybe I should have made this a double."

"But one day," I continued relentlessly, "that may be a possibility."

"I can't deny it."

"So this thread," I stood up, reaching high up and letting it hang to the living room carpet, "is composed of three billion letters formed in bar codes and this is what human life is made of."

"Not only human life," he replied bemusedly, "but all organic life. The only difference between that string you're holding and one for a chimpanzee, a spider, an orange, or an ear of corn is its length and the configuration of letters."

"So all life-forms emanate from this same thread full of bar codes?"

"Yes, you could say that."

"Including George Washington, Liberace, Bill Clinton, and Bruce Willis? They all came from threads like these?"

"Yes, a string of DNA, whose polymorphisms, if you'll excuse the technical term, create the differences between individuals."

"Including mental differences, the variances of the software in our brains that makes each of us not only look different, but think and act differently?"

"Yes, I would imagine so."

"And this string of DNA, this thread, hasn't changed much in the past 50,000 years and so what I'm holding here could just as easily have belonged to a caveman as to Adolf Hitler?"

"Well, I'm no anthropologist, but you can assume that the DNA string hasn't changed very much, since humans first became humans."

"And so the predispositions for our very basic, limbic instincts—sex, power, territoriality, nurturance and survival—are encoded on this thread."

I waved it up and down and drew some stares from others at the party, including Roslyn's cousin, who looked at me as if I were just let out of an asylum. Maybe I don't have to talk to her again, I said to myself.

"I can't comment on that. I'm a gene man, not a brain man. But I can tell you that the structure of the brain is definitely encoded on the DNA, so whatever your brain includes when it first comes out of the womb is a result of that coding. And now, my friend, it was very nice to meet you." He rose and grabbed my hand as I quickly switched the thread from my right hand to my left.

"I definitely need a double, now."

After I thanked him for his time and as he was walking away, he turned and said, "Don't call me, I'll call you." Then he laughed uproariously again.

An incident like this actually happened, although I had to recreate the conversation from memory. In times of trouble, I often revert to the thought that I am nothing more than a string of DNA, which became fertilized into a temporary human, who lives on a planet that is lost in space. There are times when this thought can actually be quite comforting.

It is apparent that our innate human drives, our basic instincts are encoded in our DNA and we pass them forward from generation to generation relatively unchanged, although they are shaped by conditioning during our lifetimes.

And to begin focusing more on the subject of this chapter, it is also apparent that these innate, core limbic drives, the five we have described thus far—power, sex, territoriality, nurturance, and survival—have limbic expectations built into them, with the intensity of those limbic expectations correlating to the intensities of the drives themselves.

A Number Seven on the power scale, for instance, will have more intense expectations for achieving and then defending positions and trappings of power to enhance status than Number Twos. Number Sevens on the territorial scale will have more intense expectations for acquiring and defending their own space and their possessions within that space than Number Twos.

Number Sevens on the sexual scale will have more intense expectations for having sex, with id-implied reproduction than Number Twos. Those higher on the nurturance scale will have greater expectations for attachment than those lower. And those higher on the survival scale will have greater expectations for security.

But nature apparently decided that the hydraulic force driving our limbic expectations wasn't enough for our caveman brain to get the job done. It added the concept of reward and punishment, which Freud first described as the "pleasure-unpleasure principle," and later shortened to the "pleasure principle." In essence, this means that if we meet our limbic expectations, we will be rewarded with positive feelings . . . happiness, joy, contentment, and such. If we do not meet our limbic expectations we will be punished with depressive feelings including sadness, misery, shame, and the like.

Seymour Epstein in his paper "Emotion and Self-Theory" in the *Handbook of Emotions* put the point as follows: "One of the most widespread assumptions among students of human behavior is that the most fundamental of all motives is the "pleasure principle"; the maximization of pleasure and the minimization of pain."[2]

The Encyclopaedia Britannica, through its *Britannica CD*, describes the theory even more simply:

> The id is oblivious of the external world and unaware of the passage of time. Devoid of organization, knowing neither logic nor reason, it has the ability to harbor acutely conflicting or mutually contradicting impulses side by side. It functions entirely according to the pleasure-pain principle, its impulses either seeking immediate fulfillment or settling for a compromised fulfillment. . . . Although id impulses are constantly directed toward obtaining immediate gratification of one's major instinctual drives . . . sex, affection [nurturance], aggression [power, territorial], self-preservation [survival] . . . the ego functions to set limits on this process.[3]

What a great description of the id as Inner Dummy. What the pleasure-unpleasure principle means in a nutshell is described by psychology professors Craig A. Smith and Richard S. Lazarus in their paper "Emotion and Adaptation" in the *Handbook of Personality Theory and Research*, as they describe the emotions that are triggered by the id in response to events. My comments are in the parentheses:

> Emotions punctuate almost all the significant events in our lives. We feel proud when we receive a promotion [met expectation of our power program], we become angry when we learn that our homes have been burglarized [unmet expectation of our survival program], we are joyful at the births of our children [met expectation of our nurturance program]; and we experience profound grief at the death of someone we love [unmet expectation of our nurturance program].[4]

It appears that our limbic expectations have been incorporated into this limbic reward-punishment system that we share with the higher animals and which also covers the strictly biological need of hunger. We eat when we feel hunger and we'll be rewarded with a feeling of contentment. When we eat something we really like, we might be rewarded with a feeling of elation. If we don't eat, we'll be punished with pain and anxiety. If we don't eat something we really like that's put in front of us because we're on a diet, we'll be punished with feelings of disappointment and frustration.

When I shared this information with my friend Bob Schwartz, he replied, "Oh, goodie, now I know why I feel good when I eat vanilla ice cream. What else are you discovering? Why we feel good when we have sex? Why do I even have to know why I feel good? If that's my Inner Dummy, then I say hats off to it."

Back to the grindstone, the same system that makes Bob feel good after eating his vanilla ice cream will reward us with positive, happy feelings when we meet our mental limbic expectations, including having sex, with the intensity of those feelings correlating to the intensity of the expectations. If we do not meet those expectations, we will be punished with lousy, depressive feelings, with the intensity dependent on the same correlation.

We see these feelings of reward and punishment acted out in front of us everyday, rarely giving a second thought that they may be the autonomous response of a limbic brain designed for the primal wilderness.

How many times have we all witnessed a sporting event such as a regular-season basketball game on television, where the producers make sure we witness the winners leaving the court with a feeling of elation and bounce in their steps? The losers are also shown, leaving with heads down, looking dejected.

If you were able to walk up to one of the winners and say, "What are you so happy for? Tomorrow you might lose," they would look at you as if you had lost your mind. Their Inner Dummy, their id, is making them happy. They want to feel the reward.

Conversely, if you walked up to one of the losers and said, "What are you so sad for . . . this is just one game of many, you played very well, you tried hard, cheer up," they might thank you for the words of encouragement, but their Inner Dummy is impervious to logic, oblivious to the external, rational world and so it would continue to punish the loser with depressive feelings. "You lost, so feel bad, this is your punishment" the Inner Dummy is in effect saying, if it could talk. "Don't bother me with reasons."

An excellent illustration of how the feelings of reward and punishment can vary in intensity according to the intensity of the limbic expectation would be envisioning the same two teams playing, but this time in a major championship game.

At the end of the game, the winners' positive emotions are exponentially greater than they were when they won a regular-season game. They are crying with happiness, pouring champagne over themselves, hugging each other, totally jubilant. The reward is extreme. In the losers' locker room, we see scenes of total dejection, heads hung in despair, tears streaming down faces. They are being punished by their ids, their Inner Dummies, with extreme depressive feelings that may linger for months or even years.

You can't eliminate those feelings simply by walking up to a player on the losing team with a long thread in your hand and say: "Now, now, cheer up. Look at this thread. It represents what you are genetically. How you played on the court today is simply a manifestation of what were in your genes on this thread and how you and those around you nurtured and conditioned them. Your genetic predispositions and their shaping were not exactly up to par today. So what? What's the big deal? Don't you know that we live in a gargantuan universe and just to get to the next star traveling at 400,000 miles an hour would take 7,000 years? You know what that tells us? It tells us we're not only lost in space, we probably don't even know the reasons we were even born. There is a great possibility that we are totally insignificant. Measured against all that, what does the outcome of a lousy basketball game mean?"

Of course, the player's blank stare and depression would continue. You are trying to reach his Inner Dummy that is intent on punishing him and it is impervious to rationality. It is just as futile trying to reach this player with rational arguments as it is Sarah, who won't get in an elevator because of her phobia, or Ellen, the fifteen-year-old girl who weighed eighty-two pounds, who thought she was fat and had to be forced to eat.

We see scenes of limbic reward and punishment every day of our lives and hardly give them a second thought because we perceive them as an integral part of our humanness. Many of us are taught at the earliest ages by ambitious parents that winning is everything no matter what it is we endeavor to do. And it is in our youth that for the most part, the intensities of our core limbic expectations are set.

"You are no good, you will never amount to anything," we might be told by our father at the age of ten, after we just failed a math quiz in school. This is the kind of statement that might become a limbic memory within our id, our Inner Dummy and remain with us for years, if not for a lifetime, perhaps raising both our metaphoric power program and its limbic expectations.

As one result, if as adults we become defense lawyers in a case we perceive as important, and a jury announces a verdict of guilty for our client, we may be punished with feelings of depression that are beyond the bounds of rationality. As we ride home in our car, completely dejected, we might recall what our father said to us when we were only ten and believe that he was right, no matter what victory we had just the week before. We then may become desperate for an important victory, which could be long delayed because our confidence level has suffered a setback.

But when a victory does come, we may be rewarded with an elation that may rise beyond the bounds of rationality. We might do something like go to our favorite bar, which is packed with people, and buy everyone a round of drinks we really can't afford.

Or, if the victory came from our hometown team competing in a championship game, we might go out with a group and create rioting on the streets and loot stores.

It is apparent that our system of rewards and punishments is one more source in our minds that creates irrationalities, inner craziness in otherwise apparently normal people.

In a closer look at the reward side, after a long search I located an excellent book on the subject called *Pleasure Beyond the Pleasure Principle*, edited by associate clinical professors of psychiatry Richard A. Glick and Stanley Bone. The book is a compendium of papers by fifteen contributors, including the two editors, all focusing on various areas of the pleasure-unpleasure principle. One of the most interesting papers was authored by Norman Doidge, M.D., instructor and researcher in clinical psychiatry, with the menacing title of "Appetitive Pleasure States: A Biopsychoanalytic Model of the Pleasure Threshold, Mental Representation, and Defense."

Fortunately Dr. Doidge wrote at a level I could understand and his concept of the "pleasure threshold" was an insightful moment for me. He described the pleasure threshold as being a level at which the chemistry of our brains begins to allow us to experience pleasure. If we have a lower pleasure threshold, it is easier for us to derive pleasure from positive situations we encounter. If we have a higher threshold, it is more difficult for us to derive pleasure from positive experiences and so we might more readily turn to artificial substitutes such as alcohol and drugs. He pointed out how the chemistry of pleasure appears to be part of our limbic system: "Those limbic areas that lead to pleasurable responses are dubbed pleasure centers, in contrast to other well-defined pain centers. These pleasure centers are thought to be part of normal brain reward systems."[5]

Later, in Doidge's paper, the point is made that "depression may be seen, in part, as an impairment of the ability to obtain pleasure." And, that enthusiasm is the result of having a lowered pleasure threshold. Doidge writes:

Enthusiasm is described as a passionate state of mind that has some of the buoyancy of euphoria and the activity of mania. . . . The enthusiastic person does not merely feel good or even very good, but great—in fact, "the greatest." There is a sense of exuberance, richness, an abundance of good fortune, yet with it all, there is some awareness that one is exaggerating; but it is enjoyable, and one is reluctant to give it up.[6]

It would appear from Dr. Doidge's paper that there is a scale for the pleasure system that is similar to the nurturance scale in that there are troubles and irrationalities on both sides. To make this clearer, I have transposed what Doidge considers to be low and high. Thus, a Number One to Two on the pleasure scale would be depressed and unable to feel any pleasure at all. A Number Three to Four would find it difficult to feel pleasure and may use alcohol or other drugs to help generate the feeling of pleasure. A Number Five to Six on the pleasure scale would be like most of us. We feel pleasure in normal circumstances. We might have a drink or two at times to relax, but we aren't relentlessly pressed by our pleasure centers to overdo it. We take pleasure in our families, our children, our work, as we attempt to maintain balance in our lives.

A Number Seven to Eight might be the enthusiast, the optimist who thinks everything is great, who wonders why you don't feel the same way he or she does, needs no artificial substances to reinforce their feelings and whose brain chemistry is keeping them on a continuing "high." A Number Nine to Ten would be manic, someone whose sense of excitement and enthusiasm may border on lunacy.

My friend Bob Schwartz, for example, would probably be at least a Number Seven. No matter where he travels, he tells me that "that trip was the best one I ever had in my life." If he goes to some new restaurant, he usually says something like, "that whitefish was the best whitefish I ever had in my life." Years ago, I remember a trip he took behind the Iron Curtain with his then wife, while the cold war was still at its height. He was gone for two weeks visiting a number of countries, including the USSR. It rained the entire time, and the finest meal he had was boiled potatoes and eggs in Moscow. He was arguing much of the time with his wife whom he later divorced and he came back with walking pneumonia. So I knew I had him when I said, "Well, tell me what kind of time you had on this trip."

He replied, "To tell you the truth, that was the best trip I ever took in my whole life."

This is at least a Number Seven.

The *pleasure scale* would also explain my brother-in-law Harold who is always happy, enthusiastic, and uninhibited. Everything is "the greatest," as described by Doidge, and having an alcoholic drink appears to be only a social chore for Harold.

The scale would also describe a neighbor I had years ago who you just couldn't make happy. When he had his first child, he looked in the crib and said something like, "Oh, that's nice." When we played in neighborhood softball games on the same team and won, and we were cheering and such, he would mope off. He was a heavy drinker and so perhaps he was a Number Three or low in his ability to feel pleasure.

The point is our reward system, which is apparently housed in our limbic brain, our Inner Dummy, is susceptible to the chemical imperfections of the limbic system and can result in manifestations of inner craziness in otherwise apparently normal people.

As Stanley Glick and Norman Bone pointed out in the introduction to their anthology: "Neuroanatomical and neurotransmitter research makes clear that feeling states and their hedonic qualities are also part of man's biological heritage."[3] In other words, our emotions, both good and bad, are the result of our brain chemistry. The feeling of sadness, for example, will develop when specific neurotransmitters emitted by the appropriate brain neuron cells are accepted by the receptors on adjoining cells. We react emotionally in accordance with our brain chemistry. However, our ego, our rationality, our power to think and reason can in many instances transcend this limbic chemistry or work to alter its makeup over time.

What is confusing to me and apparently to the academics who have studied the subject as well, is the relationship between the instinctive drive theory and the system of reward and punishment. Why do we need both? Why does a strong power program with its hydraulic pressure require in addition, rewards and punishments to help drive us toward its goals? Is this a design feature intended to reinforce the gravity that the limbic brain ascribes to these drives? Attain them and you will feel great. Fail them and you will feel miserable.

Or, might it be that one's level on the pleasure threshold, the point at which we are rewarded with good feelings, determines our levels on the instinctive program scales? Under this theory, an Adolf Hitler would be practically pleasure impaired and so his limbic power and territorial programs, which were apparently his primary motivators, needed to be a Ten, because it was only through the acquisition of enormous amounts of power and territory that he could begin to feel rewarded by the chemicals of his brain.

Oh well, these are just thoughts.

Professor of clinical psychiatry and psychoanalyst Charles Brenner in his paper "On Pleasurable Affects," made the following observations:

> One discovers, for example, unconscious fantasies of triumphing over one's rivals, of being loved for one's competence, of being cheered by one's audience, all of which suggest that at least part of what passes for pleasure in function is in fact related to the unconscious gratification of drive derivatives. . . .
>
> Pleasure in being virtuous derives, at least in part, from the fantasy of having won one's parents' love—that is, from an instinctual source.[8]

But origins aside, there are a number of imperfections of the reward side of the reward-punishment system that results in rewarding us for doing stupid things. For example, the brain is capable of rewarding us with pleasant feelings when we carry out hateful and sadistic acts. In his paper "Hatred as Pleasure," professor of psychiatry Otto F. Kernberg writes:

> It is of course, well known that hatred, a derivative of rage, may give rise to highly pleasurable aggressive behaviors, sadistic enjoyment in causing pain, humiliation, and suffering; and the glee derived from devaluating others.[9]

Most of us have known people who derive pleasure from sadistic acts. I recall knowing the head of a company who enjoyed firing people. "It gives me a high for the day," he would tell me. When I would question him about this, he could see nothing wrong with his feelings. "I don't fire anyone unless they deserve to be." Fortunately, my relationship with this person was short-lived.

Kernberg points out that:

> A strange process occurs in the patient under the domination of primitive hatred: a common defense against the awareness of such hatred is the very destruction of the patient's capacity to be aware of it, so that the patient's mind can no longer "contain" the awareness of a dominant impulse.[10]

And so in a strange combination of events, the Inner Dummy on the one hand, might punish us with feelings of hatred and revenge, when we aren't meeting its expectations, thus making our lives less peaceful and harmonious. And then in taking our revenge, it does an insidious thing by making our vengeful acts of hatred and the aggression actually feel good. This might have been a fine limbic brain design when we were in the primitive wilderness, but it can play havoc in a civilized society when a lone gunman or two can walk into a school classroom with a machine gun and smile and enjoy himself while gunning down students and teachers.

Kernberg described a poignant example of this apparent flaw in the reward side of the reward-punishment system:

> Lanzmann (in Gantheret 1986) has described the unmitigated joyful hatred in the faces of Polish peasants who, jokingly, made warning signals with their hands to the Jews who were entering the Treblinka concentration camp in sealed trains, warning signals graphically indicating that their throats would be cut.[11]

It is not out of the question that within the next two hundred years, we will know the physiology and connections of the brain well enough that we can get in there and make chemical adjustments to rid ourselves of some of its imperfections. In the meantime, if you see someone enjoying himself or herself humiliating another person in front of others, step in there and say, "Come on, your Inner Dummy is screwed up. It's making you do this. It isn't right. Take control, knock it off."

Of course, the problem is, as Kernberg puts it, that most of the people who enjoy themselves doing hurtful things are not aware of the problem. Perhaps this is another example of an "unaware limbic capturing," which would make any rational argument useless. I have frequently discussed with Dr. Hefter the problem of reaching people who are unaware of their problem. He tells me that it is difficult to convince these people to even make the attempt to change themselves with therapeutic approaches. If they do agree to meet with a therapist or even a non-mental health professional such as a church minister, a Jesse Jackson, for example, or the likes of former president Jimmy Carter, the challenge of reaching them can be formidable. Think about what they might have said to an Adolf Hitler or Joseph Stalin that would have caused them to change their behaviors. Unfortunately, neither the power of reason nor the message of a saving spirituality can reach everyone, particularly the Number Tens. You would think that the search for answers to this dilemma would be a top worldwide priority, but it remains near the bottom of the totem pole.

And now to another apparent and major imperfection of the reward side of the reward-punishment system: its propensity to drive those of us who are vulnerable to serious addictions that may be injurious or even lethal. Most of us have minor addictions . . . coffee, tea, hiking, bicycling, working out, work, gardening, opera, art, golf, and so forth. A minor addiction might be defined as one that would make us uncomfortable in some way if we were deprived of its activity or presence. Our reward system apparently senses some advantage to our Inner Dummy when we are initially exposed to activities of this kind—a *release of tension*, a satisfaction of a limbic drive—and captures us with an addiction, which might be quite positive for us. Even a minor addiction to sex can be positive in a monogamous relationship when both parties are up for it.

The problem emerges when an imperfection within our reward system makes us become totally addicted to an activity to the point that it is either detrimental to our health or our careers, or relationships with others or all of the above. The addiction of compulsive gamblers or sex fanatics might be likened to the gorilla who can only hit a golf ball 400 yards and has no sense of nuance. We start out harmlessly and before we know it, we are being driven beyond rationality. The Inner Dummy controlling our reward system notices that gambling or sex is satisfying appropriate drives and begins providing us with such rewarding feelings that we become addicted.

Just as brutish are severe addictions to substances we imbibe, particularly drugs and alcohol, which can lead to death. The limbic brain, designed for primitive living, is apparently unaware of cocaine, heroin, and scotch, among other addictive drugs. It probably thinks these are harmless herbs found in the jungle that make us feel good and so must be good for us. The id, the Inner Dummy, is apparently oblivious to the discoveries of the external world.

Norman Doidge's paper "Appetitive Pleasure States" includes an introductory quote from Dr. Freud about how these drugs actually affect the brain:

> But there must be substances in the chemistry of our own bodies, which have similar effects, for we know at least one pathological state, mania, in which a condition similar to intoxication arises, without the administration of any intoxicating drug.[12]

It has since been learned that drugs and alcohol do mimic the brain's biochemical reactions that create pleasurable feelings without any signal from our emotional sentinel that something great has happened in our lives. In other words, the drugs and alcohol emulate the exhilaration of being a member of a championship basketball team. The brain chemistry triggered to create the "high" that results is probably similar.

The problem, however, is that the brain is apparently capable of absorbing only so much euphoria. As most cocaine addicts will tell you, as time goes on, it takes more and more of the drug to activate the pleasurable feelings of the reward system. Soon, depressive feelings emerge quickly after an immediate high, more of the drug is consumed, and an overdose can take one's life. The Inner Dummy, unaware of its own brain chemistry, continues to elevate the platform or pleasure threshold that is required to reward us for doing something stupid in the first place.

While our brain chemistry reaction might differ between the various drugs, including nicotine, with which we might become addicted, the process is generally the same. And as most of us have been told, some drugs are more addictive than others and some of us are more vulnerable to individual addictive substances than others. When the right combination of addictive drug and vulnerability merge, the reward system of our Inner Dummy can unwittingly begin leading us on the path to death.

Still another major imperfection of the reward system is an inability to feel pleasure at all, a Number One on the pleasure scale that was previously described. Michael Stone in his paper "Anhedonia and Its Implications for Psychotherapy" described the disorder as follows:

> Anhedonia connotes, etymologically, the absence of pleasure. Clinically one uses the term to signify a patient's inability to experience pleasure. Fortunately, few patients are so lacking in this capacity as to merit the appellation literally.[13]

This imperfection of the reward system deprives us of most of our pleasurable feelings, making us destined to go through life unhappy, sad, and depressed. Very little that happens to us can make us happy and when it does occur, the happiness doesn't last very long. The absence of pleasure might be partially or wholly genetic, or it might be a punishment generated by our id, our Inner Dummy, perhaps because we have failed in some way to meet its expectations, senses no hope for our future prospects and so deprives us of feeling the positive emotions of reward. Or, as previously stated, it might be the mechanism that drives us to become Tens on the power, territorial, sexual, and nurturance scales.

Of course, most of us benefit from the reward-punishment system if we are meeting our limbic expectations. The positive feelings of contentment will form a relatively consistent base, from which short-term feelings of reward and punishment will emanate.

For example, if we are Number Fives on the power, sexual, and nurturance scales, have good jobs, and a nice home and family, we will be relatively content. But in all probability, every week we will be encountering singular experiences that will give us temporary feelings of elation and dejection. We miss the train and we might feel dejected for an hour or two. Our car is stolen and we might feel dejected for a month or two. We make the train after being stuck in traffic thinking we'll miss it and we might feel elated for an hour or two. We buy the new car we've always wanted and we might feel elated for a month or two. The combinations of events and resultant feelings of varying intensities of elation and dejection appear to be practically endless and for each of us they apparently differ. But presumably we will eventually fall back to our base level of contentment or discontent at the time.

Finally, there are the bonuses of the reward system, in addition to the love, affection, altruism, elation, and such we might feel when we are meeting expectations. As Ellen Handler Spitz put it in her paper, "Reflections on Psychoanalysis and Aesthetic Pleasure," "We gaze at art, we listen to music, we attend theatrical performances, we read and recite poetry because these experiences give pleasure."[14]

While Spitz offers no evolutionary theories for this bonus feeling, one reason that makes the most sense to me, having seen it a number of times in reference materials, is that our feelings of euphoria that may be generated by the arts, including music and poetry, is a therapeutic device, described in chapter 30, that allows us to release "limbic tension," just as this tension might have been released during our primitive lives by viewing the summer beauty of the forest or by painting on the walls of caves.

So much for the reward side of reward and punishment, its imperfections and irrationalities as well as its bonuses. However, it is the punishment side that really takes the cake when it comes to irrationality and inner craziness. It follows in chapter 22, the one after another encounter with Dr. Freud.

COMMENTARY BY DR. HEFTER

The idea of reward as a constituent of limbic expectations, and thus built into the limbic system genetically is reasonable, and although hypothetical at this point, provides a point for beginning to try to understand the meaning of pleasure and reward. That there are pleasure centers in the brain is generally accepted in the scientific community currently. As often occurs in human history, the misfortune of some people contributes to the advance of scientific knowledge and perhaps the increased welfare of others—thus studies of substance abuse have helped researchers discover basic scientific truths.

It is also true that whatever genetic basis there may be for the experience of reward and pleasure, there are still many unanswered questions about the course of the experience of pleasure as individuals develop out of infancy. Certainly different people have varying inherent capacities for experiencing reward, but the opportunities for having that experience may differ greatly depending upon one's circumstances. A painful illness can militate strongly against the feeling of reward regardless of what an individual's previous capacities were.

This chapter discusses the pleasure that some people have when imposing pain on others. There is also the situation in which having pain inflicted on oneself provides a sense of pleasure—a state frequently described as masochism. It is difficult to explain this phenomenon on a genetic basis. Rather, this appears to emanate from events in an individual's life which have somehow distorted the brain's chemistry.

NOTES

1. Bill Carter, *The Late Shift: Letterman, Leno, and the Network Battle for the Night* (New York: Hyperion, 1994), p. 197.

2. Seymour Epstein, "Emotion and Self-Theory" in *Handbook of Emotions,* ed. Michael Lewis and Jeanette M. Haviland (New York: Guilford Press, 1993), p. 313.

3. *Encyclopaedia Britannica* CD, keyword "id."

4. Craig A. Smith and Richard S. Lazarus, "Emotion and Adaptation," in *Handbook of Personality Theory and Research*, Pervin, ed. Lawrence A. Pervin (New York: Guilford Press, 1990), p. 609.

5. Norman Doidge, "Appetitive Pleasure States: A Biopsychoanalytic Model of the Pleasure Threshold, Mental Representation, and Defense," in *Pleasure Beyond the Pleasure Principle: The Role of Affect in Motivation, Development, and Adaptation*, ed. Robert A. Glick and Stanley Bone (New Haven, Conn.: Yale University Press, 1990), p. 155.

6. Ibid., pp. 157–58.

7. Glick and Bone, "Introduction," *Pleasure Beyond the Pleasure Principle*, p. 5.

8. Charles Brenner, "On Pleasurable Affects," in Glick and Bone, *Pleasure Beyond the Pleasure Principle*, pp. 195–96.

9. Otto F. Kernberg, "Hatred as Pleasure," in Glick and Bone, *Pleasure Beyond the Pleasure Principle*, pp. 179–80.

10. Ibid., p. 181.

11. Ibid., p. 186.

12. Sigmund Freud quoted in Doidge, "Appetitive Pleasure States," p. 138.

13. Michael Stone, "Anhedonia and Its Implications for Psychotherapy," in Glick and Bone, *Pleasure Beyond the Pleasure Principle*, p. 198.

14. Ellen Handler Spitz, "Reflections on Psychoanalysis and Aesthetic Pleasure," in Glick and Bone, *Pleasure Beyond the Pleasure Principle*, p. 221.

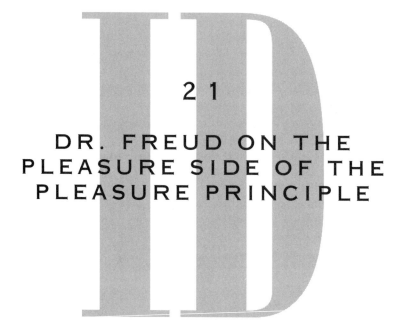

2 1

DR. FREUD ON THE PLEASURE SIDE OF THE PLEASURE PRINCIPLE

At the church funeral of an Ohio man who shot his wife and then himself, the relatives of the couple asked the organist to play "My Way."[1]

Samuel Ollander, the director of research for the agency, knocked on the closed door of the conference room, holding what appeared to be small signs, whose facings were covered by layout paper.

"Come in," he heard Dr. Freud reply.

Ollander opened the door a crack and said, "I hope I'm not disturbing you, doctor. I just have one quick item to review with you."

"No, not at all, Mr. Ollander. Come right in, I am happy to see you."

"You look to be in a fine mood today, Dr. Freud," Ollander said as he walked to a chair across the conference room table from the doctor.

"Yes, yes I am, indeed. Perhaps it is because of ego gratification. I have been reading a number of very current books that are quite supportive of my earliest theories about instincts, drives, and principles."

"I didn't realize your theories were that much in question."

"How very kind of you, Mr. Ollander. Unfortunately, many of the books and papers written since my death seemed to focus on how wrong I was. Not long after my death, it was motivation and affects, motivation and affects, this seemed to be the hue and cry. Many psychologists, particularly from the 1960s through the 1980s, felt that instincts and drives were only a temporary genetic happening that were soon erased by the conditions of nurturing thereafter. They felt that in my writings I placed far too much emphasis on their influence throughout adult life."

"And now this reasoning is beginning to change?"

"Well, not all together, but I note many references," he pointed to the books that were open, but facedown, piled in front of him, "now state that my theories need fresh reappraisal, that motivation and affect can be dramatically shaped by the core instinctual drives whose intensities are initially shaped by our genes, and whose strength may withstand the more traumatic experiences of our conditioning. It is all interesting, is it not?"

"To say the least."

"And now what would you like to review with me? I hope it is not another bathroom scale." Freud smiled faintly at the thought.

"No, no, sir, it is not another product. I will not be involved in those until it's time for consumer research to test their potential acceptance. No, this has to do with a focus group of consumers we are having tonight to test a concept for the pleasure side of your pleasure principle."

"Oh, yes, and I assume you are aware, Mr. Ollander, that I first called this the pleasure-unpleasure principle, one of its main foundations being that where there is a lack of pleasure there will be unpleasure and vice versa. And perhaps the fact that I shortened it to the pleasure principle preordained my role today in helping your agency communicate the concept of the id. Perhaps I have been unconsciously aware of what marketing is."

Ollander smiled shyly.

"You may be quite right, sir. In any event, what we want to test tonight are phrases that reflect irrational pleasures that are motivated by the drives of the Inner Dummy and which are apparently reinforced by pleasure-unpleasure or limbic reward and punishment."

"Irrational pleasures you say?"

"Yes, the kind of pleasure one gets from doing drugs, or consuming too much alcohol, or engaging in illicit sex, or the pleasure one gets from hating or hurting someone else . . . that kind of irrational pleasure."

"I see, and what do you intend to call this kind of pleasure?"

"Tonight we are testing three concepts." Ollander looked at Freud cautiously. "And they are written out on these cards I brought with me. Now brace yourself, Dr. Freud, I appreciate your reluctance to accept the framework of these statements. However, I must stress as we all have, who have been in contact with you here, that we need simplicity if the concepts are to be understood by the average person . . . in the case of irrational pleasure, from the teenager on the corner buying drugs to the business executive on the verge of becoming addicted to cocaine or gambling."

"You are quite right about my reluctance, but I understand what you are trying to do. So see," he nodded toward his hands grasping the arms of his chair, "I am quite braced."

"Okay, of the three statements, the one our creative writers prefer is . . . ," he uncovered the first of the signs so that Dr. Freud could view it, "*Dummy Bliss.*" He paused and looked momentarily at Dr. Freud who showed no reaction.

He continued. "The second statement is . . . ," he uncovered the second sign, "*Dummy Joy.*" Again he looked at Dr. Freud for reaction and could gauge none.

"The third statement is . . . and by the way, the creatives are still working on this and so we might have one more to test . . . the third statement is . . . ," he uncovered the sign, "*Dummy Delight.*"

Ollander then went to a bulletin board on the wall across from Dr. Freud and tacked the three cards to it so they could all be viewed at the same time.

"What do you think?" Ollander asked tentatively.

Freud pondered, rubbing his beard and staring at the signs. Then he responded, "Quite frankly, I don't know what to think, which might be interpreted to mean that you people are beginning to reach me."

"Well, that would be excellent news, because you can see our problem. We can't call the illicit sex of a married man or woman or a cocaine high an 'irrational pleasure.' It would be much too tame. But if we ascribed these pleasures to be the manifestations of an Inner Dummy, whose programs were developed for primitive living, but remain with us to this day, we might make some headway.

"We could tell people on the edge, in a magazine ad or a TV commercial, 'Look, what you're feeling is *Dummy Bliss.* That bliss can be addictive. Your limbic brain likes the feeling and may slowly suck you in to doing more and more until you are addicted and your life is in shatters. This side of your brain is not always acting in your behalf and may, in fact, be your worst enemy.' "

Ollander rose from his chair and began pacing the room, intent on what he was saying.

"You might reply to yourself," he continued, talking to an imaginary consumer, "that you can withstand addictions. But how do you know? Some of the strongest men on earth have succumbed and we will tell you their stories. Are you following me, Dr. Freud?"

"Yes, so far."

"Please excuse me from rambling, everything I'm saying will eventually be condensed to a few lines of copy by our creatives. But we will definitely add the point in our message that the hope we have as humans is our power to think. We have this Inner Dummy inside us because it has been provided to all the higher animals, of which we are one, but only humans have the power to think. This is what makes you the teenager on the corner different from the chimpanzee in the zoo down the street. You can think. You can exercise power over your Inner Dummy, you can gauge what it is telling you, to do drugs, to steal, to hate, to hurt your friends to get ahead, but you are empowered to make the final decision, and do the right thing, even though it might take a tremendous effort to do it. The rewards the Inner Dummy can grant you can be tremendously tempting and its strongest drives can be enormously difficult to ignore, but it can be done, either by direct confrontation or through help from others.

"And when you have succeeded you actually become a hero. A hero for winning the battle against your own Inner Dummy that is imperfect, yet an integral part of your mind."

Ollander paused in place, took a breath and looked searchingly at Dr. Freud.

"I'm afraid I have gotten too worked up," Ollander said.

"No, no, not all. Your change of character as the subject possesses you is interesting to observe."

Ollander smiled shyly and said, "Well, I only have one thought to add."

"Go ahead, my dear Ollander, please."

"Okay, I would continue saying to our imaginary consumer, particularly the wayward teenager on the corner . . . look, without utilizing the strong will power provided by the thinking side of your mind, this Inner Dummy inside you can work to pull you back to how we all thought and acted as cavemen, when we were battling it out with strange tribes wanting to kill us and take our possessions and the wilderness animals which surrounded us and wanted to eat us. This Inner Dummy, in all probability, was designed to help us survive and in the process we had to act like animals. But we must have evolved much too quickly, because in the civilized world of today with our computers and cell phones, this Inner Dummy within us has not been modulated enough. It still needs to be tamed when we are young and controlled when we are adults."

Ollander came back to his chair and slumped in it. "I don't know," he said dejectedly. "Maybe this idea won't work, either. Maybe the world will continue in its terrible ways."

"Now, now, Ollander," Freud replied encouragingly. "Maybe the concept will work."

Ollander's head snapped up. "You mean, you like it?" he asked.

"I can't say I admired every word. I am still finding it hard to reconcile myself to the concept of the id as Inner Dummy. Or the subconcept of Dummy Bliss," Freud could hardly spit out the words. "And I still hold the right to make my decision until the final presentation to me of the entire program. But I do like what you are trying to communicate to people who are lost or confused about drives and feelings that appear to make no sense. They think there may be something wrong with them, which is not the point. The point is what can they do to help themselves without all this self-guilt. Yes, I do think you are onto something."

Ollander rose from his seat enthusiastically. "Well, that is encouraging, to say the least," he said. "I'm sure that just your modest support will help me as I review these three concepts in our focus group tonight." He walked to the bulletin board and removed the three signs.

As he walked to the conference-room door, he said, "Thank you very much for hearing me out, Dr. Freud."

Freud, who was already burying himself in his books, looked up, eyes gazing out above his glasses, and said slyly with a wink, "My *pleasure*, Mr. Ollander."

NOTE

1. This two-line story was in a newspaper column I clipped out, but can't locate. However, the story was too good to leave out. Please trust me that I reported it precisely as written.

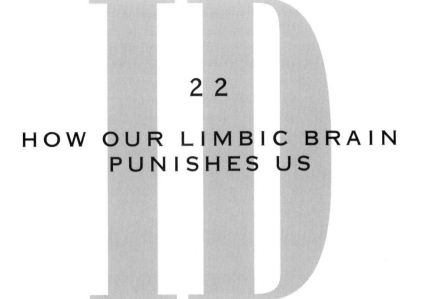

2 2

HOW OUR LIMBIC BRAIN
PUNISHES US

On the morning of June 28, 1914, in the Bosnian town of Sarajevo, a chauffeur misunderstood his instructions, made the wrong turn, tried too late to correct his mistake and in so doing, delivered his passengers, the Archduke Francis Ferdinand, heir apparent of Austria-Hungary and his wife Sophie, into the direct sight of Gavrilo Princip, who fired two shots at them and mortally wounded them both. This single event set off a series of vengeful political actions based on power and territorial challenges that culminated with the start of World War I. By the end of the war, in November 1918, more than 65,000,000 men had been mobilized for the opposing armies, of which 8,000,000 died and 21,000,000 were wounded.[1]

In her book, *Therapist's Guide to Clinical Intervention*, Sharon L. Johnson created a "List of Feeling Words," divided between "Pleasant Feelings" and "Difficult/Unpleasant Feelings."[2] I counted 116 "Pleasant Feelings," such as peaceful, thankful, passionate, engrossed, determined, tenacious, spirited, thrilled, confident, devoted, loved, joyous, optimistic, and cheerful. I counted 139 "Difficult/Unpleasant Feelings," including ashamed, powerless, fearful, crushed, desperate, confused, embarrassed, miserable, sulky, infuriated, enraged, insensitive, suspicious, menaced, rejected, and tense.

243

In addition, I added about sixty more unpleasant feelings from a perusal of a pocket dictionary, putting the total at approximately two hundred. The limbic brain's portfolio of feelings apparently includes far more to punish than to reward us, which could be interpreted to mean that if there is any Ultimate Designer it is not exactly trusting of our good sense.

To gain a better understanding of how the punishment is triggered, we might envision these feelings as being programmed onto a metaphoric hard disk in our brains, ready to be punched up by the emotional sentinel that Daniel Goleman described in his book *Emotional Intelligence*.[3]

For example, let's imagine that we have a significant other whom we love and cherish and who has just returned from a two-week trip out of town. He or she begins a conversation about the interesting events of the trip, which we listen to rationally interested as we put the silverware out on the kitchen table. Our emotional sentinel is at rest. It is presumably only triggered when one of our limbic-drive expectations has been fulfilled or disappointed.

But then our significant other abruptly stops talking, looks us in the eye, perhaps with a tear or two welling up, and tells us that he or she is leaving us because of a new love. Bang!! This is an unfulfilled expectation for each one of our core limbic programs: power because our status is in jeopardy; territorial because our home is in jeopardy; sex because our reproductive potential is in jeopardy; nurturance because our primary attachment is in jeopardy; and survival because our security is in jeopardy.

For our emotional sentinel, this would be the equivalent of sensing a four-alarm fire. It begins punching an array of punishment buttons, which we might metaphorically envision as a series of letters on an imaginary keyboard in our brains.

For example, it might begin by punching the letters "c" and "r" on our mental keyboard, which causes our brain chemistry to react to make us feel crushed. And then in series, it begins to punch other letters, "e" and "n," which creates the chemical reaction to make us feel enraged; "t" and "o" to make us feel tormented; "d" and "e" to make us feel depressed; "p" and "e" to make us feel perplexed; "s" and "h" to make us feel shamed; "e" and "m" to make us feel empty; "a" and "n" to make us feel anxious; "v" and "i" to make us feel victimized; "d" and "i" to make us feel disillusioned; and "r" and "e" to make us feel resentful. And all this is probably just for starters. Think of some of the other feelings that might emerge: discouraged, diminished, miserable, stupefied, lost, vulnerable, frustrated, grieved, distrustful, misgiving, appalled, humiliated, rejected, threatened, scared, suspicious, jealous, hateful, and dulled.

Did somebody say that the brain was our friend?

At the time of my first divorce, I felt all of this and remember wishing that I had a broken leg instead because at least I would have known how to deal with the pain.

The Inner Dummy definitely does not like its expectations to be disappointed and the stronger the disappointment, the more punishing the pain. Learning without prior warning that a significant other, a live-in or a spouse, to whom we have devoted much of our life and love and in other ways have become deeply attached is leaving us for another, can be as painful as being clubbed on the head and more punishing because of the diversity of the deriding feelings and their propensity to linger long after the initial pain is inflicted.

Or, imagine that we are summoned to our boss's office and are summarily fired for being the odd person out in a downsizing. If we imagined that a new job would be hard to find because of our age, or a recession, or the characteristics of our skills, or we don't meet the needs of the current job market, or whatever, our emotional sentinel would probably punch many of the same letters it would if it was alerted that our significant other was leaving us for someone else.

So, too, would a variation of these same buttons be punched if a loved one died, or with other variations if we lost a contest that we deemed critical to our career or self-esteem.

One of our problems as thinking humans is that while we know we experience these depressive emotions when we meet with severe disappointments, most of us are unaware that they are chemical reactions of brain connections that are computerlike in their emergence, with the intensity of the feelings dependent on the intensity of our limbic programs applying to the specific disappointments. As one result, when we are feeling depressed or hurt in some way, we may blame it on our weaknesses rather than on autonomous changes in our brain connections beyond our immediate control.

David M. Buss of the University of Michigan Department of Psychology said the following in his article "Evolutionary Personality Psychology," published in 1991, in *Psychology*:

> It does not seem to be generally recognized in personality and social psychology that all observable behavior is the product of mechanisms residing within the organism, combined with environmental and organismic inputs that activate those mechanisms.[4]

Peter C. Whybrow, director of the Neuropsychiatric Institute of UCLA, in his book *A Mood Apart*, put the issue as follows:

> The limbic system, which generates emotional behavior, is also one of the subsystems operating in the brain. However, the idea that emotion is a physical phenomenon has been a more difficult idea for people to accept.[5]

Many of us think that the emotions we feel, whether rewarding or punishing, are the result of a soul force that inhabits our bodies, and that our consciousness is the embodiment of our soul. Others of us believe that the irrational, immoral, or unethical things we do are the result of demons or evil spirits that invade our souls during our time on earth.

If there is an afterlife, during which the ultimate answers are revealed to us, beliefs like these may turn out to be true. There is no rational evidence for what happens to us, if anything, after death. Any theory, even one that appears totally unreal, could turn out to be true. Dr. Freud, who has been transposed in time to talk to a modern ad agency, refuses to discuss this issue.

However, regardless of spiritual belief, it is generally recognized that our imperfect bodies house our consciousness, whether perceived as a soul force or not, and that this consciousness resides in our brains, the "mechanism" referred to by Dr. Buss.

But while most of us agree that our bodies are imperfect, we are loath to admit that our brains are imperfect as well. The subtitle of the paperback edition of my book *Brain Tricks* was "Coping with Your Defective Brain," which turned out to be a poor choice because a great majority of people, I learned, apparently refuse to admit even to this possibility, preferring to relegate their irrationalities, if they admit to them at all, to "human nature," as if this were some ethereal entity unto itself.

But it should be obvious to most of us, if we pause to think about it, that the mechanism in our brain that makes us sense pain, both from mental and physical causes, can be viewed as imperfect in its design, because in many instances the pain it generates can be inappropriate to the injury, being either too severe or too lingering or both, or in the case of sociopaths either nonexistent or so intense as to be unbearable.

The first time I really thought about this was in the 1970s, when I fractured my foot while skiing. The intense pain lasted for about a week, as I tried to keep the painkilling medication to a minimum. I remember asking the question why the pain had to be so intense without letup? Why couldn't the brain's pain mechanism just signal me that I broke my foot with some initial pain and then remind me intermittently with additional short shocks of pain that it was still broken and I couldn't walk on it. And why, of all things, didn't the brain, designed to provide us with the reenergizing force of sleep, shut off the pain so that I could get to sleep easily in the first place and then keep it from waking me up all night, in the second.

I recall coming across a paper on pain about a year or two later that I have since misplaced, which said, in essence, that our pain mechanism was similar to those of other higher animals and hadn't been altered despite the evolutionary growth of our thinking power. The constant feeling of pain, the paper said, was essential to alert unthinking animals that whatever limb or body organ was injured, couldn't be used. Pains from organs such as the stomach were signals not to eat until whatever was wrong righted itself. Severe pains in the chest or back were signals that something was wrong and that we needed to lay still or slow down until the body's mending capabilities had a go at the problem.

This made some sense until I recalled the incessant pain my mother felt for five years as she suffered from cancer. What signal was this giving? That the form should lay still for all that time to give the body menders more energy in their battle with the cancer? Why couldn't the pain be more intermittent, or activated only when potentially harmful movement was about to take place? Why in a position of unmoving repose couldn't the pain let up?

And so I take it as a First Amendment right to voice the opinion that as part of the concept of the imperfect human body, the design of our brain's pain mechanism is imperfect as well. Further, that the same imperfections that apply to our painful physical injuries apply to our painful mental emotions as well.

Why should the victimized significant other whose story we related previously, be made to suffer so many negative, punishing emotions, which, as most of us know, can last for a disproportionate length of time and might leave the imprint of limbic memories that can alter the shape of our personalities? Perhaps one hundred years from now, we'll have learned enough about the brain to get in there and make slight adjustments at birth, both to our physical and mental pain mechanisms as well as to readily observable imbalances in the limbic system, just as we might perform male circumcisions, without considering this to be an unwarranted intrusion. In this sense, will irrational pain eventually be perceived as superfluous as our foreskins?

Just asking.

In the meantime, the unpleasure side of the pleasure-unpleasure principle is no picnic and apparently consists of a long continuum of punishments to remind our rational side when our Inner Dummy senses that its expectations have been disappointed—as if we needed this.

Let's begin with the less painful of the punishing feelings, the discomforting self-conscious emotions of shame, guilt, and embarrassment.

Shame and guilt, according to human development and family studies professor Karen Caplovitz Barrett in a paper included in the book titled *Self-Conscious Emotions*, edited by June Price Tangney and Kurt W. Fischer, are "social" emotions, in that they are designed to motivate people to follow society's guidelines. She implies that these feelings are included in our emotional portfolio as an aid to hierarchal harmony. There is apparently a fine line between the two. Shame, she pointed out, appears to be the most physically obvious. "The shameful person avoids looking at others, hides the face, slumps the body, lowers the head and/or withdraws from contact with others,"[6] she writes.

The emotion appears to signal that the shameful person is communicating "deference and submission to others, and indicates that the person feels 'small,' 'low,' or unworthy in comparison to others." Guilt apparently builds on the emotion of shame. Dr. Barrett says that, "Guilt-relevant behaviors act to repair the damage caused by the person's wrongdoing. . . . [G]uilt often moves the individual to tell others about the wrongdoing, and thus to show them that he or she understands the standards and wishes to follow them."[7]

This might be easier to understand in terms of Bill Clinton and his affair with Monica Lewinsky. We could sense in his four-minute admission to the nation that he was feeling shame, even though his body wasn't "slumped." However, many of us sensed that he wasn't feeling any real guilt. Instead, we perceived him as angry at Kenneth Starr for exposing him. He might have said in his address, "I not only feel ashamed at what I did, but I am guilty as charged. I apologize for what I did and I have learned enough from the personal trauma of this terrible experience to be able to swear to you that this will never happen again." This would have signaled us that he knew that the acts he performed in the Oval Office, of all places, were wrong, no question about it, that he was asking for forgiveness and would now follow the standards that we had expected of him in the first place.

Does that make sense? Evolutionary psychologists might suggest that when someone steps out of line and acts against the rules of his group—which have been absorbed and imbedded in the superego, another Freud metaphor for a segment of our minds—the punitive feelings of shame and guilt are designed to be triggered in the more limbically balanced of us. This would then motivate confession, which then, sooner or later, presumably leads to forgiveness. And so the tribe moves on to another day's business in relative harmony.

Of course, if someone is a Number One or Two on the Nurturance Scale, their predisposition for displaying shame or guilt would be close to nil and so perhaps Bill Clinton was a Two. You'll recall that this program had a compartmentalization about it so that even a Two could have a strong attachment to his or her children.

One might think that shame and guilt would be strictly human feelings, but it is apparently a punishment design of the limbic system we share with the higher animals. The books written by the primatologists are full of examples of the shame and guilt felt by chimpanzees and gorillas. A chimp may attempt to sneak food away from another chimp much higher on the herd's hierarchal scale, but the higher-ranking chimp spots it. A quick scuffle ensues or a harsh sound or gesture is made, with the result that the lower-ranking chimp "slumps" away, obviously shamed. Then he comes back and grooms the higher-ranking chimp in apparent expiation of his shame or guilt.

Dogs, like chimpanzees, are among the higher animals, and those of us who have had dogs as pets are well aware of their emotions, including their capacity for manifesting feelings of shame or guilt. In Jeffrey Moussaieff Masson's book *Dogs Never Lie About Love*, he quotes R. H. Smythe, author of *The Mind of the Dog*, as follows:

> . . . certain dogs, especially heavy breeds, wag their tails in an up-and-down direction when they are ashamed or feel guilty, or know they are about to be scolded, thumping the floor as the tail descends. A dog who does this is anticipating punishment, and will remain in a lying position, indicating humility. . . . Dogs love to be forgiven. They bear no grudge and are happy when they see that you don't harbor any ill will, either.[8]

So maybe Bill Clinton should have taken some tips from observing his dog, Buddy.

With regard to embarrassment, there appears to be only a shade of difference between its definition and that of shame. It is apparently less of a limbic punishment than shame. In his paper "Embarrassment: The Emotion of Self-Exposure and Evaluation," Michael Lewis points out that

"Almost all theories speak of embarrassment as an unpleasant feeling having to do with some form of the discrediting of one's own image, either through the loss of self-esteem, the esteem of others, or both."[9]

Moving beyond the self-conscious emotions, we get to the more punitive feelings unleashed upon us by the Inner Dummy, apparently in revenge for not meeting the expectations of its programs. We could dwell on each of them, as we have the self-conscious emotions, but then this book would become too heavy to hold while resting in bed. So I will merely list, for your information, the punitive emotions as detailed by Sharon L. Johnson, in *Therapist's Guide to Clinical Intervention*, which she calls "difficult/unpleasant feelings":[10]

ANGRY	DEPRESSED	CONFUSED	HELPLESS
irritated	lousy	upset	incapable
enraged	disappointed	fatigued	alone
hostile	discouraged	uncertain	paralyzed
insulting	ashamed	indecisive	useless
sore	powerless	perplexed	inferior
annoyed	diminished	embarrassed	vulnerable
upset	guilty	hesitant	empty
hateful	dissatisfied	shy	forced
unpleasant	miserable	stupefied	hesitant
offensive	detestable	disillusioned	despair
bitter	repugnant	unbelieving	frustrated
aggressive	despicable	skeptical	distressed
resentful	disgusting	distrustful	woeful
inflamed	abominable	misgiving	pathetic
provoked	terrible	lost	tragic
incensed	in despair	unsure	in a stew
infuriated	sulky	uneasy	
bad	pessimistic	dominated	
worked up	a sense of loss	tense	
boiling			
fuming			
indignant			
cross			

INDIFFERENT	AFRAID	HURT	SAD
insensitive	fearful	crushed	tearful
dull	terrified	tormented	sorrowful
nonchalant	suspicious	deprived	pained
neutral	anxious	pained	grief
reserved	alarmed	tortured	anguish
weary	panicked	dejected	desolate
bored	nervous	rejected	desperate
preoccupied	scared	injured	pessimistic
cold	worried	offended	unhappy
disinterested	frightened	afflicted	lonely
lifeless	timid	aching	grieved
	shaky	victimized	mournful
	restless	heartbroken	dismayed
	doubtful	agonized	
	threatened	appalled	
	cowardly	humiliated	
	quaking	wronged	
	menaced	alienated	
	wary		

To these, I have added the following punishing emotions, which I came across scanning a pocket dictionary, as previously noted, and were not in Johnson's listing: jealous, suicidal, antagonistic, flushed, sickened, regretful, hopeless, outraged, annihilated, violated, shocked, manipulated, reproached, chastised, forsaken, friendless, patronized, slighted, abandoned, discomforted, depleted, rebellious, agitated, contemptuous, longing, combative, paranoid, violent, denied, discredited, dishonored, disgraced, unstable, weepy, hysterical, unraveled, mortified, intimidated, despondent, humbled, squeezed, wrathful, imprisoned, scornful, envious, embittered, contrite, pitied, dirtied, unstable, disrupted, demeaned, abandoned, melancholy, chagrined, dissatisfied, slighted, scornful, stressed. And I've probably missed a lot more as I scanned the pages.

How can the punishment meted out by the metaphoric Inner Dummy get any worse, you might ask? Well, it does.

Dr. Freud in his chapters has complained that the concepts of the Inner Dummy are simplistic. So accepting that, let's now *really* get simple and envision that the punishments we may have to endure, as a result of misfortunes in our lives that are inconsistent with the expectations of our id, consist of three basic levels.

The first level of punishment would encompass the *punishing emotions* that we have just described, and which we might have to endure for minutes, hours, days, years, or even a lifetime and in varying intensities, depending on the strength of the traumas and our vulnerabilities to them. But through most of them we remain rationally grounded. We might be grief stricken, heartbroken, terrified, enraged, or whatever, but we can still go to work or raise our kids and get through the day.

The second level of punishment would be that of *neuroses* which can make us irrational in specific or general behavioral areas and that *The Oxford Companion to The Mind* describes as "more or less fixed and resistant to modification through the normal processes of learning."[11] They include neurotic depression, phobias, anxiety disorders, obsessive compulsive behavior, hysteria, and post-traumatic stress, disorders, which may make it far more difficult to get through the day. Personality disorders, which Dr. Hefter tells me are not included under the definition of neurotic disorders, should be included at this level of punishment.

The third level of punishment would be that of *psychoses* which may, for the most part, take us out of reality, such as schizophrenia and psychotic paranoia, in which we are frequently not able to distinguish between fact and fantasy. One might imagine that in the brutish world of the id, a psychosis might be a crude device for providing us with comfort, since we may no longer know what is going on in the real world.

We have already covered the first level of punishment, the punishing emotions. Among the primary neuroses of the second level, we have also previously covered anxiety disorders and phobias as being false alarms or limbic spikes of the survival program. Remember Susan, who had multiple phobias that included fear of crossing streets, becoming lost, riding escalators, heights, water, thunderstorms, or traveling. Put her into any of these situations and she might experience extreme panic attacks.

Or remember the person in clinical psychologist Helen Kennerly's book, *Overcoming Anxiety*, who said: "I always worry and I never relax nowadays. There is never a moment when I am free of aches and tension and my mind is always focused on worries. It makes me so tired and irritable and I have not been able to sleep or work properly and have not felt well in months."[12]

Or recall the descriptions of serious depression, in which the person experiences extreme despondency, hopelessness, lack of ambition, withdrawal, restricted social activity and interests, and intense variations of other emotions including guilt and which may be the result of misfortunes, such as the case of Mike Wallace after General Westmoreland brought a lawsuit against him, or my Uncle Seeme, who couldn't get over the loss of his wife, or it may not be traceable at all. Some theorists call depression a "frozen stage of rage." This would imply that the rage one is punished with following an extreme disappointment or frustration of a core instinctual drive becomes frozen and transforms to the symptoms of depression described.

We haven't as yet covered obsessions and compulsions, which in his book *Tormenting Thoughts & Secret Rituals, The Hidden Epidemic of Obsessive-Compulsive Disorder*, psychiatrist and OCD treatment specialist Ian Osborn points out that: "A compulsion is a repetitive act that is clearly excessive and is performed in order to lessen the discomfort of an obsession."[13]

The operative words are "clearly excessive." Many of us are obsessed with activities in our lives, which may actually be helpful in performing them. Obsessive-compulsive disorders go far beyond this. Osborn divides compulsions into two groups: behavioral (observable acts) and mental (thought rituals).

The two most common behavioral compulsions, Osborn says, are washing and checking. He speaks of people who will wash their hands incessantly, never sure they are completely rid of germs. Then he describes a young wife with a checking compulsion who said:

> I stand there and turn the light switch off and on, off and on, off and on, off and on. I can't make myself stop. It's crazy. What happens is that I have the thought that maybe I didn't completely turn it all the way off. . . . I know this doesn't make sense. . . . I might stay there for ten or fifteen minutes. One time the light switch started smoking. Now my husband swears at me and yells, "Leave the light switch alone or you really will start a fire."[14]

Another behavioral compulsion, Osborn points out, is requesting reassurance. "The OCDer [his label for people with obsessive-compulsive disorders] asks over and over again "I didn't hit anybody with that car, did I? . . . This lump doesn't mean I have AIDS, does it?" There are also behavioral compulsions to hoard, rub, touch, and tap.

Mental compulsions include repetitive counting, repeating of prayers, and even compulsive, devastating thoughts as described by a "gentle, civic-minded man," who recounted how: "I'll see a little boy across the street and then the thought will come into my mind to run over and strangle him. Nothing will get rid of that awful idea. . . . Now things are even worse, because now whenever I see a baseball game on TV, it brings the terrible thoughts right into my mind."[15]

An OCDer I saw interviewed on television said he was tortured by the thought that he was going to molest his daughter, which entered his mind repeatedly. The statement was made, however, that OCDers with these devastating thoughts hardly ever act on them, small consolation to those who are affected.

Some theorists contend that the predispositions for this behavior stem from genetics, or early parental rigidity and overemphasis on control of expressions, anger, and hostility, or from later interactions with adults in an authority position who require fanatic adherence to their demands. At some point the id, the Inner Dummy of those who are vulnerable, can no longer cope with the fanaticism and seeks outlets in the form of compulsive behavior that may have no bearing on the original problem or conflict.

Freud theorized that the urge to compulsively repeat is "an urge inherent in instinctual life to restore an earlier state of things."[16] In other words, the id, the Inner Dummy has been severely disappointed in some way and it is creating repetitive actions in its crude, brutish way to restore normality, even though the actions may have nothing to do with the original causes.

My friend Bob Schwartz asked me, "How can you call a lot of hand washing punishment? I wash my hands a lot."

"Forty or fifty times a day?"

"Not that many."

"Some people wash their hands that many times a day and if that isn't a punishment inflicted by the Inner Dummy then I don't know what is."

"Then what about your line calls when we play tennis?"

"What about them?"

"You make lousy line calls and that punishes me."

This is how we carry on a conversation.

Next come the *personality disorders*. At the risk of again being simplistic, these disorders (and as Dr. Hefter reminds me, many other psychological disorders) appear to reflect to a great extent what psychiatry labels *defense mechanisms*. These are processes or changes we usually make unconsciously, in our personalities to help us cope with mental punishment being inflicted on us by our Inner Dummy, whose expectations have been disappointed or unfilled. We might exert our power of reason to simply repress those unfilled and bothersome drives, stifle them, and ignore them. But this defense isn't always effective, because the drives remain and may reemerge in other forms. Freud commented on this in his *Autobiographical Study*, in which he said:

> The ego drew back, as it were, on its first collision with the objectionable instinctual impulse; it debarred the impulse from access to consciousness and to direct motor discharge, but at the same time the impulse retained its full cathexis [concentration] of energy. I named this process *repression*; it was a novelty and nothing like it had ever before been recognized in mental life. It was obviously a primary mechanism of *defense*, comparable to an attempt at flight, and was only a forerunner of the later-developed normal condemning judgement.[17]

Beyond repression we might also create personality defenses whose aim is to make our life more comfortable. All of us probably create *personality interfaces* that are aimed at protecting our self-esteem in vulnerable areas and/or reinforce a needy, limbic program drive. For example, an acquaintance of mine is forever telling jokes. One day over coffee I asked him when he started telling these jokes, one after the other. He said it started in high school when he wasn't accepted by the group of kids he most wanted to be with. He was terribly disappointed, saddened, and frustrated. It might be assumed that he was being punished by his Inner Dummy because his power program wasn't being fulfilled and he was losing status. And so he started telling jokes and became good at it and he was eventually accepted by the group he was targeting. And he's kept at it ever since, even though he is almost seventy, because he believes his basic personality is boring and that people will reject him if he doesn't keep telling jokes. (Did someone say the id has no sense of time?)

This is a common defense. So is the positive glad-handing that some people affect. They come at you with this big, wide, positive grin and grip your hand like they were tightening a vise. Another defense is the way we dress ourselves. Some people might dress in ways that might help them protect against their feelings of low self-esteem and/or reinforce their status by projecting an image of power at one extreme, or a professorial air of intelligence at the other.

Most of our defense mechanisms are relatively harmless—someone who inappropriately dominates a conversation or is inappropriately quiet.

However, when they are carried to an extreme they can contribute to several *personality disorders* that can be envisioned as part of the second level of punishment inflicted by a relentless Inner Dummy, which requires a defense that includes a new system of beliefs in order to be comforted—or, as Dr. Freud might put it, a defense to keep the id from flooding us with displeasure.

It is thought that many of the following personality disorders begin to emerge in childhood and there appears to be some controversy over the word "disorders." According to V. Mark Durand and David H. Barlow, in their 1997 book, *Abnormal Psychology: An Introduction,* "a number of researchers are convinced that many or all of the personality disorders represent extremes on one or more personality dimensions."[18] In other words, depending on how extreme the disorder is, it might be difficult to determine if they are just ordinary quirks of our personalities.

Nonetheless, as we read the descriptions of these disorders, we might visualize the circumstances of our early or later lives that might have caused our id or Inner Dummy to sense that something was wrong and worked to create warped outlooks in our minds. The challenge of treating these disorders is discussed in chapters 30 and 32.

AVOIDANT PERSONALITY DISORDER

We view ourselves as inept or incompetent and we don't want to be reminded of it so we avoid contact with other people who we think might demean or hurt us with comments or actions. We are extremely sensitive to being judged in a negative way. Since we don't know where the hurt might come from, we simply avoid other people as a general rule. This is far beyond being shy.

SCHIZOID PERSONALITY DISORDER

We don't necessarily view ourselves as inept, but we would rather remain aloof from others. We see ourselves as self-sufficient; we would prefer to be loners. We avoid close relationships because we think the other parties simply might be trying to get their hooks into us. We find we are actually happier when we are isolated. We can become anxious when we are forced into contact with others.

ANTISOCIAL PERSONALITY DISORDER

We go beyond being avoidant or schizoid in our outlook of liking to be alone in that we are capable of violating social norms. We feel little or no guilt stealing money from our mother's purse or from our best friend or pushing someone we don't like into a mud puddle. Lying and cheating is like mother's milk to us and we may not be able to separate what's true from what isn't. We may feel chronic anger over other people having possessions that we think we deserve.

DEPENDENT PERSONALITY DISORDER

We find that we can only function properly when there is a strong, dominant personality in our lives on whom we can depend. We may see ourselves as weak and ineffective and our strategy, unlike avoidant personalities, is to latch on to someone we perceive as protective. We may be obsessed with the thought of losing this person and if we do, it may be enough to cause us to fall into a clinical depression.

PASSIVE-AGGRESSIVE PERSONALITY DISORDER

We find that we enjoy the benefits being given to us by authority figures, we appear to thrive under their supervision, but we also have a need for autonomy, being in control on our own, which simmers just under the surface. I've seen a number of these personalities in the business world. They are properly submissive to their managers, but the minute their managers get into any trouble at all, they will turn on them, leaving the managers to wonder about the vagaries of life and loyalty.

PARANOID PERSONALITY DISORDER

We are mistrustful beyond the bounds of reason. We see other people from the get-go as devious and deceptive even when we might have known them for years and observed nothing but benign behavior. We fear that at any moment, given the opportunity, these other people might rise up and try to manipulate or control us. We have a pervasive anxiety about other people and we are probably not having a nice time.

HISTRIONIC PERSONALITY DISORDER

We may believe we are inept, incompetent, or unattractive, but instead of avoiding people we put on excessive displays of emotion or we might dress seductively in an effort to become the center of attention. Histrionic is usually defined as excessively dramatic or theatrical. We may make great promises to others in an effort to gain their approval, but then forget all about them. We may feel chronically anxious about being rejected and when we are, we may become very angry or depressed.

NARCISSISTIC PERSONALITY DISORDER

We believe we are princes and princesses. We are beyond arrogant. We believe we are entitled to special treatment and are above the rules that govern others. Anyone who doesn't see us as special, we believe should be duly punished. We want the best table in the restaurant and instant recognition from the maître d'. Once seated with our guests, we feel no compunction in talking loudly on our cell phones, disturbing others around us. In an office garage, we might park in someone else's reserved spot if it's closer to the elevator. We will become instantly angry when our wishes are thwarted. We will become jealous of others who we see as being given better treatment. I don't know why it is, but in my life I have come in contact with a number of narcissistic personalities and they all make my teeth grind.

BORDERLINE PERSONALITY DISORDER

I don't know why they call this "borderline." When I first came across it, I thought people with these disorders were on the borderline of the other disorders. However, it's much more serious than that. If we have this disorder we probably have a poor image of ourselves, similar to some of the other disorders, but we react differently. Our moods are unstable and turbulent. We are extremely impulsive. We usually don't know what we're going to be doing next. One minute we want to be with people, the next minute we don't. We may disappear for weeks. And worse, we may take to mutilating ourselves, cutting our arms or wrists or burning or hitting ourselves. And we may be vulnerable to suicide. This is "borderline?"

Did you recognize anyone you know in these descriptions?

While many of us have these disordered personality traits, the most normal of us, those who are primarily in the middle of the bell curves of the limbic scales, are not prone to the more serious irrationalities that these disorders create.

As was noted in their descriptions, these personality disorders while providing some comfort to an Inner Dummy that is dissatisfied in some way, carry emotional baggage of their own. The Inner Dummy apparently adapts these mechanisms, but then will revert to inflicting punishing emotions when the mechanisms themselves aren't performing satisfactorily in the face of new, limbic disappointments. For instance, the dependent personalities' primary attachment leaves them and they may be punished with severe anxiety and panic attacks.

Is there no ultimate escape?

The last of the *second-level neurotic punishments* to be covered is called *post-traumatic stress disorder*. This is the punishment that we are inflicted with when the Inner Dummy senses that we have been seriously injured or threatened with injury. The Oklahoma City bombing comes immediately to mind. Not only were the people who were in the building and survived subject to this punishing disorder, but so were the people who simply observed it from the outside.

In their book *Evolutionary Psychiatry*, psychiatrist and Jungian analyst Anthony Stevens and researcher and lecturer John Price describe this disorder:

> [It] follows exposure to an extreme traumatic stressor involving direct personal experience of an event that involves actual or threatened death or serious injury. . . . The person's response to the event will have involved intense fear, helplessness, or horror. Characteristic symptoms include persistent re-experiencing of the traumatic event, avoidance of stimuli associated with the trauma, and persistent symptoms of increased arousal. . . . For a soldier, fire-fighter or steeplejack, such avoidance may be incompatible with continuation of his professional role.[19]

They explain that the "adaptive function," which pertains to hypothetical reasons for the development of the original limbic brain design, "of such an extreme and enduring reaction is presumably to discourage the victim from ever exposing himself to a comparable danger."

I thought the reason would be more complicated than that.

To give you a better idea of the punishment that a post-traumatic stress disorder can inflict, following is a quote from the *Encyclopaedia Britannica* about "Shell Shock," the post-traumatic stress disorder that can afflict soldiers who have been in battle, that I happened to run across looking up a reference:

> What one man tolerates well under military stress can prove overwhelming for another. In acute combat reactions, prominent symptoms include psychomotor expressions of anxiety (e.g., tremors), sleep disturbances, restlessness, exaggerated tendency to startle, and such bodily manifestations as heart palpitation and increased perspiration. Conversion symptoms such as headache, fatigue, backaches and functional cardiovascular and gastrointestinal symptoms are frequent. There may also be signs of depression, guilt feelings, withdrawal, apathy and scattered amnesia. The battle dream is a frequent and outstanding feature; irritability is quite common and sometimes leads to destructive behavior.[20]

In other words, the battle first scares the hell out of us, which is bad enough, but then the Inner Dummy carries on from there with the senseless punishments just described.

Finally, we come to the *third level of punishment*, the *psychoses* that the Inner Dummy can inflict on us, which is presumably its way of offering *final comfort* by attempting to take us right out of reality, when it is really furious with us for not doing its bidding.

Psychoses, according to the *Oxford Companion to the Mind* is broken down into two main classifications. The first is *organic*, if the condition seems to result from a physical abnormality, a brain tumor or a "chemical derangement." The second is *functional* or nonorganic, which the book points out: "the majority of psychiatrists do seem to believe . . . are true medical diseases and that, one day, physical causes will be found for them—and that as a result, rational effective treatments will become available."[21]

Dr. Hefter adds to this point, "In recent years we have been seeing increasing evidence of biochemical, anatomic, and physiological factors involved in functional maladies. The effectiveness of medication may be further indications of the existence of these factors."

The *Oxford Companion* then points out in a nutshell the primary differences between neuroses and psychoses as follows:

> One [viewpoint], held by some but not all psychoanalysts, argues that the functional psychoses are not in principle all that different from the neuroses; it is merely that the fixation points are earlier, the regressions deeper, the infantile traumas more massive, the defense mechanisms more primitive.[22]

There are apparently three primary forms of functional psychoses, which if we are afflicted by them, our outlooks might be affected as follows.

SCHIZOPHRENIA

The label actually covers a number of different disorders from which we might suffer only in part.

1. We might suffer from *delusions* such as the leader of the Heaven's Gate cult group apparently did, who thought that suicide would result in his group finding a spiritual home behind the Hale-Bopp comet circling the earth. These delusions can be so strong that our belief in them becomes rock hard, as a willingness to commit suicide attests. Or we might think we are king of Europe and constantly try to recruit people for our castle court.

2. We might suffer from *hallucinations*. We hear voices that are clear as a bell, but no one is in the room. For example, the voice of our long-dead father might give us directions as we drive down the road and lash out in anger if we make a mistake. Or we see a large rabbit accompanying us, as motion-picture star James Stewart did in the movie *Harvey*.

3. We might suffer from *disorganized speech*. Somebody asks us why we are taking a walk and we might reply, "Yes, I like taking a walk. The sun is out and my cousin Loretta got a traffic ticket yesterday and I know the judge will be unfair and the mayor doesn't like airplanes."

4. We might suffer from *negative symptoms*, which means we don't display emotional reactions. Someone talks to us and we'll react with a flat toneless voice and vacant eyes. We might be apathetic to the point that we'll never clean our room or take a shower. Or we might not be able to feel any pleasure, like people who are clinically depressed.

One of the problems of schizophrenia and other disorders is that we usually have no idea we have a problem. The id, the Inner Dummy, literally makes us believe that what we are seeing or doing, or how we are reacting to events, no matter how distorted, is perfectly normal. The treatment of schizophrenia is described in chapter 32. However, we should touch on the fact that there are also subtypes to this disorder as follows:

1. If we are afflicted with the *simple type*, we will show a gradual reduction in our relationships and interests, and our level of activity diminishes. We may retreat to a simpler role in life. For example, if we are the manager of a factory department, we might end up loading trucks.

2. If we are afflicted with the *paranoid type*, we may act perfectly normal, except we have delusions and/or hallucinations about people or events that are going to persecute us.

3. If we are afflicted with the *catatonic type*, our motor responses will be affected. We might reflect odd mannerisms like sticking our tongues out excessively or at the opposite extreme, we might remain in a rigid, "catatonic" pose.

4. If we have the *residual type*, we would have recovered from a bout with schizophrenia, but there are some residual effects. We may no longer suffer from hallucinations or delusions, but we still might have beliefs that are unreal and prefer to avoid social contact.

BIPOLAR DISORDER

This is sometimes called "manic depressive disorder." If we are afflicted with this disorder, we may experience cyclic attacks of depression and manic (or inappropriate exuberant) behavior. We've discussed the depressive state previously. Typically we would feel hopeless and worthless; our feelings of pleasure would be drastically impaired; just being alive during waking hours might be a torment. In the manic stage, we might show great humor and charm and be sexually promiscuous. We might consider ourselves rich, strong, and very healthy and spend large sums of money we may or may not have in just a few days. However, if something thwarts our warped expectations, we can turn instantly from charming and smooth into hostile, irritating, and sarcastic. In other words, we can become downright mean. As with schizophrenia, we might not have the slightest insight into the abnormal nature of our mood.

PARANOIA

If we are afflicted with the psychotic version of this disorder, we may cling to a system of paranoiac beliefs that are apparently absurd or delusional to others, but which we think are the real thing. We are not afflicted with disorganized speech or thinking, as the schizophrenic might be, because we can be perfectly logical in defending our false beliefs. If we see a police car pass in front of our house, we might think with perfect logic that this is the scout car for an invasion of Latvians who intend to machine gun our house. Just the mere possibility of an event can be taken by us as conclusive evidence and you can't argue us out of it. We know. We might even consider ourselves as a savior of the world and our entire mission in life is to unmask the culprits who are attempting to undermine our society.

OTHERS

There are additional psychoses, such as multiple personalities, a condition which is considered controversial in the world of psychiatry and is listed in the *Diagnostic and Statistical Manual of Mental Disorders IV*, published by the American Psychiatric Association as Dissociative Identity Disorders. However controversial the condition is, my niece Judy, who assists with group therapy of people with manic-depression and other disorders, tells me she knows of one person, we'll call her Molly, who has more than ninety personalities and Judy has witnessed most of them.

The basic theory behind multiple personalities, she tells me, is that when the pressures of life become so painful, the mind is capable of creating a second personality, presumably to give us a fresh start against whatever the stressful environment is that we are facing. However, the basic vulnerabilities that allowed the outside stress to trigger intense, punishing emotions apparently remain and so new personalities may continue to be created, in a continuing quest for a fresh start. If this reasoning is correct, we might view the process as another brutish relief mechanism provided by a harshly disappointed Inner Dummy. Instead of taking us out of reality into a delusional world, it provides us with another personality to give us another go at it.

There are more than three hundred mental disorders listed in the *Diagnostic And Statistical Manual of Mental Disorders IV*, some of which are obviously organic, such as certain forms of dementia (Alzheimer's, for example) and mental retardation. There are also mood disorders, adjustment disorders, dissociative disorders, substance-related disorders, sexual disorders, and sleep disorders, all of which are in the world of professionals like Dr. Hefter, and which are beyond me to comment.

However, when it comes to the functional disorders that can be attributed to the varying forms of environmental stress, the operative words that trigger serious neuroses or psychoses are apparently "vulnerability" and "life events."

In their book, *Cognitive-Behavioral Therapy of Schizophrenia*, Drs. David C. Kingdon and Douglas Turkington, both on the staff of England's Bassetlaw Hospital, said:

> The more vulnerable the person is, the less stress is required to precipitate illness; a person with a strong family history of schizophrenia may be in this position. Conversely those who are less vulnerable will require greater levels of stress or combination of stressors. However, other factors . . . may interfere with the termination of episodes, so a simple reduction of stress or vulnerability is often not sufficient to enable a person to return to the previous state. . . .
>
> Events also may not occur at discrete times: For example, family arguments may be significant events but may be cumulative in effect, and moving a home involves a series of traumas (e.g., buying, renting, or selling the present home; packing; and unpacking) over a period of time.[24]

In this sense, we might view a Number One on the survival scale who has no real sense of compassion or guilt and is practically impervious to fear, to be less vulnerable to family arguments, for example, than a Number Seven or Eight, who feels the requisite social emotions with extreme intensity and might become more stressed under the identical situation. If this person, according to Kingdon and Turkington, had a genetic predisposition for schizophrenia, or for that matter, the other psychoses described, then their chances of being taken out of reality would presumably be far greater than others without the predisposition.

Are the pertinent emotions, neuroses, and psychoses set forth in this chapter the end of the punishments that the Inner Dummy can inflict upon us when we are vulnerable and don't meet its expectations? Not quite. There is one more, described after the next, brief encounter with Dr. Freud.

COMMENTARY BY DR. HEFTER

As described in this chapter, self-punishment is in many instances a way in which the individual's brain/mind attempts to deal with the experiences of anxiety. The concept of defense mechanisms developed by Freud (and his daughter, Anna Freud, in particular), among other things relates to the "punishing" of oneself through the inappropriate or excessive utilization of such defense mechanisms. David describes the issue in terms of "hard-wiring," and inherent responses arising in the limbic region of the brain. Freud, depending upon which period of his work is involved, talked about these issues in terms of the id (David's "Inner Dummy") or the unconscious. Freud also believed, however, that ultimately all mental illnesses would be found to be organic in their nature.

In the world of current mental-illness research, the major quantity of resources is focused on the biochemical, physiological, and genetic underpinnings of mental functioning, rather than the more "psychological" issues. For example, the structure, function and development of neurons, including those in the limbic region, are the objects of significant attention. This relates directly to the points raised in this chapter about the autonomy of the brain connections. In addition, however, the questions of how noninherent factors are involved, and how they affect the inherent factors, and what contribution each category of factors makes to our behavior, are still very much open ones.

It is also true that even when much more information is obtained from further study the issue of free will, choice, the idea of the soul, the mind, etc., will likely never be resolved by scientific investigation.

It is interesting why pain, whether physical or mental, is at times so intense and/or prolonged when it need not be from the standpoint of its usefulness for the individual, or apparently for humans as a species. It is perhaps from an existential perspective, a reminder of the unexpectedness of much of life. There may be systems of thought and belief that indicate a value in the intensity of pain experience, in terms of a social good, but from a clinical perspective the degree of pain felt by an individual often seems excessive.

NOTES

1. Various World War I sources. It's an old story.
2. Sharon L. Johnson, *Therapist's Guide to Clinical Intervention: The 1-2-3's of Treatment Planning* (San Diego: Academic Press, 1997), p. 183.

3. Daniel Goleman, *Emotional Intelligence* (New York: Bantam, 1995), p. 17.

4. David M. Buss, "Evolutionary Personality Psychology," *Annual Review of Psychology* (1991): 461.

5. Peter C. Whybrow, *A Mood Apart: The Thinker's Guide to Emotion and Its Disorders* (New York: HarperPerennial, 1997), p. 129.

6. Karen C. Barret, "A Functionalist Approach to Shame and Guilt," in *Self-Conscious Emotions*, ed. June P. Tangney and Kurt W. Fischer (New York: Guilford Press, 1995), p. 41.

7. Ibid., p. 41.

8. Jeffrey M. Masson, *Dogs Never Lie About Love: Reflections on the Emotional World of Dogs* (New York: Crown Publishers, 1997), p. 105.

9. Michael Lewis, "Embarrassment: The Emotion of Self-Exposure and Evaluation," in Tangney and Fischer, *Self-Conscious Emotions*, pp. 201–202.

10. Johnson, *Therapist's Guide to Clinical Intervention*, p. 183.

11. Richard L. Gregory (ed.), *The Oxford Companion to the Mind* (Oxford: Oxford University Press, 1987), p. 549.

12. Helen Kennerly, *Overcoming Anxiety: A Self-Help Guide Using Cognitive Behavioral Techniques* (Washington Square, N.Y.: New York University Press, 1997), p. 34.

13. Ian Osborn, *Tormenting Thoughts and Secret Rituals: The Hidden Epidemic of Obsessive-Compulsive Disorder* (New York: Pantheon Books, 1998), p. 37.

14. Ibid., p. 41.

15. Ibid., p. 45.

16. Sigmund Freud, excerpt from *Beyond the Pleasure Principle*, in Peter Gay, *The Freud Reader* (New York: Norton, 1989), p. 603.

17. Sigmund Freud, excerpt from *An Autobiographical Study*, in Gay, *The Freud Reader*, p. 18.

18. V. Mark Durand and David H. Barlow, *Abnormal Psychology: An Introduction* (Belmont, Calif.: Brooks/Cole, 1997), p. 372.

19. Anthony Stevens and John Price, *Evolutionary Psychiatry: A New Beginning* (London: Routledge, 1996), p. 105.

20. *Encyclopaedia Britannica*, vol. 23, p. 962.

21. Gregory, *Oxford Companion to the Mind*, p. 658.

22. Ibid., p. 658.

23. *Encyclopaedia Britannica*, vol. 23, p. 965.

24. David C. Kingdon and Douglas Turkington, *Cognitive-Behavioral Therapy of Schizophrenia* (New York: Guilford Press, 1994), pp. 31–34.

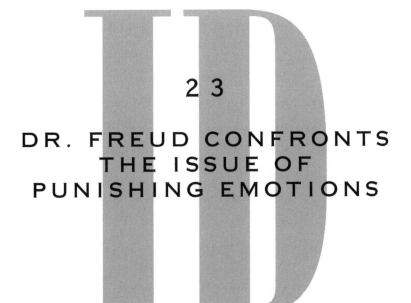

2 3

DR. FREUD CONFRONTS THE ISSUE OF PUNISHING EMOTIONS

West Fraser, an artist, was commissioned by the White House Historical Association to create a new painting of the White House. He was told, however, by the National Park Service that he could not do the painting from his position of preference at nearby Lafayette Square Park, because structures are not permitted in the park. The service maintained that an easel on a tripod is a structure.[1]

Samuel Ollander poked his head back into the conference room barely two hours after he had left Dr. Freud.

"Dr. Freud?" he coughed out softly.

Freud, who was busily making notes on a long, yellow legal pad while a finger on his opposite hand was pressing down a page of an open book, looked over his glasses and said, "Yes, Ollander."

"Oh, I'm sorry to interrupt you again, sir, but the creative group came up with another item they wanted me to show to the focus group of consumers tonight and I just wanted to pass it by you quickly, for your reactions."

"More Dummy Bliss, Ollander?" Freud said as he smiled faintly, putting down his pen and turning the book facedown.

"Almost, sir, but not quite," Ollander said, relieved at Freud's attempt at flippancy. He entered the conference room, again holding three cards whose faces were covered by layout paper.

He sat down, with the cards and a notepad in front of him, and continued:

"I just want to say, sir, before I show you these concepts, that we are all deeply indebted to you for your assistance in helping make the complexities of this campaign easy to understand for the average person."

"No problem at all, Ollander, this is what I am supposed to be here for, distasteful as it has sometimes been. Now tell me what you are going to confront me with today," Freud pointed to the cards Ollander was holding.

"Yes, sir. Our creatives thought we needed a branding concept for the irrational and senseless punishments inflicted by the Inner Dummy, similar to the concept of Dummy Bliss, which had to do with the irrationalities of our reward system."

"Irrational and senseless punishments?" Freud asked quizzically.

"Well, yes, the punitive emotions inflicted upon us by the Inner Dummy when what happens to us in the real world doesn't live up to its expectations. In our view, these punitive emotions become irrational and senseless when their array of feelings and intensity go far beyond the bounds of what the situation warrants."

"I'm not sure I'm following you, Ollander."

"Okay. Let's look first at some typical misfortunes that many of us may face at one time or another in their varying forms. Our creatives made a list of some typical examples, which I might just read off to you."

"Yes, yes, go right ahead," Freud said looking interested.

Ollander thumbed through some sheets on his notepad. "Fine, here they are. For example, a teenager becoming totally distraught when the girl he wants to take to the prom turns him down. Or a daughter becoming distressed when she tells her father of a job promotion and he, instead of congratulating her, puts her down. Or the budding concert pianist who learns one day that he simply isn't good enough. Or the executive who loses a job promotion to his or her equal in the next office. Or the law student who fails to pass the bar. Or the football player cut from his team. Or the politician who loses an election. Or the farmer whose farm is put up for auction. Or the teacher who is passed over for tenure. Or the wife who learns her husband is having an affair. Or your close friend who now shuns you. Or your drill sergeant mother who wants to control your every move."

Ollander paused. "Those are just some typical examples, sir."

"Yes, I understand now where you are leading," Freud said. "Please continue."

"Well, these are the types of situations, dilemmas in countless variations, that most of us face at times in our lives, some situations more often than others, particularly minor misfortunes, and some more enduring than others. The point is, just the feeling of disappointment should be enough to bear when we've had a setback or misfortune strikes. But no, the Inner Dummy, like some totalitarian brute, punishes us with burning, distressful, hurtful emotions that might last for days or weeks or longer and confuse our thinking, just when we need clear thought processes to plan our reactions and next steps.

"My wife," Ollander continued, "has a friend whose husband was killed in an auto accident. She didn't come out of her room for *two years*. She was positively disconsolate. Now I have nothing against an emotional mechanism that grieves us when someone close to us dies. I think it helps the process. But to stay two years in one room? That is beyond the bounds of rationality."

Ollander paused and Freud replied with some hint at humor, "And so at least one of those cards in front of you, I imagine then, is labeled *Dummy Punishment*."

Ollander hesitated, looking surprised at Freud's comment, then said, "Well no, but maybe we should add it."

Freud broke into a grin. "Oh, go ahead, Ollander, and show me your offerings. I am only teasing you a bit."

"No problem, sir," Ollander said shyly. "And you can tease me all you want. My wife tells me that being teased is good for me because I am so uptight. So you see? Your teasing," he said chuckling shyly, "can be part of my treatment program."

Ollander reached for the cards. "Here, let me show you the first one." He held the card in front of him and uncovered the layout paper. "This one, as you can see, is *Dummy Torment*." He looked at Freud as he did with the reward cards, looking for a reaction, but found none.

He put the card aside, picked up the next one, and uncovered the layout paper. "This one has a certain resonance to it, *Dummy Distress*." Again he looked probingly at Freud, who showed no reaction.

"One of our creatives suggested that there would be a certain consonance to using *Dummy Delight* for irrational rewards and *Dummy Distress* for irrational punishments. Do you have any opinion on that, sir?"

"I'm afraid I do not, thank goodness."

"Okay, then, sir," Ollander replied quickly. "Here is the last one, which a number of the creatives like because it is so direct." He uncovered the card. "It reads *Dummy Pain*.

"You see?" Ollander continued. "It gets the point across immediately. Here, I'll put them on the bulletin board." He then pinned them to the bulletin board behind his chair.

"Do you have any preferences, Dr. Freud?"

"I prefer not to comment on a preference, but it would appear they all go beyond my theory of unpleasure."

"In what way, sir?"

"My theory didn't address the issue of unpleasure as irrational. I viewed unpleasure as an entity of our biological makeup that resulted from repulsed instinctual drives, without directly referencing the imperfections of the system, the irrationalities, which I alluded to in other contexts."

"I'm afraid I don't understand."

"Let me put it more simply, then. You are contending that the punishments, the unpleasure unleashed by a frustrated, unfulfilled id is biologically irrational, a defect in the design of our brains, so to speak. I never alluded to any biological imperfection in my thoughts about the pleasure-unpleasure principle that I can recall."

"So you disagree with the concept?"

Freud thought for a moment. "No, I believe not. The idea of a biologically imperfect system is one I have alluded to in other contexts. Associating it with the pleasure-unpleasure principle would be quite acceptable to me. The idea of biological irrationality is interesting. Further, you are dealing in a metaphoric world utilizing easily understood labels and supporting concepts, much as I did, unknowing of the marketing world, when I developed the labels and supporting concepts of the id, ego, and superego. The basic contention between your agency and me is that my labels are barriers to a popular understanding of their conceptual meanings and need to be simplified. I gave my word that I would keep myself open on the issue, as we've discussed."

"Thank you, sir. And I might add that the creatives are already at work on structuring the outline of a Dummy Pain creative positioning, using that specific phrase, pending the reactions of the consumers to the three alternatives tonight."

"And this creative positioning would be used for what purposes?"

"The same as the Dummy Bliss positioning, sir, to be able to explain the concept of Dummy Pain in advertising or in a manual in a way that will provide comfort to those who are suffering from it."

Ollander thought for a moment, then continued:

"For example, we want to tell the teenager who was turned down on a date for the prom, or whose father won't give him or her an encouraging word, or whose mother or sibling is constantly criticizing him, or who failed an exam, that the pain they might be feeling is totally out of balance to the real world."

"Please expand on that."

"I mean, we want to tell them that they are living in an imperfect world with an imperfect Inner Dummy, which retains the caveman arsenal of punishing emotions that were originally designed to keep us in line under nomadic, tribal conditions. But today, we are living in a modern, civilized, industrialized world, with advances in science, which should have worked to considerably enlarge our perspective. The knowledge that we have gained about our lives and circumstances in the last one hundred years has literally filled millions of books and should have helped more of us understand and accept what is really important in life . . . to strive for contentment with our families and friends, to be kind and thoughtful to others, and to work to transcend or sidestep the irrationalities of life that constantly beset us."

Ollander paused, looking at Freud questioningly.

"Continue, Ollander, continue."

"Thank you, sir. In any event, very little of any of this has permeated our Inner Dummy, which sits heavily under our rationality, ready to punish or reward us in accordance with its own primitive rules. We don't make as much money as our friend or a neighbor and it may punish us with jealousy and frustration and maybe even feelings of hatred. Dummy Pain, we should say to ourselves, is an outrageous travesty, when its intensity goes beyond the bounds of reason. So we failed the bar exam. So what? Try again. And then again, if necessary. And if we don't pass it ultimately, well, then, let's become a legal aid, if we are so smitten with the practice of law. What difference does it make what our vocations are under the concept of a galactic/genetic perspective, if our overriding objective is to seek contentment during the very short stay we have on this planet as embodied humans? Keep working to find what makes you happy.

"Then there is the social injustice to this pain, the loss of status we feel when it is necessary to tell others close to us of our failures, which adds to the punishment when the support we might require isn't energetically returned."

Ollander rose from his chair and began pacing as he continued:

"The idea, therefore is to view this Dummy Pain for what it is. An imperfection of the human condition, a result of limbic organs that haven't kept pace with our rational evolution. So the general idea then is, if you haven't caused any real harm, if you haven't hurt others in the process, if you have been caught in a negative life event which you didn't create, then face that pain as an injustice, a travesty, and do whatever you can to rationalize it, transcend it, sidestep it, avoid it, release it. Fight back, in other words. And if that fight means avoiding situations or the people who give you the most pain, then avoid them as much as possible. And that would even include your mother or your father, if they are obviously abusive and irrational. Becoming a parent doesn't make a somewhat mentally disordered person the embodiment of an idealized parent figure, and there are no screening tests for parenthood. You might have gotten the wrong pick in the lottery for parents . . . or siblings or close friends, for that matter."

Ollander stopped, returned to his chair and looked up at Dr. Freud.

"You look perplexed after all that, Ollander."

"I am indeed, sir," Ollander said as he calmed down. "There is one major problem to all of this theorizing."

"Which is?"

"Well, this makes a good deal of sense for normal people who are in the middle of the bell curves of the limbic drives and aware that the world is replete with irrationality. But what about those who have been limbically captured by their core instinctual drives, their limbic programs and belief systems, to the point that they themselves cannot view reality in specific areas of their lives and may trace the causes of their Dummy Pain to the wrong sources? They are unaware of their capturing.

"How can we tell people like this to avoid the situations or the people who are causing or may potentially cause their pain, including their parents or whoever. They may be just the very situations and people they need."

"It's not so simple, is it, Ollander?"

"No, it's not, sir. And to make our communications even more complex, there is no universal remedy for healing Dummy Pain quickly, although a rational understanding of its imperfect, mechanistic source may go a long way. I am afraid the ads or the manual, if we are able to develop one, will take a great deal of work."

"To say the least. But even the simplest of efforts would be of the highest importance if properly constructed, Ollander."

"You think so?"

"Yes, I do. The ultimate purpose of the psychoanalytic methodology I designed was what? Of course it was to relieve the mental pain of the patient. So I am in sympathy with the purpose of your manual because it parallels the purpose of my work, even though I might continue to disagree with your metaphors that work to make concepts so simplistic. In the wrong hands, they might do more harm than good."

"Well, thank you again, Dr. Freud," Ollander said as he stood and began removing the cards from the bulletin board. As he reached the door, he said. "I'll let the creatives know that you agree with the difficulties of the task. And I'll be sure to let you know the results of our consumer panels on the alternative brands for Dummy Bliss and Dummy Pain."

"Please do," Freud replied, now turning his interest back to his books.

As Ollander opened the conference room door, Freud looked over his glasses and said. "Oh, Ollander."

"Yes, sir," Ollander paused in the doorway.

"The color of your shirt doesn't match your pants."

"What?" Ollander replied startled, looking down at his shirt and pants, then looking back inquiringly at Dr. Freud.

"Just teasing," Freud chuckled, "part of the treatment, and at no charge, by the way."

"Oh, yes, sir, thank you, sir," Ollander replied, blushing. He quietly closed the conference-room door behind him.

NOTE

1. Zay N. Smith, *Chicago Sun-Times*, September 24, 1998, p. 28.

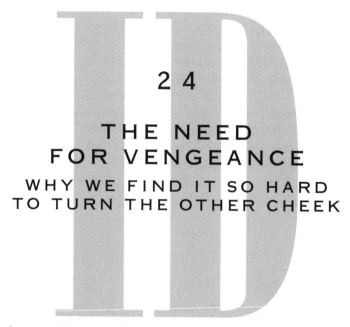

2 4

THE NEED
FOR VENGEANCE
WHY WE FIND IT SO HARD
TO TURN THE OTHER CHEEK

A dentist in Wiesbaden, Germany, walked into a bar, reached into the mouth of a woman who failed to pay her bill and repossessed her dentures.[1]

Let's consider again the plight of the significant other at the beginning of chapter 22. Her partner, with whom she was deeply in love, came home one night from an out-of-town trip and, after some small talk, broke the news to her that he was leaving her because he had fallen in love with someone else. You'll recall some of the punishing emotions we imagined she might have felt: crushed, enraged, tormented, depressed, perplexed, shamed, empty, anxious, victimized, disillusioned, resentful, discouraged, diminished, miserable, stupefied, lost, vulnerable, frustrated, grieved, distrustful, misgiven, appalled, humiliated, rejected, threatened, scared, suspicious, jealous, hateful, and dulled.

Then another pervasive feeling began to emerge in the form of a compulsion to seek revenge. He has cartons delivered to the apartment so he can begin packing. She throws them out. He looks in the closet to put on his favorite shirt. She has cut it to shreds. He tries to make a purchase with his credit card, but learns she has already used up the limit. The acts of vengeance continue long after he moves out. Whatever she can do to make his life difficult, she will probably do. If they were married, for example, she will drag him through court, going after everything she can, including his frequent-flyer miles.

If the situation were reversed and she were the one who found another love, the acts of vengeance might have been similar. He cuts her favorite outfit to shreds. He throws out the moving cartons and so forth. The punishing emotions play no favorites when it comes to sex or sexual preference.

The more intense the limbic drives that were disappointed the greater the intensity of the punishing emotions, including revenge. The partner who walks out on a Number Ten on the power, sexual, and nurturance scales may be in danger of being physically harmed, along with his or her new significant other.

Is this any way for our lives to be structured?

What was the evolutionary idea behind revenge? Why was its drive designed into our limbic brains in the first place? For it is a trait whose core origins we apparently share with the higher animals. Threaten or strike an alpha chimp or gorilla and it's highly improbable that they will turn the other cheek.

Randolph M. Neese, associate professor of psychiatry at the University of Michigan, in his paper "Evolutionary Explanations of Emotions," which appeared in *Human Nature* in 1990, offers this theory about the origins of anger and revenge:

> When the other person defects by not providing help in return, or cheats by doing less than is fair, anger is the usual response. Anger includes not only threats to abandon the relationship, but also spiteful threats to harm the other person, often at great cost to the self. Anger is not a reasoned negotiating ploy; it is an agitated, irrational, unpredictable state of aggressive arousal. . . . How can anger possibly be adaptive? Why not just ignore the person who will not cooperate and look instead for a different reciprocity partner? The answer may be that anger is worthwhile precisely because relationships are valuable.
>
> Anger signals that a defection or potential defection has been detected and will not be tolerated. Its most basic function is to protect against exploitation. But by increasing the cost to a potential defector, the threat of spiteful retaliation also, paradoxically, helps to preserve the relationships. This helps to explain why the angry person is unpredictable and irrational.[2]

What Dr. Neese appears to be saying is that just the thought that the person we may be planning to wrong in some way will react with unpredictable anger and retaliation may in itself be enough to prevent us from doing the deed. This might have been a useful evolutionary, peace-keeping device for our lives in the caves.

The operative question appears to be: "Why not just ignore the person who will not cooperate and look instead for a different reciprocity partner?" Or, why not turn the other cheek and just walk away? In a civilized world, wouldn't this be the most appropriate thing to do?

The apparent reason that most of us can't do this is that we still hold this primitive, caveman emotional baggage in our heads, which we might consider to be part of the reward-punishment system of the Inner Dummy, which triggers feelings of rage and revenge when the strongest of its limbic expectations are not being met. It "expects" our significant other to remain loyal to us. It "expects" not to be fired from our jobs. It "expects" to win the important contest. It "expects" not to be run off the road by a reckless driver. When expectations such as these are jolted, an array of punishing emotions are triggered, with probably the strongest being sheer rage, and a compulsion for revenge. We literally can become captured by them.

In his paper "An Argument for Basic Emotion" in *Cognition and Emotion*, Paul Ekman of the University of California described the theories of Richard Lazarus who, ". . . succinctly described what he called a 'psycho biological principle' ": "Once the appraisals have been made, the emotional response is a forgone conclusion, a consequence of biology."[3]

In other words, once our emotional sentinel grasps that something is going on that we don't like—our significant other telling us that she is leaving us, a boss firing us from our job—the game is over insofar as the Inner Dummy is concerned. It will react in these instances with some level of rage in accordance with its programming, a "consequence of biology," a "foregone conclusion." Lazarus's concept would ascribe the same reaction to events happening that are good for us. We get promoted instead of fired, we win the big games. The "consequence of biology" may be that we feel ecstasy, with the level established by our capacity for feeling pleasure.

There is obviously a rage and revenge threshold because all of us don't reach our "boiling point" at the same level of frustration. We might thus envision a metaphoric *rage and revenge scale*, in which Number Ones and Twos might only rarely experience the feelings of rage accompanied by a compulsion for revenge. Number Fives experience the feelings normally, while Number Tens would pop off at any little thing.

The Number Ones are favorites of motion-picture plots. I recall one western in which a stoic Clint Eastwood played a rancher with a calm and peaceful demeanor. Nothing seemed to rile him. Then one day he comes home to find his wife and daughter brutally molested and murdered by four outlaws. He still doesn't show much emotion outwardly, but we are led to assume that rage and revenge are consuming him, as he saddles his horse and begins tracking down the outlaws and proceeds to kill them one at a time. And we enjoy watching him do it because as Dr. Hefter pointed out in one of his commentaries, our feelings can easily be stirred by fantasy.

A Number Five on the *rage and revenge scale* might accurately describe those of us with an average "boiling point." We don't "fly off the handle" at every little thing, but we would probably have intense feelings of rage and revenge if our significant others abruptly told us one night they were leaving us for other people, or we unjustly lost a job we needed, or a loved one was robbed and beaten, or we were the victim of a cruel hoax.

The term "Number Ten" would properly describe those people who indeed "fly off the handle" at every little thing. If they don't get the right table at a restaurant, they fly into a rage and threaten to get the maitre d' fired. If their car isn't fetched promptly by a garage attendant, they might threaten to get him fired. If you honk at them on the road because of the way they are driving, they might try to sideswipe your car.

Revenge can thus be viewed as more of the inner craziness that can reside in the minds of apparently normal people.

Cognitive scientist Steven Pinker in his book *How the Mind Works*, in a chapter on "Hotheads," makes this observation:

> The lust for revenge is a particularly terrifying emotion. All over the world, relatives of the slain fantasize day and night about the bittersweet moment when they might avenge a life with a life and find peace at last. The emotion strikes us as primitive and dreadful. . . . But in many societies an irresistible thirst for vengeance is one's only protection against deadly raids. . . .
>
> Most legal theories, even from the highest-minded philosophers, acknowledge that retribution is one of the legitimate goals of criminal punishment, over and above the goals of deterring potential criminals and incapacitating, deterring, and rehabilitating the offender.[4]

Pinker's last paragraph about retribution might explain why, during the O. J. Simpson trial, the major cable television talk shows appeared to center on people who wanted him locked up and behind bars, concerned that even his stay in jail during his trial was being made too comfortable. These were people apparently higher up on the rage and revenge scale. Apparently, their Inner Dummies became attached to O. J., just as if he were part of their own lives, or in "fantasy," as described by Dr. Hefter. They reacted to his plight just as they might to a neighbor they have known for years, who appeared obviously guilty of a heinous murder and they now wanted punished badly.

However, culture and conditioning are obviously major factors in determining what it is we are enraged by. For example, if O. J. were a nomad in Somalia and murdered his ex-wife and her friend, there would be no media coverage at all, let alone a trial. All O. J. would have needed to do to settle the matter was provide one hundred camels to the family of his ex-wife and one hundred camels to the family of the friend. Done deal.[5]

In many cultures throughout the world, murder is recognized as a singular act of passion that deserves far less punishment than thievery, for example, which might cost you a hand or an entire arm. The settlement of a murder of passion becomes a negotiation between the families involved, with the murderer making restitution to the family of the victim. If the restitution is not fully made, then the family of the victim is free to murder the murderer.

Robert Wright, writer and senior editor of the *New Republic*, in his book *The Moral Animal* makes the point that our "retributive impulse," as he aptly labels it, is part of our focus on ourselves, our selfishness, which is ultimately aimed at surviving long enough so that we can mate and pass copies of our genes onto the next generation. He makes the observation:

> Retribution helps solve the "cheater" problem that any moral system faces; people who are seen to take more than they give are thereafter punished. . . . However lowly its origins, it has come to serve a lofty purpose. This is something to be thankful for.[6]

I don't know if I would be exactly thankful. Wright's retributive impulse has also led to countless wars, as one side seeks to take revenge on another, frequently for the most absurd of reasons, leading to millions of needless massacres and deaths. For relatively current reference, check out the massacres and "ethnic cleansings" that have taken place in and around Bosnia and Kosovo in eastern Europe. Or, read the following excerpt from *Days of Darkness: The Feuds of Eastern Kentucky*, by Pulitzer Prize-winning columnist John Ed Pearce, which describes some of the irrationalities created by the retributive impulse in the years following the Civil War:

> Returning Rebel and Yankee soldiers clashed. Duels were fought, homes burned. Freed slaves found themselves at loose ends. . . . Night Riders and Vigilantes terrorized the countryside by night, driving blacks across county lines, burning their homes, lynching those who resisted and threatening to kill any whites who tried to help them. Blacks accused of crimes against whites were routinely hanged, usually without trial. . . . The near chaos presented an ideal atmosphere in which to settle old scores, real or imagined . . . lawmen were hard put to keep the peace.[7]

I'm sure that Robert Wright wasn't thinking of episodes like this when he said the retributive impulse was something to be thankful for. And wasn't it Jesus Christ who disagreed with the concept of "An eye for an eye, a tooth for a tooth," and said such things as: "Do unto others as you would have them do unto you," "Love your enemies," and "Turn the other cheek"?

Obviously Jesus found the retributive impulse repugnant and a hindrance to the establishment of "peace on earth." I am on Jesus' side on this one. I find the retributive impulse to be needless and repugnant in a world in which our thinking power should allow us to transcend what is apparently a natural instinct designed for primitive life centuries ago, when we didn't have police forces to maintain authority and harmony.

Unfortunately, the primitive instincts that caused cheating, stealing, betrayal, and such on the savannahs, still are with us today, despite our advanced technology and governmental structures. Our Inner Dummies, in other words, haven't progressed with the rest of us. The only thing that appears to work to keep many of us in check is the fear of retribution.

The one thing we have made some small progress on is how we apply legal retribution, at least in Western cultures. Corporal punishment, including whipping, starvation, and the stocks, and other forms of torture are no longer used. So isn't this a step in the right direction? But a myriad of formal punishments continue to exist, including imprisonment; fines; suspensions; censures; excommunication; threat of loss of jobs, family, or esteem. I found this interesting statement in the *Encyclopaedia Britannica*: "The individual who has inflicted harm on another, runs the revenge argument, must be made to suffer in return; for only an act of vengeance can undo the harm that has been done and assuage the suffering of the people."[8]

It would appear that our system of punishments is aimed at our survival program. If we are higher on the survival scale and vulnerable to normal fears and somewhere in the middle of the power scale and aren't quite so driven, the system of retributive punishments probably works marvelously for us. But if we are a Number One on the survival scale and oblivious to fear of retribution and a Number Nine on the power scale and intensely driven, the game is probably over. We will doubtless bend the rules or worse.

The upshot is that until we've learned enough to make physical adjustments to our imbalanced limbic programs, or until we learn more effective ways to condition ourselves, primitive punishments will continue to be required to restrain a primitive Inner Dummy.

But there is more to the story. In what appears to be a unique twist to our nature, carrying out a retributive act might reward us with the feeling of irrational joy, Dummy Bliss, in other words. It is probably Dummy Bliss that we are feeling when we watch Clint Eastwood and the other good-guy Hollywood heroes track down the murderers of innocent people and kill them. It is also probably Dummy Bliss that the lynchers of African Americans felt, as they saw their victims hanging from trees in the throes of death. We were stupidly being rewarded by the Inner Dummy for a retributive job well done.

Further, those of us high enough on the metaphoric rage and revenge scale might even become addicted to this form of Dummy Bliss. After a messy divorce, we might continually seek court orders that severely limit access of our ex-spouse to the children. We might know rationally that the children could be hurt by our actions, but our addiction to the irrational joy we feel can override our rationality, much like an addiction to cocaine. As a result, the retributive acts may last for years, even after the death of the ex-spouse as we now make irrational claims against the estate or hurt in some way the second wife of the ex-spouse, now a fellow widow or widower. As with any addiction, there is never enough.

We also see irrational joy or Dummy Bliss exhibited in criminal trials when an alleged perpetrator is pronounced guilty and sent to prison for many years. The prosecutors and the families of the victims are whooping with joy, while the parents and children of the criminal are crying their eyes out. In the culture of the United States, a jury trial can take on the nature of a professional football game. Seeing justice done is not the main issue, victory is. If justice were the sole issue and the defendant is pronounced guilty of the crime, the plaintiffs should walk out of the courtroom as glum as the parents and children of the criminal, knowing that we still have to resort to primitive, retributive punishments to keep the primitive drives of our Inner Dummy in check.

Most of us recognize that the drive we feel to seek revenge after we have been seriously wronged is difficult to control. That is one reason why we view with such awe the successes of Mahatma Gandhi and Martin Luther King Jr., both of whom succeeded, for the most part, in convincing their followers to follow a path of nonviolence in achieving their respective revolutions.

Freud didn't have much to say in his writings about the adaptive, evolutionary nature of revenge. But he did talk about the hydraulic nature of aggression, which he described as a drive that constantly seeks release.

Gary Brodsky, on the other hand, author of *The Art of Getting Even*, put it this way:

> There is no worse feeling than to be treated contemptuously by a fellow human being, and where you're helpless to respond. There is, however, no better feeling than taking the time to perfect a fitting revenge, and to carry it out successfully. Perhaps you have tried all legal resources, you've tried to work things out personally and professionally, with little or no results. Now is the time to get down to business, and plan a secretive revengeful scheme. . . . When the unsuspecting victim falls into your custom-tailored trap, your load is lightened considerably and you can go on living your life.[9]

In other words, he is implying that an act of vengeance can be a great release for the hydraulic rage and revenge pressure building within our metaphoric Inner Dummy. Here are some of Brodsky's suggestions for carrying out acts of revenge:

> Say that you go into a men's room in a restaurant or other public place and there's somebody you don't like in there. Take a cup of water and hit him in the crotch with it. The guy will stay in there for six hours, until the water dries.[10]

But what if the rest room has an automatic hot-air dryer? And what kind of cup of water takes six hours to dry? No matter, Brodsky is having fun. Here's another act:

> Take a jar of petroleum jelly, and coat your enemy's shower floor with it. Sure this is nasty. But if the victim's actions toward you deem it necessary, go ahead and do it. You'll be glad that you did. As soon as the person turns on the water and steps in the shower—slip, bang, boom.[11]

Brodsky also commented on the power of prayer in creating acts of revenge: "This method hasn't worked for me. I suggest that you take a more direct approach."

In author George Hayduke's book, *Make 'Em Pay: Ultimate Revenge Techniques from the Master Trickster*, he says:

> Sherry of Palm Springs has a true vandal's way of getting back at some-body's furniture when the host/hostess . . . has been nasty to her. . . . If they have a beanbag chair, she makes a small slice in it with her razor knife. Or she makes several slices. The weight of the next occupant and gravity will carry this stunt to completion.[12]

It might be tempting to write off Brodsky's and Hayduke's books and others like it as low-brow efforts, not fit for the more intellectually aware in society, including academics. But these men could just as easily write special editions for the scientific community, which is not at all immune to the retributive impulse. In his book *Great Feuds in Science*, popular-science writer Hal Hellman makes the following observation:

> Certainly, one of the major drives in science is just the pleasure of finding things out, learning something new about the world around us. If scientists were saints, they might be satisfied with that; for the most part, they are not driven by monetary gain. If they discover something, however, they generally want the world to know it. Visions of a Nobel Prize may dance before them.
>
> All such cases, then, offer the opportunity for priority conflicts, and some ferocious battles have resulted.[13]

This is just my own observation, but it would appear that most people who have really intense rage and revenge reactions are those higher on the limbic scales, the Number Eights, Nines, and Tens. Perhaps this was another design of nature aimed at imbuing primitive, cavemen leaders with high enough levels of rage and revenge for fright to be instilled in their followers, thus diminishing the incidence of challenges.

In today's world, it might be preferable if we could find a fair and equitable way to order these people to attend anger-control workshops. We would all probably be better off.

I was discussing with my friend Bob Schwartz the problems that exist with the irrational joy in the carrying out of a retributive impulse.

"I don't know," he said, "when we play doubles and I'm at the net and you hit a high overhead right at me and happen to hit me, I enjoy the thought of getting a high ball that I can hit back hard, right into your stomach or lower."

"But what sense does that make? I don't try purposely to hit you."

"I didn't say it made sense. I only said that when you hit me, I enjoy the thought of hitting you back. In your stomach or lower."

"But shouldn't we do something about it?" I replied.

"Like what?"

"I don't know, like creating a chemical of some sort that we can inject right into the rage and revenge center in our brains, if we can locate it, that changes things."

"Changes what?"

"Changes the process in some way. When some misfortune happens to us and we begin to feel rage and revenge, we just shout something out, which signals those new chemicals in our brain and the feelings immediately subside."

After a pause, Bob said, "I have an idea."

"Yeah?"

"Well, you know Harold Allen, when he misses a shot he cries out 'Oh, sugar.'"

"I know, I can't stand that. Whenever he says that in his proper and prim way, I shout at him, 'Harold, the word is "shit." Say "Oh, shit." You'll feel better.' Then he gives me a disapproving look like I'm some kind of heathen."

"Wait, but listen. The minute we feel that rage and revenge building, like after you try to hit me on the head with a tennis ball, we simply cry out 'Oh, sugar,' and that chemical that was injected in your brain reacts immediately to remove the rage and revenge."

"Then what happens?" I asked.

"Well, all of a sudden I wouldn't enjoy the thought of hitting you back in the stomach or lower. I would think to myself calmly that he didn't mean to hit me. Why should I become upset? After all, the idea is to win the game. You apologize, I accept it, and there isn't a smidgeon of vengeance for your action left in my brain. That's the process."

"That's a pretty good idea," I replied. "The idea then, in general, is to stay focused on your objectives and not be detracted by foolish acts of revenge."

"Exactly."

"But how do we even create a chemical like that? Do you have a chemistry set"?

"No, but I think my grandson has one. Should I ask him?"
And that's how our conversations go. But you get the point.

COMMENTARY BY DR. HEFTER

Vengeance as a human characteristic, whether only wished or actually implemented, is probably programmed into the human limbic system. With some people it may not be experienced consciously, because the feeling of vengeance may be repressed the moment it approaches awareness. This is more evident in some societies than in other ones. And yet even in cultures that appear to discourage it strongly—those that encourage "turning the other cheek"—the strength of the exhortation is testimony to the intensity of what is discouraged. The basis for vengeful feelings being so ubiquitous may be a consequence of its evolutionary value in indirectly preserving particular genetic transmissions.

With respect to our inclination to feel and/or act in a vengeful manner, and the presence in some societies of teachings to minimize it, there may well be indirect expressions of it. Thus resentment and feelings of wanting revenge against cruel parental figures, for example, may find expression in harsh parenting toward one's own children or harsh behavior toward youngsters in general, under the guise of teaching children that "life is tough and they'd better learn how to deal with it," beyond what common sense dictates.

NOTES

1. Zay N. Smith, *Chicago Sun-Times*, August 3, 1998, p. 24.

2. Randolph M. Neese, "Evolutionary Explanations of Emotions," *Human Nature* 1, no. 3 (1990): 277.

3. Paul Ekman, "An Argument for Basic Emotions," *Cognition and Emotion* (March 1992): 188.

4. Steven Pinker, *How the Mind Works* (New York: Norton, 1997), p. 413.

5. Waris Dirie, *Desert Flower* (New York: Morrow, 1992), p. 11.

6. Robert Wright, *The Moral Animal: The New Science of Evolutionary Psychology* (New York: Pantheon, 1994), p. 339.

7. John E. Pearce, *Days of Darkness: The Feuds of Eastern Kentucky* (Lexington: University of Kentucky Press, 1994), p. 139.

8. *Encyclopaedia Britannica*, vol. 16, p. 863.

9. Gary Brodsky, *The Art of Getting Even* (Edison, N.J.: Castle Books, 1990), p. v.

10. Ibid., p. 3.

11. Ibid., p. 6.

12. George Hayduke, *Make 'Em Pay* (Secaucus, N.J.: Carol Publishing Group, 1986), p. 72.

13. Hal Hellman, *Great Feuds in Science: Ten of the Liveliest Disputes Ever* (New York: Wiley, 1988), p. xii.

25

DR. FREUD ON
IRRATIONAL VENGEANCE

In Bangladesh, approximately eight hundred Muslim militants chanted in protest of author Taslima Nasrin's contention that Islamic laws should be changed to give women more rights. The chant: "Arrest infidel Taslima and hang her."[1]

I t was now after 6 P.M. of the same day and Dr. Freud was still in the conference room poring over his reference books. The door was open since most of the agency's employees had left for the day.

Wendy Smith of the agency's public relations department poked her head through the door and said, "Hi, Dr. Freud, it's me."

Freud looked up, obviously irritated at being disturbed, but when he saw it was Wendy, he immediately relaxed and broke into a smile.

"Oh, Wendy, my dear. Come right in."

"Oh, good," Wendy gushed as she entered the room, carrying one art board covered with paper. "Do you mind if I sit down?"

"Not at all. Make yourself comfortable," Freud said, pointing to the chair opposite him across the table.

As she sat down, she said, "I hope you are in good health, doctor."

"Well, in my condition, it really doesn't matter, does it? Living, dying, quite frankly, it's all the same to me." Freud broke into a deep laugh as he thought about what he had said. Then, composing himself, he asked, "Now tell me, what can I do for you?"

"This will just take a moment, really. Samuel Ollander is ready with his first focus group tonight, reviewing the concepts of Dummy Bliss and Dummy Pain, which he told me you haven't accepted outright, but haven't dismissed, either."

She paused, waiting for a reaction from Freud, but detected none.

"Anyway," she continued, "Sam called me and said that the creatives had come up with another concept late today that he would like to test with the other concepts tonight. He asked me to run it by you first, before we send it over to him, if that is okay."

"That is fine, my dear. Please proceed."

Wendy placed the art board on the table and uncovered the paper shielding the headline, which read: "Dummy Vengeance."

"Do you get the idea?" Wendy asked.

Freud was staring at the headline.

"I'm not sure."

"But don't you see? It complements the concepts of Dummy Bliss and Dummy Pain, in that it reflects the irrationality of vengeance, which prolongs the disturbance of one's peace of mind."

"You'll have to clarify that for me, my dear."

Wendy paused, then said, "Okay, let me give you an actual example. When this concept was first explained to me by the agency writer assigned to it, an incident that happened to me just this last week came immediately to my mind. I mistakenly parked my car in someone else's parking space in my apartment-building garage. I was tired; I really don't know how it happened. Anyway, the next morning I came down and there was this nasty note placed under the windshield wiper saying how stupid I was to park in the wrong space. But worse, the person had apparently taken a sharp object and made a deep scratch along the entire length of my car."

"That is terrible."

"Yes, and when I complained to the building management about it, and they confronted the person who is assigned to that space about the scratch, he denied it. But I know he did it, in a moment of Dummy Vengeance. Do you get the idea?"

"Yes, now I do."

"Oh, good. Well anyway, it certainly crossed my mind to go back to that parking space and scratch that man's car in retaliation. I mean, there are many people who would do that, but it would just be another round of Dummy Vengeance. Do you see how well the phrase works? And if I actually went ahead and did scratch his car, then he would feel compelled to do something back to me and a feud might start between us."

Wendy paused and looked searchingly at Freud before she continued. "And then something odd would happen."

"Like what, my dear?"

"Well, each time either one of us succeeded in perpetrating a harmful act on the other, we would not only feel a release, but a rush of joy . . . irrational joy. It would be a form of Dummy Bliss, actually, to which we might become temporarily addicted as we continue with our vengeful acts of 'getting even.' He and I might even laugh and joke about these acts of vengeance to our friends, but deep down it will be creating disharmony in our lives that we could both do without."

Freud continued to stare at the headline on the card, stroking his beard. "It is an interesting concept, my dear."

"I think so," Wendy said, brightening at Freud's positive remark.

"I mean," she continued, "it really isn't that much of a stretch to go from my parking-space incident to feuds between nations or groups of people, like between the Israelis and the Palestinians. One act of terrorism leads to perpetual rounds of it. Talk about Dummy Vengeance, people getting killed and all." She paused and then continued. "Or back to situations in our everyday lives, what about families? Because of a senseless argument and then one vengeful act after another, family members might end up not talking to each other for years. In wealthy families, the arguments and vengeful acts can turn into lengthy lawsuits that may tear the families apart forever. Why can't these families just sit down and work things out? Don't you think with men like Jesus or Mahatma Gandhi or Martin Luther King Jr. if they were still alive, acting as mediators, that these feuds could be settled? Of course they could be, any feud could be with sensible compromise. But what gets in the way? Guess, Dr. Freud, guess what gets in the way."

"I hesitate to say."

"Well then, I will. What gets in the way is Dummy Vengeance. These feuds no longer become a matter of finding a compromise, they turn instead into a steady concentration on developing strategies for hurting the opposite party. What can I do to hurt him? What can I do to hurt her? What can I do to hurt them? That is what people think when they become addicted to this insidious Dummy Vengeance. Don't you agree?"

"I must tell you, Wendy, that you are beginning to sound very much like Samuel Ollander when presenting your case."

"I take that as a compliment, doctor. I have a very high opinion of Sam."

"That is good, so do I."

Wendy thought a minute.

"I don't know," she continued, "with all of these concepts developing from your study of the id, which we are branding as the Inner Dummy, I have felt an amazing enthusiasm well up within me."

"I can certainly see that."

"You see, sir, in our advertising campaign we can say to the world, look . . . these are all physical attributes of your brain. This Inner Dummy of ours is controlled by chemical reactions. The feelings that emanate from it are all chemical happenings. And that includes Dummy Pain and Dummy Bliss and Dummy Vengeance. Just because you feel these things doesn't mean they are always acting in your best interests. Once you have a perspective that allows you to see Dummy Vengeance for what it is, to take just one of the concepts, you don't have to follow its dictates. You can see its irrationality. So hold on, lock yourself in a room, if you have to, let it simmer down, let your rationality assume control, and then react in a reasoned, civilized manner. That, I think, is part of the message we want to send."

Wendy paused again, looking at Dr. Freud thoughtfully.

"So, Dr. Freud, can I send this sign over to Sam to test with the focus group tonight? Does it have your approval?"

"Yes, my dear, I believe it does, pending my final approval of the entire campaign, of course. The feeling of revenge can be overwhelming at times, and whether a simplistic approach to releasing or neutralizing it will be effective remains to be seen. But there can be no harm in Ollander showing this to his group of consumers."

"Well, then, thank you, Dr. Freud," Wendy said as she stood up to leave. She stared at him a moment, then said hesitatingly, "Sir, you wouldn't like to come along with me when I deliver this to Sam? His group is just down the street. Then right after, I am meeting my girlfriends again, at that bar I told you about. I've told them all about you and they are just dying to meet you. I know you will have a wonderful time. I certainly know that I will, being with you outside of this room."

Freud stared at Wendy and began to feel some embarrassment. "Ah, I don't know, my dear. Some other night, perhaps. I do have a lot of studying to do, unfortunately," he said as he pointed uncertainly down to his books.

"Another time, then," Wendy said, looking disappointed. "Good night, sir."

"Good night, Wendy. And please give your friends my fondest regards."

"I'll do that," she said as she left the room.

Again, Freud wondered if he should have gone with Wendy. He could feel something stirring, and after all, at least for the time being, he was no longer dead.

NOTE

1. Zay N. Smith, *Chicago Sun-Times*, September 21, 1998, p. 22.

2 6

SHAPING OUR
LIMBIC DRIVES

GENES AND THE TRAUMAS OF LIFE

In his Personal Memoirs, *Ulysses S.* Grant *described as follows the disputatious nature of Confederate general Braxton Bragg: "On one occasion . . . he was himself acting as post quartermaster and commissary. He was first lieutenant at the time, but his captain was detached on other duty. As commander of the company he made a requisition upon the quartermaster— himself—for something he wanted. As quartermaster he declined to fill the requisition. . . . As company commander he responded to this, urging that his requisition called for nothing but what he was entitled to, and that it was the duty of the quartermaster to fill it. As quartermaster he still persisted that he was right. In this condition of affairs, Bragg referred the whole matter to the commanding officer of the post. The latter, when he saw the nature of the matter referred, exclaimed: 'My God, Mr. Bragg, you have quarreled with every officer in the army, and now you are quarreling with yourself!' "[1]*

W hat makes us the way we are? Is it our genes or our environment? Is it nature or nurture? The enigma, for the most part, remains a contentious issue among academics. The five limbic programs we have described thus far are part of the enigma.

291

The behaviorists, beginning with John B. Watson in the 1920s, believed that while we had a genetic component, the slate was wiped clean by our environment. In his book *Nature and Nurture*, psychology professor Robert Plomin described the thinking of behaviorists like Watson as follows:

> From the start, behaviorism denied any role for hereditary differences. In his book, *Behaviorism*, published in 1925, John B. Watson concluded "that there is no such thing as an inheritance of capacity, talent, temperament, mental constitution and characteristics. These things again depend on training that goes on mainly in the cradle" (pp. 74–75). Although Watson recognized hereditary influence on physical traits, he denied any influence of heredity on behavioral traits and said that given sufficient environmental control, he could train any healthy baby to become a doctor, artist or thief, regardless of the child's heredity. Few would accept Watson's dictum today; nonetheless, his emphasis on nurture rather than nature continues to affect the social and behavioral sciences.[2]

Watson's beliefs remind me of the movie *Trading Places*, released in 1983, which focuses on a callous, one-dollar bet made between billionaires, one contending that he could take a man out of the gutter and train him to be president of their large investment company, the other believing that this would be impossible, that a person can only be as talented as his genes allow him to be. "It's all in the genes," he said.

Unfortunately the movie never resolved the issue, hardly addressing it after the opening scenes, but the initial suspense did serve to get our attention, because none of us is really sure how much our parents' genes determine what and who we've become, how much is attributable to their influences or those of others, and what we do all on our own.

One school of thought contends that genetics is paramount because it gives us a brain that determines the level of our predisposition for improvement after we are out of the womb. For example, we may emerge so mentally retarded that we are hardly aware of reality and so what our parents and others in our lives do for us may be immaterial, since we are unreachable in any event. Since any of us might have emerged in this state, it is theorized, then genetics is preeminent because from a base level of retardation, it determines how much our later conditioning might be allowed to shape us.

Most academics today believe that there is both a genetic and environmental basis to who we become as adults. To begin with, if we have older siblings, most of us emerge from the womb looking and acting different than they do. As Robert Plomin put it in *Nature and Nurture*:

Among behavioral geneticists, there is a saying that parents are environmentalists until they have more than one child. With one child, it seems possible to explain anything that happens. However, when their second child turns out to be different in many ways from the first child, parents realize that they did not treat the two children differently enough to account for the behavioral differences that are so apparent between them. With their second child, parents become more accepting of the possibility of hereditary differences.[3]

Plomin later points out that the genetic relatedness of identical twins is 100 percent: "they are essentially clones from a genetic point of view." Parents and their offspring are considered first-degree relatives and have a genetic relatedness of 50 percent. In other words, the child has only 50 percent of the genes of either parent. Genetic relatedness would then decrease among grandchildren to 25 percent, great-grandchildren to 12.5 percent, great-great grandchildren to 6.25 percent, great-great-great grandchildren to 3.12 percent and among great-great-great-great-grandchildren to 1.06 percent.

As an interesting aside, in many cultures of the past and some to this day, girls marry at the age of twelve and have a child at the age of thirteen. If in one such family, each succeeding generation of firstborns were women who married at twelve and had a child at thirteen, a woman could become a great-great-great-great-great-grandmother at the age of ninety-two. When she looked at the most recent offspring with a genetic relatedness to herself of just above .5 percent she'd be hard pressed to find any similarity.

So tell me, what is all this concern many of us have about keeping our names and heredity alive, when at the age of ninety-two we could be looking at offspring who might be almost as remote from us as our next-door neighbor, who could have descended from our same family tree, but our forebears just lost track of? I saw one statement made by someone in authority who said that only six generations ago, all of us who have survived within our cultures were somehow related.

My first ex-wife, Phyllis, had bright red hair. No one in her family had red hair and her parents didn't know of any ancestors who had red hair, although there was some hint that perhaps a great-great-grandfather living in Russia had red hair. The point is, when the genetic threads of two humans combine in the birth process, only 50 percent of the genetic content of either parent is included on the genetic thread of the newborn. And significant numbers of these might be repressed if the specific hereditary element, which geneticists sometimes call *phenotypes*, is *recessive* and the one received from the opposite parent is *dominant*.

Thus, Phyllis's red hair may have been passed down as a phenotype on the genetic threads of her forebears, but may have remained recessive in comparison to its dominant counterpart that created brunettes, until her parents created an egg in which the phenotype for red hair on her genetic thread became at last dominant. Anyway, that red hair certainly attracted me, when I first saw her, so hats off to those red-hair phenotypes. According to science writer William Wright, author of *Born That Way*, "Geneticists have come to consider behavior (or behavioral tendencies) as just another phenotype."[4]

The passing along of behavioral phenotypes through several generations before they emerge may be one reason two mild and meek parents may bear a child with a high power drive and low capacity for feeling guilt or compassion, who is aggressive, disobedient, and violent when opposed. The parents, unable to quell the aggression, become embarrassed and wonder what it was they did, when in fact it was probably only the luck of the genetic lottery. Like Phyllis's red hair, these behavioral phenotypes might have been extant on the genes carried through many generations and only now emerged in their present combination through a matter of sheer chance.

John Watson, who died in 1958, might have altered his theories about the environment if he had lived long enough to see the major studies done on the subject, particularly those centering around twins reared apart. These studies have helped provide geneticists with their best clues for determining the weight that both genetics and environmental conditioning have on our behavioral propensities.

There are two types of twins, fraternal, referred to by academics as *dizygotic* or DZ, for short, and identical, referred to as *monozygotic* or MZ. Fraternal twins derive from the fertilization of two eggs, which according to writer Lawrence Wright in his *Twins, and What They Tell Us About Who We Are*, is an "event that may take place at different times and occasionally by different fathers." Identical twins derive from a single egg. He goes on to say:

> Theoretically, DZ twins (fraternal) are no more alike than ordinary siblings. MZ twins (identical) are thought to result from the splitting of a single fertilized egg or zygote. It is a form of asexual reproduction. MZ twins have identical genes—they are clones—whereas DZ twins share an average of only fifty percent of their genes, thus creating a statistical opportunity that provides a basis of comparison for nearly every human quality.[5]

The study referred to most frequently in books on this subject was the Minnesota Study of Twins Reared Apart, which began in 1979, when Professor Thomas J. Bouchard Jr. first learned from a newspaper article about a pair of twins who were adopted by different families. Laurence Wright, in the same book, described the discovery as follows:

> It was odd enough that both of the twins were named Jim, but it was utterly uncanny that each man had married and divorced a woman named Linda, then married a woman named Betty; the names of their firstborn child were James Alan Lewis and James Allen Springer, each had owned a dog named Toy. The article went on to say that both Lewis and Springer enjoyed carpentry and mechanical drawings and had spent family vacations on the same beach in Florida. Both had worked part time in law enforcement . . . shared a taste for Miller Lite beer and chain-smoked Salem cigarettes.[6]

Thus began the fascinating study at Minnesota of twins reared apart, which, as of 1997, according to Wright, "included 132 individuals who are identical twins; two sets of identical triplets; another two sets of mixed triplets," plus a number of fraternal twins.

In his book *DNA Destiny*, brain researcher R. Grant Steen made the following observation about the split twin study:

> Overall, about 50 percent of all personality traits that could be assessed by testing were shared between identical twins, even though these twins shared no environment. These shared traits must be the result of shared genes, which is astonishing evidence for the heritability of personality. In fact, identical twins reared together were no more similar for personality traits than were identical twins reared apart, which is convincing testimony to the power of the genes in determining personality.[7]

In many of the books on this subject, each of the authors seems to put a unique twist on the implications of the Minnesota study as well as other studies relating to the origins of genetic behavior. For example, William Wright, in *Born That Way*, made the following observation:

> With humans, the assumption is that a certain minimal level of shelter, diet and nurturing places the developing child within the normal range of environment, the range in which the genome would express itself as nature intended. On the other hand, a child who has been beaten, starved,

or chained in a closet clearly fell outside the normal range and, developmentally speaking, all bets were off. The environment must push genes pretty far before they react with any changes whatsoever in the organism.[8]

And so the question remains which influence is stronger for each individual, genetics or the environment, since no two individuals are alike? The puzzle reminds me of the famous apocryphal quote about the power of advertising: "I know that half of my advertising works. The problem is I don't know which half."

Academics studying personality traits have now developed tables of correlation that indicate the degree to which specific traits are influenced by genetics versus the environment. R. Grant Steen in *DNA Behavior* writes:

> Several different tests showed that even something as nebulous as social attitudes are about 40 percent heritable, while the extent to which twins adhered to the same traditional values was 53 percent heritable. The biggest single difference that could be found between the twins was in "nonreligious social attitudes," which are apparently much influenced by education, but were still 34 percent heritable. . . . Several years ago, a compilation of four different studies, which together involved over 30,000 pairs of twins, suggested that extroversion and neuroticism are both about 50 percent heritable . . . agreeableness is less heritable at about 39 percent.[9]

Steen also stated: "Good evidence seems to show that the heritability of personality traits declines with age. This is consistent with the interpretation that we can indeed learn and grow as we age, and that some of this learning or the changes in our standing as older adults can modify personality traits."

In other words, we need not go through life being totally victimized by our genetics, which should be good news for a normal person with parents who have lunatic behavioral traits.

The fact that our personality traits might change over time reminded me of John D. Rockefeller Sr., who, according to Ron Cherkow's book *Titan*, was absolutely ruthless as a young businessman,[10] certainly a Number Eight or Nine on the power scale. Yet, after he succeeded in making an enormous fortune, he focused on philanthropy and his ruthlessness diminished and eventually ceased or was unnoticeable.

We might surmise that this happened because the expectations of his power drive were met, which released him from its "captivity," allowing a natural kindness, wit, and sense of humor to emerge. How many other kindly, elderly, and successful men have we seen whose present demeanor belies years of ruthlessness? On the other hand, how many Number Tens have we seen who are still clamoring for more power and wealth on their deathbeds, held "captive" by their power drives until the very end.

Simply living long enough may be one of the remedies we might seek out in our battle against our Inner Dummy, when it makes us act irrationally and nothing else we or anyone else have tried to alter it has worked.

Psychology writer Judith Rich Harris in her very interesting book, *The Nurture Assumption: Why Children Turn Out the Way They Do*, published in 1998, summed up the entire issue of nature versus nurture as follows:

> People differ from one another in many ways; some are more impulsive, others more cautious; some are more agreeable, others more argumentative. About half of the variation in impulsiveness can be attributed to people's genes, the other half to their experiences. The same is true for agreeableness. The same is true for most other psychological characteristics.[11]

Between the ages of fourteen and twenty, I was a camp counselor during the summer months, most years with a cabin full of boys ranging from ages five to eight. Invariably there were always one or two boys who were model campers—up on time, made their beds, were active and sportsmanlike in conduct—and one or two boys who were extremely difficult—hard to get out of bed, fussy about what they ate, obdurate during activities, and intent on harassing the pet dogs of the owners. Then there were the boys in the middle, not exactly model campers, but not real problems either. During parents' day I would recall thinking that most of the parents of the problem boys were just as nice as the parents of the model boys. I wasn't giving much thought to nature versus nurture back then, but the observation always stuck.

So how much is nature and how much is nurture that makes each individual what she or he is, now that we know that both are involved? Based on what geneticists have learned from their research, one might propose that a baby emerging from the womb already has the intensities of its limbic drives in set positions on the scales, ready to be adjusted up or down, by the conditioning of his or her environment.

As child psychologist Kenneth Wenning put the obvious in his book *Winning Cooperation from Your Child!*:

> Studies show that children are born with different temperaments. Some children are born friendly, outgoing, flexible, and cooperative. Other chil-

dren are difficult, rigid, and aggressive. Your child's temperament plays a role in how he or she behaves and how well he or she follows your rules.[12]

I had dinner with Dr. Hefter one evening and we began discussing the influence that the environment might have on an individual's genetic propensity in relation to the core limbic instincts or drives. I told him about the correlations of the twin studies, but that I couldn't find any research that indicated why certain personality traits of one individual might be shaped more by the environment than those of another individual. He then referred to a concept of "genetic loading," which I found to be extremely insightful.

In a nutshell, this would mean that a child born with an extremely high setting on the power scale—for example, a genetic Eight, Nine, or Ten—would be less subject to the influences of the environment than someone lower on the scale. In other words, a stronger genetic predisposition—a higher "loading"— would be more capable of withstanding assaults or other influences from the environment, than a weaker genetic predisposition or "loading."

The genetic weaponry of a power-driven child might be further enhanced if he or she was born with a low genetic predisposition on the nurturance scale, with little capacity for exhibiting shame, guilt, sensitivity, compassion, or an ability to form attachments in general. Being in the midst of a warm and caring family might have little effect on this child, certainly not as much as a child in the middle or higher ranges, who might be more predisposed to a nurturing influence. On the nurturance scale, a high "genetic loading" would thus mean a lack of it, which in the wilderness might have proved to be an advantage.

This transposition might also apply to the survival program, with a strong "genetic loading" protecting a low setting on the survival scale, which offers a natural lack of fear. This might be exemplified in the child who more easily takes punishment from a parent who beats him incessantly, even for the slightest of transgressions, and practically dares the parent to give him more.

If a child has extremely low survival and nurturance settings in combination with a high power drive, the potential would exist for the child to become the metaphoric "bad seed," no matter what strategies the parents might apply. While the child might otherwise be pleasant and well mannered, one day he might walk into the school library with a gun and begin shooting whoever's in sight, because of some small slights by his fellow students that his Inner Dummy perceived as major onslaughts.

We would soon find the parents in the courtroom wracked with guilt, thinking they did something wrong, when in actuality it was probably all in the luck of the draw, with genetics and its strong "loading" factor playing the major role. The environmental punishment inflicted by the boy's *peers*, the kidding and the taunts, might have been just enough to push him over the edge. Judith Rich Harris contends in *The Nuture Assumption* that the influence of peers *can be more destructive than the attitudes and actions of parents*.

In a nutshell, one might summarize the concept of "genetic loading" as follows: the higher the "loading," the less effect the environment might have; the lower the "loading," the more effect the environment might have. It's an interesting theory.

If the first sixty-four-thousand-dollar question of this chapter was the issue of nature versus nurture, the second such question has to do with how we can change the nature of these settings for the better or the worse. Whatever combination we have of these instinctive settings at any time in our lives, probably from the age of three or four on as many parents would attest, is what shapes our personalities. Most of our hundreds of personality traits, it would appear, build upon this handful of basic instinctive settings. So, in attempting to change the settings, we would be tinkering with our personalities as a whole, which most of us recognize as one of the most difficult of all tasks.

We have heard the comment "Look at how Fred has changed, being nice to his employees." The response: "No, no, he's just out to get them to work harder this month, or something like that. You can't change a leopard's spots."

Changing those spots can be difficult, indeed.

It is apparent, however, to most of us, from our own observations, that the one thing that can change those spots quickly and dramatically is a *traumatic event*.

In this sense, a reply to the response about Fred might be, "No, no, you're wrong, you can change a person's spots. Fred's little daughter died six months ago, and I tell you it has changed him. He is kinder, more considerate, less power driven. We have all seen it."

In the jargon of this book, we might describe a traumatic event as an intense, dramatic assault that strikes with enough force to get through to the heretofore impervious Inner Dummy to change its stubborn limbic settings. The amount of change that takes place would presumably be controlled by a combination of the intensity of the trauma and the vulnerability or the strength of the "loading" of the limbic programs involved.

Most of us can remember traumatic incidents in our lives that appeared to reshape our outlook or those of others. It might have been the death of a parent, a sibling, or a child. It might have been being abandoned by a parent or another loved one. It might have been a violent encounter, sexual abuse, a serious car or other accident, an armed robbery, or being in the front lines in a battle. It might have been a flood, a tornado, a hurricane, or a severe earthquake. It might have been an insightful spiritual moment; a turning to Jesus, for example, which changed the lives of St. Francis of Assisi, Charles Colson, and countless others. It might have been a marriage to or an association with the "right person." It might have been a new job or an avocation, where we are recognized for our abilities. It might have been a "cathartic insight" that took place during one moment after months or years of psychotherapy. It might have been the loss of a fortune or a painful divorce that caused a dramatic change in our lives. Or it might have been a revelation that simply came to us while eating breakfast one day.

While we have recognized that traumas can be life-changing events, unfortunately, as psychiatry professor Judith Lewis Herman points out in *Trauma and Recovery*, depending on their intensity and our individual vulnerability to them, traumas can cause hysteria, depression, and other disorders, in the course of altering our personality traits for the better or worse.[15] Further, we might be apparently normal, in the mid-ranges of all of the limbic scales, when a painful trauma might only change us for the worse. On the other hand, a traumatic event may involve little pain at all, such as a spiritual awakening or a "cathartic insight," which might alter personality traits without disturbing our mental balance.

Military basic training or "boot camp" might be viewed as an example of a *controlled trauma* because its objective is to alter strong or distinctive personality traits so that one no longer thinks as an individual with choices, but as a member of a military unit that will follow orders without question, even under the imminent prospect of death. In the vernacular of the world of limbic drives, one might view the goals of basic training as raising or lowering as necessary, one's positions on the power, territorial, survival, and nurturance scales, so that one is a Two, Three, or Four. In other words, low enough on the power and territorial scales to give up status and space to the greater needs of the military unit; low enough on the survival scale to be more confident and less fearful, and low enough on the nurturance scale to be toughened and less sensitive.

I went through basic training in the army during the 1950s and personally witnessed its effects on myself and the other men in my platoon. Some of the immediate techniques that affected our power and territorialism included shaving our hair; wearing identical clothing; living in an open barracks with strangers; being relentlessly intimidated by a tough sergeant; made to adhere to a strict, demanding schedule; and for a final indignity made to use toilets without booths.

My friend Bob Schwartz told me that when he was going through basic training, he would wait to go to the bathroom until 2 A.M., so he could sit and read his newspaper without other people watching him. I learned to enjoy this same experience chatting with my seatmates after a while as if we were all having dinner together.

Fear, intimidation, lack of sleep, and loneliness are the four factors that boot camp experts point to as their initial modus operandi in getting all recruits to conform, with the toughest of the recruits getting the roughest treatment. At the same time, the training is aimed at making recruits less fearful and more self-confident with such techniques as body-building exercises and instructions in self-defense.

Of course, of all the institutions on earth, none is more visible than the military in general when it comes to an illustration of the power scale. Uniforms and insignias designate your position, from lowly buck privates to varying designations of sergeants, lieutenants, captains, majors, colonels, and generals. If you are a buck private and formerly the CEO of a large company, as happened with some who were drafted during World War II, you still have to salute a lieutenant who might have worked for you as a clerk. Power and rank is everything in the military, including the types and numbers of medals you wear on your chest, which are an additional status symbol.

I saw many men who entered basic training as Number Eights and Nines on the power scale come out as ostensibly changed men, properly deferential and obedient. I saw others on the lower and opposite end of the scale come out with a prouder bearing and more self-confidence. I saw men on both extremes of the scales come close to "cracking" under the pressure, with one or two suffering breakdowns. The process of "cracking" the high-power recruits was referred to as reaching their "breaking points." The idea apparently was to "break" and thus "tame" the high-powered trainees, just as you might a spirited horse, and the process probably has similarities.

The military also works to *raise* power drives by sending potential leaders to academies like West Point, where the aim is to transform them through a combination of a "boot camp" atmosphere with its intimidation, and leadership training. So obviously, the military's idea of a controlled trauma environment can work both ways.

While my descriptions don't do justice to the traumatic environment of a "boot camp," they do make it apparent that it takes a traumatic event or process to raise or lower our position on the five limbic scales, including the sexual, which wasn't part of the basic training process in the 1950s, but has intruded itself today in the coed military.

Rape, for example—whether the victim is a female recruit or a male in prison—and other forms of sexual abuse can create a trauma that can affect not only our position on the sexual scale, but on all of the other scales as well. A rape may make us more fearful or phobic (survival), less sensitive to others (nurturance), more concerned with who occupies our space (territorial), and less or more driven to power. Judith Lewis Herman in *Trauma and Recovery*, writes that "traumatic events overwhelm the ordinary systems of care that give people a sense of control, connection, and meaning."[14] Coincidently, she also describes the concept of a "breaking point," as related to the varying forms of torture experienced by prisoners of war. She implies that those who are less fearful—in limbic parlance, lower on the survival scale—would take longer to reach a "breaking point," than those more fearful. Interestingly enough, Dr. Herman compares the traumas experienced by prisoners of war as being similar to those of wives being held captive by the demands and intimidation of their power-driven and violent husbands.

In terms of "breaking points," we have seen how the nurturance program in general remains highly vulnerable to change under traumatic conditions. Recall how Iris Chang's *The Rape of Nanking* describes how perfectly normal Japanese men quickly became "desensitized," a form of "breaking point," by the horrors of war and were able to learn quickly to kill children with bayonets.[15] Some actually appeared to enjoy themselves in an extreme example of Dummy Bliss. As Dr. Herman put it: "Traumatic events call into question basic human relationships. They breach the attachments of family, friendship, love, and community. They shatter the construction of the self that is formed and sustained in relation to others."

Many of us will wonder, when we've learned that someone we know has been involved in a traumatic event, "How did they come out of it?" Did it "break their spirit"? We might ask this not knowing that we are using an idiom for recognizing a reduction in the power program. We appear to know innately that traumas change us in some way. And we can surmise that these changes are rooted in shifts in the intensity of our core limbic drives.

The *New York Times* in an interview with the Miami Dolphins quarterback Dan Marino, after he recovered from an injury to his Achilles tendon which almost ended his career, reported that he said: "After I hurt my Achilles, that kind of woke me up a little bit." The newspaper also reported, "There are signs, too, that Marino has mellowed from his fire-eating days of bristling at almost anybody who erred."[16]

We can also recall motion pictures we've seen about the land-hungry western rancher who will force neighbors into foreclosures and bankrupt-cies, or threaten to kill to get them off the land. But then one day his son is murdered in a gunfight and instead of taking revenge, the father "sees the light," and becomes fatherly to his neighbors.

Some of us are obviously more impervious to this kind of change than others. Clinical psychologist Emmett Early in his book, *The Raven's Return: The Influence of Psychological Trauma on Individuals and Culture*, made some interesting observations about the relationship between the intensity of a trauma and the vulnerability of the individual:

> It is generally believed that the less consciousness or strength of identity the individual has, the less intense the trauma stimulus needs to be to overwhelm the individual. . . . A low-intensity trauma can, at the right time, or in a sequence that follows previous traumas, create a trauma response that is beyond the level expected by an objective observer.[17]

We might easily substitute the phrase "genetic loading" for strength of identity, even though that "loading" might have been strengthened or weak-ened by the influences of environment, particularly if the genetics were in the mid-ranges to begin with.

Dr. Early then goes on to present nine levels of trauma that relate the vulnerability of the individual to the intensity of the trauma, either actual or perceived. His first three levels illustrate mild mishaps to children, at which age the "threats to person are perceived as endless." In other words, when we are children, the traumas we encounter are greatly magnified.

One of the best examples of a person who was less vulnerable to a trauma and who might be viewed as an extreme, "genetically loaded" adult would be Adolf Hitler, who might be portrayed as the prototypical Number Ten on the power scale. You just couldn't walk up to him and say, "Adolf, you are killing millions of people out there. Let's go out and have a beer and talk about it." A Number Ten is not only impervious to rational persuasion but apparently to the most visceral of traumas as well. Hitler remained unmoved until the final moments of his life when his armies and cities were devastated and millions of his own people were dead because of his actions.

He personally survived a bomb blast, an assassination attempt. Rather than "softening" him, it served to "harden" him. While he was probably affected with punishing emotions because of his failures—his id had to be some kind of classic case—he presumably remained a Number Ten until the very end, never bowing to defeat or admitting that he was wrong in any way.

If Hitler were that western rancher and his only son was killed, he would have probably hired an army to wipe out all the remaining settlers around him. And those in the next county as well, just for good measure.

Not all behavior modification requires a trauma. As humans we have the ability to think, to be aware of our environment. If a group of people we respect tells us something about our personalities that is holding us back from advancing in our careers, or being content in our families, or among our friends, we have the capacity to become aware of it, to understand that since we have an Inner Dummy within us, we are susceptible to being "captured" by emotions, feelings, and drives that may be irrational, bothersome, or insufferable to others. If we recognize these problems and admit to them, there are remedies we might use short of a self-induced trauma to change our outlook. But before we get to these remedies, there is one more program that we need to describe. I have avoided it till now because it is the only limbic program that, as humans, we don't share with the animals. It is one that we have all to ourselves and it throws Dr. McLean's theory of the triune system of the brain up for grabs.

Of course, we first need another visit with Dr. Freud.

COMMENTARY BY DR. HEFTER

The interaction of genetic factors and environmental influences is an old story by now. My guess is that it has been known implicitly for thousands of years, but that for narcissistic, political (in the broad sense), and economic reasons, an emphasis has been placed on one or the other. To say "they were born that way" in describing individuals one looks down upon can be seen as a way of saying "our genes are better than yours, and therefore we have a natural right to have whatever we get."

Marxist theory articulated the importance, in its own language, of "nurture" as the dominant force in constructing a society. Perhaps one of the reasons for the relative failure thus far of the longevity of governments based primarily on nurturance almost exclusively is the nonrecognition of the crucial role played by heredity factors. Regimes overly emphasizing what we are born with, of course, may be making the opposite error, and fail ultimately because they do not recognize well enough how potent non-hereditary factors are. For example, French royalty drastically misperceived what was fermenting in the country in the late 1780s, leading to the subsequent French Revolution.

The issue of trauma as a factor in personality is being given increasing recognition in the scientific community. A particular area of interest is the possible effect of trauma, or for that matter any nongenetic, experiential factor, on the biochemical makeup of the individual, including the neurological system. There is evidence that life experiences, both negative and positive, may contribute to an alteration of neural receptors and transmitters. In other words, the genetic base may be modified. The emerging information in this area may well lead to a demonstration on the molecular level of what our common sense has been telling us for a long time. It also obviously puts greater emphasis on our potential to improve our therapeutic approaches.

NOTES

1. Ulysses S. Grant, *Personal Memoirs* (1885; reprint, Lincoln: University of Nebraska Press, 1996), p. 388.

2. Robert Plomin, *Nature and Nurture: An Introduction to Behavioral Genetics* (Belmont, Calif.: Brooks/Cole, 1990), p. 7.

3. Ibid., p. 8.

4. Robert Wright, *Born That Way: Genes, Behavior, Personality* (New York: Knopf, 1998), p. 6.

5. Lawrence Wright, *Twins: And What They Tell Us About Who We Are* (New York: Wiley, 1997), p. 11.

6. Ibid., p. 44.

7. R. Grant Steen, *DNA and Destiny: Nature and Nurture in Human Behavior* (New York: Plenum Press, 1996), p. 169.

8. Wright, *Born That Way*, p. 60.

9. Steen, *DNA and Destiny*, p. 170.

10. Ron Chernow, *Titan* (New York: Random House, 1998), n.p.

11. Judith R. Harris, *The Nurture Assumption: Why Children Turn Out the Way They Do* (New York: Simon & Schuster, 1998), p. 23.

12. Kenneth Wenning, *Winning Cooperation from Your Child: A Comprehensive Method to Stop Defiant and Aggressive Behavior in Children* (Northvale, N.J.: Jason Aronson, 1996), p. 17.

13. Judith L. Herman, *Trauma and Recovery: The Aftermath of Violence from Domestic Abuse to Political Terror* (New York: BasicBooks, 1992), p. 33.

14. Ibid.

15. Iris Chang, *The Rape of Nanking: The Forgotten Holocaust of World War II* (New York: BasicBooks, 1997), p. 56.

16. Charlie Nobles, *New York Times*, August 6, 1998, p. C4.

17. Emmett Early, *The Raven's Return: The Influence of Psychological Trauma on Individuals and Culture* (Wilmette, Ill.: Chiron Publications, 1993), p. 11.

27

DR. FREUD'S ENCOUNTER
WITH A PUNCHING BAG

An armed robber in Colorado Springs, Colorado, who robbed nineteen stores in twenty-eight days had his holdup note laminated.[1]

D r. Freud looked up suddenly as Peter Norton, vice president of sales of the Manchester Doll Company, burst into the conference room, carrying a large, wrapped object, followed by Jenny Kagan, the company's communications director.

"Hey, hey, Dr. Freud," Norton boomed out as he laid the object on the conference table and walked around to shake hands, not noticing the look of irritation on Freud's face. He took Freud's hand in a hard grip and said, "My, sir, how I have missed you. There hasn't been a day gone by when I haven't talked about you. Isn't that right, Jenny, sweetheart?"

He looked over his shoulder at Jenny, who was looking sympathetically at Dr. Freud.

"That's right, Peter," she said laconically, winking at Dr. Freud as Norton turned back to him.

"She's a great looker, isn't she, Dr. Freud?" Peter said leaning close to

Freud's face and breathing out the fetid breath that Freud had come to loathe.

"Peter, for god's sake," Jenny said, "give the doctor a little breathing room, won't you? You're right in his face."

"Ah, I just wanted to get close to this great man. You don't mind, do you, doctor?" Norton replied. But before Freud could respond, Norton dropped his hand and began walking around the table, saying, "And anyway, we don't want to take any more of your time than we have to, do we, doctor?"

Freud now attempted to compose himself and said, "I'm afraid, Mr. Norton, that nobody informed me of your visit. They usually do. And how are you today, Jenny? You I am always happy to see. Norton I am never too happy to see."

Norton, now alongside Jenny, slapped the table hard with his hand and burst out, "That is great, doctor, just great, you have such a tremendous wit." Norton was guffawing. "My god, Jenny, isn't that a great wit?"

Freud and Jenny were now looking sympathetically at each other.

"Again, doctor," she said, "my advice is to ignore Norton's remarks. The man has absolute zero sensitivity."

"Hey, Jenny, just agree to go out to dinner with me one night," Norton said, "and you'll see how sensitive I can be. But after dinner, once I get you home, whammo."

"Norton, you would do all of us an immense favor if you would just drop dead."

Norton looked at Freud, "She is great, isn't she, doc?" Freud looked embarrassed and didn't respond.

"Aren't you interested in what we have in the package?" Norton asked, pointing at the large, wrapped object on the conference table.

"To tell you the truth, Mr. Norton, I am not interested at all."

"Playing coy, again, aren't you, doc? Well, don't worry, you're going to love it. It's another Dr. Freud Inner Dummy product and it's hot out of the model shop. The minute I saw it demonstrated, I wanted to surprise you with it. That's why we didn't make an appointment or anything because I knew you'd be just as thrilled as I was."

Jenny looked away from Norton unbelieving, shaking her head.

"Okay, Jenny, dear," Norton said to her, "get your camera out, I'd like to get a shot of the doc with the product when he first sees it, you know, for our publicity people. I can see the photo caption in my mind, 'Dr. Freud's first reaction to a new Inner Dummy product.' The trade press will eat the photo up, help us get distribution in all the right retail outlets."

"Please, Norton," she replied. "Don't you think you ought to show this thing to the doctor first, before we start taking photos?"

"Are you questioning my keen sense for publicity, Jenny?" Then looking at Dr. Freud, he continued, "Women, what do they know about these things?"

"*Norton,*" Jenny shouted with indignation, "the reason I don't carry a gun in my handbag is that there is a 100 percent chance that if I had one right now I'd shoot you in that big mouth of yours."

She began yanking the camera out of her bag, throwing accessories on the table.

"Excuse my anger, Dr. Freud," she said through gritted teeth.

"Quite justifiable, my dear," Freud responded, "quite justifiable."

"Doesn't she look pretty when she's angry, doc?"

"Norton, please shut up, otherwise I'm walking right out of here."

Norton looked at her momentarily. "Ah," he said quietly, "I see I have really upset you. I apologize my dear, I was only trying to have a little fun."

Jenny, now adjusting her camera, didn't look up. "Just shut up," she said.

"I will indeed, except for the demonstration of our new product," he said, brightening up and looking enthusiastically at Dr. Freud. "Are you ready, doc?"

"Does it matter?" Freud replied.

"Oh, you're great, sir, really great." First he pulled a laptop computer out of one of Jenny's shoulder bags. Then he lifted the package and began unwrapping the paper covering it. Holding it upright on the table, he said, "Can you guess what this is, sir?"

Freud was gaping at the object, dumbfounded, while Jenny snapped a photo.

"Well, I'll tell you what it is. We are calling this the *Dr. Freud Inner Dummy Punching Bag.*"

"What?" Freud gasped.

"That's it, sir, it's a punching bag, but not just an ordinary punching bag—it is computerized. Here, let me set it up."

Norton put the punching bag, which was apparently inflatable, on the floor. It had an attached, plastic base that appeared to be filled with sand or gravel. The bag itself, above the base, was a round cylinder about four feet high. Attached to it was a smaller circular bag, shaped like a face. The bag had two electrical connections at its base. Norton plugged one into the wall. The other line he connected to the laptop.

"This won't take but a minute, doc," Norton said as he booted up the computer. "You know, I am deathly afraid of computers, but I wanted to prove that the program for the punching bag is so simple that even I could do it."

After a moment, a color photo image began appearing in the face-shaped head of the punching bag, looking almost lifelike.

"You want to know who this guy is, doc?" Freud didn't respond, staring in a trance at the punching bag. "Well, I know you're too excited to talk. But I'll tell you anyway. The name of this guy is Werner Davis. I used to work for him at the Collins Doll Company and he fired me for no cause at all, no cause. And so I dislike him, I dislike him intensely. It was a year ago and it was hard for me to find a new job, because he spread the word around the industry that I was lazy. Lazy? Can you imagine that? Me lazy? Well, I really dislike this guy and this is one of the big ideas behind this punching bag. If you really dislike somebody, you can scan their picture into the computer, which transmits it to the head of the punching bag. Then as you punch the head, the face will actually change, become more distressed as you punch it."

Freud, now showing some interest in the product, said, "Change? What do you mean, change?"

"I mean the face changes. You see how happy Werner Davis looks now?"

The photo image had a smiling face.

"Well, watch what happens."

Norton slipped on some thin boxing gloves and began hitting the face. A voice was heard from the computer speaker, which said, "No, no, don't hit me."

Norton continued hitting the bag and looked over at Freud. "The voice is actually Werner's. Our computer people synthesized it from a tape I had of him conducting an office seminar."

As Norton continued hitting the bag, he said, "Now watch the face. And turn up the speaker volume, dear," he said to Jenny, who adjusted the volume. Then, as Freud watched, Werner's face began to change from a smiling face to a distressed face.

"Amazing," Freud said.

"I knew you'd love this once you saw the whole demonstration," Norton said to Freud, looking back as he kept punching.

"But it even gets better."

Finally, Werner's face literally began to cry with weeping coming from the loudspeaker. "I give up, Peter," the voice from the computer speaker said, sobbing. "Please stop it, I was entirely wrong, you were right, I never should have fired you. You were never lazy. It was an excuse I made up. I was stupid . . . please, stop hitting me."

Norton gave the punching bag a few more punches and then stopped as the face continued its sobbing expressions and the speaker kept repeating, "I was stupid...please stop hitting me."

"You see?" Norton said, looking at Dr. Freud, sweat dripping off of his face. "I feel just great. Just great. I got even with that SOB even though it was just a computer simulation. You get the idea, Dr. Freud? You can hit an ordinary punching bag when you're really angry at someone to give you a release. This is far better, I can tell you, than just hitting that ordinary punching bag without any personality."

"Amazing," Freud repeated.

"You know, Norton," Jenny said, "if I had a picture of you right now, I'd scan it in and hit that bag with your lousy face on it until I dropped."

Norton brightened immediately. "But don't you see, my dear, that's the idea. Isn't this wonderful? Isn't this just the greatest thing?"

Then Norton looked slyly at Dr. Freud. "And I have a surprise for you, sir."

"I hope not another crazy product."

"No, sir. Now watch the punching bag and see whose face now appears on the screen."

Norton bent over the laptop and Werner Davis's picture disappeared.

"Watch carefully now, Dr. Freud."

Just as he said this, the face lit up again and Freud gasped, "My god," he said. "That is Carl Jung."

"Exactly, sir. And as I recall, you became very upset with him, extremely angry, is that not correct?"

Freud didn't respond immediately. He was looking at the face of a smiling Carl Jung on the punching bag.

"Want to take a few punches at him?" Norton asked.

"*Ach, Gott,* no. That is barbaric."

"Okay, I'll do the job for you. Jenny, turn up the volume again." She did and Norton began punching Jung's face, with the voice coming out of the computer begging for mercy.

"My god," Freud said, his face whitening. "That is Jung's voice."

"Correct, sir. Our computer people did it from a tape that Dr. Jung made in 1960, shortly before his death."

As Norton continued punching, Jung's face began turning from a smile to a frown and his voice said, "Please, Herr Freud, I didn't mean to betray you. It was stupid of me. You were right in your theories, I was wrong to get messed up with the mystics. Please, I am begging you, stop hitting me."

"You want me to stop, doc?" Norton asked over his shoulder as he kept punching away, with Jung now turning into a sobbing wreck, pleading for forgiveness.

Freud leaned on the table, watching intently, engrossed in what was taking place.

"Well, enough, doc?"

Finally, Freud said, "*No, keep hitting that no-good bastard.*"

Norton burst out laughing as did Jenny. He stopped punching, took off his gloves, and said, "Well, you see what I mean? This product has some real potential."

Freud, now embarrassed, slumped back in his chair.

"Please," he waved at both Norton and Jenny. "Please, excuse me. I am embarrassed, I got carried away. Please, take that thing out of here."

"That we will, doc, that we will," Norton said wiping his sweating face with a large handkerchief. "But you've got to admit it has possibilities."

"Oh, my god," Freud replied.

"Come on, Peter," Jenny said, "let's get out of here. We've taken enough of Dr. Freud's time and you can see he is upset. I apologize for this intrusion, doctor, and for Norton's abrupt demonstration, with no warning and his use of Dr. Jung's picture. There was no call for that."

Freud replied weakly, "It is okay, my dear. He was only doing his job. But now, if you will both leave me for a while, I have some thinking to do."

"Hey, no problem, doc," Norton replied as he disconnected the bag and began wrapping it up. "But what can I tell my design guys and model makers? Do we have a winner here or do we have a winner?"

"Please, Mr. Norton, that decision will have to await the final presentation of all the concepts."

"I understand. Well, good day, doc. Hope to see you again, soon. Here, Jenny," he said, handing her the computer, "you take the laptop." She took it and placed it in her shoulder bag.

Then she said to Dr. Freud, "My apologies once again, doctor. I hope we didn't disturb you too much."

"There is no problem, Jenny, and it was very nice seeing you again."

They both left the room and Freud was left staring into space, entranced by what he had just witnessed. Then he began to smile. That traitor Jung got just what he deserved.

NOTE

1. Zay N. Smith, *Chicago Sun-Times*, November 2, 1998, p. 30.

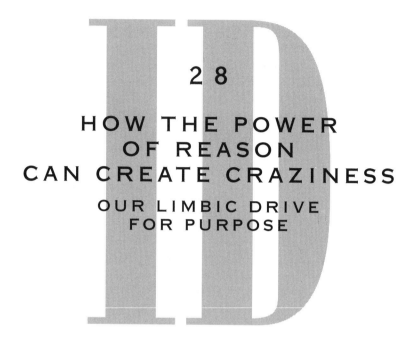

2 8

HOW THE POWER
OF REASON
CAN CREATE CRAZINESS
OUR LIMBIC DRIVE
FOR PURPOSE

The Quebec Commission for the Protection of the French Language sent letters to all the merchants in Montreal's Chinatown warning them that all Chinese signs must now be in French.[1]

I was vacationing at a hotel in Hawaii when I received a call from the tennis shop. A visitor in for just one day was looking for a game of singles. "No problem, I'll be right down," I replied. When I got there, I found a tall, gaunt, serious-looking, middle-aged man waiting for me with a large tennis bag, indicating he possessed a number of rackets and a penchant for winning. Uh-oh, I said to myself, this is going to be a long afternoon.

More than two hours later, worn to a frazzle, the two of us adjourned to the bar at the beach. His first name was Edwin; I never did catch his last name. We had hardly said ten words on the court, which wasn't much fun, since I like to kibbitz and needle when I play. I was thinking that I would get my diet drink down quickly and bid farewell.

However, when I asked Edwin what he did to make a living, he said he was a physicist who worked at a laboratory housing one of those enormous accelerators that are designed to help researchers find the smallest of the elemental particles, the building blocks of the universe.

I immediately perked up and told Edwin that I was writing a book and would he mind answering some questions I had in language I could understand about the concept of time.

He smiled and said, "That's an unusual request, but no problem. I feel I owe you something for keeping you out on the court for so long."

"Didn't mind it a bit," I said, as I feigned a severe limp walking to the end of the bar, where I grabbed a ballpoint pen and some napkins to make notes.

Edwin laughed. "Hey," he said, "it wasn't that bad."

"I'm glad to see you have a sense of humor, Edwin. We didn't have a whole bunch of laughs on the court."

"Oh, I apologize," he said gently. "The minute I get on a tennis court I transform into a Bjorn Borg, all serious and intent on winning. I'm not always that way, although I have been told I'm a bit intense."

"No problem. It's always interesting to meet someone who can be transformed by what he does or who he's with. It's not uncommon."

He laughed gently, again. "That's good to know," he replied. Then after he sipped his drink, "So, okay then, what are your questions?"

I gulped down some soda and began. "Remember, you've got to keep this real simple."

"I will."

"Okay, the first question is about 'imaginary time.' Now, as I understand it, science calls time 'imaginary time,' because it perceives the passage of time as relative, depending on how fast one might be going at any given instant. The faster we travel, the slower time will pass, which is a bit dumbfounding. So my question is, what is the difference between imaginary time and real time? And remember, you have to answer in words an infant could understand."

Edwin chuckled. "Of course, well, let me think how to put this." He paused momentarily. "Let's just say there is no such thing as real time or absolute time. All time is indeed relative and what we sense as time is indeed imaginary. If we could travel, as Einstein envisioned himself doing, at the head of a light beam, time would literally stop. If you were wearing a wristwatch, it would also literally stop."

"So you are confirming that time is capable of actually stopping. This is what you are saying."

"That is what I'm saying."

He paused in thought and then continued.

"Let's imagine that this bar we're sitting in is part of a spaceship. As our spaceship takes off and flies into space, the more speed we would pick up, the slower the time we are experiencing would pass. And as we would begin to pick up speed up to the rate, say, to one-tenth the speed of light, or hundreds of millions of miles per hour, time would noticeably begin to slow down."

"Which includes clocks slowing down."

"I mean the whole shebang, the whole concept of time slows down. You and I and those with us in the spaceship would begin to age a lot slower than those who we left behind sitting around the pool," he pointed behind him. "If we returned in, say, ten years, after continually traveling that fast, their clocks might be three or four years ahead of the clocks we took on the flight. They would literally be three or four years older than we were at the start of the flight."

"I just can't get this. How do you know all this?"

"You asked me to keep this simple, right?"

"Yes."

"Did you ever read the Stephen Hawking book *A Brief History of Time*[2] which he wrote for the average person?"

"Yes, I read it."

"Did you understand it?"

"Hardly more than a few pages."

"Out of the whole book?"

"The whole book."

He smiled. "So I am supposed to outdo Hawking in my ability to communicate simply."

"Yes, I have trouble following the concepts of physics or really anything that borders on the mathematical."

"I see."

"So if you are successful in making me understand, I'll buy the drinks."

Edwin laughed. Now it was a soft, gentle laugh I would have never imagined he had on the tennis court.

"Okay, well then, I'll make an attempt. In Hawking's book, which I would reread if I were you, he mentioned a test in 1962 in which highly accurate atomic clocks were used at the top and bottom of a water tower. After the testing period was up, it was found that the clock at the bottom of the tower actually ran slower, since it was closer to earth and not traveling through space as fast as the clock at the top of the tower."

"How much difference in time was there?"

"It was infinitesimal. But enough, certainly, to prove the theory of the relativity of time."

"So what you're saying is that if I stayed in my high-rise apartment all day and all night, that I would age less than someone who lived on the ground floor and my clocks would actually run slower, even my electronic clocks."

"Exactly, but the aging difference would be so slight as to be hardly noticeable, even over a period of many years. Even for astronauts, who travel through space at 25,000 miles per hour, where time would pass significantly slower than in your high-rise apartment, the differences in aging over a few weeks or even years would be hardly noticeable."

"So what would be noticeable?"

"Well, as I said, when you're traveling hundreds of millions of miles an hour, then the differences certainly become noticeable."

"And at the speed of light, time actually stops."

"Yes, I said that."

"And what happens if we ever learn to travel beyond the speed of light?"

"We can't travel beyond the speed of light, which is in accordance with the general theory of relativity."

"Why can't we? What would happen to us?"

"Okay, let me put this as simply as I can. If you shot a bullet out of a gun standing still, the bullet would travel at 700 miles per hour, or whatever speed bullets travel at. Now, if you were standing on the front of a speeding train going at 100 miles per hour, and you shot the gun, the bullet would be traveling at 800 miles an hour. Do you follow that?"

"Yes, of course, the bullet is getting a 100-mile-an-hour boost from the train."

"Exactly. Now, if you did the same thing with a flashlight, shooting out a light beam from the front of a train, the speed of the light would not change. You could be on a train going 100,000 miles an hour, and light will still travel at the same speed as if it started from a flashlight you were holding standing still on the ground. Did you follow me?"

"I think so. You're saying that we can't propel the speed of light beyond 186,000 miles per second, or whatever, no matter what we do to try to accelerate it."

"Correct. The speed is precisely 186,282 miles per second."

"But why is that? Why can't light travel faster?"

"No one knows; that is just the way it is. And at the point that the spaceship we're sitting in might reach the speed of light, time would literally stop."

"And we would look just as we look right now, traveling all that fast."

"No, of course not. If you used Einstein's famous equation, $E=mc^2$, the mass of objects increases vastly as it nears the speed of light. As a matter of fact, at the speed of light, the mass of your body would become infinite, so you couldn't even reach that speed as a human."

"Careful, I am obesiophobic, you know, fearful of getting fat."

Edwin broke out in his soft laugh again, now with his shoulders shaking. "Well, anyway," he said, "you get the gist of the idea."

"Okay, another question. What about black holes? I understand that like traveling at the speed of light, if we were to fall into a black hole, time would also stop."

"Correct again. A black hole is the result of a burned-out star falling in on itself. When this happens, the gravity that is created is forbidding. Hawking in his book compared it to the weight and mass of a mountain being congealed into a particle the size of the nucleus of an atom. That minuscule particle would weigh as much as the mountain. It would be so heavy, that if you placed it on the surface of the earth, it would instantly plunge down to the center of the earth."

"A nucleus you can't even see, that heavy?"

"Yes. Now, the more mass an object has, the more gravity it creates. So you can imagine the mass and gravity of an enormous black hole. The gravity would be so intense that a beam of light from your flashlight would be drawn back into it. Light cannot escape a black hole and so neither could time, which would stop with it."

"So the speed that light can travel equates directly with time."

"Roughly speaking."

"So what you're saying, Edwin, is that if I got caught in a black hole, I wouldn't have any more birthdays."

He laughed, "Yes, that is correct, you wouldn't have any more birthdays."

I thought for a moment.

"So in a nutshell, what you're saying is that time is basically an illusion for us, since it is not what we think we are experiencing. It is just part of a big show being staged for us, for whatever the reasons. Our stage is an earth that is lost in an immeasurable universe, but with props such as a pleasant sky and clouds to give us a sense of reality. Bodies and other organisms made from bar codes form the cast of characters to keep us company and help us reproduce and survive. The illusion of time is to make us think we are moving forward into the next act, which we envision for life in general as being an infinite series of acts. And all of this and more is synthesized by the software of our brains in a way that makes us think something important is taking place."

"That's more philosophy than physics, I'm afraid."

We then said a few parting words, I signed for the drinks, and we went our separate ways.

I thought this story, which was true, although I had to reconstruct the dialogue, was an appropriate beginning to this chapter because it illustrates how we have developed a system of passionate beliefs that creates purposes, missions, ideology, and other convictions that fill out the written script of the role of humans on a stage that is primarily illusory.

These zealous beliefs are products of our pure reasoning power. You don't find chimpanzees and gorillas hurrying off to religious services or taking stands on gay marriages. But oddly enough, the strongest of our beliefs, once set in place, reflect limbiclike characteristics. The highly stringent and restrictive religious beliefs of a fundamentalist Catholic or Moslem or Orthodox Jew, for example, or the beliefs of someone who has been caught in the clutches of a spiritual cult, are as impervious to rationality as was Sarah's fear of elevators. These beliefs as a drive system also have the expectations of the other limbic drives. Satisfy them and you will be happy—"my prayers have been answered." Disappoint them—your son does something diametrically opposed to certain of your zealous beliefs—and you will be punished with depressive feelings.

In *Brain Tricks*, I labeled this phenomenon metaphorically as the *purpose program*, a sixth limbic program that devolved from our intelligence. However, in the course of writing the present volume, two points became apparent to me regarding this drive. First, that this human drive to absorb and reflect beliefs does indeed put in question the triune theory of the evolving brain as developed by Dr. Paul McLean, thus confirming the views of some of his critics as detailed in chapter 3. Second, the level of intensity or zeal we have to define a purpose or mission for ourselves in this world, both spiritual and nonspiritual, may apply as well to an entire array of beliefs we might hold dear, ranging from abortion and capital punishment to the worthiness of a corporate stock or a politician or our system of justice or a professional football team or our alma mater or a set of values we hold dear. Television talk shows are stocked with guests who are obviously selected because they have zealous outlooks about the different sides of the issues being discussed.

This purpose program, using the metaphor now to include our sense of purpose, mission, and other strong beliefs, appears to have the same bell curves as the limbic drives we share with the higher animals—power, sex, territorial, nurturance, and survival. At the lower levels, the Twos and Threes would be relatively ambivalent in their beliefs. At the higher levels, the Eights and Nines would be fanatical in their beliefs; aggressive in their defense; and subject to id-based jealousies, hatreds, and vengeance, among other punishing emotions, when challenged. The Tens would be willing to commit murder. It seems clear, then, that our pure reasoning power alone, which is the primary characteristic that raises humans above the higher animals, is also capable of creating inner craziness among otherwise apparently normal people.

This then raises the question, how can we have five core drives or programs—power, sex, territorial, nurturance and survival—that presumably emanate from our limbic organs—our id, our Inner Dummy—since we apparently share them with chimpanzees and other higher animals, and one drive, *purpose*, that emanates from our cerebral cortex?

Most of the academic references to this psychological drive to absorb and reflect a limbic-like closed system of zealous beliefs have to do with rituals and religion. Robin Fox, for example, in his 1971 paper titled "The Cultural Animal," as described in chapter 10, believed that "man in isolation would not only develop a translatable language and laws about property, incest and marriage, customs of property and so forth, they would also have beliefs about the supernatural and practices relating to it."[3]

It turns out that anthropologists have been unable to find any society on earth, no matter how isolated or when it existed, where some form of ritualism wasn't practiced. It is as if we have a genetic predisposition for ritual, including the practice of atheism. If a belief relating to spirituality doesn't exist we presumably create it and then pass it along to our children.

Dr. Freud in his paper, "The Future of an Illusion," said the following:

> When the growing individual finds that he is destined to remain a child forever, that he can never do without protection against strange superior powers, he lends those powers the features belonging to the figure of his father; he creates for himself the gods whom he dreads, whom he seeks to propitiate [accommodate], and whom he nevertheless entrusts with his own protection.[4]

But what was it in our cerebral cortex, the seat of our intelligence, that created outlooks emanating from both spiritual and nonspiritual beliefs that became impervious to rationality? Some of the greatest intellectual heroes of history—Socrates, Galileo, Freud, and Einstein, to name a few—were initially scorned or even killed because of their beliefs. They were unable to penetrate an impervious wall of authoritarian beliefs. Why wasn't the rationality we developed, a human gift, left unencumbered by evolution, open to all the larger questions of life? This had me stumped until I discussed the question with Dr. Hefter.

The first thing he reminded me of was that we are speculating about a working brain that we can't tear apart to see what makes it tick while it's still alive and we are in the midst of pondering a belief or hating a neighbor or whatever. Our observations about the mental side of the brain, aside from the physiological, are, for the most part, theoretical and metaphoric. Even Dr. Freud's concept of the id, ego, and superego are metaphoric. They are figures of speech that provide analogies to help us comprehend the enormous complexity of the human mind.

Dr. Hefter then hypothesized that our basic instinctive drives, which, in a metaphoric sense, we can more easily envision as being housed in an id, are relentless in their pursuit of fulfillment and pleasure or reward. It is therefore likely, he said, that as humans developed the power of thought, these instinctive drives saw it as just one more new tool for pursuing their fulfillment. We might become attached limbically to a religious belief, for example, because our survival program senses that it makes us feel *secure* and have less fear, or because our power program senses that it gives us meaning, a feeling of empowerment and thus higher status.

I thought this was an excellent insight.

Next, I went back to psychiatrist John Bowlby's book *Attachment* and noted his observation that when we attach ourselves to people who we perceive as more powerful than we are, we frequently attach ourselves to their system of beliefs as well. He said:

> During adolescence and adult life, a measure of attachment behavior is commonly directed not only towards persons outside the family, but also towards groups and institutions other than the family. A school or college, a work group, a religious group, or a political group can come to constitute for many people a subordinate attachment-"figure." In such cases, it seems probable, the development of attachment to a group is mediated, at least initially, by attachment to a person holding a prominent position within that group. Thus, for many a citizen, attachment to his state is a derivative of and initially dependent on his attachment to its sovereign or president.[5]

This would help explain why his millions of followers became attached to or "limbically captured" by Adolf Hitler's lunatic beliefs about the superiority of Aryan blood. You certainly couldn't address a group of Nazis, dangling an eight-foot string of thread, and tell them: "Look, let me try to explain things to you, here. We all came out of this same genetic string and the differences between one race of humans and another are basically insignificant and immaterial. All this string has on it is a bunch of genetic bar codes. And get this, an ear of corn is created from this same genetic string, although it's somewhat shorter and the bar codes on it are a little different. So if you are going to hate Jews, Gypsies, Negroes, homosexuals, and basically everyone in Europe east of Germany's borders, you should probably hate ears of corn as well. The point is you are simply being captured by your limbic purpose program and it is time to get off of it because you are causing needless deaths and suffering among tens of millions of people."

Those Nazis would have stared at you as if you were the one with lunatic beliefs. They were not only presumably limbically attached to their beliefs, and thus impervious to logic, they obviously nurtured them as if they were their pet dogs.

It is apparent that we can become limbically captured by or attached to beliefs, both spiritual and nonspiritual, that the attachment is probably facilitated if a specific leader figure is associated with them, and that they may empower us, give us comfort, or satisfy our instinctive, drive reward system in other ways, regardless of how irrational and warped our outlook becomes, or in how many other ways we are apparently normal.

This would help explain the Heaven's Gate cultists who committed mass suicide in the belief that their spirits would reside safely behind the Hale-Bopp comet. They were just as much victims of a rationality that had been captured, or as Dr. Freud put it in his *Future of an Illusion*, "an ego that has been overwhelmed," as Ellen who weighed eighty-two pounds but looked in the mirror and thought she was fat, and so would eat nothing. Or, the president of the company I described earlier, who wouldn't make an acquisition because it was recommended by an executive vice president, who he thought was out to get his job, when in actuality the executive vice president was only trying to support him. Or, wealthy John McDonald III, who went into a panic because I gave a ten-dollar tip to a valet. Or Bob Schwartz, who wouldn't eat a steak at a barbecue because he thought the cook was sweating too much and might have dripped on it.

As pointed out previously, the territorial, power, and nurturance programs could be considered part of the survival program, because, taken together, their ultimate aim is to improve our chances for surviving in the primitive wilderness long enough to reproduce and nurture our young. Survival and reproduction comprise the evolutionary endgame. But separating off our territorial, power, and nurturance helps us understand ourselves. And so, too, does separating off our drive for purpose (the drive shared only by humans) to cover our propensity to attach to spiritual and nonspiritual beliefs.

I recall working with a bright young woman fresh out of the University of Michigan (we'll call her Amy) who fell in love with and married an Orthodox Jew and then became one herself.

"You can't be serious about this," I remember saying to Amy when she told me about it.

"No, I am serious."

"But as a woman, you'll be subjugated. You'll have to sit upstairs in the synagogue where the women are segregated."

"No, it's not upstairs; we sit in our own section on the main floor."

"But you're still segregated and subjugated. You are acquiescing to what the women's rights movement has fought so hard against in this century."

"It's not that bad."

"Yes it is. And don't forget, you won't be able to drive on Saturdays or turn on the lights, or whatever else Orthodox Jews aren't supposed to do, and there are pages upon pages of perfectly normal things you're not supposed to do."

"We bought a home near the synagogue. We can walk."

"But you'll have to keep a kosher house. Every steak you eat from now on will taste like a doormat."

She laughed. "It's not that bad and I enjoy keeping kosher and making kosher foods."

"But you realize that there are 1,500 different religions and sects in the United States alone, at last count, and upward of 5,000 worldwide, each believing that their religion has all the answers and all the others don't. It's obvious from this fact alone that no single religion has the answers. The ultimate answers, even if there are any, are still up for grabs."

"We respect other religions."

"But that's not the point. You are devoting a good part of your life to a spiritual belief that is in disagreement with 5,000 other such beliefs. This is nothing but an enormous leap of faith. How can you sacrifice your life to a narrow set of beliefs? Why don't you pick a denomination that lets you flip the light switch on Saturdays? How can you be sure about what you're doing?"

"Howard [her husband] and I are sure. We believe in Orthodox Jewish ways and laws. We feel comfortable with them. We like following them."

"So you're not going to give this up."

"No."

Doesn't this conversation remind you of the one with Sarah in front of the elevators?

It has always puzzled me that some of the most intellectual men and women in the world have fundamentalist religious beliefs that restrict their lives in so many ways, and which they believe in fanatically. While you might argue the law or mathematical equations or art or music or great literature with them with rational equanimity, if you begin questioning their spiritual beliefs, all arguments fall on deaf ears, including the fact that since we are lost in space and time and the origins of our genetic engineering remain unknown, that life obviously remains a mystery, that no one has the answers. Over time, they have apparently become obsessed, captured by their beliefs, their "egos overwhelmed."

Some, like a good friend of mine, Larry Dore, who ran large corporate sales and marketing operations, and is a devout Catholic, is aware of the rational questions relating to his beliefs and is open to discussion, but he will tell you that he won't give up his spiritual beliefs because they are ingrained and they give him comfort and strength. And why should he give them up, if life is indeed a mystery? Why not be captured by a spiritual belief system with pat answers if this makes you happy?

Freud, who was an atheist, in a paper he wrote in 1907, entitled "Obsessive Actions and Religious Practices," described the resemblances between the ceremonies of believers and the ceremonies of neurotic obsessives.

> In view of these similarities and analogies, one might venture to regard obsessional neurosis as a pathological counterpart of the formation of a religion, and to describe that neurosis as an individual religiosity and religion as a universal obsessional neurosis.[6]

Of course, he was probably describing our metaphorical Nines and Tens on the purpose program, certainly not the Amys or Larry Dores of the world, who become deeply attached to their spiritual beliefs, but are not neurotically obsessed or blinded by them.

Further, if you substitute in the quote from Freud above the word "mission" for "religion," the statement about obsessional neurosis could apply to *nonspiritual* missionary zeal as well. We have all seen statements of mission, which is another compartment of our drive for purpose. I recently saw a statement from a newly appointed publisher of a magazine, which was ranked third in circulation in its field, who said, "My mission is to make this the greatest magazine of its kind in the world." The article described the concerns of the current magazine staff about the new publisher, because he had a history of firing or exploiting people as if they were inanimate pawns on a chessboard. It also described how the man was a workaholic, the victim of three divorces, because he was married to his work, which he considered to be his primary mission. I'm sure if we could talk to his ex-wives or children they might agree that he had an obsessional neurosis. And yet, sitting around a table with his friends, he might appear apparently normal.

Most of us have missions to which we attach ourselves that are in the range of normality. Perhaps our mission is to save enough money to send our children to college. Or maybe it's to own our own home. Or to work to become perceived as a gourmet cook. Or to own a business of our own. Or to become a scratch golfer. Or to run for elective office. It is when these missions consume us in some way, capture our rationality, and have the potential for harming others or ourselves, that an inner craziness can begin to surface.

I ran across a fellow whose mission was to climb seven of the highest mountains in the world. He had two more to go. However, he told me that on a recent climb he had almost lost his life and the two mountains he had yet to climb were the most dangerous.

"Well, my god, why don't you give this up?" I remember saying to him.

"Not on your life. I set this goal and I'm sticking to it."

"But you almost got killed and you're no spring chicken."

"I don't care. I'm off in the spring."

I haven't heard anything since, so I assume he survived.

The point is that there is apparently a scale of intensity that governs our propensity to attach to the missions we establish for ourselves. And there is undoubtedly some "blurring" between the limbic programs that create totally irrational missions, such as the genocides that have been committed throughout history. No doubt Hitler was a Number Ten on both the power and purpose scales, which warped his rationality and drove him to have millions killed in order to "purify" the Germanic race—the Race Hygiene Program he called it.

The same combinations of limbic power and purpose drives undoubtedly existed in the minds of Idi Amin, Joseph Stalin, Pol Pot, or the generals of World War I on both sides of the battle who incessantly threw thousands of soldiers to their deaths to capture some lonely ridge or other plot of land, only to lose it the next day. In one such battle, more than 30,000 soldiers were killed in a single day. Talk about the Inner Dummy.

But it was probably more purpose than power that motivated the soldiers of Iran in the war against Iraq in the 1980s, who were told by their commanders that their deaths in battle would qualify them to enter heaven immediately, after being handed a cheap amulet. And so they charged the Iraqi positions en masse and were killed by the thousands. The Japanese kamikaze pilots of World War II were obviously more concerned with purpose than power, as they readily volunteered to sacrifice their lives by flying their planes into U.S. warships. Talk about an all-consuming mission.

Then there was the war between Armenia and Azerbaijan, which ended in 1994. The dispute centered around the small enclave of Nagorno-Karabakh, and resulted in the loss of 35,000 lives and forced hundreds of thousands of families from their homes. Certainly the soldiers on both sides had to have a strong sense of mission, probably reinforced by the drive to acquire or defend territory.

Then there was Slobodan Milosevic of Yugoslavia, who in the face of massive bombings of his country continued his "ethnic cleansing" of Kosovo, probably driven by relatively equal drives of purpose, power, and territory.

Then there is the irrationality of our attachment to the missions motivated by war itself. I sometimes stare mystified at the countless documentaries on television about wars and the weapons of wars, from the Civil War to the present, wondering when the commentator will break in and say, "But isn't this madness? Isn't this weapon of destruction madness? Isn't it madness that we fought this war at all? Why can't we just figure out ways to get along?" But you seldom hear words like this. We have apparently become "attached" to the concept of war as a natural part of our existence. And so it remains as unquestioned today, among most of us, as it was hundreds of centuries ago.

It would thus appear that our metaphoric purpose program, which theoretically should be based on the intellectual capacity of humans, is as dangerous to our survival when carried to extremes as the other core limbic programs we share with the higher animals. What a wasted opportunity for the human species!

And finally we come to the third compartment of this program, the stubborn beliefs we have about the general issues within our lives, that don't involve spirituality or a sense of mission, but which can also cause chaos in our lives. It is apparent that the higher we are on the metaphoric purpose scale, the greater our propensity for becoming attached to one side or another of a given issue, including values, and the more we are unable to see any outlook but our own, apparently another form of obsessional belief.

I recall working with a man who had a strong opinion about everything. I tried to avoid asking him questions because he always had pat answers. But one night, unavoidably, we wound up having dinner alone and so to stimulate myself, I came right out and said, "You seem to have an opinion on everything, don't you?"

"That's right. I think it's important to take stands, to have an ideology, to not be wishy-washy."

"Okay," I said, "I'll give you a few minutes of glory. Hold on while I find a newspaper. I'm going to give you a chance to spout off." I left the table and quickly found a newspaper. Returning, I began flipping through the pages, looking for issues of the day. "Here's one," I said. "O. J. Simpson is planning on getting married, again."

"That bastard should be dead and not with any lethal injection, but electrocuted."

"So, you think he was guilty?"

"Guilty?" He laughed mockingly. "Of course he was guilty. A bunch of clever lawyers got him off, that's all."

"But you weren't at the crime scene. The evidence was all circumstantial. Simpson had never committed a violent crime before or since, to anyone's knowledge. How can you know for sure?"

"He was guilty; next subject."

"Okay, give me a second here. Oh, this is a good one. Church minister is excommunicated for performing a gay marriage between two homosexuals."

"The son of a bitch should be shot. Forget gay marriages, homosexuality itself should be outlawed. Those people should be forced into therapy to change their ways."

"You've got to be kidding on that one."

"No, I'm serious. Just the idea of homosexuality makes me sick. We shouldn't give people the choice."

"So you think this is a lifestyle they choose, that there is nothing genetic or biological about it."

"Absolutely."

"And you think there is nothing sick about heterosexual males and females writhing around in bed together exuding all kinds of fluids?"

"Hey, are you gay?"

"No, I'm just trying to make a point. We are driven to our sexuality by organs in our brains and gonads and I think that what one is driven to do is almost always beyond our choice and depending on the intensity of the drive, our ability to exert control over the drive may also be beyond our control, so to speak. And ultimately, what difference does it make anyway? When the sun burns out and life on earth ceases to exist, who will be left to worry about how we performed sex?"

"Well, you're just wrong, but you can't see it. Next subject."

"All right, just one more. I can't take much more of this without being drunk, and I have to drive."

"That's your problem."

Why did I feel like hitting him in the mouth?

"Okay, here's one. Dr. Kevorkian strikes again. What do you think about allowing people who are terminally ill and in excruciating pain to call Dr. Kevorkian?"

"It's sick, totally sick. All life is sacred. When God wants us to die, then we'll die."

"But what about surgical operations, heart and liver transplants, that prolong our lives? Is this going against God's will?"

"That's different."

"Why is it different?"

"Because we are trying to save lives, not kill people."

"So it isn't God's schedule at all that's involved."

"Not when you are trying to save lives."

"So terminally ill people should just be forced to suffer, not be allowed to make the ultimate choice themselves?"

"You're damned right. Next subject."

"No more subjects. I'm going home."

Most of us have run into opinionated know-it-alls. High on the purpose scale, they are apparently more vulnerable to absorbing even the most bizarre beliefs.

There is a sports columnist for a metropolitan daily newspaper who will frequently make the most absurd observations about sports team members and their owners, particularly after losses, presenting only his opinions and rarely facts. One day, I saw him on a plane and struck up a conversation. It turned out he was a polite and quiet guy. I asked him what drove him to his incessant and obviously biased attacks on specific people. He said it was just part of his business. It's what created readership. Surveys showed that his readers liked his attacking, opinionated reporting style, whether they agreed with him or not. It is no surprise to hear that many of us can be attracted to contentiousness. Perhaps, as previously suggested, having strong opinions empowers us in our own minds. It gives us status. More inner craziness.

The compartmentalization of our purpose program between our beliefs in spirituality, mission, and other nonspiritual beliefs appears obvious. For example, one might be a noted academic, relatively open to both sides of most issues, but devout and closed-minded in a spiritual belief. Or, one might be agnostic in spiritual beliefs but have a steely mission to succeed in some venture or be strongly attached to one side of several issues. Or, one might be generally ambivalent about most issues, but an ideologue about a political system.

I didn't post a quiz relating to a purpose scale on my Web site because of the complexities caused by the compartmentalization of the drive. However, I have created the following *miniscale*, to indicate that there is apparently a bell curve to this singularly human program of ours. As with the other limbic scales, there is no academic research to support it. It is presented as a rough guideline only.

Here it is:

NUMBER ONE:

You are probably ambivalent in the extreme. You have few if any beliefs, either spiritual or nonspiritual. You have no missions in life, no goals. You take things day to day, generally try to stay out of the way, and let the breaks fall where they may.

NUMBERS TWO AND THREE:

You may have goals for your life, but they are probably soft goals, aside from assuring the safety and nurturance of your family, if you have one. You may have a spiritual belief, ranging from atheism to fundamentalism, but you are relatively open and feel that you could change your mind if you came across facts you felt were relevant. You may have opinions on a number of issues, but you are not zealous in your convictions and probably don't express them, except when asked.

NUMBERS FOUR, FIVE, AND SIX:

About where most of us are at. You do have a sense of mission. You may have beliefs relating to spirituality, ranging from atheism to fundamentalism, and whatever it is, you are strongly attached to the conviction. You probably have strong beliefs on varying issues, but you are usually able to see both sides of an argument. You work hard to keep an open mind. You don't enjoy standing around a cocktail party, preaching and defending your beliefs in heated arguments.

NUMBER SEVEN:

You have a strong sense of mission for your life. Once you take on a task, you will become absorbed by it. Whatever your belief about spirituality, ranging from atheism to fundamentalism, you are zealous in your attachment to it. You probably have definite convictions and will argue vehemently in their defense. It would be hard for you to accept an opposite point of view, even when the facts presented to you are obvious. It takes time for you to change your mind.

NUMBER EIGHT:

You are zealous in whatever missions you have formulated for yourself, whether they involve work, family, or avocations. You won't accept failure at anything. You will keep trying, even if your efforts involve years. Whatever you believe about the spiritual world has become an intensely zealous and unshakable belief for you. You have intense convictions about most of the issues that involve life in general and like to preach about them. You rarely, if ever, will change your mind about anything. Arguing with you is hopeless.

NUMBER NINE:

You are a fanatic. You probably have established an array of missions for your life and are obsessed with pursuing them. Nothing will stand in your way. Making others suffer in pursuit of your missions is like mother's milk to you. You are also fanatic about your convictions and you probably have a lot of them. It's your way or the highway. You are fanatic in your views about spirituality, regardless if they are atheistic or fundamentalist. There is nothing about life that you haven't figured out. You are right, everyone else is wrong. You probably sometimes wonder why, with all your knowledge, you are not more popular.

NUMBER TEN:

Time to check in somewhere. You are everything a Number Nine is, but on top of that, you would be willing to commit murder to further your beliefs. You are like the father, previously noted in this book, who intends to find and murder his daughter because she ran away from an arranged marriage. You cannot countenance what you perceive as betrayal. You would have no feelings of compunction if you were called upon to beat people into submission if they don't believe as you do. You can be maniacal.

As noted, we might be ambivalent about most things, a Number Two or Three, but zealous or even fanatic about a spiritual belief. Or we might be ambivalent about spirituality, but zealous or fanatic in the missions we undertake. It is part of the compartmentalization of this program.

I find myself to be between a Number Three and Four, across the board. I'm still waiting for most answers.

COMMENTARY BY DR. HEFTER

The relationship of unconscious factors to the rational processes is a source of continuing scientific and more generally, universal speculation. The dividing line, if indeed one exists, between "id"-determined activity and behavior resulting from principled commitment to a cause, will always be prone to uncertainty, and the likelihood is that often there is a mixing or coexistence of the two. The issue is not whether one kind of activity is good and another is bad, but rather how can we better recognize the appearance of one or both. In terms of a political perspective, this recognition is extremely important in a democracy, where information is essential to appropriate decision making.

It is likely that scientific developments will increasingly lead to more detailed conclusions about brain activity. Those developments, involving anatomical and microscopic observations of the brain as well as indices offered by measurements of brain activity, may well lead to more informed hypothesis about the relationship between the more rational and the more "Inner Dummy," id-based aspects of our brain.

NOTES

1. *Ottawa Citizen*, December 27, 1997, p. B5.

2. Stephen W. Hawking, *A Brief History of Time: From the Big Bang to Black Holes* (New York: Bantam, 1988), n.p.

3. As quoted in Edward O. Wilson, *Sociobiology* (Cambridge, Mass.: Belknap Press of Harvard University Press, 1980), p. 284.

4. Sigmund Freud, excerpt from *The Future of an Illusion*, in *The Freud Reader*, ed. Peter Gay (New York: Norton, 1989), p. 699.

5. John Bowlby, *Attachment* (New York: BasicBooks, 1982), p. 207.

6. Sigmund Freud, excerpt from *Obsessive Actions and Religious Practices*, in Gay, *The Freud Reader*, p. 435.

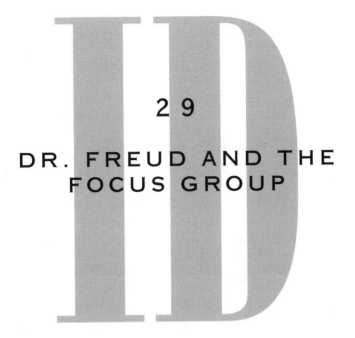

29

DR. FREUD AND THE FOCUS GROUP

A Virginia man was sentenced to eleven months in jail for writing bad checks. However, he was released after only three weeks, when jail officials discovered that the cost of eleven months of the kosher meals he required would be $23,000.[1]

"This way, Dr. Freud," Wendy Smith said excitedly, as she led Dr. Freud through the research facility where Samuel Ollander was conducting his latest focus group. "Samuel is going to be thrilled when he learns you are here."

What am I doing here? Freud wondered. How did I get talked into this? He was following closely behind Wendy, observing the curves of her body and thought fleetingly that maybe the idea of calling the id the Inner Dummy might not be such a bad idea after all.

Wendy approached a heavy closed door and carefully began opening it.

"We have to be quiet, Dr. Freud," she said, turning back to him, "because Sam is already working with his group of consumers. This is the observation room where clients and people from the agency sit to watch what is taking place."

Freud followed her into the darkened room, which was empty. Much of the light came through a long window along one wall through which Freud could see Ollander sitting at a large, round table with three men and three women, each wearing a name tag that denoted only their first names in large letters. A microphone hung over the table.

"That's a two-way mirror, Dr. Freud," she said. "We can see them, but they can't see us. They know that people are here and watching them, however. Sam tells them right away that a two-way mirror is used so they won't be distracted by the reactions of the people watching them. They also, of course, know the session is being taped. The microphone is in full view."

Freud nodded.

A long table was placed close to the window, with several cushioned folding chairs behind it. On a platform behind the chairs were a handful of additional, more comfortable chairs. Freud could hear Ollander's voice through the loudspeaker system in the room.

Wendy pointed to two chairs in the middle of the table. "Why don't we just make ourselves comfortable here," she said. "We can watch what's happening for a little while and then we can head over to meet my friends at the restaurant bar just down the street. I can't wait to show you off."

Freud nodded again as he sat down.

What am I doing? he thought. What is the matter with me? He wasn't even sure how much younger Wendy was than he. How do you count time? From the day you died? Do you count the intervening time? And what is time, after all? How old am I really, at this point? But if time is only an illusion, does it even matter? His body was a molecular retransformation of some sort, he knew. And with it, unfortunately, came the brain and the limbic system with all of its torturous expectations and demands. The spirit is so much better when it is uninhibited by the brain, he thought, free and unfettered and peaceful, which was about all he could remember. The brain, he had learned, has a blocking mechanism that immediately shuts out any remembrance of "the other side." Once you are in a body, inhabiting a brain, you become immediately concerned with the here and now, survival and reproduction. Reproduction, he said again to himself, looking at Wendy. *Ach.*

Wendy wrote out a short note and left the room. Freud watched as she entered a side door of the research room and handed Sam her note. As she left, Sam looked at the two-way mirror and nodded, almost imperceptibly, acknowledging that he knew Freud was watching.

"Pardon me, Sam, but the phrase *Dummy Convictions* is just as stupid, in my opinion, as this whole idea of an Inner Dummy." The words echoed through the loudspeaker system and Freud looked out to see that it was a large, older man named Ed doing the talking.

"Why don't you just hold off there, Ed," said a woman named Rita, who was almost as large as Ed and about the same age. "We promised Sam, here, that we wouldn't comment much until he got through with his presentation."

"That's okay, Rita," Sam spoke up. "Any of you can put your two cents in now at any time."

"Well, I think it's all just stupid," Ed said.

On a large bulletin board on one side of the room, Freud noticed a large sign that said "Inner Dummy." On another one just behind Ollander was a sign that said "Dummy Convictions." Ollander had two additional signs in front of him, facedown on the table.

"What is stupid about it, Ed?" Ollander asked.

"This whole concept of the Inner Dummy, that's what's stupid," he replied.

"I presume, therefore, that you don't think *you* have an Inner Dummy inside your head?" The question was asked by a middle-aged, thin man whose name tag said he was Leonard. He was fondling a pipe, leaning back easily in his chair, legs crossed and looking studious.

"Hell, no, I don't have an Inner Dummy in my head," Ed replied directly to Leonard. "I've done some pretty stupid things in my life, but I think it's a cop-out to say that 'Oh, I screwed around on my wife because of my Inner Dummy.' Give me a break."

Ed broke out into laughter and some of the others laughed with him, but not Leonard.

"Hey," a man whose tag said he was Howard broke in, "that is one hell of an idea." He spoke fast with a slight stammer. "I think I'll go home tonight and try something like that on my wife. 'Honey,' I'll say, 'do you mind if I mess around with your sister Evelyn because my Inner Dummy finds her very attractive and it is driving me to have sex with her. Is that okay? After all, it is not my fault, it is my Inner Dummy that wants to do it.'"

"If you came home and tried that on me, buster, you'd be dead meat," this from a young, urbane-looking woman named Edna.

"You see what I mean?" Ed said excitedly. "This whole concept is ridiculous."

"Does everyone feel that way?" Sam asked. "What about you, Jeannie? You haven't said anything."

Jeannie, a small, middle-aged woman said, "I think the concept is marvelous."

"Oh, brother, I'd love to sell you a used car," Ed said.

"Hold on, Ed," Ollander said. "Tell us what you like about it, Jeannie." She moved closer to the table, hands crossed in front of her.

"I agree with Ed, that we can't use the concept as a cop-out. But the idea that we have this primitive mechanism in our brain that we designate the Inner Dummy as a label, has a great deal of value. I am a teacher and like most teachers, I have difficulty articulating why some of us are driven to do irrational things. I think this helps. And far from being a cop-out, I think the job of parents and teachers is to help children learn to control their emotions. And as adults, much of the judgment made by others about us is how well we manage our emotions. I think it will be far easier to communicate that many of the emotions that compel us to do something that is apparently irrational is housed in the metaphor of the Inner Dummy, whose mental processes include primitive drives that in some of us are stronger than in others and need to be controlled or managed. I think this concept may be a clarifier to that extent."

"Well said," Leonard replied. He sat back, tapping his unlit pipe against his teeth. "The concept of the Inner Dummy could be a catalyst for a broader understanding of the origins of the irrational mind. It becomes a burden that most of us share, and as Jeannie said, it must be managed."

"Don't include me on this," Ed said. "I don't have any Inner Dummy. What you see is what you get."

"Unfortunately," Howard commented.

"Hey, why don't you just shut your big mouth," Ed blurted out, agitated.

"Please, men, let's keep some order here," Sam said. "And Howard, let's not get into anything that is personal."

"I apologize, Sam." Then looking at Ed, he said, "And I apologize to you, too, you big boob. Here I am a salesman, supposedly open to all sorts of people. And yet if I were to call on you, the minute you opened your big mouth I'd be right out the door."

Ed, who was extremely overweight, began struggling to get out of his chair.

"Hold it, hold it," Sam said urgently. "Please, gentlemen. Ed, get back in your chair. And Howard, please apologize to Ed . . . nicely."

Howard thought momentarily.

"Ed, in the interests of getting out of your presence as quickly as possible, I apologize."

"Too bad," Rita interjected. "That would have been an interesting matchup. Blubber versus blabber."

Ed looked at her in anger. "Blubber, look at you, and you're talking to me about blubber?"

Rita laughed, "Just more of me to love, as the old saying goes."

Sam stood up. "Okay, maybe the best thing is to get back to the discussion of the subbranding of irrational beliefs." He walked over to the bulletin board holding the sign that said "Dummy Convictions." He stood there until he had their full attention.

"Okay, as I said before, we are looking for the best designation that would describe irrational beliefs, missions in life, ideologies that either have no basis in fact and/or in some ways can be harmful to others."

"Like those poor people who committed suicide to get behind the Hale-Bopp comet," Rita interjected. "Or that Jonestown deal when Jim Jones persuaded people to poison themselves."

"And their children, too," Howard added. "Don't forget that. I think it was cyanide."

"Yes, exactly," Sam said, "two perfect examples of the type of irrational belief we are attempting to describe with one quickly recognizable, two-word phrase."

"Well," Ed broke in, "I'll agree that those people had really dumb Inner Dummies."

"Look at that," Howard said, "an insight."

"Hey . . ."

"Or what about the balloonists who attempt to traverse the world to set a record?" Leonard broke in. "What drives them to it, risking their lives over the wide expanses of oceans and mountain ranges to set some meaningless records? That's part of what you mean isn't it, Sam?"

"Yes, that would be included as an irrational mission or obsession, particularly if these people had families that they would leave behind or made others to suffer in some way in order to pursue their obsessions."

"Sam," Jeannie broke in with a sly smile, "would this include an older spinster without a family who was determined to stay up night after night, week after week, in order to be the first person to read the Bible backward and does harm to no one?"

Leonard looked at Jeannie with new interest. "Well put, Jeannie. What say you to that, Sam?"

"You tell me, Leonard," Sam replied.

"Well yes, that would definitely be a Dummy Conviction, in the sense that she may be ruining her own health in this senseless quest to establish a meaningless record. In my opinion, I would put her up there with the balloonists or the people who want to row a boat across the Pacific. These are all selfish quests to establish credentials in a world that in itself is obviously meaningless."

"Meaningless to you, buddy, not to me," Rita replied. "And it will be even less meaningless when I get home tonight and serve the pot roast I have simmering to my husband, who is working a second shift and will love every inch of me for it," she said as she looked tauntingly at Ed.

"Well, what about that abortion doctor who was killed by an anti-abortionist the other day?" Edna said, stiffly. "That was really stupid. That would certainly apply as a Dummy Conviction. Someone who is pro-life and willing to kill. I can't imagine what makes people do these things. And all these marches, particularly in shopping malls. Sometimes you can hardly get inside a store."

"What makes them do it? Their Inner Dummy, dearie, that's what we're all sitting around the table jabbering about," Rita said.

"Oh, but I do agree with Edna on her point, " Jeannie said. "I am personally open on the issue of abortion, but to see someone who believes it is okay to kill another who disagrees with him over the right of a fetus to live, that is the result of a Dummy Conviction, all right."

"You have the idea, then," Sam said addressing the group as a whole. "I'm sure we could stand here for hours, listing hundreds of obsessive beliefs we know others have, that are or may border on the irrational. But time is running short now, and I want you to look at two more alternative subbrands for the designation *Dummy Conviction*. Let me put one other sign up here and see what you think of it."

He uncovered one of the two signs he was holding and held it over his head. It said "Dummy Beliefs."

The group stared intently at the phrase.

"Any comments?" Sam asked.

"I think it's better," Leonard said.

"Why?" Sam asked.

"Because it would be easier to walk up to somebody in our research lab who was certain he had the answer to hydrogen fusion when it was obvious that he didn't and say, 'Roy,' or whatever his name was, 'there is nothing there. You are the victim of a *Dummy Belief.*' "

"But if he was convinced," Rita followed, "of this hydrogen thing, wouldn't that be a conviction? And if you are obviously wrong, wouldn't that make it a Dummy Conviction?"

"Hey, there's a brain behind all that blubber," Ed said mockingly.

Rita looked at him. "Ed, are you married?"

"Yes."

"My condolences to your Mrs."

"Okay, okay, let's get back on the track," Sam said. "What do you think, Howard?"

"Dummy Conviction, Dummy Belief, it sounds the same. All you're doing is describing somebody's crazy ideas. You should come around with me on some of my sales calls if you want to see some crazy ideas. Stupid ideas, I should say. Just today I called on a hospital run by the county. It needed at least $5,000 worth of office supplies. I said to the purchasing agent, 'If you order today, you'll get a 10 percent discount.' 'Sorry, Howard,' he replies to me, 'I can't order until next Monday, the opening week of the month. It's in the book.' And he points to his procedures manual. I said, 'But, Henry, you can pay later. The point is, you're going to lose $500 for waiting. That's taxpayer money you're wasting.' He said, 'Sorry, we go by the book here.' Now call what that guy was thinking Dummy Convictions or Dummy Beliefs, he was just plain stupid. Maybe we should just call these people *Dummy Bureaucrats* who follow *Dummy Regulations*."

Edna broke in, "I think, Sam, that Howard has illustrated that neither Dummy Conviction nor Dummy Belief is the encompassing designation you are looking for. Maybe you need both. I'm involved in social work for the county and his story is a familiar one."

"Or maybe several designations," Leonard added. "How about *Dummy Goals*, or *Dummy Missions* or *Dummy Obsessions*, or *Dummy Ideology*, or simply *Dummy Ideas* as four more under the group. That way we could say to the balloonist who is risking his life, you have this *Dummy Obsession* to carry out this *Dummy Mission*, making your family sick with worry. To the cultist who wants his members to commit suicide to get to a better life in another world, we can say, 'That is a *Dummy Delusion* you have. Get off of it.' Do you see what I mean?"

"I don't know, I think people will get too confused with all these Dummy statements," Ed said, apparently forgetting his initial opposition to the concept as a whole.

Sam said, "These are definitely some interesting thoughts. Let me show you the last card I have." He put it up and it read "Dummy Delusions."

"Look at that," Jeannie said to Leonard. "Great minds working in the same direction."

Leonard looked away shyly. "Oh, please, it was just a wild thought."

"Holy moley, the guy's a psychic," Ed said. "You guessed what was on the hidden card."

"Please, let's drop it," Leonard replied.

"Sam," Jeannie said, "I think we have all struck on something here.

This concept cannot be described by one designation. It needs several, whether they include the ones you have," she pointed to the bulletin board, "or others. The scope is too wide."

"You may be right, Jeannie," Sam said. "Maybe we need our creatives to take another crack at this."

"Maybe you need a *Dummy Dictionary*," Leonard added. "In it would be all the appropriate Dummy designations, not only for irrational beliefs, but for other irrationalities as well. Dummy Bliss, for example, the concept you described when you began your presentation. Maybe you need a wider range of phrases to describe that."

"A Dummy Dictionary," Rita exclaimed. "Why Ed, that would be the perfect book to keep at your bedside."

"You know, if you weren't a woman—"

"I'm not a woman," Howard broke in, gruffly.

"Men, ladies, please," Sam implored the group. "Now we need some order here." He looked at his watch. "We only have twenty more minutes to wrap this up and I think you've come up with some terrific ideas. Let's take the remaining time to discuss them in detail . . . and calmly, please."

"Dr. Freud? Dr. Freud?" It was Wendy, standing behind him. Freud was staring through the two-way glass, mesmerized.

"Dr. Freud," she raised her voice.

He snapped his head back. "Ah, Wendy, I am sorry. Watching this was fascinating. Are these groups always so passionate?"

"I'm afraid not," Wendy said. "Many of them are just plain boring. It depends on the group members screened for us by the research company. They were screening for a cross-section of educational levels and it appears as if they were successful. The characters were interesting as well, although we did have two no-shows."

"No-shows?"

"People who said they'd be here, but didn't show up."

"Are they paid for doing this?" Freud pointed at the window.

"Usually, but it's not very much unless we have a panel of professionals in a specific field of work, who demand a fee. Tonight I believe each of the group members was paid $50, plus a free buffet dinner of deli items, if they wanted to partake."

"Very interesting, indeed," Freud muttered, stroking his beard.

"I think we can go now, sir. Sam just wanted you to get a taste of these focus panels to help you with your decision on the final concepts, when they are ready for presentation to you, early next week. He wanted you to see how ordinary people react to them."

"I see, I see," Freud said, lost in thought.

Wendy grabbed his hand.

"Come on, Dr. Freud, my friends are waiting for you. You are about to become the hero of the night."

Her grip tightened on his hand.

"Yes, yes, but we won't stay long, will we? I must get back to my work."

"Dr. Freud, that is a Dummy Obsession you have. Now let's go have some fun."

What am I doing? Freud wondered to himself again, as Wendy led him out of the room, her hand tightly gripped in his.

He pointed his eyes up tightly at his forehead and said in a mutter, visualizing that he was talking to his id, "Get a grip on yourself."

"What was that, Dr. Freud?"

"Nothing, my dear," he sighed. "Nothing at all."

NOTE

1. Zay N. Smith, *Chicago Sun-Times*, October 8, 1998, p. 34.

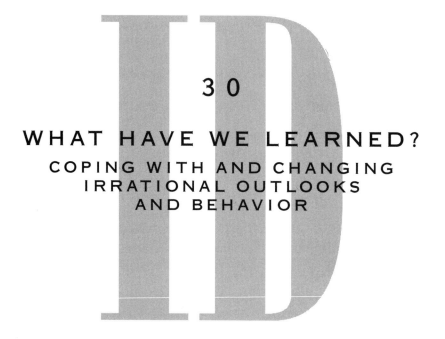

3 0

WHAT HAVE WE LEARNED?
COPING WITH AND CHANGING
IRRATIONAL OUTLOOKS
AND BEHAVIOR

The U.S. State Department reported that there are 60 million to 70 million land mines worldwide in about 60 countries, far fewer than the previous estimate of 80 million to 100 million land mines in about 70 countries. The report stated that the amount of land rendered unproductive by land mines is "unacceptably large."[1]

Dr. Freud probably framed the challenge of adjusting personality and other psychological disorders most succinctly in a phrase from *New Introductory Lectures*: "Where id was, there ego shall be."[2]

This is obviously the objective for those of us afflicted with irrationalities of one sort or another, which may emanate from intense instinctive-drive levels or the punishment inflicted upon us by those drives when their expectations weren't met. But short of the traumas of real life that may change warped outlooks, as described previously in chapter 26, the road toward any serious behavioral change can be long and hard.

The Inner Dummy appears, in its metaphoric sense, to be a clingy mechanism of the mind that once it has in its clutches a biological need or

342

a missionary idea or an anxiety or phobia or a relationship that may be tragic, or a desire for revenge that generates feelings of jealousy and hatred, it will engulf them behind its strong and thick castlelike walls that may be impervious to any sense of reason.

To get some idea of the strength of the id or Inner Dummy, think back to a time in your life when you attempted a crash diet or tried to stop smoking. If you'll recall, your Inner Dummy proceeded to force you back to overeating or smoking by unleashing a repertoire of punishments, ranging from pangs of physical pain to feelings of depression, frustration, discouragement, misery, despair and fright—basically varying forms of torture.

When a rational desire alone is disappointed, our mental punishment is far less severe. For example, we may be writing a school or business report and can't find some words that will express our thoughts better. We may feel some frustration over our inability to have found the right words, but we soon shrug it off.

Simply put, our ego center of pure reasoning alone hasn't the punishing ammunition of our Inner Dummy, which is capable of figuratively delivering mental knockout blows when we don't meet one of its more intense limbic-drive expectations. The spouse described on page 244, whom we love and appears happy, tells us one night she or he has fallen in love with someone else and wants a divorce. The Inner Dummy triggered, punishing response results. *Pow, Boom, Bash, Sock.* Our boss calls us into his office and tells us that someone who has been working for us has been promoted over our heads and is now our boss. *Pow, Boom, Bash, Sock.* We stand with our small children at our side and watch as the farm our family has lived on for generations is put up for auction. *Pow, Boom, Bash, Sock.* We are on the fourth date with someone we really like, are falling in love with, and expect this to be a night of commitment, when she looks up and says after dinner, she's decided you are obnoxious, ugly, and a big bore, so goodnight. *Pow, Boom, Bash, Sock.* It is our big chance; we have practiced this presentation for hours in front of the mirror. We have it down pat. Then we walk out on the stage, stand in front of the podium, and look up and see an audience of three thousand strangers. *Pow, Boom, Bash, Sock.* It is the last three seconds of the championship basketball game. The other team is ahead by one point. We don't want the ball, we want someone else to take the last shot. The play is called; we're not part of it. Relief. But something happens that thwarts the inbound ball. We get it and have to shoot. *Pow, Boom, Bash, Sock.* You are an alcoholic trying to go on the wagon. Your beautiful date drags you into a bar in a posh hotel and orders champagne for both of you, before you can say a word. The glasses come. You stare at yours. *Pow, Boom, Bash, Sock*. You are President Clinton and you know you have a Number Nine rating on the Sexual Scale. A young, attractive intern begins flirting with you. Your Inner Dummy reacts by activating all the pertinent sexual glands, but through enormous will, you control yourself. Then one day the young intern opens her jacket and you see that below her waist is nothing but thong underwear. *Pow, Boom, Bash, Sock*.

Or, what about the adolescent sensitive to her weight, who gets on the scale one morning to find that she is ten pounds over what she considers to be her normal weight. *Pow, Boom, Bash, Sock*. Or the student who needs to tell his strict and ambitious parents that he just flunked out of school. Or the golfer who needs to make a two-foot putt to win the tournament for his team. Or the obsessive-compulsive whose wife threatens to leave him if he doesn't stop aligning light switches at the top and bottom of a stairway. Or the cheap business executive who discovers when he gets home that he overtipped a waiter by twenty dollars. Or the claustrophobic in a crowded elevator that gets stuck between floors. Or the person who loses his job and falls into a depression. All of them are or about to be punished with *Pow, Boom, Bash, Socks*.

Do you get the idea? And when it comes to examples of situations that can trigger harsh, punishing responses from our Inner Dummies, we're barely at the tip of the iceberg. The question is, what can we do to prepare ourselves to better handle situations like these? What could President Clinton have done to prepare himself so that seeing the thong underwear on a young intern he found sexually appealing would not have overcome his willpower (ego defenses) and aroused him to action? What could the public speaker have done to avoid anxiety as she stared out across a sea of three thousand strange faces? What can the spouse who has learned his wife is leaving him do to ameliorate the dozens of punishing emotions he is beset with? Or the sensitive man whose date has just rejected him? As we seek answers, we find that there are no easy ones. Whatever we attempt to do to change our behavioral reactions or to build up defenses against them will require a lot of hard work for many of us and success is not always assured. No single form of therapeutic intervention will work for everyone. What works for your next-door neighbor might not work for you.

Perhaps by the year 2400 we'll be able to go to a "Mental Equilibrium Store" and buy a divorce chip or a championship-game chip or a sexual-defense chip, or whatever type of chip is appropriate, so that after we have encountered a situation that has severely thwarted the expectations of our Inner Dummy, we can insert the chip in a patch next to our ear that will diminish the punishing emotions, bring back our equanimity and maintain it through the upset, just as we use a seasickness patch today, preparing for rolling seas on a cruise. Who knows? It's possible.

There isn't anyone on the planet who doesn't have a psychological or personality disorder of some sort. We are all afflicted by something that in a consensus vote of apparently normal people would be voted as an irrationality. Even Sigmund Freud went so far as to have his wife put toothpaste on his toothbrush in the morning. Consensus irrationality? I think so. A college friend of mine who became a psychiatrist used to throw over the table on occasion when his wife made a mistake during a bridge game. Or what about the university professor who would swear profanities in his car, when even elderly ladies innocently cut in front of him? Or my first ex-wife, Phyllis, who made my bed at 5 A.M. one morning, when I got up to go to the bathroom? Or a woman I know whose young daughter is under the illusion that she knows everything and has to be in charge of everything, leading to one confrontation after another?

There appears to be a continuum in most of the common personality and other psychological disorders, ranging from the mildly annoying to the psychotic. The sixty-four-thousand-dollar question is at what point on the continuum is some form of remedy desirable?

Psychiatric professor Jerome Kroll, in his book *The Challenge of the Borderline Patient*, put it as follows:

> It is not clear when a particular trait, such as suspiciousness, should be considered abnormal, or when a particular person who exhibits a pattern of traits or behaviors in excess, such as suspiciousness and argumentativeness, should be considered abnormal.... If we consider a trait such as aggressiveness displayed by a trader in the pit of the Chicago Board of Trade—"where as many as 700 traders shout their orders and elbow for position two hours each day while trying to remain on two feet" it might not be viewed as pathological in that particular context... however such aggressiveness most likely would be seen as highly aberrant, and therefore pathological, if displayed by a monk or nun living in a religious community.[3]

Dr. Kroll also questioned why in the Personality Disorder section of DSM-III (*Diagnostic and Statistical Manual of Mental Disorders*), "a criterion for antisocial personality disorder should be defined as ten or more sexual partners within one year." He makes a good point. If this were the criterion used in a court of law, then Wilt Chamberlain, the former NBA basketball player who claimed to have twenty thousand sexual encounters during his long career, should long ago have been committed to an institution.[4] It is apparent that along the continuum of mental disorders there are many gray areas.

Think back to the experience of Jerilyn Ross in her book *Triumph over Fear*, when she experienced a panic attack while dancing in the Cafe Winkler in the city of Salzburg, Austria, with floor-to-ceiling panoramic windows. "The pull was so strong I thought I was going to jump out of the window. Everything started to spin. I felt as though I was on the verge of completely losing control of myself," she wrote.[5] Is she a candidate for treatment, in this case perhaps a therapy known as "systematic desensitization"? Of course.

But what about those of us with the same phobia, but lower on the continuum at a point where it may be defined as an inhibition, who would only feel some mild discomfort and stay away from the windows? Or someone with a mild form of anthropophobia (a fear of being with people), who would only experience a discomforting inhibition upon entering the room? Is some kind of remedy called for? Probably not. Most of us experience phobias or inhibitions of one sort or another, but we just grit our teeth and bear it.

It is apparent that in this sense, there is a continuing battle for our sense of reason between our pure rationality, our ego, and our Inner Dummy. When John McDonald III grabbed my wrist in front of the restaurant when I was about to give the valet a ten-dollar tip and said, "Don't give him the money, give him five dollars instead," he was deadly serious. This is what his sense of reason was telling him, even though the valet looked to be in poor shape on a very slow night and I could afford the money. His Inner Dummy had captured him, but it was an "unaware" capturing. In all the years since, I have been unable to convince him that giving the valet ten dollars was the right thing for me to do. Yes, we talk about it to this day. Does that tell you something about my Inner Dummy?

Then there was Bob Schwartz at the barbecue, who refused to eat a tantalizing steak because he saw that the chef was sweating and might have dripped a drop or two on the steak. And so he had a salad. His was an "aware" capturing in that he understood what was happening, and wonders to this day why he went ahead and did it. Yes, we still talk about it.

Hitler was obviously a victim of an "unaware" capturing of his reasoning power by an Inner Dummy that should be a charter member of an *Inner Dummy Hall of Fame*, if we decide to establish one. His outlook on the world was totally warped by intense limbic-drive expectations, which obviously captured his power of reasoning to the point that he was unaware that his outlooks and actions were distorted.

Or what about Ellen, the fifteen-year-old who weighed eighty-two pounds and refused to eat because she thought after eating a meal that she had grown fat?

And yet, you could put John McDonald, Bob Schwartz, Hitler, Ellen, Jerilyn Ross, and Albert Goldstein, the schizophrenic who in early 1999 killed a girl in a New York City subway station, on beach chairs reading books on an island in the Caribbean and never know that they had phobias or disorders of any kind. The Inner Dummy is only alerted when the emotional sentinel described by Daniel Goleman in chapter 4 is activated by a physical encounter or a thought that triggers it. It is then capable of flooding the mind with irrational thought and/or the punishing emotions of anxieties, stress, depression, or a combination on the list of more than two hundred.

At that point, it appears as if the strength of our "ego defenses" determines if our power of reason becomes captured. For a man like Hitler, who as previously observed was probably driven by an Inner Dummy that was a Number Ten on the power, territorial, and purpose scales, combined with a Number One on the nurturance (practically zero capability of compassion) and survival (little fear of taking risks) scales, there isn't much any "ego defense" can do. It is all over when a man like this gains a position of great influence.

At the other extreme, Bob Schwartz is not walking around all day thinking about germs. He is not obsessed by them. But if he sees a chef over a grill preparing steaks and dripping sweat, his mild phobia against germs will be signaled by his emotional sentinel and it may be enough to overpower his "ego defenses," which are also telling him of the probability that sweat dripping on his particular steak is small, that if indeed a drop or two does land on the steak, that it would probably contain less germs than a tuna sandwich. However, these rational thoughts are overcome by the Inner Dummy, which has an agenda of its own and is saying, in effect, "don't touch that steak," and wins the conflict.

In the same way, the recovered alcoholic we just spoke about, whose beautiful date drags him into the bar of a posh hotel and orders two champagnes, may not have enough "ego defenses" to just say no. His Inner Dummy's reward system will pull out all the stops to motivate him to recreate the feelings of reward attained by having alcohol in his bloodstream. As anyone recovering from any serious addiction can tell you, the process can be long, hard, and painful. The Inner Dummy has all the ammunition when it comes to delivering punishing emotions and it is persistent in its memory. Even after a long and successful fight of abstinence, it may still not be over. The limbic memory of the rewarding feelings of the addiction remains. And so when you put a glass of champagne in front of our recovering alcoholic at the posh bar, his emotional sentinel activates the limbic memory, and all the wrong emotions emerge. Whether or not our man takes the drink depends on the battle between his Inner Dummy and the state of his "ego defenses" on this particular night. If he is tired or beleaguered or somewhat depressed he might relent and drink the champagne, which will quickly lead to the consumption of one glass after another, since merely the taste of a potential reward that has been repressed is apparently enough to exponentially increase the pressure of the id-based drive expectations involved. On another night when our recovering alcoholic might be feeling well rested, exuberant, in control of himself, he might push the champagne away and order a mineral water and lime instead.

In making a decision, either voluntary or forced by our family or others, to change the effect of behavioral outlooks that may be harmful to ourselves or others, we can probably boil down the strategies available to three basic categories:

- Avoid whatever or whoever is triggering the punishing emotions.

- Create "ego defenses" that work to keep the punishing emotions out.

- Work to change the intensities and the expectations of the limbic drives involved so that whatever punishing emotions we are being afflicted with are relieved or dissolved.

My apologies to Dr. Freud, Dr. Hefter, and all their modern contemporaries in the fields of psychiatry and psychology for making this appear so simplistic. Of course the solutions are much more complex. But in reading literally dozens of books about various forms of therapies to cope with and/or alleviate irrational actions and behavior in otherwise apparently normal people, these three categories appear to encompass all of them. The strategies we might pursue, however, may emanate from a combination of all three. We'll describe the first two in this chapter.

ENVIRONMENT CHANGE

The first category of strategies involves changing our environment in some way so that we are in much less danger of being exposed to whatever may trigger the id-based drives that we are trying to avoid. For a recovering alcoholic, this might mean, among other things, staying away from places where alcohol is served. For a cocaine addict, it might mean staying completely away from friends or others who are users. Or if we have a phobia against heights, it might simply mean staying away from tall buildings. If we feel stress and anxiety when we visit our families or our in-laws or certain friends, it means staying away from them as much as social harmony allows. If our boss on the job is stressing us out, it means making the decision to get another job and then looking for opportunities to do so. It also might mean getting into a new relationship, one that is supportive, if we perceive the one we have now as destructive.

One psychological phrase for this category of strategies I found in reference books is "environmental stimulus control." Another is "avoidant coping style." In a chapter entitled "Self-Management Methods" in the book *Helping People Change*, the authors of the chapter, psychology professor Frederick H. Kanter (also an editor of the book) and Canadian psychologist Lisa Gaelick-Buys, wrote the following:

> Numerous clinical reports have described the use of alteration of physical or social environments to prevent a response. For example, cigarette cases or refrigerators have been equipped with time locks that make access impossible except at preset intervals. Persons on weight reduction programs have been advised to keep only as much food in the house as can be consumed in a short time, thus eliminating late evening snacking. . . . Mothers put mittens on small children to reduce thumb sucking, students find isolated areas for study, some persons do not carry credit cards, others play loud music or flee from houses that hold past memories, all in order to control undesired behaviors or fantasies.[6]

Most of us would have difficulties making major changes in our environment. Our attachment to jobs, families, other people, and communities might make it as painful to change as to stay and endure the existing pain. But some change is definitely an option.

A person I knew many years ago was so pained by the actions of his father, who made an attempt to steal money from a trust established by his grandfather, that he disowned his father as well as most of his other relatives. He then became addicted to drugs and had difficulty holding a job. I heard just recently that he is living in a small town miles away from everything and is doing quite well. So, in some circumstances a major environmental change may work.

In an extreme example of environmental change, outdoor writer Jon Krakauer in his book *Into the Wild* attempts to uncover the motivations of

Chris McCandless, who was so anxious to bury himself in the wilderness of Alaska that he did so without adequate preparation and lost his life. In making comparisons to others who have sought solitude, Krakauer describes fifth-century Irish monks known as *papar* who

> sailed and rowed from the west coast of Ireland . . . in small open boats . . . without knowing what, if anything, they'd find on the other side. The papar risked their lives—and lost them in untold droves—not in the pursuit of wealth or personal glory or to claim new lands in the name of any despot. As the great arctic explorer and Nobel laureate Fridtjof Nansen points out, "these remarkable voyages were . . . undertaken chiefly from the wish to find lonely places where these anchorites might dwell in peace, undisturbed by the turmoil and temptations of the world.[7]

Krakauer prints a note left behind by McCandless in the shelter in which he died:

> And now after two rambling years comes the final and greatest adventure. The climactic battle to kill the false being within and victoriously conclude the spiritual revolution. . . . No longer to be poisoned by civilization he flees, and walks alone upon the land to become lost in the wild.[8]

McCandless gave up all contact with his family, including his parents and all the attachments of civilized life, to find "spiritual freedom," as he and others like him called it, in the wilderness. How different is this from people who hole up in their apartments or homes for months or even years at a time to escape the travails of life?

To even begin attempting this type of avoidant coping style probably requires a low nurturance scale, a Number One or Two. Krakauer quoted one of his characters: "We like companionship see, but we can't stand to be around people for very long. So we go get ourselves lost, come back for a while, then get the hell out again."

I recall a friend who told me that he loved to run into the woods and stay there for hours, sitting at the foot of a tree. Before long, the thoughts that were bothering him would return, and so he would hike out. The limbic brain isn't easily left behind, as people who try to break the cigarette habit by throwing out all cigarettes in their homes know. It is usually only the first step in what can be a long and painful process. The Inner Dummy isn't easily thwarted.

"EGO DEFENSE" STRATEGIES

The second major category of strategies comprise those that strengthen our "ego defenses," to allow us to withstand whatever long-term punishing emotions are triggered by id-based drives when their expectations aren't fully met. One of the greatest "ego defenses" of all time is a strong religious belief, particularly if we have achieved the leap of faith that allows us to fall on our knees and pray to our God when we feel we are becoming beset and converse with Him in a meaningful way. What happens when we have succeeded in a leap of faith and fail to meet a limbic-drive expectation—we didn't get the job we wanted, we are in the midst of a divorce, we lost a championship game— is that we can rationally attribute the disappointment to "God's will," and our Inner Dummy will actually buy the argument. "Oh, so you're telling me that expectation I wanted and you failed to meet was God's will," our Inner Dummy might say to us. "Well, okay, if that's the story then there will be no frustration or depression for you today, but tomorrow is another day."

In her book *The Therapy Sourcebook*, therapist Francine M. Roberts writes the following about the value of spirituality:

> Often, a connection to a higher power or God presence fosters a sense of being connected to a whole, of being at one with all that is in existence. Faith in God can help us to believe that there is some reasoning behind events that occur, and that good will prevails over evil. . . . Believing in a higher power may offer a sense of being nurtured or guided. We often view God with a parental interpretation.[9]

There are billions of people throughout the world who believe in one of more than five thousand religious belief systems, with the depth of their beliefs ranging from mild interest to orthodox fundamentalism. Many families teach their children the religious belief that was taught to them, in the belief that they are handing down a tradition. It might be better for harmony between religions to view the teaching of a religious belief as an "ego defense system" that will help the children bear the disappointments of their limbic drive expectations with the minimal triggering of punishing emotions. Religious schools and textbooks might spend less time on their traditions and more time cultivating an environment that will create a leap of faith.

Although I am not a religious person myself, I sometimes watch evangelist events on television and get a thrill when I see people walk to the front, "giving themselves to Jesus," because I know if they mean it, they will find comfort.

Probably the second most popular "ego defense" mechanism, after religion, is the consumption of alcohol. It is second because in many Middle East and eastern countries, alcohol isn't consumed with the passion it is in the West because their religions and cultures forbid or de-emphasize it.

If we are mildly inebriated, the effect is a numbing of our rational consciousness and Inner Dummy so that we feel its punishing emotions less. If we are drunk, we may hardly feel these emotions at all.

Franklin D. Roosevelt took great pride in being able to prepare the ideal martini, which he consumed with family and friends each night before dinner. "It must be cocktail hour somewhere in the world," I have frequently heard at the end of tension-packed business meetings that end early in the afternoon.

The problem with alcohol and other narcotics as well as mind-easing prescription drugs is that some of us may become addicted to them. On the one hand, they work in numbing the Inner Dummy, but at the same time, the reward system of the Inner Dummy may become so taken with the rewarding emotion produced that it addicts us and begins using our mind-altering alcohol, narcotics, and other drugs not at five in the afternoon, but at eight in the morning. Nothing is easy or surefire for an Inner Dummy that may, at times, be likened to a loose cannon in an all-out war. It can backfire.

Another form of "ego defense" is working to build our willpower. We may become part of an organization or a culture with militant characteristics, where through months or years of regimentation, we build our rational will to resist tempting limbic-based drives and/or endure their punishing emotions.

Victorian England set a standard for resisting temptation with a culture that included maintaining a stoic attitude and rational discipline in the face of adverse or tempting situations, the veritable "stiff upper lip." Children of Victorian families were trained, through parenting and boarding schools, not to let their emotions show, to take punishment without a whimper, to watch stoically during a father's death, to resist immoral sexual advances, and so forth. And while there were failures in the system, the stuff of old English movies, that revealed the whims of human nature behind the stiff manners and airs, it did show that in many of us, the rational will can indeed be strengthened through training.

In this sense we have the picture of the U.S. Marine, proud and true, standing at attention in full dress uniform at his post, while someone stands in front of him shouting profane expletives about his mother to test his resolve, and he shows no flinch or change of expression. The image of the marine is one who has been trained to take it, who has the "right stuff." "Pour it on," I recall an old friend of mine, an ex-navy officer and former member of the FBI, saying in his position of running a major distribution chain, as he was getting some bad news. "Pour it on," he would say on the telephone to the branch manager he was talking to, "you haven't made it sound bad enough." Paul Murray, who passed away many years ago, was proud of his ability to take bad news with equanimity. I used to say to him, "Boy, I wish I could be more like you." Bad news used to just wipe me out. Today, if Paul were alive, I'd say to him, "Boy, I wish I had your 'ego defenses.' "

What Paul and others like him appeared to have was high self-esteem that was developed through training, in becoming proficient in their work and in surrounding themselves with supportive families and friends. Self-esteem, as pointed out in chapter 18, relates to high confidence. And so working to develop higher levels of self-esteem and self-confidence is a strategy for strengthening your "ego defenses."

This line of reasoning might be enough to justify a decision to go back to school to get a master's or doctorate, or to acquire some specialized skill. Or to enroll in one of those jungle survival boot camps. Or whatever else we think might work for us in building our self-esteem, if we think it needs building. We are investing in a stronger "ego defense."

Does that fly? Not all the time, unfortunately. I've known many dysfunctional people with doctorates. The operative phrase in strategizing against the Inner Dummy, whether avoidance, building "ego defenses," or working to change the limbic drives themselves, is this: *Nothing works for everyone.* Each of us has to find those strategies that work for us.

Strengthening our "ego defenses" can also mean working to occupy our minds so that punishing and stressful thoughts and emotions are kept at bay. How often have we seen people recovering from various addictions or a divorce or other traumatic events, throwing themselves into their work, occupying themselves for twelve to eighteen hours a day? The Inner Dummy appears intent on "overwhelming our ego," as Freud said, and which bears repeating, punishing us with its emotions when we disappoint it. Occupying that ego with activities that require rational focus can apparently help keep those emotions out. For example, in his book *Flow*, University of Chicago psychology professor Mihaly Csikszentmihalyi described a number of techniques for quieting and enriching the mind, ranging from Yoga and meditation to sex, art, and athletics.[10]

Then there are the transcendental and holistic teachings offered by such people as Deepak Chopra, physician, author, and lecturer, who work to create a perspective in the mind through meditation, proper nutrition, and other self-care techniques and belief systems that allow us, among other things, they say, to view life with a calmer outlook, lower our levels of stress, and thus improve our physical as well as our mental health.

Holistic teachings also include many of other "ego defense" techniques, ranging from the "Power of Kabbalah," an ancient Judaic body of thought, whose proponents claim "can lead towards prosperity, success and genuine peace," to the "Japanese Tea Ceremony," which its proponents claim "brings forward consciousness, tranquility and graciousness," to "Reiki Training," which is an "oriental healing art form of spirituality."

There are undoubtedly hundreds, if not thousands, of activities if we include all the occupations in the world that can be therapeutic and can work to calm those Inner Dummies that appear to take great satisfaction in punishing us. The idea in most of the therapies that follow is to occupy our consciousness, since it is believed that the mind can only visualize one thought at a time.

MEDITATION AND YOGA

The idea is to defend your consciousness against the intrusive thoughts of your Inner Dummy. The mantra or word you use, repeating it over and over in rapid succession, to begin your meditation sessions, is apparently aimed at filling your consciousness. Teacher of meditation Dr. John Harvey in his paper "Meditation," included in the *Big Book of Relaxation*, said, "Meditation is a conscious effort to focus the mind in a non-analytic manner and to avoid discursive [meandering] or ruminative [gnawing] thought."[11] Outside thoughts that come to you are ordered out—"Get out," we might say to ourselves. Once we are trained in this technique, the saying of the mantra soon trails off into a soothing state of mind, sans Inner Dummy meandering and gnawing thoughts. Yoga is a form of meditation and there are many books that describe its techniques.

RELAXATION TECHNIQUES

Yoga and meditation would fit in this category as well. There are workshops and books galore that offer techniques for dealing with and controlling stress and anxiety in our lives. Of course, some of us learn to relax sitting in front of a television with a remote clicker or watching our favorite soap operas. We become absorbed with what is on the screen and may feel less uptight about our cares of the moment. My son Barry, who is a pilot, finds flying therapeutic. My other son, Andy, who works for Microsoft, will sit for long periods of time, eyes glazed, working on a spreadsheet. Others of us relax with video games or card playing. Our focus on the games keeps the Inner Dummy out of our consciousness and so we consider this relaxing. Visualization is another technique. One process is to lie back with soothing music and think of the calmest spot you've ever visited, while working to relax your body. I use this sometimes, visualizing my favorite scene in Hawaii. Writer Jenny Sutcliffe, author of *The Complete Book of Relaxation Techniques*, observes: "The main benefit of relaxation is, paradoxically, a negative one: when you are relaxed, you are not stressed."[12]

PET THERAPY

Many people find pets therapeutic, not only because they occupy the mind, but because for many of us, they can fill our expectation drives for nurturance and purpose. When you consider all the millions of dogs, cats, birds, and other pets kept by households throughout the world, pet therapy has to rank right up there as not only an "ego defense," but as a drive fulfillment for the Inner Dummy. Now there are even dogs trained to provide therapy. In her book *Therapy Dogs*, author Kathy Diamond Davis says, "In general, therapy dogs provide people with emotional benefits through the use of the dogs' social instincts and social skills."[13] I know at least one person who would rather be with her dogs than people and knowing many of the people she knows, this makes perfect sense.

ART THERAPY

Creating art can be highly therapeutic for those of us who have the skill for it, which I don't. The idea apparently is that once focused on the project, we can go for long stretches without stressful, anxious thoughts fed to us by an Inner Dummy that sometimes won't let us alone. You can probably add in here such activities as quilting, knitting, woodworking, stamp and coin collecting, and the thousands of hobbies, crafts, and collections and other avocations available to us in which we can lose ourselves. Note: There is a complete book on the subject called *The Art Therapy Sourcebook* by Cathy A. Malchiodi.

MUSIC THERAPY

Music probably ranks right up there with religion and alcohol as one of the world's most popular "ego defenses." In his book *The Healing Energies of Music*, college teacher and counselor Hal A. Lingerman writes, "I believe that great music, carefully selected and experienced, can be a unique agent for healing, for partnering joy and sorrow, for empowerment, attunement and inspiration, and for expanding one's spiritual consciousness."[14] I like Al Jolson songs.

DANCE THERAPY

Sometimes called "Movement Therapy," it suggests that dancing can be a form of therapy. The next time you are on a dance floor in the wee hours, you can tell your friends or parents that this is therapy. In her book *Dance Therapy and Depth Psychology*, analyst Joan Chodorow writes, "The use of dance as a healing ritual goes back to earliest human history, but dance therapy is a relatively new profession. The American Dance Therapy Association, founded in 1966, defines dance therapy as the psychotherapeutic use of movement."[15] Many years ago when I attended the University of Wisconsin, I won a Charleston dance contest and I know I felt a lot better.

EXERCISE THERAPY

People I've known who are joggers, bicyclists, and swimmers tell me that after the first few minutes of the exercise, they actually begin to feel meditative. Others who play tennis or racquetball tell me that hitting a ball as hard as they can releases the frustrations of the day or week. I know when I am upset about something, I hit the tennis ball harder. There is also, obviously, therapeutic value in competitive sports, being active in a bowling league for example, or baseball or soccer or whatever. During the event, the mind is focused, the Inner Dummy shuts out, except when it is driving you crazy because you made a mistake in the game itself. Is there no ultimate relief?

FRIENDSHIP AND LOVE THERAPY

I've known people who at night will talk on the phone for hours with their friends and family. They find it therapeutic. I've also known couples who are completely supportive of each other and talk out every problem they have, either their individual problems or ones emanating from the relationship. This may be one of the best therapies of all. Of course, if you have an Inner Dummy that makes you fall in love with people with severe personality disorders, then I would try another strategy.

SLEEP THERAPY

For some reason, the Inner Dummy is less on edge after a good night's sleep. If you are tired, it is more apt to make you cranky, mad, irritable, someone to avoid. Maybe it doesn't like the idea that you didn't get enough sleep and this is actually a form of punishment. The problem is that it punishes everyone around you as well.

GOOD NEWS THERAPY

This is referred to by Francine Roberts in the *Therapy Sourcebook* as "Life Experiences."[16] For example, if we have problems with self-esteem, our identity might be reaffirmed after sessions with a therapist. Or we might get a job promotion that we have worked hard for. Or we might fall in love with someone who puts us on a constant high. In other words, if life treats us kindly, our Inner Dummy is apt to punish us less than when it doesn't. I for one, find it therapeutic when I get good news. I seek out good news and try to avoid bad news. Of course, bad news will always find you. The idea then is to look for good news as a balancing effect. This works for me, although there might be long periods of bad news, which I work hard to stop, using any technique suggested to me, short of throwing amulets in a river.

EDUCATION THERAPY

For most of us, the process of learning something new focuses and exercises the rational side of our mind. I've known people who never stop going to school. Of course, curiosity may also have something to do with this. However, if you are one of those who is always taking classes on one subject or another and someone is criticizing you for spending too much time doing it, tell them that this is your form of therapy and to get lost.

BIBLIOTHERAPY

There are pros and cons to self-help books. Some experts, like Richard M. Restak, who has written many books about the brain, are not high on them, believing that their effects are temporary. On the other hand, I recall reading a self-help book more than twenty years ago and still remember the central thought of facing an inhibition and just burrowing through it, a strategy I still use. If you can find a central thought from a self-help book that helps you build an "ego defense," then reading it was worth the effort. I'm also including bibliotherapy in the next section because books that might be prescribed for us by a professional may help change the way we think, to alter our limbic drives. That is the true definition of the term "bibliotherapy."

When I came across a book titled *Using Bibliotherapy in Clinical Practice* by university social worker John T. Pardeck,[17] I was thrilled because this is my favorite therapeutic ego defense—reading books. And so, if you don't mind, when people ask me what I do to keep my Inner Dummy at bay, I will tell them I use "bibliotherapy" in that sense of the word. It sounds better than just, "I read books." Does this sound like I have a problem with my self-esteem?

DOODLE THERAPY

In a New Age book called *Would the Buddha Wear a Walkman?* authors Judith Hooper and Dick Teresi say, "Some therapists would like to analyze your doodles. Gregory M. Furth, a Jungian therapist who works in New York City, uses drawings to 'hitchhike with the client's unconscious.' "[18] The term "unconscious" may be considered to be another word for the id or Inner Dummy. Aside from the description of doodle therapy above, I know people who love to doodle simply for its therapeutic value. So definitely include doodling in your arsenal of potential "ego defenses," now that you know it is a formal therapy.

AROMATHERAPY

I found a number of references about aromatherapy, so it must have some value. There is something about the right kind of smells that may soothe you, it turns out. On the other hand, being in the presence of the wrong kinds of smells can be an irritant. So the idea must be to avoid those. Am I stating the obvious?

DAYDREAMING

According to the book *Would the Buddha Wear a Walkman?* "If you're in Waking Dream therapy, you're encouraged to discourse at length with all the 'invisible guests' in your unconscious be they wise hags, sulky children or queens."[19] Isn't this great news for daydreamers? Now when your parents or teachers or boss scolds you for daydreaming, you can claim that you are engaged in Waking Dream Therapy.

There are probably hundreds of other activities that might be described as ego defenses, including finding a job you love and absorbing yourself in it. As previously pointed out no single "ego defense strategy" works for everyone. What provided magic for your next-door neighbor may fall flat for you. The proponents of many of the more unusual movements, doodle therapy included, have engendered success in enough people to create a following, so no method that isn't harmful to others should be belittled when it comes to creating periods of time when a disappointed Inner Dummy and its punishing emotions can be held at bay. *The Therapy Sourcebook* is an excellent reference for the many forms of therapy that are available to us.

Working to change our irrational outlooks, which can lead to irrational thoughts and actions is a lot more difficult than avoiding them or developing "ego" defenses to endure them. We'll discuss what it takes in the next two chapters, following a brief encounter with Dr. Freud.

COMMENTARY BY DR. HEFTER

In pointing out the extensive array of activities that an individual can utilize in order to better cope with the powerful unconscious drives searching for need gratification, David is, in effect, offering a primer for allowing people to function in a civilized manner. His emphasis on the fact that different individuals may employ different means of strengthening their respective ego or rational coping skills is especially warranted. Not infrequently a person will attempt to engage in an activity recommended by another person because it worked for that individual, only to discover that it is not helpful and perhaps even worsens a situation. For example, not everyone with an alcohol abuse problem is helped by involvement in AA, not everyone benefits from relaxation training, the therapist who was a godsend for your best friend may rub you the wrong way, and so forth. In addition, a technique may not be of value at all for an individual at one point in his life, but proves to be of significant utility at a later time. It is important to keep trying to develop appropriate control over the Inner Dummy, David's pseudonym for the id. This does not mean denying it, nor does it mean never allowing it to have gratification—what is meant is learning ultimately how to integrate it with the rest of what one is.

NOTES

1. *New York Times*, September 4, 1998, p. A7.
2. Sigmund Freud, excerpt from *New Introductory Lectures*, in *The Freud Reader*, ed. Peter Gay (New York: Norton, 1989), p. 100.
3. Jerome Kroll, *The Challenge of the Borderline Patient: Competency in Diagnosis and Treatment* (New York: Norton, 1988), p. 7.
4. *Ottawa Citizen*, June 15, 1998, p. F1.
5. Jerilyn Ross, *Triumph Over Fear* (New York: Bantam, 1994), pp. 5–6.
6. Frederick H. Kanfer and Lisa Gaelick-Buys, "Self-Management Methods," in *Helping People Change: A Textbook of Methods*, ed. Frederick H. Kanfer and Arnold P. Goldstein (New York: Pergamon Press, 1991), p. 336.
7. Jon Krakauer, *Into the Wild* (New York: Anchor Books, 1997), p. 97.
8. Ibid., p. 163.
9. Francine M. Roberts, *The Therapy Sourcebook* (Los Angeles: Lowell House, 1998), p. 277.
10. Mihaly Csikszentmihalyi, *Flow: The Psychology of Optimal Experience* (New York: HarperPerennial, 1990), n.p.
11. John Harvey, excerpt from "Meditation," in *The Big Book of Relaxation*, ed. Larry Blumenfeld (Roslyn, N.Y.: Relaxation Co., 1994), p. 9.
12. Jenny Sutcliffe, *The Complete Book of Relaxation Techniques* (Allentown, Pa.: Quarto, 1991), p. 7.
13. Kathy Diamond Davis, *Therapy Dogs: Training Your Dog to Reach Others* (New York: Macmillan, 1992), p. 1.
14. Hal A. Lingerman, *The Healing Energies of Music* (Wheaton, Ill.: Quest, 1995), p. vii.
15. Joan Chodorow, *Dance Therapy and Depth Psychology: The Moving Imagination* (New York: Rutledge, 1991), p. 1.
16. Roberts, *The Therapy Sourcebook*, pp. 266–67.
17. John T. Pardeck, *Using Bibliotherapy in Clinical Practice: A Guide to Self-help Books* (Westport, Conn.: Greenwood Press, 1993), n.p.
18. Judith Hooper and Dick Teresi, *Would the Buddha Wear a Walkman?* p. 116.
19. Ibid, p. 119.

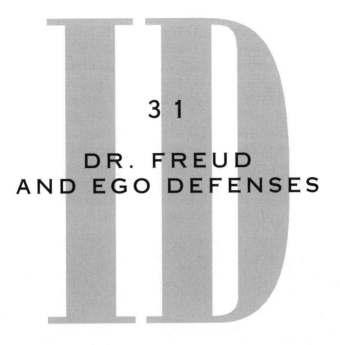

3 1

DR. FREUD
AND EGO DEFENSES

An estranged couple in Fresno, California, drew guns and wounded each other after the husband was late for a marriage counseling session at a church.[1]

Dr. Freud was walking toward the agency conference room when Samuel Ollander overtook him from behind.

"Excuse me, Dr. Freud," he said tapping him on the shoulder, "I was just coming to see you."

"Ah, Ollander, I'm sorry we didn't have a chance to chat after your discussion with that interesting little group last night."

"Yes, sir, I did look for you, but you were gone."

"That was Wendy's doing, she wanted me to meet some friends and I have to admit to having a tad too much wine. So you'll excuse me if I am a bit groggy."

"Not at all, sir, I just wanted to show you one more concept before the final presentation to you, which I understand is scheduled for tomorrow afternoon." Ollander pointed to a card he was holding.

"That is correct. I am prepared to render a decision at that time."

"Well, we're all hopeful that your decision will be positive, sir."

"We shall see, Ollander, we shall see. Now why don't we step into the conference room and you can show me what you have."

They began walking the few steps to the conference-room door.

"You say this is something new," Dr. Freud said as they entered the room.

"Yes, sir, it is. It just came in from the creatives this morning. I could have waited until the presentation, but I wanted you to see this beforehand."

"Very well, Ollander," Freud said offhandedly as he sat down. "Go ahead with it."

Ollander sat opposite Dr. Freud and began.

"The idea, sir, was to come up with a subbranding theme that would cover what someone might do to handle the stress in their lives, the pressures that might result from one's vocation or avocation or being subjected to the irrational thoughts and actions of others. An irrational parent, for example, or a boss or a spouse. It is you yourself, I believe, who made the statement that the pressures generated by the id require discharge."

Freud thought for a moment.

"With that short statement, you show that you cannot avoid oversimplification, try as you might, Ollander."

"I didn't mean to upset you."

"No, you didn't upset me. To use your simplifications, a minor event, an argument with one's spouse, can create id-based pressure, but time alone or a slight fit of temper might suffice to release that pressure. However, pressures build in accordance with the intensity of the trauma experienced and the vulnerability of the individual at the time. Some combinations of these two facts can result in the pressures enduring over long periods of time, if not for a lifetime, particularly when there is no respite or relief from the source of the trauma. In other words, it is a complex subject."

"Oh, I do know that, sir," Ollander replied. "What we are focusing on with this subbranding," he shook the card he was holding facedown in his hand, "is indeed simplistic, but we think it is essential to the campaign. We will be testing it with a handful of other materials we hope will be ready by tonight, with another group."

"I hope this is not another idea for a Dummy Punching Bag, Ollander," Freud replied with a chuckle.

Ollander smiled, looking embarrassed. "Oh no, sir, it's not another product."

"Okay, then, show it to me, let's get the pain over with . . . or should I say the Dummy Pain." He paused and grinned. "Maybe you are finally getting to me, Ollander."

"Oh, I hope so, sir. Anyway, here it is."

Ollander turned over the card, which read: "Dummy Diverters."

Freud looked puzzled.

"Dummy Diverters, sir. Of course we'll test alternate concepts. But it means finding therapeutic thoughts or activities that will protect or relieve the Inner Dummy from stress, the normal anxieties of life that emanate from job pressures, having to deal with irrational people and other causes, as we just discussed. Do you understand?"

"I'm not sure I want to."

"Well, like music or art, sir. They would be Dummy Diverters. They may have the capability for diverting our stressful thoughts. A long trip somewhere might be a Dummy Diverter, or doing Yoga or meditation or reading books or working in your garden or becoming absorbed in a hobby. Or finding a strategy for avoiding a mother-in-law who is annoying you without disturbing the family's harmony. That strategy might be called a Dummy Diverter as well."

"Certainly, Ollander, you can't be serious."

"I am serious, sir. Just think of how many people there are in the world who find activities in their lives that are comforting to them, but who may be criticized by others for becoming overly absorbed with them, even something as harmless as stamp collecting for example. Well, now, with the advertising exposure we will give to this concept they can simply say . . . ," Ollander stood up and held up the sign, ". . . they can say, 'What I am doing is simply a Dummy Diverter, an Inner Dummy Diverter, to use the full euphemism. This is my way of handling life. You might have your way of handling your lives and you don't see me criticizing your Inner Dummy Diverters.' Do you get the idea now, sir?"

"I'm afraid I do."

"One of our creatives even had the idea of coming up with a logotype for the phrase Inner Dummy Diverter that hotels, recreational facilities, and other outlets or forms of therapeutic activities can put in their own ads. They can say, 'Come visit us in the Caribbean and relax. We are an Authorized Inner Dummy Diverter. Or come join our Yoga class or exercise class . . . we are Authorized Inner Dummy Diverters.' Do you see the possibilities?"

Freud leaned his head in his hands in his now familiar pose. He didn't say anything.

After a moment, Ollander said, "Dr. Freud, you are all right, aren't you?"

Freud looked up. "No, Ollander, I am not all right. Every time I try to reach some accommodation with the nonsensical materials you show me, you come up with something even more outrageous. I cannot believe you need these simplistic concepts to communicate my very basic thoughts about the id. Why can't you just distribute some of my books?"

"We could, sir, we could. But we are attempting to reach a mass audience with this campaign and your books are written primarily for those interested in academic concepts. If I may say so."

He paused. After a moment Dr. Freud said, "Go ahead, Ollander, spit it out."

". . . If I may be so bold, sir, I think the Inner Dummy campaign is the way to go, and it needs to include concepts such as Dummy Diverters."

Freud looked momentarily at Ollander and then in a dismissive voice said, "I'm sorry, Ollander. I know you mean to do the right thing. Let's not get into a discussion about it now; I have a lot to think about, as you know. Now, is there anything else I can do for you?"

"No, sir, not at the moment," Ollander replied, picking up the card and moving toward the door. "Thank you, sir."

Just as Ollander was leaving the room, Freud said, "Well, there is one thing you should know, Ollander."

"And what is that, sir?" Ollander peeked back through the door.

"In my day, I used to take a month every year to walk the mountains of Austria and I found that experience to be highly diverting."

Ollander stared at Freud.

"That was a joke, Ollander. I am still trying to lighten you up. Now get on with you."

Ollander smiled weakly and left.

NOTE

1. Associated Press, *Chicago Sun-Times*, April 24, 1998, p. 34.

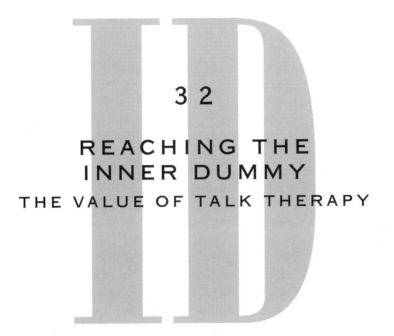

3 2

REACHING THE
INNER DUMMY
THE VALUE OF TALK THERAPY

Rough estimates for those killed in warfare during the past twenty years include the following: 2,000,000 in Afghanistan, 650,000 in Rwanda, 250,000 in Bosnia, 150,000 in Liberia, 175,000 in Burundi, 75,000 in Algeria, 50,000 in Chechnya, 57,000 in Sri Lanka, 1,500,000 in Sudan, 37,000 in Turkey, 500,000 in Angola, and 14,000 in Sierra Leone. These are only partial figures.[1]

The third category of strategies for working to change the effect of our irrational outlooks is the most difficult. While avoidance keeps us removed from triggering points, and "ego defenses" help keep the punishing emotions of our Inner Dummy at bay, this third category of strategies involves working directly on our minds to *change the nature* of our Inner Dummy.

What we, in essence, decide to do when we utilize this category of strategies is to create a "controlled trauma" that will change the outlooks of our id-based drives so that their expectations are either raised or lowered as needed to alleviate the punishing emotions that are besetting us . . . because in real life we are somehow disappointing those expectations, which may be totally irrational.

For example, we may decide we can no longer endure the torment of going into high-rise buildings in our job as a building inspector. We are aware we have the phobia and we are willing to give it up. And so we begin to see a behavioral psychologist who puts us through a series of well-established steps to desensitize the intense and irrational expectations of these specific fears. Or perhaps our marriage is failing and our spouse, who calls us a power-obsessed "control freak," tells us we either seek therapy for our problem or she is leaving. And so even though we think we are perfectly normal, we go, because the expectations of our nurturance program are driving us to remain attached. Or perhaps we are tired of washing our hands forty to fifty times a day. And so we seek treatment for this compulsion. Or maybe we can no longer stand the fit of jealousy we suffer when a spouse is late coming home, or maybe we want to get rid of our "road rage," or our binge eating, and so we seek treatment. Or maybe we are tired of having more than one personality running our lives. And so we seek treatment for multiple personality disorder, also known as dissociative identity disorder. Or we are severely depressed, feel hopeless, can hardly make it through the day, and so we seek treatment, which might mean after the proper diagnosis, having medication prescribed for us. Or, we are tired of the nightmares we suffer, which began with our days in combat in the Vietnam War, and so we seek treatment for them.

Or perhaps we are fed up with becoming dejected and depressed when we are not the center of attention. Or we are fed up with being so sensitive to criticism that we find ourselves avoiding people unless we are certain of their support. Or we are fed up with our adulterous affairs, which threaten our family. Or we are phobic about appearing clumsy, silly, or shameful to others in public to the point that it gives us panic attacks. Or we are fed up with our manic episodes, periods which last about one week, when we are euphoric and expansive, think we can advise presidents, and spend more money than we should. Or we understand that the voices we hear talking to us are not real, that they are delusions, and we want to let the voices go. Or we are fed up with our violent behavior and the cruelty we exhibit to people and animals.

When conditions like these are serious enough, environmental changes and the initiation of "ego defense" strategies are not enough. And so we voluntarily seek out treatment for our problems or are virtually forced to do so by those close to us.

The key with voluntary treatment is that we are aware we have a problem. We have not been so captured by our limbic drives or their imbalanced rewards or punishments, that we understand that things are not right. If we are the victims of an "unaware limbic capturing," we are not aware of our irrationalities; one of our few hopes is that we are pressured into treatment by those close to us. As Dr. Hefter pointed out in chapter 20, it is difficult to convince people like this to make the attempt to change themselves with therapeutic approaches. And once they do visit a therapist, the initial approaches taken by the therapist to establish a relationship conducive to treatment presents enormous challenges.

It is apparent that all disorders are biologically based. In the end, our behavior is determined by the activities of the neurons in our brains and their transmitters and receptors that form specific connections that work somehow in concert to create specific outlooks.

What is less clear is the weight of biology in causing mental disorders from the genetic get-go, as discussed in chapter 26. We know that some forms of schizophrenia and manic depression have a genetic basis that make some people far more vulnerable to these diseases than others. And as we learned from the Minnesota Study of Identical Twins Reared Apart, along with other research that at least half of our behavioral tendencies are genetically based. And this can include the propensity for specific psychological disorders. The strength of our other genetics and the nature and strength of the traumas we meet along with the experiences of our lives are the primary factors in determining whether these propensities come to fruition.

One of the great problems of our society is determining who is mentally ill and who is not. Before I began writing this book, I never doubted that there were millions of neurotic people walking around in the world, people who have been conflicted in some way and were being punished for it, with, for example, depressive feelings or unreal outlooks. I thought it was the more neurotic of us, the "Woody Allens" of the world, who formed the primary client base of trained psychologists and psychiatrists, while still leading lives in our everyday world as otherwise apparently normal people.

However, I was unaware that the more mentally ill among us were also walking around in our everyday world. I was under the impression that seriously afflicted schizophrenics, manic-depressives, and such were in institutions, under the care of trained professionals. When I mentioned this to Bob Schwartz, he stared at me as if I were the one who was delusional. "You didn't know this?" he said. "How could you not know this? Look at who comprise the homeless, the people in shelters. A lot of them are psychotic."

"How do you know this?" I replied.

368   BATTLING THE INNER DUMMY

"Because I read *People* magazine."

Of course, that explained everything.

The National Institute of Mental Health estimates that about 57 million people, or 20 percent of our population of 270 million, have a mental disorder in any given year and that 6.5 million are disabled because of it.[2] In other words, one in five persons who might otherwise act apparently normal have a mental disorder. About 3 million people are victims of a manic-depressive disorder and about 5 million have some form of obsessive-compulsive disorder. Another 2.7 million have schizophrenia and we are probably only skimming the surface here. Schizophrenia captured the limelight in early 1999, after Albert Goldstein, age twenty-nine, with a history of the disease, who reportedly stopped taking his medication, was accused of pushing Kendra Webdale to her death under a New York City subway train on January 3 of that year.

The *New York Times*, in an article about the incident dated January 11, reported the following:

> When someone with a mental illness kills, images are evoked of a crazed and wicked population that should be separated from the rest of society, even though research confirms that the mentally ill are generally no more dangerous than anyone else. . . . This tragedy reinforces the notion that there is too little money and too few programs to serve a needy population that is no longer kept in hospitals.[3]

The point is that Albert Goldstein could at times be perfectly cogent. And so can most of the other neurotics and psychotics in the world. When we see this cogency, we begin to believe that the mentally disordered through an act of will alone can fix themselves in some way. As a result, there is a taint surrounding seeing a therapist, particularly among men higher on the power scale. It is as if going to a therapist is divulging a weakness, the thought being that if you see a therapist you are not a "real man."

Marv Albert, the network-television sports commentator, who, in 1997, had a forcible sodomy charge brought against him because of an encounter with a girlfriend in a Virginia hotel room, and then lost his high-paying job with NBC, was quoted recently in a column by Phil Rosenthal in the *Chicago Sun-Times*, describing the things he had been doing with all his free time, among which:

> I was seeing a therapist, which was very helpful. I'm one who, in the past, didn't believe in that, and I found it was very helpful to me to get through

the whole situation. And I just feel much better about myself. I think I'm
a better person now and I look at things a bit differently.[4]

In my experiences in the business world, Albert's initial attitude was typical. I knew of a few executives who saw therapists, but they did their best
to keep the visits secret.

When we have an ankle sprain or a tumor or an ulcer we have no
problem going to a doctor's office because doctors specialize in the physical
aspects of our bodies and can often show us with X-rays or MRIs or whatever what is wrong with us. "Oh, so it's a hernia," we might say. "Well, let's
get it fixed." We let it be known to our friends, acquaintances, and business
associates that we are "going in for surgery."

"Good luck," they'll frequently reply. "Do you want us to send you
some flowers?"

"Don't bother," we'll say grinning. "I'll handle the pain without looking
at a bunch of daisies."

And yet the pain caused by punishing emotions can be just as severe
as the pain caused by a physical malady and may even be sensed by the
same pain center in the brain. But many of us will deny treatment and suffer
needlessly.

Author Anne Sheffield in her book *How You Can Survive When* They're
Depressed, wrote about the depressive experience of author William Styron,
"who documents his descent to the edge of suicide in *Darkness Visible, A
Memoir of Madness* (Vintage 1992)." Following is the passage, as reported
in her book:

> Styron writes that one evening he chose to abandon his room and come
> downstairs to attend a dinner party his wife had arranged, at which he sat
> in "catatonic muteness." "Then," he says, "after dinner sitting in the living
> room, I experienced a curious inner convulsion that I can only describe as
> despair beyond despair. It came out of the cold night; I did not think such
> anguish possible. . . . I felt my heart pounding wildly, like that of a man
> facing a firing squad, and I knew I had made an irreversible decision. . . .
> I had not as yet chosen the mode of my departure [suicide], but I knew that
> step would come next, and soon, as inescapable as nightfall."[5]

I know some people who would have walked up to Styron at the dinner
party, after he revealed his feelings, and say, "Oh, come on, snap out of it. Grow
up, will you? Look at how well you write. What is this depression business?"

It is the intermittent rationality that fools all of us. Styron was probably able to greet the guests cordially and at times speak cogently about some issue of the day, even as he was in deep mental pain and no one was pressuring him. Many of us think that if our rational mind is able to emerge among all the symptoms of mental disorders to discuss the New York Mets, then we should be able to fight our disorders ourselves and fix them.

I thought that Anne Sheffield offered an excellent example related to her by a group-support leader of how rational and even charming sufferers of severe manic depression can be in their "up" or manic state:

> If you're married to or living with a manic-depressive, don't bother with couples therapy or marriage counselors while he or she is in an up phase. (Many) manics also have a problem with sex, but it certainly isn't one of low libido. On the contrary, manics often sleep with anyone they can get their hands on, and . . . they have a very high success rate in getting their chosen partner into bed. *Chosen* is perhaps the wrong word to use here because . . . anyone of the opposite sex looks great to them, and the more the merrier. Mania seems to turn every one of its sufferers into a charmer with charisma and a great sense of humor. Manics also give the appearance of listening to every word that every man or woman lets fall from their lips, a big help when you're looking to make out.[6]

How many motion pictures have we seen where one of the characters is a smooth, rational charmer, who at some point in the plot, begins violently assaulting the heroine, who must run for her life, only to be saved by the hero?

The problem boils down to the fact that we can't X-ray or MRI the Inner Dummy and learn if there is a problem with the neurons or their transmitters and receptors as we might see a fracture in a broken arm. And so the diagnosis made by a psychiatrist or other trained psychotherapists needs to be deduced from interviews and observations, making therapy, according to Dr. Hefter, at times as much an art as a science.

Nonetheless, there are any number of disorders, from a phobic fear of heights to delusional schizophrenia, that are not difficult to diagnose and for which processes are available, including psychotherapy and medication, that can alleviate the symptoms. The fields of psychiatry and clinical psychology have not done a great job of public relations. If they did, people like Marv Albert might have gone into therapy before he committed the acts that caused him to lose his job as a high-paying sports commentator, considered one of the best in the business. Perhaps therapists, as suggested in the previous Dr. Freud chapter 11, would do better if they called themselves *"Inner Dummy Specialists."* If this were so, visualize this conversation between two female college students.

"I heard you broke up with Fred."

"Yeah, he turned out to be another nut case."

"One in a long string, as I recall."

"Absolutely."

"So, what are you going to do about it?"

"I'm seeing an Inner Dummy Specialist."

"Good idea."

"Yeah, when I'm through, the specialist tells me, I should be able to find someone, finally, who doesn't enjoy a destructive relationship."

"But will your Inner Dummy allow you to fall in love with someone normal?"

"My specialist says it's possible."

"Let me know if it works. I'll want the next available appointment. My Inner Dummy definitely needs a specialist."

Okay, so maybe the specialist phrase isn't such a good idea. But the point is, as you review the following methods of therapeutic treatment available to change the outlooks and ameliorate the punishing emotions of the Inner Dummy, it would be beneficial to think of them as techniques for getting through to the right brain connections of our limbic organs so that we can change them in a way that will improve ourselves, much as physical therapy allows us to modify cells to mend a sprained ankle.

As pointed out previously, it would appear that the objective of all forms of therapeutic intervention in attempting to change distorted outlooks into rational ones is to get the *Inner Dummy to bite on it, to buy off on it so that the chemical connections that are rearranged to create the new more rational outlooks become more or less permanent.*

In a paper entitled "Medication and Psychotherapy" in the *Handbook of Psychotherapy and Behavior Change*, the authors made the following point regarding the chemistry of the brain:

> The actions of drugs on mental processes and behavior have generated new knowledge concerning long-standing questions about the relationships of brain and behavior and of mind and biology. The fact that defined chemical substances can influence aggression, anxiety, guilt, performance and so on creates opportunities for research on the neurobiological substrate of mental functioning and behavior.[7]

In a sense, whether we utilize therapists or not, the objective is to find strategies that will get the job done, to get the Inner Dummy to bite, including the use of prescribed medications that rearrange for the better those brain connections that affect our mental processes. What follows is a summary of the main strategies of psychotherapy, with apologies again to Dr. Freud, Dr. Hefter, and all their contemporaries throughout the world, past and present, for attempting to reduce entire libraries of reference works to this form of simplicity.

"Psychotherapy" is the term generally used to define the entire spectrum of therapy. In an edited volume titled *Theories of Psychotherapy*, psychology professors Paul L. Wachtel and Stanley B. Messer included their own paper, which began with the following observation:

> As Jerome Frank (1973) elucidated in his influential book, *Persuasion and Healing*, psychotherapy is an institution with roots that are both broad and deep. Historically, its development can be traced to the shamans, rabbis and faith healers that have responded to the spiritual and psychological needs of humankind at least since the dawn of recorded history. More currently, Frank suggested it has strong affinities . . . with a variety of practices of persuasion, including some—such as "thought reform practiced by totalitarian regimes"—that are far from benign.[8]

This last sentence adds strength to the third cause of psychological disorders discussed previously, our *vulnerability* for becoming attached to dysfunctional ideas and beliefs handed down to us by parents or other authority figures. Frank apparently believes that Adolf Hitler and Vladimir Lenin were practicing a form of perverse and distorted psychotherapy on their followers that caused so many of them to become accomplices in irrational killings.

The paper also stated:

> The proliferation of therapeutic schools—one estimate runs as high as 400 . . . is itself a cultural phenomenon because psychotherapy as a business and a form of secular counseling is one of the defining characteristics of the cultures. . . . The various schools of psychotherapy, to be sure, differ in significant ways. They differ in practice, in values, and in the intellectual traditions to which they link themselves. . . . And yet, Frank argued, they also have much in common.[9]

However, there appears to be some disagreement with regard to a definition of the term "psychotherapy," and how many forms of therapy there are. Frank claimed as many as four hundred. But then I saw one estimate by Edward Shorter, in a September 1998 issue of *American Heritage*, that claimed there are 130 kinds of psychotherapy. Regarding a definition of the term, clinical psychologist Petruska Clarkson, in a paper titled "The Nature and Range of Psychotherapy," which she edited with British psychoanalyst Michael Pokorny, and which was included in *The Handbook of Psychotherapy*, states:

> Definitions of psychotherapy are legion, and none is entirely comprehensive nor entirely satisfactory. . . . In their textbook of psychiatry, Henderson and Gillepsie (1956) regard psychotherapy as any therapy of the mind, appearing to include talking therapy . . . but, by their eighth edition of 1956, psychotherapy has become specific to psychoanalysis and its derivatives. . . . Holmes and Lindley offer a definition: "The systematic use of a relationship between therapist and patient—as opposed to pharmacological and social methods—to produce changes in cognition [awareness, knowing], feelings and behavior. . . . All these definitions rely on the idea of bringing about changes in the personality and manner of a person's relating by the use of essentially psychological techniques.[10]

So there is apparently some terminology confusion in the field. In general, however, the many "schools of therapy" appear to be broken down into *insight-based therapy* including psychoanalysis, but taking other forms as well, and *action-based therapy*, in which therapists take whatever happened in the past for granted, and use varying methods of rational persuasion to change irrational thoughts or outlooks to rational ones, not an easy job. Today, the two forms of therapy are frequently combined. Did you get all that? If not, read on as I attempt to make it clearer.

PSYCHODYNAMIC THERAPY

An underlying hypothesis of psychodynamic therapy, which is insight-based, is that the memory of intensely painful, traumatic incidents that caused our current irrational outlooks have been "repressed" in some way. For example, we might have been bitterly rejected and made fun of in the schoolyard at the age of ten by a friend who we thought betrayed us. The memory of the event became so painful that it was impossible to forget, so we ended up "repressing" it. In other words, we didn't forget it, we somehow buried the memory in our unconscious.

It appears that the id, the Inner Dummy, in an uncharacteristic act of generosity, helps us to "repress" the memory so that it doesn't keep popping up in our minds and creating punishing emotions. But the Inner Dummy, apparently, wants us to pay a price for such generosity. And so one result of the repressed memory of a trauma is that it may drive us toward creating defense mechanisms, which in the case of the schoolyard incident may make us extremely shy and reclusive as an adult, at which point it is hampering our career. When we have to appear at meetings and give presentations, we become practically panic-stricken and wonder why. Defense mechanisms, unlike many phobias or inhibitions, develop as part of our id-based unconscious and become such a natural part of our personality that we are unaware that there were underlying causes. And so we turn to a therapist practicing psychodynamic therapy, which he uses to help us uncover the repressed memory of the trauma. During the process of this form of therapy, the therapist uses "interpretations," suggestions of what the client's conflicts might be in an attempt to penetrate the Inner Dummy. Was it a single schoolyard incident at a point in our lives when we were extremely vulnerable? Was it the father that ignored or belittled us over many years and who has since died, but our Inner Dummy is still trying to please? Recall that the Inner Dummy, unaware of time, awareness, or logic may be unaware that your father has died. You are, but it isn't. Sometimes, when the client disagrees with the therapist's conclusions, this is called "resistance," and needs to be interpreted by the therapist. In a sense, the therapist is working against his client's resistance, the barriers erected by the Inner Dummy, in an effort to get to the bottom of it all. With apologies to Dr. Hefter and his contemporaries, it is as if the therapist is playing the role of a Sherlock Holmes in an investigation aimed at finding the culprits.

Another part of the process is called "transference." In some instances, the therapist in effect becomes an authority figure in the client's life. The therapist is perceived by the client as an important figure from the client's life, perhaps as a parental figure. Within this unique relationship, the client has more freedom to transfer his or her conflicts to the therapist, or, in other words, to let it all hang out. Freud in many of his works repeated the importance of resistance and transference. The expectations of this form of therapy is that at some point, if things go well, we will experience an "insight," an awareness of a rush of feelings of relief as we realize what we did not know previously, that our entire life has been shaped by a ridiculous schoolyard event.

Hey, don't laugh. Something like this happened to me and shaped my early relationships with women. Just look at my lousy record.

Dr. Hefter emphasized the point to me that both repressed memories and defense mechanisms are part of the unconscious. In other words, the Inner Dummy may be manipulating us and we haven't got a clue.

My second ex-wife, Barbara, who tried psychodynamic therapy for quite a while, said she acquired four or five traumatic "insights" during the period of the therapy, which she used to call "Ah-hahs." I recall that one of her "Ah-hahs" was about her father, who her insight told her was disappointed he never had a son and wasn't sure how to interact with Barbara as an adult woman who didn't like hunting or fishing, which he did. Or it was something like that. Anyway, I remember her coming home the night of her "Ah-hah" as happy as I'd ever seen her. "It wasn't my fault," I remember her saying.

PSYCHOANALYSIS

There are some differences between psychodynamic therapy and classical psychoanalysis. One is that in psychodynamic therapy, the client and the therapist sit across from each other and there may be considerable interaction between the two. In classical psychoanalysis, the client is probably asked to recline on a couch, with the therapist sitting behind him or her, out of view. Often there is little overt invervention from the therapist, with the technique being to allow the client to project on his or her own as the therapist seeks to pick up clues.

During the process of my first divorce in 1972, 1 visited a psychoanalyst for a while and sort of liked not having to look at him as I poured out everything that I was feeling, none of which was good. I stopped going to him for a number of reasons, one of which is that we started playing tennis together and I thought he was trying a bit too hard to beat me.

Immediately thereafter I began seeing a therapist who sat across the desk from me and interacted with me as I again poured out all my anguish, trying to determine what it was in my past that made me the disinterested lout my first ex-wife said I was. (Note: After the divorce, we became friends.)

Science writer Morton Hunt also writes the following in his book *The Story of Psychology* about how early psychoanalysts do talk from time to time in psychoanalysis, but that,

Many patients were aware chiefly of their silences and refusals to answer questions and were infuriated—but unable to break away. One analyst

wrote of treating an attractive young woman "who bawls me out unmerci-
fully almost every hour, calling me immature, a quack, cold, a sex maniac,
and so on, yet at the end of the hour she gives me a deep, longing look and
says softly, "See you next time." . . . Occasionally an analyst might even let
a patient who was unable to voice his or her thoughts lie silent on the
couch for the whole hour, or even a number of hours, without trying to help
the patient break through—yet would charge for the time spent. Humorists
and satirists made this seem a common occurrence, although it was actually very rare. Apart from a sense of obligation to help the patient, most
analysts would have found such hours of silence unendurable.[11]

Psychoanalysis doesn't always have to take months or years of lying on
the couch. Hunt points out that:

By the 1970s and 1980s, a handful of psychiatrists and psychologists
were developing the techniques of "short-term dynamic therapy," based
on psychoanalytic principles. Focusing on a single current problem troubling the patient, these methods do not use free association, probe the
unconscious, strive for insight, or overhaul the personality; they rely
chiefly on the patient's transference. Unlike the psychoanalyst, the therapist actively confronts the patient with the evidence that he or she is
behaving toward the therapist in an unrealistic way carried over from
other relationships.[12]

This sounds a bit like "Behavior Therapy," which is action based,
growing ever more popular and easier to understand. Further, there is a
trend away from the use of single therapies such as psychoanalysis and
toward the integration of therapies, so that a therapist might use a combination in seeking a solution.

SELF-PSYCHOLOGY

The concept of self-psychology was developed by Heinz Kohut in the early
1970s. This method of therapy, which Dr. Hefter tells me added a major
dimension to the fields of psychoanalysis and psychotherapy, appears to
focus more on the therapist being highly empathetic to patients, understanding and accepting of the problems they've had. The theory in its most
simplified form appears to be that despite "defects"—for example, not
having had an empathetic caretaker when they were young—and disorders

which have led to their current problems, patients can learn to have fulfilling lives if they begin to feel as if they are understood. Kohut felt that many therapists in psychoanalysis communicate a "censorious and disapproving" attitude to the patient. He believed that "empathetic understanding" is a potent therapeutic agent and built the structure of his therapeutic methods around creating this feeling in his patients.

A clinical psychologist I visited during the 1970s, soon after my first divorce, could have used a dose of Kohut's methods. Talk about "censorious and disapproving." She looked at me as if I were a lunatic. Of course she had sent me to take the Rorschach test, in which dozens of inkblots are shown to you and you are instructed to tell the person conducting the test what first comes to your mind. The person giving me the test was a woman in at least her seventies, and of the fifty or so inkblots that were shown to me, I named at least forty of them as reminding me of a vagina. I recall that she started backing away from me about midway through the test. So maybe the results of the test, which were duly reported back to my therapist, colored her view of me. I'm sure if I were to take the test again today, now that I'm older and less intense, the results would be far different. I hope.

BEHAVIOR THERAPY

When I first began the research for this chapter, I was a bit dubious about the effectiveness of behavior therapy in general because of my own personal problems and experiences. I just couldn't see my fear of eating fatty foods or how much I weigh being overcome by mere rational persuasion. The barrier wall protecting my Inner Dummy from rational thought is doubly thick, I suspect. But after delving into this form of therapy, reading book after book and talking to people who have successfully used it, I lost some of my skepticism. Then I tried some of the mind techniques on some of my own phobias, inhibitions, and other irrationalities and found some success, without really trying hard.

For example, I no longer weigh myself each day, dreading what I'd find the scale reading. In this sense, I would be the perfect candidate for the Dr. Freud Inner Dummy Bathroom Scale, which always weighs eight pounds less and when you're really overweight, reads out: "You don't want to know, check back tomorrow." I also now eat some fatty foods that I would crave but never touch, but only two or three times a month and I haven't gained any weight. Yes, I did step on the scale before writing this.

I also used some procedures from Rational Emotive Therapy (described shortly) to improve my tennis game. Instead of thinking I was going to lose when falling behind, I began to use this method of therapy, devised by Dr. Albert Ellis, to believe I was going to win and it improved my confidence level in seesaw matches. So there you are. Is this enough to convince you to read further?

Behavior therapy as such became more popular in the 1960s and 1970s. In the *Comprehensive Textbook of Psychiatry*, Dr. John Paul Brady writes the following:

> In this approach to clinical problems, emphasis is placed on observable, confrontable events and especially the behavior of the patient, rather than inferred mental state and constructs. To understand the individual patient and their difficulties, the clinician seeks to relate their various behaviors and especially those problematic behaviors called symptoms to other observable events of a physiological or environmental nature.[13]

In terms of what this form of therapy attempts to do, the following from *Behavior Therapy* by John C. Masters, Thomas G. Burish, and Steven D. Hollon of Vanderbilt University, with David C. Rimm, appears to sum it up in language easier to comprehend:

> Often, behavior therapists deal with behaviors that are maladaptive, that are obviously self-defeating and interfere in some way with the welfare of others. Perhaps just as often, the behavior therapist is called upon to assist a client with a specific aspect of personal growth or improvement in the absence of what others would describe as "psychological problems." Thus, for example, individuals not notably lacking in assertiveness might, nevertheless, seek assertion training. Those who have poor social skills might profit immensely from social skills training through contingency management or cognitive procedures.[14]

So while in psychodynamic therapy and psychoanalysis, the greatest focus is on finding the underlying causes, including past traumas that might have caused or furthered the disorder and using that insight and its ramifications to begin a healing process, behavior therapy, for the most part, ignores the causes. Instead, it focuses on the problems, the disorders that exist right now, the irrational thoughts and outlooks that result from those disorders, and through a series of therapeutic techniques, attempts to modify these thoughts and outlooks, which will result in modified behavior.

Going back to an example used earlier in this chapter, if we are shy and reclusive and have gotten to a point in our careers where those characteristics are beginning to hamper us, behavioral therapists, unlike psychodynamic therapists or psychoanalysts, would not take us back in time to determine what traumas in our childhood or as adults, repressed or not, caused this behavior. Instead, the behavior therapist would go to work on finding ways to reduce or dissolve entirely the fears that are triggered by our Inner Dummy when we are thrust into a social gathering of strangers or have to give a presentation or have to interact intensely with a customer, or whatever the irrationality, without focusing on the history of the individual.

There is apparently a limit as to how far behavior therapy can go in treating more serious disorders of depression, obsessive-compulsive disorders, or schizophrenia, even though books have been written about the subject.

What follows is a listing of the types of therapies used under the broad heading of behavioral therapy. I will use only a handful of references that best describe these theories in the most abbreviated form.

SYSTEMATIC DESENSITIZATION

Systematic Desensitization does basically what it says. Through a series of small steps, a "hierarchy" as some therapists call it, we are exposed to situations that trigger our fears, our phobias, anxieties, and inhibitions in such a way that these reactions are gradually desensitized. Here is an excellent description of this therapy from *Helping People Change*:

> Desensitization is accomplished by exposing an individual in small, graduated steps, to the feared situation while the person is performing the activity that is antagonistic to anxiety. The gradual exposure to the fear stimulus can take place either in the person's fantasy, where she or he is asked to imagine being in various fear-related situations, or it can occur in real life (in vivo). . . . The response that is most typically inhibited by this treatment process is anxiety, and the response frequently substituted for the anxiety is relaxation and calmness.[15]

If Sarah wanted to do something to ease her phobia about riding in elevators, systematic desensitization would probably be the therapy of choice. As you'll recall, the *Encyclopedia of Phobias, Fears, and Anxieties* lists hundreds of phobias, including fear of heights (acrophobia), fear of bathrooms (bathroom phobia), fear of visiting barber shops (barber's chair syndrome), fear of noise (acousticophobia), fear of going into the water, (aquaphobia), and fear of being alone (menophobia).

If one has a fear of heights, the therapist usually begins the sessions with small steps, perhaps walking the client up to the first floor and getting them to feel comfortable there. Then they go to the next floor and so on. As pointed out in chapter 18, these fears are real. A few years ago in Hawaii, after listening to a woman merely tell the story of seeing a shark near her on the beach, I developed a shark phobia. What nonsense. There hasn't been a shark attack on the beach I visit there as far back as anyone can remember. But my fear was real. It has since abated, but I could imagine going through systematic desensitization sessions with a trained therapist who might get through to my Inner Dummy after a number of sessions that it's okay to go in the water.

Morton Hunt in *The Story of Psychology* described the case of a married woman who was phobic about touching a penis. Therapist Joseph Wolpe worked up a "hierarchy in which the least fearful situation for her was seeing a nude statue in a park thirty feet away." He then brought her closer in imaginary scenes until after the twentieth session she "reported that she was enjoying sexual relations with her husband and having orgasm about half the time."[16]

In many of the books I perused about desensitization techniques, the authors usually included the number of sessions it takes, most frequently between fifteen and twenty-five. However, most of the experts point out that this technique of therapy, like all other forms, may not work for everyone.

AVERSIVE CONDITIONING

This form of therapy uses a series of punishments or some kind of discomfort when we are attempting to eliminate some activity, such as cigarette smoking, that we know is not good for us.

One common form of this therapy is used in weight-loss training where participants are forced to pay money to the group if they don't meet their goals. The following is a quote from *Behavior Therapy, Concepts, Procedures, and Applications* by Geoffrey L. Thorpe of the University of Maine and Sheryl L. Olson of the University of Michigan:

> Suppose that a client joins a group of people who are trying to help each other lose weight. Every participant deposits $10 at the outset. Each week that a client loses weight, $1 is refunded. On weeks when there is no

weight loss, there is no refund. Is forfeiting the money a form of punishment? To behavior therapists, it is, and its use can be justified if (1) the client voluntarily accepts it and (2) it works.[17]

The authors also described punishments for people who want to quit smoking cigarettes—"every time he thinks of lighting one he snaps a thick elastic band that is tightly stretched around his wrist." I don't know, I'm not sure this would have worked for me. A hammer to the head, maybe, but not a rubber band.

As the authors point out:

> When it is used, it is because positive reinforcement is not always effective in treatment plans aimed at treating destructive behavior. . . . Disadvantages of punishment are that it can evoke negative emotional responses, it can produce aggression and it can disturb the patient's relationship with the caregivers.[18]

OPERANT (REWARD) CONDITIONING

Operant conditioning primarily uses rewards rather than punishment in seeking to change undesirable behaviors, although in some texts I note that Operant Conditioning includes the use of both rewards and punishments. However, I'll take the easy way out and project this form of therapy as reward based.

In the book *Clinical Behavior Therapy*, psychology professors Mervin R. Goldfried and Gerald C. Davison, in describing the use of operant conditioning, or reinforcement, among less disordered people, talk about "the smile of the therapist" as being a positive reinforcement.[19] Most parents are familiar with aversive therapy and operant conditioning. When I was young, my aversive therapy was a good spanking on the behind by my mother when I was bad and compliments and cookies when I was unusually good. So you get the idea. The developers of this form of therapy have made a science out of what we all understand. It would appear that the use of punishments is aimed at the survival program of our Inner Dummy, which wants to keep us safe and alive to reproduce.

Of course, animal trainers use rewards primarily to create specific actions. If we could eliminate our cerebral cortexes, which give us the power to think, more of us might then rely on animal trainers to adjust our aberrant behaviors. This isn't as strange as it sounds. Monty Roberts, author of *The Man Who Listens to Horses*, contends that his form of training, which involves nonverbal communication that is apparently aimed directly at the Inner Dummy and is more nurturing than confrontational, can work well between parents and children and employer and employees.[20]

COGNITIVE THERAPY

For quite some time I remained confused over the difference between behavior therapy and cognitive behavior therapy. I thought they were basically the same. It turns out that they are not. Behavior therapy includes other therapies, including those just described, as well as cognitive therapy.

Cognitive therapy, like some other behavior therapies, is a relatively recent invention and aims directly at changing irrational outlooks and thoughts that we might have to rational ones. It attempts to convince us that the outlooks of our Inner Dummy, when distorted, are not accurate.

Cognitive therapist Aaron T. Beck, whom I mentioned in chapter 18 dealing with anxieties and phobias, was one of the founders of cognitive behavioral therapy along with Albert Ellis. Beck, for example, lists the following distorted outlooks that create and maintain depression:

—"the cognitive triad": the depressive's distorted view of himself or herself, his world and his future ("I'm not good," "My life is disappointing," "Things will never improve").

—"silent assumptions": unexpressed beliefs that negatively affect the individual's emotional and cognitive responses ("If someone's angry, it's probably my fault," "If I am not loved by everyone, I'm unworthy");

—"logical errors": overgeneralization (taking one instance to represent a pattern), selective attention (focusing on some details and ignoring others), arbitrary inference (drawing conclusions unwarranted by logic or the available evidence), and others.[21]

Sound familiar? Do you know people whose outlooks are similarly shaped?

Beck relates these distorted outlooks to the creation of automatic thoughts. For example, those of us who are prone to overgeneralize might automatically think that if our spouse did not come home in time for dinner, he or she doesn't love us anymore. I've seen people in the business world, who get a sharp response from a customer, believe without a doubt that they will lose the customer, who was only blowing off some steam.

I've also seen people practically fold when they get some bad news, under the distorted outlook that they are no good to begin with and that "things will never improve."

Probably all of us have distorted outlooks of one form or another, which shape the quirks of our character. The problem emerges when these distorted outlooks are intense and enduring and are hampering our lives in serious ways.

Someone I know, for example, thinks that anyone who does harm to him in any way is bad and villainous, including strangers who cut their cars in front of him on the road. He has an "I'm always a victim, everyone is out to get me" outlook. In the hands of a cognitive therapist, this person would first need to admit that he has this problem, which he does. His is not an "unaware limbic capturing." The therapist would then aim not so much at replacing his negative outlook with a positive one, but at putting his outlook to the test so that when the therapy is over, this person will understand that there is no basis in fact for him to have such an outlook. He would come to realize that other people are not what his Inner Dummy is making him think they are.

The process is not an easy one.

Think of Dr. Beck sitting in a room with Joseph Stalin, attempting to change his warped outlooks to more rational ones. Does this give you an idea of the difficulties?

I have known people in business who needed only slight adjustments in their thinking to be highly successful. I recall sitting with one man in my office, explaining the whole picture to him, how strong he was in so many areas and how he was being held back by an irrational power drive combined with insecurities that gave him a warped outlook in his business dealings. He always wanted to be in total control, found it difficult to delegate, and when he did, usually became jealous of any success his subordinates achieved, rarely giving them credit for anything.

Despite my best efforts in telling him exactly what his problems were, with which he actually agreed, he couldn't change his irrational outlooks and eventually lost his position. On the other hand, I have seen people adjust their thinking when we sent them to counseling firms who confronted them in different ways. I recall asking the head of one of these firms at lunch one day exactly what he did with one person who transformed herself from a shy, reclusive executive to an assertive manager, even though her voice and demeanor remained low-key. I watched her deliver a presentation after this change and noticed a new, positive energy even though her voice remained quiet and you almost had to strain to hear. So it became obvious to me that some change through cognitive therapy was possible. A passage from *Psychology: An Integrated Approach* states:

> Cognitive therapy is collaborative in that the aim is to have an open and relatively equal relationship between therapist and client, with an agenda negotiated from the outset. Sessions will involve the therapist uncovering and challenging the client's thoughts, and will be aided by homework given to the client to carry out between sessions. Commonly, clients will be asked to record their negative thoughts and so learn to identify when they are having them. Sometimes negative thoughts can be tested out in the session using Socratic dialogue, a logical question and answer sequence, and sometimes they can only be tested out by the client carrying out some test or exercise in between sessions.[22]

Cognitive therapy is also viewed as "time limited." In other words, before you even begin the therapy, the therapist can give you some idea of how many sessions, or "interviews," as Dr. Beck calls them, it will take to get specific problems resolved, usually, as previously pointed out, fifteen to twenty-five sessions.

Someone I know who is being treated with cognitive therapy for depression sent me one of her homework forms, called a "Thought Record." The headings on top of this form included the following:

- SITUATION: What were you thinking about?

- FEELINGS: Specify, Rate 1-100

- AUTOMATIC THOUGHT: What was going through your mind just before you started to feel bad? Any other thoughts?

- FACTS THAT SHOW IT'S TRUE

- FACTS THAT SHOW IT'S NOT 100% TRUE

- MORE BALANCED THOUGHT

- RATE FEELING NOW 1-100

In reading the comments on the chart that this person noted following disturbing incidents, it's possible to see how the combination of work with the therapist and written, consistent forms of homework might eventually work to change a distorted outlook.

Albert Ellis, one of the founders of this therapeutic movement, took cognitive therapy into a more confrontational, in-your-face type of format called Rational Emotive Therapy (RET). He said the therapist should "make a forthright, unequivocal *attack* on the client's general and specific irrational ideas . . . try to induce him to adopt more rational ones in their place . . . and keep pounding away, time and again at the illogical ideas which underlie the client's fears."

In the book *Behavior Therapy: Techniques and Empirical Findings*, John C. Masters, Thomas G. Burish, Steven T. Hollon, and David C. Rimm made some interesting observations about Ellis:

> [He] believes that humankind has a biological predisposition toward irrationality. He bases this view in part on the apparent pervasiveness of irrational thinking (across cultures, across centuries) and the unwillingness of people to give up irrational ideas, even in the face of insight.[23]

Ellis is apparently referring to the type of "insight" we might achieve in psychodynamic therapy, what my ex-wife Barbara called an "Ah-hah"; it ultimately may not work to change the irrational outlook. In other words, you may get the "insight," the "Ah-hah," you experience feelings of exhilaration and relief, but a month or two later, you may learn that the insight didn't make any lasting difference in changing the irrational outlook that was targeted.

The book also listed "examples of irrational ideas" targeted by Ellis and his colleagues, which it said "is not exhaustive," but it does provide concrete instances of the main material focused on in RET. I thought a handful of these irrational ideas were worth listing as the products of the warped outlooks of an Inner Dummy, which has no sense, to repeat the phrase, of time, awareness, or logic:

> The idea that you must—yes *must*—have sincere love and approval almost all the time from all the people you find significant.
>
> The idea that you must prove yourself thoroughly competent, adequate, and achieving; or that you must at least have real competence or talent at something important.
>
> The idea that people who harm you or commit misdeeds rate as generally bad, wicked, or villainous individuals and you should severely blame, damn, and punish them for their sins.
>
> The idea that life proves awful, terrible, horrible, or catastrophic when things do not go the way you would like them to go. . . .

The idea that if something seems dangerous or fearsome, you must become terribly occupied with and upset about it.[24]

Ellis believes that we can successfully combat irrational outlooks such as these utilizing his techniques. Some years ago I worked with a product designer who thought he needed everyone's approval. In the car at a stoplight, he would make sure he pulled out promptly to avoid getting honked at. He usually acquiesced in most arguments about products he was working on or the procedures he was using. I once said to him, "You know, it's not necessary for everyone to love you. Not everyone will love you, no matter what you do."

This statement never registered for him, but he came to my mind as I was reviewing Dr. Ellis's work. I could see him being confronted by a rational emotive therapist and being told to repeat the statement over and over again: "I don't need anyone's approval." The idea is that with hard work, including journaling, the Inner Dummy will buy off on this rational statement so that a person like the product designer would no longer get upset when someone honks his horn or mildly criticizes him.

Cognitive therapists have developed a plethora of strategies to get their clients to realize that they have been held captive by some of these ideas and to modify their distorted outlooks with rational ones. Some of the strategies include the following from the *Handbook of Cognitive Therapy Techniques* by Dr. Rian E. McMullin, director of the Counseling Research Institute:

Cognitive Flooding:	Involves flooding us with images of what we fear or are trying to avoid so that we feel the emotions intensely and learn to deal with them.
Self Flim-Flam:	Based on the investigations of James Randi, an internationally known magician who in 1964 offered the sum of $10,000 to anyone who could "demonstrate the existence of paranormal powers under scientifically observable conditions." The therapy is to describe this concept to the client, if they aren't already aware that they have been captured by a delusional belief, and then redirect their thinking.
Forced Catastrophes:	"Under this technique, clients are challenged to follow their fears to their worst possible conclu-

	sions. When the worst is never actually realized, they are forced to acknowledge the fallacies in their prior thinking."
Switched Roleplaying:	We switch roles with the therapist, who acts out our irrational thoughts, while we try to convince them of the irrationality. "Switched roleplaying is a technique that preserves clients' self-image, [and] lowers their resistance to therapy."
Reductio Ad Absurdum:	"[Reduction to absurdity] is a method of disengaging clients from their irrational beliefs by caricaturing those beliefs until they appear utterly ridiculous."[25]

You get the idea. There are dozens of such strategies, among them symptoms-based exercises, including one for people with germ phobias in which they are prevented from washing after coming in contact with something they think is full of germs, like the doorknob of a public bathroom. The theory is apparently that after a number of these contacts with no hand washing afterward and we don't get sick, our Inner Dummy realizes that the germs are not threatening.

Sports psychologists, who are basically cognitive therapists, like to use the strategy of *visualization*, which was described earlier. If we tighten up when we have to make a simple, three-foot putt on a golf course, what golf professionals call getting the "yips," some of these psychologists suggest that we create strategic visualizations. We might imagine hitting the ball two or three times and watch it follow a specific line into the cup. Or, we might visualize that this is just a practice putt; there is no pressure.

OTHER FORMS OF TALKING THERAPY

Following are other talking therapies that I thought deserved attention:

HUMANIST THERAPIES

Humanist therapies appear to be more on the behavioral-therapy side because they don't deal much with the past, but rather work on our perspectives as they exist right now. The emphasis appears to be on guiding us to accept and take responsibility for whatever the realities of our lives are, while helping us to explore avenues for better fulfilling whatever our potentials may be.

In their book *Theories of Psychotherapy*, Wachtel and Messer included the following as being humanist therapies: "*Existential therapy* is principally about individuals seeking meaning in a meaningless world. . . . The type of meaning pursued in existential therapy involves such basic matters as love, courage, freedom, and aesthetic fulfillment. . . . In *Gestalt therapy*, meaning is said to flow directly from vivid experience from which the client creates meaning . . . *client-centered therapy* with its focus on the reflection of feelings and inner meanings engages the client in experiential search . . . in order to construct new meanings."[26]

Did you get all of that? No? It doesn't matter. Neither did I.

TRANSACTIONAL ANALYSIS

This form of therapy was the rage in the 1960s and the subject of at least two bestsellers, which I can recall. It is based on a restating of structure of Freud's id, ego, and superego. In transactional analysis, the id is the "Child," the ego is the "Adult," and the superego is the "Parent," the person who gave us our basic belief system and tells us what is right and wrong. In the actual therapy, sometimes three chairs are used, each representing one of the three characters. Patients go from one chair to the next as they realize which of the three characters they are playing in their imaginary transactions with others. The basic premise of the therapy was that "I'm okay, you're okay." So if I said something childish and foolish, this was okay, because it was my "Child" talking. I know a man, a former judge who underwent a tough divorce, who said his therapist used transactional analysis techniques, particularly the emphasis on the "child within." This man told me that he found it very helpful, particularly when he was wondering why he was thinking about or doing specific things that didn't make rational sense, to relate it to the child inside him. He found that in the car he would often be able to chuckle at himself and that this gave him some relief.

GROUP THERAPY

Following is a description of group therapy from *The Story of Psychology*:

At least a hundred varieties have existed, new ones appear every year, but many soon die out. . . . Today the general view is that group therapy is useful primarily for interpersonal and social problems, although it does also address internal ones; members of a group provide one another with support and empathy as well as with feedback on how the social self each presents is perceived and which aspects of it are welcomed and which are not.[27]

It is apparent that some of us do better in a group with a trained therapist than with a one-on-one therapist. We look around us and we see others with problems similar to ours, and this alone might have therapeutic value. Further, since we all have similar problems, we might be better able to discuss them openly as well as seek ideas from others. Many years ago, I accompanied a friend in a troubled marriage to one of his group therapy sessions, which focused on marital problems, because at the time I was having troubles of my own. I sensed that he found support in the group even as they berated him over a problem in his marriage that he brought up for their opinions. The therapist handling the session kept it on an even keel and told me later that it is common in such sessions for one member to be verbally attacked by others when they sense that member is obviously in the wrong. But when a member is obviously in the right, they will usually be quick in their support. She also said that being in a generally supportive group while discussing one's personal problems can offer what she called "therapeutic release."

In a paper entitled "Sex Therapy" by James E. Burg and Douglas H. Sprenkle in a compendium titled *Family Therapy Sourcebook*, they said: "The group therapy format has been used successfully to treat a variety of dysfunctions for quite some time." They referred to examples of group sessions that combine the "treatment of marital and sexual dysfunctions."[28] Group therapy can also mean support groups, which are used with or without a professional caregiver, to fight varying forms of addiction, as described later.

COUPLES THERAPY

I attended couples therapy sessions with my first ex-wife. Every Monday morning for more than a year, my then wife and I would show up at the therapist's office where we would relate the disagreements we had during the previous week. She wanted to go to parties, I hated them. I liked to have my family over for dinner, she disliked the idea, and thought my family always favored me. I frequently got home late for dinner, she thought I could arrange my time better. And this was just for starters. Her point of view was certainly as valid as mine. We were just very different in what we liked and disliked and how we perceived things.

The one thing I found most valuable in these sessions is that we were able to talk about our problems in a calm, cogent manner since the therapist was there and set a calming pace. Further, since you are making the attempt to work things out and paying for it, I found you tend to bring up subjects you might not talk about at home to avoid discomforting conversations. While couples therapy didn't work for us, it obviously has worked very well for many others.

In a paper titled "Transgenerational Family Therapies" by Joseph L. Wetchler and Fred P. Piercey in *Family Therapy Sourcebook*, they made the observation that in some sessions, the family-of-origin, the parents or other family members of the participants would attend in order "to decrease the amount of parental introjects projected onto his or her spouse. In effect, they are able to see their spouses without the ghosts of their family of origin occluding [clouding] their vision."[29] My first ex-wife and I never tried this, but in retrospect it might have helped. I loved her parents and would have respected what they had to say.

FAMILY THERAPY

Here is commentary from *The Handbook of Psychotherapy*, which pointed out "the many different models . . . used within the field over the last thirty years." The authors go on to say:

> In general, in all approaches the therapist is less concerned with pathology and with dysfunction and more concerned with the promotion of both latent and actual strengths in the family. . . . The therapist attempts to achieve small changes in sequence and pattern as they occur in a session. Such small changes are themselves unlikely to be lasting, unless they're repeated with sufficient intensity and frequency that they become part of a new folklore in the family.[30]

What the authors appear to be saying is that family therapy is more cognitive than traditional psychotherapy in that the therapist is not always acting to get at the root of the dysfunctions causing the problem, but on seeking out strengths the family may display within the sessions and then building on those to begin creating small changes in perception, perspective, and interaction between the family members. Makes sense to me.

NEW AGE THERAPIES

New Age therapies encompass a number of forms, but usually include some Eastern thought, including teachings of Zen, that are aimed primarily at giving us enlightened insights and a more harmonious, less-conflicted mental state. Back in the late 1970s, still feeling the pain of my first divorce and after my sessions with two psychiatrists and one clinical psychologist, I attended a New Age therapy program called *est* (Erhard Seminars Training). The seminars were being held all over the nation at that time in hotel ballrooms over two consecutive weekends. They would start at eight in the morning and last until midnight. There were about 250 people in the room, all sitting in semicircle rows of straight-backed folding chairs facing a podium behind which was the *est* trainer.

The seminars consisted of a number of mental exercises. Sometimes the chairs were cleared and the participants would be asked to lie on the floor attempting to create different forms of imagery. However, a considerable portion of the sessions were taken up with people standing up and telling their stories of woe. If during the telling anyone showed the slightest amount of arrogance or pride, if they were taking a "position," if they had sanctimonious or irrational ideas along the lines of those described previously by Albert Ellis, the trainer would come down hard on them, calling them "assholes." That was the actual word they used, which was particularly hard on the more Victorian in the group. However, no matter how hard the trainer came down on participants, the participant would be applauded by the group and then thanked by the trainer for "sharing." It wouldn't be long before he or she stood up again, joined by the more reticent in the group to tell more stories, sometimes about how they were abused by parents, spouses, and so forth. But again, if the participant showed any arrogance or gave any appearance of asking for sympathy, the trainer would come down hard on him.

This style of direct, harsh confrontation, in hindsight, was apparently aimed at the Inner Dummies of all of us sitting there. The trainers, who worked from thick binders, were relentless in drumming away at irrational "positions," or distorted outlooks as Dr. Beck might put it, that were making us unhappy in some way, in preparation for the final hours of the seminar when we would finally be given answers to life that would provide the insights we were all seeking. This was called getting "It." "It" was the hopeful word.

I recall sitting there the last night and actually getting "It" and being filled with feelings of enormous relief, I'm sure close to the feelings that we might get after a Zen enlightenment, or a coming to Jesus, or a psychodynamic insight. As I left the hotel that night, I can recall the feelings of exhilaration, which lasted about a month. Then the slow descent down into the somewhat depressive state I had been in previously began, but it never reached the lower levels I had experienced before the seminars. However, the *est* system did alter my perceptions of life just enough to change my outlooks ever since.

Oddly enough, I can't remember all the parameters of "It" today, more than twenty years later. I do recall getting the visualization that the mental side of our brains is composed of video- and audiotapes that were recordings of the more traumatic teachings and experiences of our lives. If something triggers one of those tapes, for example, a spouse telling us that we will never get anywhere, the tape that held the memory of a similar rejection by a former spouse or girlfriend or parent or other authority figure would play and we might lash out irrationally as we had been doing for years without knowing why. In other words, how we react in life is the result of tapes or imprints of our experiences that reside in our brains and which might make us think or act irrationally each time they are triggered with some variations, but with the same basic thrust. We can't control those tapes, we were told, but we can recognize them for what they are and rise above them, to "take control of our lives." Just "let the tapes run and run and run," we were advised, but simply watch them, treat them as so much garbage and enjoy the show.

I don't recall any mention of the limbic brain or limbic memories or the id, but obviously the seminars were aimed at our ids, our Inner Dummies, with a system of harsh confrontations, similar to Albert Ellis's school of Rational Emotive Therapy, but with the addition of exhaustion, which weakens our will to resist, and metaphoric insights about the workings of the brain.

My second ex-wife, Barbara, attended an *est* session about a month later and I was there to greet her on the last Sunday around midnight when she came out of the ballroom as exhilarated as everyone else. She got "It," she said. But as the weeks went by, she came down faster than I did and I didn't detect any residual effect in her from the experience.

As with many forms of awakenings, either from therapy, spiritual insight, or just daydreaming sitting on a beach, the real challenge is keeping the insights alive months and years later. The Inner Dummy may apparently *buy off* on such an insight, giving us the feeling of relief or exhilaration, but it will do its best to make it go away. That is why many programs of this sort have refresher sessions to keep the insights in place. Religions don't trust our Inner Dummies at all. They have weekly services, or "fixes," as described next, under motivational therapy.

As far as I know, *est* no longer exists. Werner Erhard, the founder of the system, was alleged to have taken money that wasn't his and fled the country, according to Steven Pressman, author of the book, *Outrageous Betrayal, The Dark Journey of Werner Erhard from est to Exile*. Pressman reported that many *est* participants felt betrayed by Werner, but I never did. Although he developed the system, apparently he himself never got "It."[31] Many of the *est* trainers began to develop systems of their own, including Landmark, which today is apparently one of the most popular.

MOTIVATIONAL THERAPY

In 1998, I noticed an advertisement in a Chicago newspaper offering a one-day seminar featuring about ten great motivational speakers, including some very well known professional coaches and retired military leaders. The seats in the stadium were very expensive as they needed to pay the fees and fund the advertising. I met one person who attended and she told me that it was one of the greatest experiences of her life.

There are any number of seminars, training tapes, and self-help books today devoted to motivational training, which is surely one more form of therapy, since their objective is to give us insights into ourselves and change our behaviors.

Anthony Robbins's book *Awaken the Giant Within: How to Take Immediate Control of Your Mental, Emotional, Physical, and Financial Destiny!* includes a conglomeration of thoughts and techniques that reminded me a bit of the *est* seminars. In the book, it appears as if he is taking dead aim at the Inner Dummy when he describes how so many of the choices we make in our lives are dependent on the pleasure or pain we derive from them. He speaks about our need to take control of our lives with rational mastery over our emotions, physical well-being, relationships, finances, and time. He makes the point that "it's your decisions, not your conditions that determine your destiny."

What he is apparently trying to do is build up or reinforce our power drive, while lowering our position on the survival scale in an effort to reinforce our self-esteem and self-confidence and reduce our levels of fear for doing what we rationally might believe is best for us. The following statement from his book helps make this point:

Remember, anything you want that's valuable requires that you break through some short-term pain in order to gain long-term pleasure. If you want a great body, you've got to sculpt that body, which requires breaking through short-term pain. Once you've done it enough times working out becomes pleasurable. Dieting works the same way. Any type of discipline requires breaking through pain: discipline in business relationships, personal confidence, fitness and finances. How do you break through the discomfort and create the momentum to really accomplish your aims? Start by making the decision to overcome it. We can always decide to override the pain in the moment, and better yet is to follow up by conditioning ourselves.[32]

The pain Mr. Robbins alludes to is obviously the punishing emotions released by the Inner Dummy when we decide to do something that is not in accordance with the expectations of its drives. If it expects us to play it safe because we've had painful experiences from risks taken in the past that didn't work out, it will make us feel pained, anguished, and depressed if we think seriously about leaving our safe job with an accounting firm to open a real-estate business in an opportune area, for example.

And so Mr. Robbins in his motivational system directs us to focus our rational thoughts, to steel ourselves against the punishing emotions of our Inner Dummy and go for it.

I recall about twenty-five years ago attending a two-hour talk by Zig Ziglar, a motivational speaker who wasn't very well known then, but today is the author of several books and in high demand. I remember that at the end of his talk, I felt like I could walk through a brick wall to make my dreams come true. The speech was given at a national sales meeting for a company with which I was working, and the salesmen who made up most of the audience were equally mesmerized.

Then, only a year ago, I was attending another national sales meeting dinner and Mike Singletary, former linebacker of the Chicago Bears, was the featured motivational speaker. We sat at the same table for dinner and I asked him how he learned to do what he was doing. He said by watching others and putting himself through long hours of rehearsal and training. This preparatory effort obviously paid off because his presentation was outstanding. After he had finished and we were walking out of the room, I happened, by coincidence, to see a sales representative I had known for many years and who had been in the audience with me, listening to Zig Ziglar almost twenty-five years before.

I said to him, "Frank, don't you ever get tired of these motivators?"

"No," he replied. "Every year I need at least two or three *fixes*. And tonight with Singletary, it was a great one."

What he was implying is that with motivational therapy—and this is probably true with other forms of therapy as well—the insights and outlooks gained can begin to wear thin from the normal experiences of life. And so we need to go back and get "fixes" from time to time, which I suppose is one of the reasons why so many religions—the world's most popular form of therapy—have weekly or even daily services, which should tell us that the people who structured the service frequencies of the major religions knew quite a bit about human nature and by inference, the obstinance and trouble-making capacities of the Inner Dummy.

We still have other forms of remedies to cover, after one more very brief encounter with Dr. Freud.

COMMENTARY BY DR. HEFTER

Although David refers in this chapter to the changes in the irrational outlooks of the Inner Dummy or id, these changes cannot be viewed totally in isolation, since they must also involve activity of those aspects of the individual's psychological makeup which constitute the ego. In other words as humans we employ our cognitive apparatus in some way even when our focus is on modifying the id. Thus cognitive therapy clearly requires the participation of more than just the limbic area of the brain even though the goal is limbic change. Family and couples therapy, for example, is fruitless without the capacity of the participants to make a conscious commitment to the therapy process itself and to rationally consider the changes required. When practiced with people (as opposed to nonhuman animals), behavioral therapies require a conscious participation on the part of the individuals involved.

It should be said that there is much overlap between therapy modalities even when not specifically acknowledged by the practitioners. There are obviously cognitive and behavioral elements in psychodynamic therapy although the particular practitioner may not think of it in those terms. Examples of such overlap could be given for all of the methodologies listed.

It is unlikely that psychotherapists who have undergone academic training at the graduate level (Master's degree, Ph.D., and M.D.) in the past thirty-five years or more have not been exposed to a variety of therapeutic approaches in their training. As a result psychotherapists today for the most part employ several therapeutic techniques during the course of psychotherapy. As David points out, it is unusual to see "pure Freudian" psychotherapists today. Even within the psychoanalytic schools the advent of ego psychology and self-psychology has influenced the practice as well as the theory of the psychoanalytic perspective. And the changing economics of mental health treatment, for example, the growth of managed care, have had a significant effect on how psychotherapy is delivered.

NOTES

1. Associated Press, *Chicago Sun-Times*, April 20, 1999, p. 24.

2. Ruth Larson, *Insight on the News*, September 7, 1998, p. 43.

3. N. R. Kleinfield, with Kit R. Roane, *New York Times*, January 11, 1999, p. A1.

4. Ron Frehm, Associated Press, as quoted in Phil Rosenthal's column, *Chicago Sun-Times*, February 16, 1999, p. 29.

5. Anne Sheffield, *How You Can Survive When They're Depressed: Living and Coping with Depression Fallout* (New York: Harmony, 1998), p. 50.

6. Ibid., p. 203.

7. Gerald L. Klerman et al., "Medication and Psychotherapy," in *Handbook of Psychotherapy and Behavior Change*, ed. Allen E. Bergin and Sol L. Garfield (New York: Wiley, 1994), p. 735.

8. Paul L. Wachtel and Stanley B. Messer, "The Contemporary Psychotherapeutic Landscape: Issues and Prospects," in *Theories of Psychotherapy: Origins and Evolution*, ed. Paul L. Wachtel and Stanley B. Messer (Washington, D.C.: American Psychological Association, 1997), p. 1.

9. Ibid., p. 2.

10. Petruska Clarkson, "The Nature and Range of Psychotherapy," in *The Handbook of Psychotherapy*, ed. Petruska Clarkson and Michael Pokorny (London: Routledge, 1994), pp. 3–4.

11. Morton Hunt, *The Story of Psychology* (New York: Doubleday, 1993), p. 567.

12. Ibid., p. 569.

13. John Paul Brady, *Comprehensive Textbook of Psychiatry*, p. 1,365.

14. John C. Masters et al., *Behavior Therapy: Techniques and Empirical Findings*, (New York: Harcourt Brace Jovanovich College Publishers, 1987), p. 1.

15. Richard J. Morris, "Fear Reduction Methods," in *Helping People Change: A Textbook of Methods*, ed. Frederick H. Kanfer and Arnold P. Goldstein (New York: Pergamon Press, 1991), p. 163.

16. Hunt, *The Story of Psychology*, p. 574.

17. Geoffrey L. Thorpe and Sheryl L. Olson, *Behavior Therapy: Concepts, Procedures, and Applications* (Boston: Allyn and Bacon, 1997), p. 77.

18. Ibid., p. 79.

19. Melvin R. Goldfried and Gerald C. Davison, *Clinical Behavior Therapy* (New York: Wiley, 1994), p. 225.

20. Monty Roberts, *The Man Who Listens to Horses* (New York: Random House, 1997). The cover jacket states: "Roberts has acquired an unprecedented understanding of nonverbal communication, an understanding that applies to human relationships as well. He has shown this between parent and child, employee and employer (he's worked with over 250 corporations, including General Motors, IBM, Disney and Merrill Lynch), and abuser and abused."

21. Aaron T. Beck and A. John Rush, with Brian F. Shaw and Gary Emery, *Cognitive Therapy of Depression* (New York: Guilford Press, 1979), p. 10.

22. Andrew MacLeod, "Therapeutic Interventions," in *Psychology: An Integrated Approach*, ed. Michael Eysenck (Essex, England: Addison-Wesley Longman, 1998), p. 573.

23. John C. Masters et al., *Behavior Therapy: Techniques and Empirical Findings* (New York: Harcourt Brace Jovanovich College Publishers, 1987), p. 393.

24. Ibid., pp. 393–94.

25. Rian E. McMullin, *Handbook of Cognitive Therapy Techniques* (New York: Norton, 1986), pp. 184–218.

26. Leslie S. Greenberg and Laura N. Rice, "Humanistic Approaches to Psychotherapy," in Wachtel and Messer, *Theories of Psychotherapy*, pp. 105–10.

27. Hunt, *The Story of Psychology*, pp. 592–93.

28. James E. Burg and Douglas H. Sprenkle, *Family Therapy Sourcebook*, p. 160.

29. Ibid., p. 31.

30. Clarkson and Pokorny, *Handbook of Psychotherapy*, pp. 237–38.

31. Steven Pressman, *Outrageous Betrayal: The Dark Journey of Werner Erhard from EST to Exile* (New York: St. Martin's, 1993). This was the general expression of the book.

32. Anthony Robbins, *Awaken the Giant Within: How to Take Immediate Control of Your Mental, Emotional, Physical, and Financial Destiny* (New York: Fireside, 1991), p. 67.

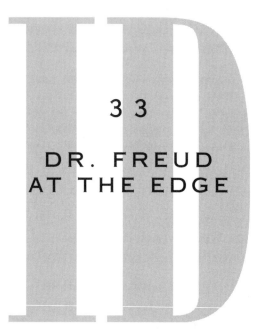

3 3

DR. FREUD
AT THE EDGE

In 1998, a group of environmentalists against the renewal by Makah Indians of an ancient tradition of hunting gray whales in dugout canoes off the Washington coast, agreed to stop harassing the Makah with cannon fire.[1]

It was late in the afternoon and Wendy Smith poked her head in the conference room, where Dr. Freud, as usual, was poring through a pile of books that lay on the table in front of him.

"Dr. Freud?" she said gently.

Freud looked up, putting a pencil he was holding carefully between the pages of one of the books out of which poked several yellow "Post-It" notes.

"Ah, Wendy, my dear," he said cheerfully. "Do you know what one of the greatest inventions has been since my demise in 1939?"

"No, sir," she answered quietly.

Freud picked up the book and said, "'Post-It' notes. What a marvelous device for a researcher. You can simply stick them on the appropriate pages of the books you are studying and jot brief reminders of the subject matter."

Wendy didn't respond. She looked glum. Concerned, Freud said, "And how do you feel today?"

"Not so great, Dr. Freud. You know . . . about last night, I . . ."

"Let's not talk about that right now, my dear. I was telling Ollander this morning that I was not up to par myself. However, I do feel much better now."

"But I . . . "

"You know, it is embarrassing for a European like me to feel a bit groggy after a modest amount of wine. What was it, one bottle, a bit more?"

"I'm not sure, Dr. Freud."

"No matter. I'm sure I'll recover. Now what can I do for you, my dear?"

"I was just wondering if there was anything I could do for you?"

Freud paused, looking searchingly at Wendy.

"Not at the moment, Wendy," he continued abruptly. "It may look as if I am working hard to bring myself up to date academically, but I am also thinking about the presentation tomorrow and what my decision will be."

Wendy looked tentative. "We are all hoping it will be positive for the Inner Dummy campaign, sir," she said. She hadn't moved from the doorway.

"We shall see, my dear, we shall see."

Wendy hesitated, still looking uncertain.

Freud said, "Is there anything else I can do for you?"

"I was hoping we might get together again tomorrow night, after the presentation, that is, if you're not busy. All my friends can do is talk about you, I mean incessantly. And I miss seeing you, too."

"But we were just together last night."

"I know, but I miss you already."

"Come, come, Wendy, we have talked about this, already. Why don't we see what happens with the presentation and afterward we can again discuss our little situation."

"So that isn't a 'no,' that I . . . we, that is, may see you tomorrow evening."

"Yes, that isn't a no," Freud said smiling.

"Oh good," Wendy looked relieved. "Well, I have to run along, I guess. You'll call me if you need anything."

"Indeed I will, my dear."

Wendy closed the door and Freud thought for a moment about Wendy and decided that his Inner Dummy would indeed become a candidate for an Inner Dummy Hall of Fame, if one were to be established.

NOTE

1. Zay N. Smith, *Chicago Sun-Times*, October 22, 1998, p. 26.

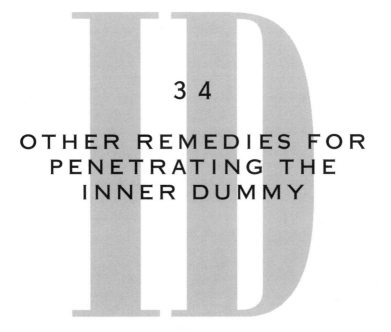

3 4

OTHER REMEDIES FOR
PENETRATING THE
INNER DUMMY

In Franklin, Massachusetts, one evening, police responded to a suspected dis-
turbance at 9 P.M. after neighbors reported hearing screaming. Officers found
that the occupants' toilet was not working and they were "yelling at it."[1]

Of all remedies designed to alleviate mental disorders, the use of psychiatric drugs in recent years has gained the most public attention.
For example, the drug Ritalin was featured on a weekly newsmagazine
cover in 1998 as a medication that attacks attention deficits and hyperac-
tivity in children. Along with Valium for anxiety and Prozac for depression,
the publicity that these drugs have generated has created an awareness
among many of us that the mental disorders of our brains are susceptible to
the powers of medicine.

In a September 1998 article in *Insight on the News*, Ruth Larson wrote
the following:

Knowledge of the brain's neurochemistry allows manufacturers to develop
drugs that pinpoint specific brain chemicals. A new family of antidepressant medications, combined with behavioral therapy, reduces symptoms

in 80 percent of patients with obsessive-compulsive disorder, to cite one example.[2]

She quotes Alan F. Holmer, at the time president of the Pharmaceutical Research and Manufacturers Association of America (PhRMA) as saying: "Pharmaceutical research has helped transform mental illnesses from a misunderstood cause of fear and shame into highly treatable conditions."

However, the increasing use of psychotropic drugs, as they are called, has led to increasing controversy in the mental-health field as some advocates view it as eventually replacing all psychotherapy. An interesting balance to the controversy was provided in an article written by Joshua Rosenbaum entitled "Talk Therapy: Ready for the Trash Heap?" that appeared in the October 1994 issue of *American Health*:

> Few psychiatrists are ready to dismiss psychotherapy altogether. But increasingly, they advocate combining talk therapy with medications and other forms of treatment. "A major goal of psychotherapy is to gain perspective on one's life, to become empathetic and see another person's point of view," says Brown University psychiatrist Peter Kramer, author of the best-selling *Listening to Prozac*. "While psychotherapy can give insight, medication can help lend this perspective."[3]

Rosenbaum includes the following comments from Dr. Michael Stone, a psychiatrist at Columbia University's College of Physicians and Surgeons, who specializes in psychoanalysis:

> "Psychoanalysis has fallen out of fashion and come under attack because of its association with elitism," he says. "But as a theory it holds up quite well." In its modern form it remains a useful way of understanding the workings of the mind and how people relate, he finds. . . . Not even Stone, however, uses psychoanalysis exclusively. He treats many of his patients with medication combined with cognitive or supportive techniques. "We pull whatever arrow we need out of our quiver to reach our patient," he explains. He adds that most of his analysis patients are ready to end therapy after three to five years.[4]

Clinical psychiatrists have traditionally seen their first task as diagnostic, determining the nature of the disorders of their patients. Their next task, if they use more than one school of therapy, is to determine those treatments most suitable for the disorders and the characteristics of the patients. Creativity is stressed because no single system of therapy will work for everyone. The strategies of therapy determined by the therapist is probably the key in determining the success level of the outcome. As Dr. Hefter pointed out, in this sense therapy can be as much art as science. "What methods do we need to pull out of our quiver to penetrate the id of this patient?" is the operative question, as suggested by Dr. Stone.

Today, the diagnostic task remains just as important as it ever was and the use of psychotropic drugs becomes one more remedial agent. In the paper "Medication and Psychotherapy" in the *Handbook of Psychotherapy and Behavior Change*, Gerald L. Klerman et al. said:

> Many pharmacotherapists [specialists in psychiatric drugs] hypothesize value for psychotherapy as a secondary, ameliorative treatment. . . . Many advocates of this approach employ a sequence in which the medication is administered first and psychotherapy introduced after the appearance of symptom reduction, stabilization of affective states and early improvement in social adjustment.[5]

In their book *Medicine and Mental Illness*, psychology professors Marvin E. Lickey and Barbara Gordon add the following:

> We believe that the effectiveness of drug therapies and talk therapies can be compared only by evaluating the results of properly conducted research. One must demand *evidence* that a particular therapy is the most effective way to provide relief from a particular illness. Are drugs better for some disorders, while talk therapies are better for others? Maybe, unlikely as it seems, psychotherapy and drug therapy are about equally effective for certain illnesses.[6]

Whatever the answers, psychotropic drugs may not do much for the father who is hostile to his children, giving them no credit for any achievement, or being abusive. Nor do they do much good in a hostile spousal relationship. John McDonald III is not going to take drugs nor will Sid Cohen, who reminded a waitress that she overcharged one dollar on a bill for meatballs that weren't served and as she was going away, called after her not to forget the eight-cent tax.

And, going to an extreme, don't expect Saddam Hussein of Iraq to take medication to ease his Number Ten power, purpose, and territorial drives that would lead his country into another war in the blink of an eye, if he could bring it off. Nor would medication have been used by Joseph Stalin,

Mao Tse-tung, Pol Pot, Idi Amin, and hundreds of other government leaders who through the centuries have ordered untold numbers of deaths. Such people wouldn't take them because they didn't think anything was wrong with what they thought.

Psychotropic drugs, therefore, will not end the craziness of the apparently normal people on this planet. They will probably not replace many forms of talk therapies—for example, family and relationship therapies—but they will play an increasing role in ameliorating the effects of depression and psychoses such as schizophrenia. And that is a blessing unto itself.

In addition, psychotropic drugs, by the very nature of their being, do indicate that psychological disorders are ultimately biological and not some gossamer injury to our souls. In *Medicine and Mental Illness*, Lickey and Gordon point out that psychotropic drugs work by adjusting the transfer of neurotransmitters—like dopamine and serotonin—over a microscopic space or synapse to receptors on adjoining cells, making them fire or not and thus affecting our thought processes, moods, and outlooks. They said:

> The ability of psychiatric drugs to affect specific synapses indicates that they are not generalized poisons that merely prevent mental illness by turning the brain off or, worse, by destroying large parts of it. It is also clear that psychiatric drugs are not all the same. Different drugs act on different kinds of synapses and have different effects on behavior and mental life.[7]

According to the article written by Ruth Larson, "There are about sixty-five drugs on the market for mental illness; PhRMA's survey of pharmaceutical companies lists eighty-five more under development to treat diseases ranging from anxiety disorders to substance abuse." She adds, "[M]edications such as Prozac, currently used to treat depression, are being investigated in connection with other conditions. Other drugs are being administered in more user-friendly fashion, such as patches."[8]

One of the major problems of some of these medications has been their side effects, particularly for schizophrenia, causing many who should be on the medications to stop taking them. As a result, drug companies have made a concerted effort to minimize side effects.

ADDICTION REMEDIES

While many of the remedies described so far—avoidance, "ego defenses," and various forms of psychotherapy, including behavioral therapy and psychotropic drugs—are used to treat addictions, it seemed to me that the subject required its own focus.

As pointed out in chapter 20 on how our id-based drives reward us for meeting their expectations, that reward system can become imbalanced and create addictions that can cause untold amounts of suffering and even death. To repeat:

The limbic brain, designed for primitive living, is apparently unaware of cocaine, heroin, and scotch, among other addictive drugs. It probably thinks these are harmless herbs found in the jungle that make us feel good and so must be good for us. The Inner Dummy is apparently oblivious to the discoveries of the external world.

As most cocaine addicts will tell you, as time goes on, it takes more and more of the drug to activate the pleasurable feelings of the reward system. . . . The Inner Dummy, unaware of its own brain chemistry, continues to elevate the platform or pleasure threshold that is required to reward us for doing something stupid in the first place.

When the right combination of addictive drug and vulnerability merge, the reward system of our Inner Dummy can unwittingly begin leading us on the path to death.

So how do you attack an Inner Dummy which has addicted us to a behavior that is overwhelming in its compulsiveness to make us continue, but is harmful to our lives? How many careers and families have been ruined because of irrational addictions?

I was addicted to cigarettes many years ago as I've previously stated, and recall quite clearly the feelings of reward when I lit up the first cigarette of the day. My Inner Dummy would flood me with exhilaration and a sense of calm. I tried to quit three times and recall just as clearly the feelings with which I was punished by an Inner Dummy that didn't want me to quit, whose reward system was apparently unaware that cigarettes over time can be lethal, even though I was rationally aware of it. I try to remember my own feelings of cigarette withdrawal when trying to understand how difficult it is for others to recover from any strong addiction.

I recall dealing many years ago with an obvious alcoholic who had become president of a small company. Everyone in the company knew of the alcoholism and the operative strategy was always to meet with the president before lunch. Meetings that took place after lunch, during which he'd normally eat alone and would guzzle down four martinis, would be difficult. He would pay attention to what you were saying and could talk deliberately without slurring, but he couldn't make decisions or remember the next day the detail that was discussed. Yet in the morning, he was an excellent executive with a good mind, and an ability to organize and delegate effectively. I learned later that upon threat of divorce from his wife, he underwent therapy, kept his job, and stayed on the wagon.

In his book *The Addictive Personality*, family therapist Craig Nakken wrote about the "trance state" of the addict, which reminded me of this executive:

> The trance state is a state of detachment, a state of separation from one's physical surroundings. In the trance, one can live in two worlds simultaneously, floating back and forth between the addictive world and the real world, often without others suspecting it.[9]

It is apparent there is a scale of intensity for each type of addiction. Someone low on the scale might be able to stop smoking or cease compulsive shopping cold turkey through willpower alone. Someone in the middle of the scale would probably need some form of assistance. This person might be able to get off of cigarettes with a patch or one of the other medications available to help addicted people recover. Someone higher on the scale would probably need therapy, possibly in conjunction with the help of a support or fellowship group like Alcoholics Anonymous. Someone near the top of the scale would probably require a prolonged visit to one of many treatment centers that exist to treat various addictions from alcohol to drugs to sex. And yet, in the severest of cases even this intense treatment might not be enough to prevent the addict from resuming his destructive behavior upon release.

Therapist Francine Roberts in *The Therapy Sourcebook* writes as follows:

> A number of therapeutic methods is available to support recovery from addiction. Psychotherapy can be combined with pharmacotherapy and fellowship programs . . . heroin addiction is sometimes treated by giving the addict legally prescribed doses of opiates such as Methadone. . . . Antabuse is sometimes used as a deterrent to discourage alcohol intoxication . . . [because the drug] causes severe nausea when taken with alcohol.[10]

Dr. Albert Ellis, who developed Rational Emotive Therapy, also developed the concept of Rational Recovery, which attempts to break an addiction by replacing distorted outlooks, which may be causing the addiction, with rational ones. Would this work for someone who is off the scale with an addiction? Perhaps it might only be the first step. On the other hand, it might be the miracle cure. Joshua Rosenbaum, writing about Dr. Aaron Beck's studies of cognitive therapy with cocaine abusers in *American Health*, quotes Beck as saying "practically all the patients were drug free after twenty-four weeks."[11]

It appears to be generally agreed, regardless of the chosen therapy, that the first step in the treatment of an addiction is admitting that you have one. Despite the newer thinking in our society that perceives someone as a hero for admitting to addiction, there appear to be many who continue to see it as a sign of weakness whatever one's genetics, upbringing, or present environment, particularly in the corporate world. So there is some risk and potential shame in admission.

The twelve-step fellowships appear to be the most popular form of addiction treatment, sometimes in combination with other forms of therapy. These fellowships, such as Alcoholics Anonymous, are basically support groups, which were described previously, and have come under some criticism because they appear to have a strong religious influence. However, they are available without charge and there is little doubt that they have helped many people worldwide.

Today the activities modeled on Alcoholics Anonymous include Narcotics Anonymous, Cocaine Anonymous, Sex Addicts Anonymous, Shoplifters Anonymous, Spenders Anonymous, Overeaters Anonymous, Gamblers Anonymous, Pills Anonymous, and Smokers Anonymous. Many books about addiction mention the twelve steps upon which these fellowships are based, but don't spell the steps out. I recite them for your reference:

1. We admitted we were powerless over alcohol—that our lives had become unmanageable.
2. Came to believe that a Power greater than ourselves could restore us to sanity.
3. Made a decision to turn our will and our lives over to the care of God as we understood Him.
4. Made a searching and fearless moral inventory of ourselves.
5. Admitted to God, to ourselves, and to another human being the exact nature of our wrongs.

6. Were entirely ready to have God remove all these defects of character.

7. Humbly asked Him to remove our shortcomings.

8. Made a list of all persons we had harmed, and became willing to make amends to them all.

9. Made direct amends to such people whenever possible, except when to do so would injure them or others.

10. Continued to take personal inventory and when we were wrong promptly admitted it.

11. Sought through prayer and meditation to improve our conscious contact with God, as we understood Him, praying only for knowledge of His will for us and the power to carry that out.

12. Having had a spiritual awakening as the result of these steps, we tried to carry this message to alcoholics, and to practice these principles in all our affairs.*

So there you are. In his book *Addictive Thinking*, psychiatrist Abraham J. Twerski pointed out that the words "higher power" can have a nonspiritual meaning. He writes:

> AA is simply saying that because addicts have no control over their chemical use, they must obtain controls from elsewhere. It is this "elsewhere" that constitutes a Higher Power. Someone who does not believe in a religious Higher Power may find other external sources of control. Many, for example, consider their AA group to be a Higher Power.[12]

James Christopher, the founder of the Save Our Selves Movement, which is a rational alternative to the twelve-step fellowship, says the following in his book *SOS Sobriety: The Proven Alternative to 12-Step Programs*:

> Yes, AA has helped countless thousands, but it has also failed countless thousands as well. Twelve "spiritual" steps, or "stepomania" as some critics have called the AA program, is not the only way. SOS offers

---

*The Twelve Steps are reprinted with permission of Alcoholics Anonymous World Services, Inc. Permission to reprint the Twelve Steps does not mean that A.A. has reviewed or approved the contents of this publication, nor that A.A. agrees with the views expressed herein. A.A. is a program of recovery from alcoholism only—use of the Twelve Steps in connection with programs and activities which are patterned after A.A., but which address other problems, or in any other non-A.A. context, does not imply otherwise.

another approach, an approach that has been utilized successfully by thousands to date, thousands who could not recover in AA.[13]

So obviously there is some controversy in the field. Christopher's book included the movement's "Guidelines for Sobriety," which are nonspiritual and so I offer them for your reference:

> To break the cycle of denial and achieve sobriety, we first acknowledge that we are alcoholics/addicts:
> - We reaffirm this truth daily and accept without reservation—one day at a time—the fact that as clean and sober individuals, we cannot and do not drink or use, no matter what.
> - Since drinking/using is not an option for us, we take whatever steps are necessary to continue our Sobriety Priority lifelong.
> - We can achieve the "good life." However, life is also filled with uncertainties; therefore, we do not drink/use regardless of feelings, circumstances, or conflicts.
> - We share in confidence with each other our thoughts and feelings as sober, clean individuals.
> - Sobriety is our Priority, and we are each responsible for our lives and our sobriety.[14]

John Bowlby might have considered an addiction to be the ultimate form of attachment. We can become addicted to an idea, a belief system, a mission in life, a person, a pet or activity, or an object, to name a few non-substance addictions. When we are forced to withdraw from a person to whom we are addicted, for example, in a divorce we don't want, the punishing feelings of "withdrawal" may include many of those we experience when we withdraw from an addictive attachment to alcohol, gambling, or cigarettes.

In perusing some Internet references on addiction, I came across the term "Internet Addiction Disorder," and a story about an introverted Texas student who became so addicted to an online game that he became suicidal and ran away from home twice. He was finally admitted to a psychiatric hospital for treatment. The same reference, which I have misplaced, discussed the formation of Internet support groups. It didn't mention the possibility, but perhaps these support groups might turn into a new fellowship, Internet Anonymous. The point is, probably all of us are vulnerable to becoming addicted to something. Even the sturdiest of us who might be kidnapped for ransom and repeatedly injected with heroin, one of the most addictive of all known substances, might become addicted to it. The key is apparently the intensity level of the reward an id-based drive experiences when we become involved in an activity that fulfills its expectations, whether it's ingesting narcotics, shopping at the mall, or surfing the Internet. At some point, if the feeling of reward is very intense and we are vulnerable to the activity, we may become addicted.

The upshot is that managing our Inner Dummies as we pass through life isn't easy. And fixing them when they go off the deep end appears to be even harder.

MISCELLANEOUS THERAPIES

In the interests of making this chapter as complete as possible I thought I would include some of the miscellaneous therapies listed in the book *Would the Buddha Wear a Walkman?* authored by Judith Hooper and Dick Teresi,[15] which appear designed to penetrate the irrationalities created by the Inner Dummy through varying techniques, in an effort to make us see reality. Following are my own interpretations of the strategies of these therapies:

Correspondence Therapy: Uses writing, including diaries and letters, notes, poetry, and manuscripts, which then can be analyzed by the therapist specializing in this form of therapy. The therapist apparently is able to pick up clues from our writings that are creating distorted outlooks and uses those in techniques that help us recognize and confront our distorted outlooks.

Exaggeration Therapy: The technique is apparently aimed at utilizing our sense of humor to see our irrationalities for what they are. The therapist attempts to poke fun at our neurotic, complaining behavior to help us see reality. I sometimes laugh at my own irrational thoughts as I raise my eyes to the top of their sockets in an attempt to confront my Inner Dummy. This kind of self-deprecating humor, I find, offers some relief, and perhaps that is the underlying theory of this form of therapy.

Implosive Therapy:

The therapist using this form of therapy makes up a story based on our own fears and phobias. Then he or she tells us the story and we listen as if we were listening to a story about a stranger, in an apparent effort to give us an objective view of our own irrationalities.

Logotherapy:

This therapy undoubtedly falls in the category of humanist therapies, since it attempts to motivate us to will ourselves to a sense of meaning. It is probably aimed at offering a life structure to people who have feelings of insignificance. Maybe I ought to try it.

Mirror Image Therapy:

This therapy utilizes a Mirror Image Projective Technique (MIPT), which involves going into a "mirror trance" and free associating. Apparently, as we look in multicolored mirrors and see ourselves, the image of ourselves can change as we simultaneously think about those in our lives who have unduly influenced or traumatized us and we are confronted with how they have become part of us. Audiotapes and videotapes may be used as part of the process.

Morita Therapy:

Under this technique you are put in a bed alone in a room. There is nothing in the room to distract you from your own thoughts—no radio, TV, phone, visitors, or even books. The therapist tells you that whatever your problems are, the solutions lie within you. You are told to think about these solutions as you "engage in 'intrapsychic' activities." This must be similar to gurus, monks, and others who put themselves in isolation to help them get in touch with their real selves, minus the irrational drives of an Inner Dummy that is triggered by sights and thoughts of sex, money, power, relationships, survival, and so on. Steven Mitchell, one of the editors of this book, suggests that this might also be an "occasion for the ego to proliferate and intensify," and he may be right.

Paradigmatic Therapy: Using this technique, the therapist actually acts out the role of authoritative figures in your life, your father, for example, who may have traumatized you with his thoughts and actions. Your therapist "acting as a 'paradigm of the world,' deliberately assumes the roles of the various disturbing others in your life." The theory probably is that your paradigm, your mindset, may be changed when you see a professional acting out the roles of authority figures in your life who are irrational, but who you haven't necessarily recognized as such.

Primal Therapy: The therapist has you recall as vividly as you can the experiences of painful childhood events, and as you do, you let out with shrill screams. The screaming is apparently a therapeutic release of the pressures that have built up within our Inner Dummy and by so doing offers us relief. You may not want to live next door to someone who is using this technique.

Realness Therapy: The technique focuses on motivating you to become "authentic." This could be a takeoff on rational emotive therapy, which works to harshly confront us with our distorted outlooks.

Anti-Expectation Therapy: Uses techniques that motivate us to perceive that our symptoms are much worse than they are. Apparently the idea is that if we make our problems seem worse than they are, then this helps us see reality. When I first saw the name for this therapy, I thought its techniques might work to lower our limbic expectations and so our Inner Dummy may be more satisfied with the results of our lives than it has heretofore and thus may stop punishing us. Maybe that is part of it.

There's more, but why go on?

SELF-HELP BOOKS

Finally, we get to the last of the major remedies for changing our behavior: self-help or self-management, utilizing self-help books, or bibliotherapy if we include a wider array of books that might be suggested to us by a therapist.

The field itself is vast. Utilizing varying references, I found that there are more than 10,000 self-help books of all types currently in print. Another 10,000 are out-of-print and may still be available in libraries. Specific authors have large followings, with their readers eagerly awaiting their next books. Many people simply have a penchant for wanting to fix errant behavior or improve their thought processes themselves.

So how effective are these books? I thought Francine Roberts, in *The Therapy Sourcebook*, comes closest to the mark when she says:

> Bibliotherapy is helpful in areas that are not highly conflicted. For example, if you have difficulty with time management, you may be able to solve it by reading a book about organizational skills.[16]

In other words, John Madden probably won't be able to resolve his fear of traveling on airplanes by reading a book on how to cure phobias. Ellen, who suffers from a severe eating disorder, would probably not be able to convince herself that she looks thin by reading a book. Someone who spends half an hour each night locking and unlocking the front door to be sure it really is locked will probably not be able to cure this obsessive-compulsive disorder by reading a book. A father who is abusive to his children, who competes with rather than nurtures them, will probably not be able to reduce his high power drive by reading a book.

"Self-Management Methods" by psychology professor Frederick H. Kanfer and psychologist Lisa Gaelick-Buys, a chapter in the book *Helping People Change*, reminds us about the difficulties of any form of behavioral change:

> Changing behavior is difficult and often unpleasant. Many clients seek assistance, but often they are motivated not so much to change as to alleviate current discomforts or threats, preferably without altering their behaviors or lifestyles.[17]

The authors then comment on the need for training in self-management, stating that, "Therapeutic tasks should therefore be designed to guarantee success by insuring that the task demands not exceed the client's capacities at the time." The remainder of the paper outlines many of the steps and tasks that are required to perpetuate a behavioral change, most of which we've already covered in this chapter, including changing what we allow into our environments.

It is not surprising therefore that they write:

> However, these [self-help] programs vary widely in quality and there is little empirical evidence for their effectiveness and validity. . . . In fact, self-help programs can have detrimental consequences. . . . Consumers can incorrectly diagnose their problems, select inappropriate methods or fail to comply with key program requirements. However, under close guidance of a helper, carefully chosen self-help resources can be integrated into the total self-management program.[18]

The authors don't comment on the efficacy of self-help books with the "less-conflicted" problems. For example, there are books on breaking bad habits that can be helpful in less than family—or career—threatening situations such as nail biting, being perpetually late, procrastination, and so forth. Books on how to reduce friction in relationships by helping each side better understand the needs of the other can obviously be helpful. And so can books on stress management, particularly those like the *Stress Management Sourcebook*,[19] where the reader is asked to do some written work, part of the journaling that is necessary for any form of cognitive therapy. And then there are books that offer useful tips on how to have better dating or sex lives, how to be better parents, how to deal with difficult people, and so forth. Finally, there are thousands of books written to help us think more positively, to motivate us, and to inspire us, forming a self-help category of their own. And let's not leave out the Bible.

I have gone through countless numbers of self-help books, trying to find inspiring insights and thoughts. It is not easy to find anything that is lasting, but the handful of lasting insights I've been able to garner from the effort has made it worthwhile. My favorite self-help book is one called *Handbook to Higher Consciousness*.[20] I began reading it and using its systems in the late 1970s, after I went through the *est* seminars. In hindsight, I can now see that the procedures recommended in this book are a self-help sort of rational emotive therapy.

For example, if you become furious every time someone in another car honks at you, according to the *Handbook*, you would need to develop a phrase that would directly contradict the cause of the anger. And so you would develop a phrase something like: "I will not get upset when somebody honks at me." You would then scream it out in the car several times after someone honked at you and you were feeling the fury. Believe it or not, this can actually make you feel better. Try it sometime when something is upsetting you. Of course, it's hard to scream out in a car when there are passengers. They may turn you over to the police. So you need to do it when you're alone.

If you're at home when something upsets you, develop a phrase that directly contradicts the cause of the upset and, according to the *Handbook*, scream it out in a wastebasket to take full advantage of its echoing effects. I believe the idea is that the Inner Dummy requires a lot of noise vibrato before it will over time and after plenty of screaming, sign off, on a rational outlook correcting a distorted one.

Please don't judge me on my affection for the *Handbook*, which I haven't read for several years, even though I do now and then scream out something in my bathroom, my substitute for a wastebasket, when I'm alone and upset, to get some immediate relief. Again, we all have to remember the operative phrase: "Nothing works for everyone." A self-help book might succeed in giving us enough insight to modify some bothersome behavior, but may do nothing for our next-door neighbor.

SUCCESS RATES

In covering the difficulties of measuring the success rates of psychotherapy alone, Andrew MacLeod, in the compendium *Psychology, An Integrated Approach*, wrote the following in discussing a study of more than

> 7,000 patients who had undergone treatment for neurotic disorders . . . (Hans) Eysenck's analysis of these data claimed that eclectic therapy (which would have meant insight therapy at that time), had a success rate of 66 percent and psychoanalysis a success rate of 44 percent. However, the crux of his argument (that the therapies were not effective) was that in order to show that psychotherapy was effective, it must be shown to have better effects than simply leaving people alone. It is known that many psychological problems do improve if given time, a phenomenon known

as *spontaneous remission* [emphasis in the original]. Any effects of therapy therefore need to be compared with spontaneous remission.[21]

Clinical psychologist David S. Holmes, in his book *Abnormal Psychology*, after acknowledging Hans Eysenck's studies, adds the following:

> The recent research on the effects of psychotherapy is much more sophisticated than the earlier research, and its results consistently indicate that psychotherapy can be more effective than no therapy or placebo treatment and that in many cases the effects of psychotherapy can be long-lasting. ... However, it is important to recognize that psychotherapy is not equally effective for treating all types of problems. For example, it can be effective for treating depression, but it is ineffective for treating schizophrenia, and its results with anxiety disorders are mixed. .... [I]t is wholly ineffective for treating the obsessive-compulsive disorder.[22]

On the other hand, the book *Cognitive Behavior Therapy for Psychiatric Problems*, by psychiatrist Keith Hawton, clinical psychologists Paul M. Salkovskis and John Kirk, and psychology lecturer David M. Clark, claims that therapy may be effective for variations of obsessive-compulsive disorders. Then, of interest is a paragraph in the article by Joshua Rosenbaum previously referred to:

> Cognitive therapy, [Aaron] Beck insists, not only is effective for problems such as drug abuse, depression and panic attacks, but also works quickly. Panic attack sufferers respond to treatment after only about eight weekly sessions. In cases of depression, he sees marked improvement in three to four months of weekly therapy.[23]

It would appear that the results of the various forms of behavioral therapy are easier to measure than other forms of psychotherapy. If the therapy was aimed at dissolving a fear of heights, without going back in time to learn what the cause was, then the success of the therapy can be judged by whether or not the person no longer fears heights when the therapy is over.

Even easier to measure, however, is the effectiveness of psychotropic drugs. Ruth Larson in "New Hope for Mentally Ill," writes:

> New drugs and treatment are helping those afflicted lead normal lives. The success rate for mental illnesses now varies between 60 and 80 percent, higher than the success rate for many other diseases.[24]

The question that would probably be asked of recipients of these drugs would be something like: "After you took the drugs for the prescribed period of time, did you feel better?" And so the research that led to the claim of a 60 to 80 percent success rate doesn't seem out of line.

It is not easy to alter the outlooks and the resulting thoughts and actions of an Inner Dummy that in some areas is out of balance. But we have a 60 to 80 percent chance of succeeding, of getting the Inner Dummy to sign off or bite on more rational outlooks, if we decide to do something about it and are prepared for a lot of hard work.

COMMENTARY BY DR. HEFTER

The arrival, particularly over the past forty years, of an array of medications used to treat mental difficulties has had a major effect in the clinical practice of psychiatry. This refers not only to the actual utilization of medications, but also to the attitudes of increased optimism with which treatment personnel now approach patients. Especially with respect to the more disabling conditions of schizophrenia, and the mood disorders including major depressions, the antipsychotic, mood stabilizer, and antidepressant drugs have markedly diminished the incapacitating consequences of these illnesses, and have permitted many people to engage in productive activity, while lessening the burden on family and friends. Antianxiety medications have been of great help to many people who have been negatively affected by crippling anxieties, panic disorders, and phobias.

The value of medications for addictions has also increased in recent years. Methadone as a treatment for heroin addiction has been a subject of controversy, for political and attitudinal as well as clinical reasons, but is viewed favorably by many patients and treatment personnel as an effective tool in the management of this condition. Other medication treatments for opiate, alcohol, tobacco, and eating addictions are being used more widely. It is important to keep in mind also, that in the treatment of addictions there are often additional diagnoses that complicate the picture, and in these situations medications can be of much value. Infrequently, however, are medications used as the sole treatment for addiction problems—they are almost always only part of a multidimensional effort involving individual, group, and milieu modalities.

Medication also has its adverse aspect, particularly in the possible appearance of side effects. In general, side effects are infrequently of serious negative consequence for the majority of people taking them. However, for the individual in whom serious side effects do occur, they can be quite troubling. For example, some of the medications prescribed for the schizophrenic disorders can cause significant neuromuscular problems. Some of the medications used to combat depression can lead to heart arrythmias, significant weight gain, and drowsiness. Many of the antianxiety medications can be habituating. There is the possibility also of problems arising from the use of some medications the patient is taking while at the same time using other substances, such as nutritional supplements or herbal preparations, prescribed for other conditions as well. Some medications are for long-term (many years) use, while others need only be taken for short periods of time. Thus it is important for a patient to be clear about how a medication is to be used and to inform his physician of other medications he is taking. If side effects arise, the patient should discuss their occurrence with his physician—not all side effects require discontinuation of the medication since a change in the dosage or a change in the time of taking the medication may be all that is indicated.

Medication, like psychotherapy and other therapeutic techniques, and like medical treatments in general, are not always effective. Sometimes a particular medication will not be helpful, but another will. For the most part, psychiatric drugs are not a cure for a problem—they serve to help an individual manage a problem and that can be of great benefit.

It is also important to realize that the psychotherapeutic relationship can be crucial in helping many individuals to continue taking medications that are prescribed. In other words, medication should be part of a treatment context and not seen as an isolated form of treatment. This does not necessarily mean frequent therapeutic sessions; it does mean the recipient of the medication should maintain ongoing personal contact with the individual involved in his treatment.

NOTES

1. Dave Barry, *Fresno Bee*, August 9, 1998, p. E4.

2. Ruth Larson, "New Hope for Mentally Ill," *Insight on the News* (September 7, 1998): 43.

3. Joshua Rosenbaum, "Talk Therapy: Ready for the Trash Heap?" *American Health* 13, no. 8 (October 1994): 60–65.

4. Ibid.

5. Gerald L. Klerman et al., "Medication and Psychotherapy," in *Handbook of Psychotherapy and Behavior Change*, ed. Allen E. Bergin and Sol L. Garfield (New York: Wiley, 1994), p. 752.

6. Marvin E. Lickey and Barbara Gordon, *Medicine and Mental Illness* (New York: Freeman, 1991), p. 10.

7. Ibid., p. 33.

8. Larson, "New Hope for Mentally Ill," p. 43.

9. Craig Nakken, *The Addictive Personality: Understanding the Addictive Process and Compulsive Behavior* (Center City, Minn.: Hazelden, 1988), p. 4.

10. Francine M. Roberts, *The Therapy Sourcebook* (Los Angeles: Lowell House, 1998), p. 27.

11. Rosenbaum, "Talk Therapy: Ready for the Trash Heap?" pp. 60–65.

12. Abraham J. Twerski, *Addictive Thinking: Understanding Self-Deception* (Center City, Minn.: Hazelden, 1997), p. 72.

13. James Christopher, *SOS Sobriety: The Proven Alternative to 12-Step Programs* (Amherst, N.Y.: Prometheus Books, 1992), p. 22.

14. Ibid., p. 70.

15. Judith Hooper and Dick Teresi, *Would the Buddha Wear a Walkman?* pp. 137–38.

16. Roberts, *The Therapy Sourcebook*, pp. 256–57.

17. Frederick H. Kanfer and Lisa Gaelick-Buys, "Self-Management Methods," in *Helping People Change: A Textbook of Methods*, ed. Frederick H. Kanfer and Arnold P. Goldstein (New York: Pergamon Press, 1991), p. 306.

18. Ibid., p. 313.

19. J. Barton Cunningham, *The Stress Management Sourcebook* (Los Angeles: Lowell House, 1997).

20. Ken Keyes Jr., *Handbook to Higher Consciousness* (Coos Bay, Ore.: Love Line Books, 1975).

21. Andrew MacLeod, "Therapeutic Interventions," in *Psychology: An Integrated Approach*, ed. Michael Eysenck (Essex, England: Addison-Wesley Longman, 1998), pp. 578–79.

22. David S. Holmes, *Abnormal Psychology* (New York: Longman, 1997), p. 140.

23. Rosenbaum, "Talk Therapy: Ready for the Trash Heap?" pp. 60–65.

24. Larson, "New Hope for Mentally Ill," p. 43.

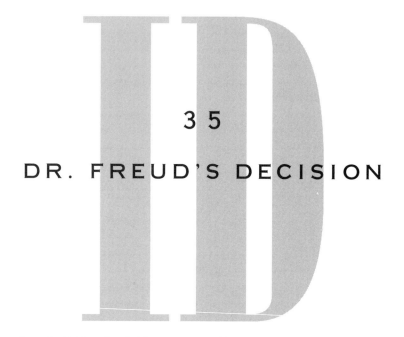

3 5

DR. FREUD'S DECISION

In early 1999, a South African soccer referee shot a player to death during a soccer match near Johannesburg, in front of six hundred spectators, after the player, angry over a disputed goal, lunged at the referee with a knife. The manager of the dead man's team was quoted as saying: "It is easy for players and referees to get hurt during games in this area."[1]

Ted Croft, head of the agency, was just finishing making his presentation to Dr. Freud in the agency's auditorium conference room. The room was sloped with five rows of theater-type chairs. Sophisticated projection equipment was installed behind a glass window on the wall behind the last row. A conference table was located in a bay at floor level, in front of a screen bordered by wall-to-wall bulletin boards. A small podium was resting on the conference table. Croft had been standing behind the podium. Wendy Smith and Samuel Ollander were sitting together next to him. Dr. Freud was sitting on the opposite side alone, facing them.

Croft had noticed that Wendy Smith could hardly take her eyes off Dr. Freud and momentarily wondered if something was going on between them.

Ah, no way, he thought to himself.

Many of the chairs in the rows behind Dr. Freud were occupied by members of the agency's account and creative staff, including writers and designers who had been working on the Inner Dummy campaign and were invited to witness the presentation to Dr. Freud. They had been introduced to him individually by Croft, before he started his presentation.

The presentation itself lasted almost two hours, as Croft reviewed in tedious detail each and every component of the campaign that had made it through the approval process of the consumer-focus groups.

The campaign's components filled the bulletin boards as well as most of the conference table. They included the story boards and scripts to be made into television and radio commercials, brochures, manuals, and print ads on such subjects as Dummy Snatched, Dummy Drives, Dummy Bliss, Dummy Pain, Dummy Diverters, Dummy Vengeance, Dummy Delusions, Dummy Convictions, Dummy Sex, Dummy Missions, Dummy Goals, Dummy Attachments, Dummy Remedies, Dummy Scales, and Dummy Status.

At the end of the conference table opposite the entrance, the products for the campaign were neatly displayed, including two Inner Dummy Dolls, the Inner Dummy Screen Saver, which was being demonstrated without sound on a computer screen, the Inner Dummy Bathroom Scale, and an Inner Dummy Dictionary. The Inner Dummy Punching Bag stood on the floor right behind the other products. Two female and two male half-bodied mannequins sat next to the products on the table and held T-shirts that read: "Would someone please fix my Inner Dummy before I fall in love with another idiot?" "My Inner Dummy needs to knock it off." "I have given my Inner Dummy its notice." "I love my Inner Dummy. I call it Ernest." "My Inner Dummy is not the real me."

A section of the bulletin board contained a handful of posters with compelling designs that read: "What is your Inner Dummy making you worry about today?" "Who is your Inner Dummy making you hate today?" "Who is your Inner Dummy making you abuse today?" "Please ask your Inner Dummy to give the rest of us a break."

A doorknob hanger was displayed that read, "Please use caution. Inner Dummy temporarily out of order."

Ted Croft had left the podium and was completing his description of the posters, pointing to one on the far right side that simply had the initials "I.D." and describing how the initials might be another pseudonym for people who aren't up to calling their ids their Inner Dummies. "They can simply call them their I.D.s," he said. "We have to do some additional research on this as an alternative designation." Then he walked back to the podium, looked at Dr. Freud, and said, "I think that just about does it, Dr. Freud. We've covered every component developed for the kickoff of the campaign. Peter Norton, as I mentioned before, is running late, but should be here any moment. He has two more products to add to our collection at the end of the table." Croft pointed toward them.

"I can hardly wait for that," Freud replied indifferently, his eyes glazed as they kept wandering over the exhibit of Inner Dummy material, stopping only when they met the stares of Wendy Smith.

"Would you like me to review any of the materials again, or perhaps Wendy and Samuel might be able to answer questions you might have. I must reiterate that we need your decision on whether we can move ahead with this campaign today, sir."

"Excuse me, Ted," Sam interrupted.

"Yes, Sam."

"Since we probably have a few moments before Peter gets here, there is one concept that was handed to me by the creatives just before this meeting and I didn't have time to discuss it with Dr. Freud and it's not on display. Perhaps I can show it to him now."

"Of course, go right ahead."

Sam reached down and grabbed a card that was resting against his chair. He faced Dr. Freud, and said, "We thought that we needed to address the problem that millions of people in this country seem to have about visiting a therapist when they have a neurotic disorder or something worse. Men, in particular, appear to view therapy as a sign of weakness. They appear to perceive it as an admission to their family, friends, and coworkers that they are helpless to fix their mental problems themselves, as if they were to blame for their biochemical imbalances."

"There are many men who visit therapists, Samuel," Dr. Freud responded.

"Yes, there are, but our research shows that many of them are embarrassed about it, while millions more, according to statistics we've seen, simply refuse to go, even though their chemical imbalances may be causing a malady such as depression that makes it almost impossible to carry on with their jobs or relate to their families."

"What is your suggestion?"

"It is just this, sir. If it bothers you to tell people that you are going to visit a therapist for a mental disorder, an anxiety, a phobia, a depression, whatever, you simply say you are going in to get an—"

Ollander turned the sign around and read it:

"—*Inner Dummy Adjustment.*"

Freud, whose eyes were already glazed from the detail of the campaign materials that Croft had already presented, buried his head in his hands.

"Oh, no," he barely whispered.

"But, sir," Ollander continued, "consumers in the telephone interviews we did this morning liked this concept. They can say to their bosses and friends, when something has happened to make them irrationally anxious or paranoid, or whatever, that 'I'm going in for a series of Inner Dummy Adjustment sessions.' Do you get it? This doesn't sound like any weakness. It is little different than saying 'I'm going in for a series of allergy shots.' Don't you see?"

Freud was still holding his head in his hands and didn't reply.

"In a typical case of depression, for example," Ollander continued, "our person can tell his co-workers and friends, 'It looks like I have been made *Dummy Depressed*, for some reason. My specialist tells me it will take six to twelve visits, perhaps with medication to overcome it. After that I'll simply go back for checkups.' You see? It is easier to talk about. Think of the millions of people who can be helped because this language makes it easier for them to seek treatment."

Dr. Freud looked over to Ted Croft. "Do I have to decide on this insanity today?"

"Along with the rest of the campaign, yes, sir," he replied.

"Oh, there is one more thing, Dr. Freud," Ollander said.

"I can't wait."

"Oh no, you're going to like this." He reached down beneath his chair and picked up a layout for a manual, which he turned to Dr. Freud. "Here it is, a *Dummy Disorders Manual*."

Freud slipped back in his chair, looking up at the ceiling in obvious pain.

"Wait, this is good, sir. It contains a simplified explanation for more than three hundred personality and other mental disorders and the nature of the Inner Dummy Adjustment, the treatment required for each one of them, based on the severity." Samuel flipped through the pages. "And see, we call the various types of therapies recommended Inner Dummy Adjustment Techniques, to be administered by the Inner Dummy Specialist you're visiting."

"Oh, Dr. Freud," Wendy Smith interrupted, "isn't this wonderful? Look at all the people we can help by lightening the approach to the problem of mental disorders and in this way motivating them to seek help. We will make you famous, Dr. Freud."

"I am already famous," Freud said, snapping out of his lethargy. "And even though I am dead, I don't want to be vilified. And I can't imagine that any professional worth his or her name will want to be called . . . that specialist . . . I refuse to even utter the full name."

"But I don't think—"

"Sorry, Wendy, for cutting you off, " Croft interrupted as he stood and motioned to Ollander to pin his new materials to the bulletin board behind him. "You can talk to Dr. Freud about this later, if you want. In the meantime, time is growing short and we have to move on."

Croft moved back to the podium and gathered his papers. Wendy looked disappointed and Freud looked at her with some concern.

"Let's just put the new concepts Sam presented to you aside for a moment and consider the bigger picture," Croft continued, directing his comments to Dr. Freud. "I am pleased to inform you that a number of charitable foundations have pledged all the money we need to get everything you see before you produced. That includes enormous quantities of the manuals, which will be offered free through a toll-free telephone number. It also includes the hundreds of thousands of dollars it will take to produce the print ads and the television and radio commercials in a compelling format. In addition, we have commitments from the major television networks and the cable television networks. They are all prepared to run our Inner Dummy television and radio commercials when they are produced as free public-service spots. We also have commitments from the major national magazines, dozens of them, which will run our print ads at no charge. Every single commercial and print ad will carry a toll-free number for consumers to request copies of the manuals. Hold up the toll-free number, Wendy."

Wendy left her seat and walked to a bulletin board behind her where a sign facing away, was resting against the wall. She picked it up and showed it to Dr. Freud. It read: 800-555-DUMMY.

"Isn't this wonderful, Dr. Freud?" Wendy said, now smiling again. "Anyone can dial this number without charge and request any of the free manuals. The donations we've received from the foundations will cover the cost of mailing millions of them and we've been promised more money if we need it."

Freud looked at Wendy and Croft, puzzled. "I am confused about what you call public-service spots."

"Public-service spots and ads, sir," Croft continued, "are commercials and print ads that are run free by the networks, individual stations, and magazines as a service for the public at large. You can imagine how many charities and worthwhile public entities attempt to get the available allotment of this public-service broadcast time and the print-ad space. But without exception, all of the media we approached became immediately convinced that our messages, which explain the nature of our id, with the branding of the Inner Dummy, will capture the public's imagination. In addition, they are also as convinced as we are that the campaign will help more people who require treatment to go get it, because they will view it as a problem with their Inner Dummy, not a generalized weakness of their minds. And there is a difference."

"Surely, Mr. Croft," Freud said, "you don't expect this collection of trivia," he pointed to the wall and table filled with materials, "to rectify the problems of serious neurotics or to even touch on the problems of psychoses?"

"No, we don't, sir," Croft replied, allowing Freud's biting comment to pass. "But there are two long-term outcomes that we think this campaign will generate. The first is that consumer awareness of the Inner Dummy will be a positive influence for the world at large in that it pinpoints the causes of the warped side of human nature in a way that nonacademics, the rest of us, can understand. And second, a broader understanding of the cause of the problem may result in the diversion of billions of dollars into brain research that will help us find acceptable ways to rid ourselves of the limbic brain's more violent, hateful, and aggressive nature. And that's just for starters."

Freud turned around abruptly and said, "What do you think, Eddie?"

Everyone in the room followed Freud's eyes to an older man sitting quietly in the farthest seat of the last row of chairs, where he was somewhat apart from others on the agency staff. No one had taken notice of him. He appeared to be about the same age as Dr. Freud, but balding with patches of thin gray hairs on the sides of his head. He was wearing a white shirt and tie, and a thick, wool cardigan sweater.

"I'm not really sure, Uncle Sigmund," he replied.

Croft, Wendy Smith, and Samuel Ollander were looking dumbfounded. Other agency staffers near him were staring at the man.

"When did he get here?" Croft asked, startled. "And why did he call you 'uncle'?"

"He has been sitting there since the start of your presentation, Mr. Croft," Dr. Freud replied. "He has heard everything. You simply didn't notice him. I would like to introduce him to you."

Freud turned around and said, "Okay, Eddie, come on down here and sit next to me." Freud patted the chair next to him. As the man stood and started walking down, Freud continued. "Ladies and gentlemen, this is my nephew, Mr. Edward L. Bernays, who was known in your country as the father of the public-relations profession. As you might remember, my wife Martha's maiden name was Bernays and Eddie is the son of her brother, Ely. In addition, his mother was my sister, Anna. So we have very close familial ties. Eddie died at the age of 103 in 1995. I asked that he be brought back for this meeting, since he is more skilled at this type of thing than I am."*

"I am glad to hear you say that, Uncle Sigmund," Bernays replied as he walked to the chair. "Uncle Sigmund and I didn't often agree. We had many disagreements during our day, particularly after World War I, when I was instrumental in getting his books published in the United States."

"Now, now, Eddie, you know that Ernest Jones and Dr. Otto Rank were more responsible for that publishing venture than you were."

"You see?" Bernays asked. "We are both dead and we are still arguing."

Freud stared at Bernays and then began his deep, quiet laugh. When he recovered he said, "You'll notice that Eddie was brought back at around the age of seventy-five, as I was."

"And you know, Uncle, I feel better already." They both enjoyed the little joke, as Eddie sat down.

Just then, the conference-room door burst open and Peter Norton of the Manchester Doll Company strode in, followed by Jenny Kagan. He boomed out, "Hello, hello, everyone; here we are, here we are, hope we're not disturbing anything." His eyes rested on Dr. Freud. "Hello. . . . Dr. Freud," he blasted, walking over to Freud with his hand extended as Freud appeared to shrivel back in his chair.

"How are you, sir, how are you?" he boomed, grabbing Freud's hand and shaking it as if it were a country water pump, and leaning close in to Freud's face where his breath once again made Freud nauseated.

"For god's sake, Peter, stand back from the man; you're practically suffocating him," Jenny barked at Norton.

"Oh, he doesn't mind, do you, sir?" Norton replied. "I can tell when someone is fond of me. Aren't you, sir? Am I right or am I wrong?"

Freud was unable to speak but looked relieved as Norton backed away.

Jenny interjected, "Norton, anyone who claims to be fond of you deserves to be a candidate for sainthood."

Norton burst out laughing as he placed the two packages he was car-

*Bernays was indeed Freud's nephew and brought the public-relations profession to prominence beginning in the 1920s, with his work for Procter & Gamble, General Electric, *Time*, and General Motors, among others.

rying on the table and began unwrapping them. "She's great, isn't she, folks? Always kidding, that's my Jenny."

"I'm not kidding, Norton," Jenny said as she took a seat next to Wendy and said hello to her and then greeted Dr. Freud, Croft, and Ollander, apologizing for Norton's gruffness.

Norton said, "You'll let me know when you're finished with you're presentation, Ted, and then I'll show these new Dr. Freud Inner Dummy products. Sorry to disturb you."

"I just finished, Peter. Your timing is great, so go ahead."

"Okay," he said as he finished unwrapping the first package. Then he looked up and for the first time noticed Bernays.

"I'm sorry, sir, I haven't had the pleasure," he said as he strode over to Bernays, who like his uncle shrank back from the physical exuberance of the large man. "My name is Peter Norton and I am the vice president of sales of the Manchester Doll Company and we have the licensing rights to all the Inner Dummy products. Aren't they great, sir? And who might you be?"

"I am Edward Bernays, Professor Freud's nephew."

"Nephew? But you look to be about the same age." Norton looked from Bernays to Freud and then back again. "My god, I know, sir—you are dead, too."

"That is correct. I am here on a special assignment to assist my uncle in making his decision since I spent my career in the practice of public relations."

"Bernays, Bernays," Norton stroked his chin. "The name is familiar."

"Edward L. Bernays Counsel on Public Relations was the name of my company," Bernays replied. "You might have heard of it, but in any event, let's not hold things up. Please show us what you have."

"Quite right, sir, I will." As Norton began striding around the conference table to take his place behind the podium, Freud glanced at Wendy, who gave him a quick wink.

Gott, Freud thought to himself. She does want to go out again after this is over. His mind raced back to the night he went to the restaurant bar with her friends and the hangover he felt the next day, proof that his body and mind were quite human again, if only temporarily in their retransformation. He couldn't believe a little wine made him feel that way. It made him feel less European.

Norton finished unwrapping the first package and held an oversized bricklike object in the air.

"And here's the first new idea, Dr. Freud. What do you think of it?"

"I hesitate to say, other than it looks like a large brick," Dr. Freud replied cautiously.

Norton burst out with a laugh loud enough to make the spectators jump. "You just won the jackpot, Dr. Freud; it is a brick. We are going to call it the *Dr. Freud Inner Dummy Throwing Brick.*"

"Oh, my god," Freud whispered.

"Now watch this," Norton went on. He turned toward the screen behind him and hurled the brick at it with all his might. It simply bounced off. He then retrieved it, brought it back to the podium, and threw it again.

"Do you get it?" he asked as he again retrieved the brick. "It's like a Nerf ball," he continued. "You keep it on your desk or on the kitchen counter at home, and when somebody or something gets you really mad, you pick it up and hurl it at the nearest wall or across the room or whatever. Or, you can set it on the floor and kick it. It can't hurt anything because it's made of a soft, foamlike substance. In this sense, the brick becomes what the creatives are tentatively calling a *Dummy Discharger.* Sam still has to check the name with his consumer groups."

He nodded at Sam, who nodded back.

"This man is obviously insane," Bernays said.

"Hold on, sir. It helps when you affix this label to it." Norton reached into his pocket and pulled out a label with a paper backing. He removed the backing and applied the label to the brick, where it read in big letters, "The Doctor Freud Inner Dummy Throwing Brick." A line beneath it read: "Throw or kick when angry. Repeat as necessary."

"Well, what do the rest of you think?"

Ted Croft replied chuckling, "Norton, you can count me in. I'll order one for me and one for my wife."

"Hey, that's great," Norton replied. "Maybe we can even have 'his' and 'her' bricks. What do you think about that idea, Jenny?"

"Beautiful. You can make a set for you and me. Only make mine a real brick."

"Isn't she just great, folks?" Norton said looking up at the spectators who were laughing.

"And what do you think, Dr. Freud?"

Freud was just shaking his head. Bernays was simply staring at Norton.

"Norton," Jenny said, "why don't you go onto the next product?"

"Good idea. Thank you, Jenny." Norton walked to the end of the table where the other Inner Dummy products were displayed and placed the brick gently next to the Inner Dummy Bathroom Scale. Then he picked up the second package he had brought to the meeting and unwrapped it. It appeared to be a large, plastic bucket with a label that Norton hid from the group as he walked back to the podium.

"This is another great product, folks. And I can tell you that my wife, Zena, the old ball and chain, tried it last night and she is ready to give it a testimonial. Now what do you think this is, Dr. Freud?"

"I have no idea," he replied in barely a whisper.

"Well, guess what." He turned the bucket around and the label on it read: *The Dr. Freud Inner Dummy Antianger & Antiworry Screaming Bucket.*

"Oh, no," was Dr. Freud's barely audible reaction.

"I knew you'd love it, sir," Norton said looking directly at Dr. Freud, "even though the name might be a little long. We need to have the creatives work on it. It was their idea in the first place and I congratulate you, gang." He pointed to the gallery and there were a number of nods back to Norton.

"And now you do want to know how it works, don't you, sir?" Norton said, again looking directly at Dr. Freud.

Bernays broke in, "Hey, talk to me, too, buddy; I'm his advisor."

"Of course, sir, of course. I was talking to you as well."

"Yeah, but you weren't looking at me."

"I apologize, sir."

"Well, we'll see. Go ahead."

"Good. The way it works is simple," Norton continued, making sure his eyes covered both Dr. Freud and Bernays. "Say you just got off the telephone with someone who said something that made you mad. Maybe it was your ex-husband, let's call him Alex, who is late with his alimony payment and told you that you were worthless as a wife and mother . . ."

Freud and Bernays exchanged glances, both wondering why Norton was using an example that assumed they had ex-husbands.

"You hang up and you are infuriated," Norton continued. "Well, you go to your Dr. Freud Antianger & Antiworry Screaming Bucket and pick out an exact phrase that will contradict your anger or worry. In this case it would be, 'Alex is irrational and so calling me worthless will not make me angry.' Do you get it? A direct contradictory statement.

"The next thing you do is put your head in this bucket and scream that statement out as loud as you can."

Norton then proceeded to put the bucket over his head and screamed out the statement four times. Then he uncovered himself, looked at Dr. Freud, and said, "The theory is that this will lessen your anger or worry.

And if you keep doing it enough, sooner or later your Inner Dummy gets the message that Alex is indeed irrational and anything he says you'll be able to laugh off."

Freud had his head buried in his hands again, and low groans could be heard.

"Or say that you have a nagging worry," Norton went on, now looking more at Bernays. "You're worried that your son, Edward, is not going to pass his college exams. Well, worrying isn't going to help him and it's going to be painful to you. So you come up with a statement that contradicts the worry, put the bucket over your head, and shout it out. Like this."

Norton put the bucket over his head and screamed four times, "I will not worry because Edward may not pass his college exams."

He took the bucket off and said, "The theory is that this will give you some immediate relief from worry. The worry will then slowly begin to reemerge, but as soon as it does, you put the bucket back over your head and repeat the statement four times all over again. And then again and again and again. After a period of time, if this technique works for you, your worry will begin to change from painful anxiety to serious concern. There is a difference between the two emotions, according to the creatives up there, who as I understand it, got this idea from a New Age therapy book. It is another form of Dummy Discharger."

"You know what, Norton?" Jenny said.

"Yes, dear."

"You look a lot better with that bucket over your head."

"You're great, dear, you know just when to inject a little humor."

"Excuse me, Peter," Croft said.

"Yes, Ted?"

"Is that the last of the products?"

"It is. Your creatives have some other products in the idea stage, but for right now this is it."

"Okay, then, why don't you take a seat. We appreciate your time to present these new products, but we'd like to get a decision today from Dr. Freud and Mr. Bernays on the overall campaign. Of course, you're welcome to stay."

"My pleasure, sir," Norton said as he left the podium with the basket and set it among the other Inner Dummy products on display. Dr. Freud was now leaning back in his chair, hands in his suit pockets, looking chagrined, but obviously relieved that Norton was finished.

"And now, Dr. Freud," Croft continued, "we have come to a moment of decision. As we agreed near the beginning of this project when you were in my office voicing objections to the concepts we were showing you, you would have the final say on this campaign when all the components were ready. Well, the best of them have now been completed and tested," Croft pointed around the room to all the materials on the bulletin board and table, "the money is in place, the media have given us their commitments, and all we need now is your approval."

Freud leaned forward again, elbows on table, his hands running through his hair. Then he looked toward Bernays and said, "Eddie, this is painful. If this campaign is allowed to commence, my academic credentials will be in tatters again. I will be a laughingstock. Please, I need your advice."

Bernays sat with knees crossed, one arm draped over the back of his chair, the other tapping the eraser side of a pencil on the table. He sat deep in thought, the room in silence.

"What about the PR?" he asked suddenly, addressing Croft.

"The what, sir?" Croft replied.

"The PR, the public relations part of this campaign. What about that?"

"Wendy, you're our public-relations director. Why don't you answer Mr. Bernays's question."

Wendy looked uncertain momentarily, but then stood resolutely.

"First of all, Mr. Bernays, I want you to know how proud I am to be able to meet you. You were in all the textbooks in the public-relations courses I took at the university."

"So you know about me," Bernays said looking pleased.

"Know about you, sir? I mean you're famous."

"Famous, you say."

"Oh, yes, sir, and certainly among public-relations professionals you would be in our hall of fame, if we had one."

"So tell me, Wendy," Bernays said, now looking very pleased, "what kind of campaign do you have in mind for this program?"

"To tell you the truth, Mr. Bernays, my department has been so busy working on the copy for the Dummy manuals and such that we haven't worked out the details of the public-relations side of the campaign."

"Well, that's inexcusable," Bernays said, as he stood up and began pacing, his mood suddenly turning sour. Wendy looked chagrined.

"I have to tell you, Uncle Sigmund," Bernays said as he paced behind the table, "that at first I thought this campaign lacked some imagination. 'Inner Dummy,' I'm thinking. I'm pretty sure that in my prime I could have come up with something better, something that would have had just as much consumer appeal, but would have been more protective of you. However, the facts are that considerable time and effort have already gone into this concept and we know from the research data Mr. Ollander presented that the concept definitely has consumer appeal."

He stopped pacing behind his chair and looked directly at Wendy.

"The public-relations program for this campaign will be critical, my dear."

"I know that, sir," Wendy replied quietly.

"First of all, we will need a spokesperson," Bernays continued, resuming his pacing. "Some acclaimed clinical psychiatrist or well-known psychologist. Someone with credentials who can communicate the messages convincingly."

Wendy was now busy scribbling notes.

"We will need television and radio interviews for this spokesperson on the national level. At the local level, we will need . . . we will need rallies, yes, Inner Dummy Rallies, where ordinary people can speak briefly to entire cadres of therapists at no charge about any problems of irrationality they have themselves or their loved ones have, where they can receive some initial advice and where our Dummy Manuals can be made available for free. Then we will need a Web site, an Inner Dummy Web site, where much of this information can be downloaded and printed out."

"Excuse me, sir," Peter Norton interrupted loudly.

"What is it, Norton?" Bernays replied, annoyed.

"I was just wondering how you know about Web sites, you being dead and all that."

Bernays relaxed and chuckled. "I have only been dead four years, Mr. Norton, and I was, in any event, updated on all communications vehicles in preparation for this assignment."

"Just wondering," Norton said.

"Now to continue . . . and you'll all pardon my immodesty if I say that in my autobiographies it was stated authoritatively that I was known throughout my career as the consummate idea man."

"I must say, Mr. Bernays," Croft interrupted enthusiastically, "you certainly haven't lost your touch."

"Thank you, Mr. Croft. Now another idea that came upon me is that we should ally ourselves with a university, create an Inner Dummy Foundation, an organization that will be capable of handling the incredible amount of field work that lies ahead. I agree with Mr. Croft that the Inner Dummy concept should be positioned as not only explaining the nature of irrationality—why a father becomes jealous of his son's success; why Hitler and Stalin and Idi Amin and Mao Tse-tung and others did what they did, killing tens of millions of people—but communicating the nature of mental illness to the world at large, taking us out of the mental Dark Ages, so to speak; allowing those who suffer from severe neuroses or psychoses to be unafraid to admit to it and seek treatment. We could—"

"Please, Mr. Bernays," Wendy said, scribbling briskly on her notepad, "could you please slow down? You have one idea after another."

Bernays smiled coyly. "In my day, I could not only come up with one idea after another, I could figure out how to get them carried out. That is an unbeatable combination, even today."

Dr. Freud said jokingly, "I see, Eddie, you have lost none of your modesty." Then he turned serious and said after a moment's hesitation, "I assume, Eddie, by your enthusiasm that you think I should give this campaign my approval."

"That has to be your decision, Uncle Sigmund. I can understand your problems with it. But if you give your consent to proceed with this campaign, you are, in fact, licensing other psychiatrists and psychologists as well to do the same . . . to risk their academic credentials in promoting a concept as simple as the Inner Dummy. And yet, sir, it is all based on your concept of the id, which you alone can take credit for. So via the Inner Dummy, your concept not only lives on, but it grows stronger and gains the general popularity it was denied as a concept that heretofore could only be comprehended by academics, students, and the most serious-minded. The Inner Dummy campaign may be simplistic, sir, but we live in a world of sound bites; it is not the same today as it was in the 1920s or 1930s, and the Inner Dummy will make one of the greatest sound bites of all time. And it will be yours in essence, Uncle Sigmund. No one will ever be able to take that away from you. And, you will be admired for allowing your complex systems of ideas to be simplified in this way."

"So what do you think I should do, Eddie?"

"My recommendation, sir, would be to go for it."

Wendy burst in. "Mr. Bernays, do you think it would be possible for you and Dr. Freud to stick around a little longer? I mean, I could certainly use your help in developing the public-relations campaign and Dr. Freud would be the perfect spokesperson."

"Please, Wendy," Dr. Freud responded, holding up a hand. "I must return as soon as I make my decision."

"But Dr. Freud, I hope not tonight. The girls are waiting for us."

"Please, Wendy, this is the way it has to be. However, I might make some arrangements for Eddie to linger a bit longer to help you out and to protect my interests, should I decide to allow this simplistic campaign with its trivial products to move ahead."

"We need your decision now, Dr. Freud," Croft spoke pleadingly. "We know it is a difficult one for you."

"*Ach*," Freud said, throwing up his hands and standing up. Then he began pacing back and forth, hands folded behind his back, head down as he thought. Every time he passed the display of Inner Dummy products, he glanced at them momentarily and then grunted. Then he walked to the other side of the table and began perusing the manuals affixed to the bulletin board, sometimes nodding in agreement, other times shaking his head in disagreement. Then he looked at Croft and said, "Excuse me a moment, I have to leave the room."

Freud left the room, with Bernays still standing behind his chair. Not a word was spoken. There was total silence. Nobody moved. Ten minutes later, Freud reentered and stood next to Bernays behind his chair.

"I hope you'll pardon my absence, but I needed an emergency communication with the Regional Higher Authorities. They have granted me, along with Eddie, an extra stay of three days to work with you in assuring that the simplified wording of those manuals and the other materials are at least in accordance with proper academic theory and that we eliminate anything that is too far afield. They have granted me these extra days and as a result I have decided to give my approval."

Pandemonium broke out in the room. Jenny Kagan was actually hugging Peter Norton. Ted Croft was dancing with Samuel Ollander. Wendy Smith came over to hug Dr. Freud and Bernays. Those in the gallery were whooping and hollering as if their team won the championship game.

Then Ted Croft looked over at Dr. Freud and Bernays and said, "Dr. Freud, Mr. Bernays, I hope you'll come with me, right now; we have some contracts to sign."

"Contracts?" Freud asked bemused. "Eddie and I are both dead."

"Sorry, sir, it's our legal department; they want us to follow standard procedures."

"Lawyers," Bernays spit out. "Even when you're dead they think they have to control you."

As the three men left the room, Wendy Smith followed them, saying, "Dr. Freud, I hope now you'll be able to join us tonight . . . and I hope Eddie can come, too. The girls will just love him, I know. It will be quite a celebration; I can guarantee that for both of you."

Freud looked at Bernays, who shrugged in consent.

"Count us in, Wendy, my dear," Dr. Freud said as he left the room, imagining that he was looking up at his Inner Dummy and saying, What is the matter with you? What is your problem? Will you ever knock if off?

NOTE

1. *Pittsburgh Post-Gazette*, February 24, 1999, p. C7.

EPILOGUE

So what was Hugh Grant thinking when he decided to have oral sex with a prostitute in his car on a Los Angeles street?

Or what was Bill Clinton thinking when he decided to take that first sexual step with Monica Lewinsky?

Or Leona Helmsley when she decided to evade a relatively paltry sum in income taxes by deducting as a business expense the cost of furnishings for her own home?

Or Adolf Hitler when he decided to exterminate millions of Gypsies, Jews, Slavs, homosexuals, and the handicapped?

Or the leader of Heaven's Gate when he persuaded his group to commit suicide so that they could reach a new home behind the Hale-Bopp comet traveling by the earth?

Or the Pakastani father when he issued a death warrant for his own daughter when she ran away instead of marrying the man he had arranged for?

Or Bob Schwartz when he decided not to have a steak at a barbecue because he thought a chef might have dripped sweat on it and had a salad instead?

Or John McDonald when he grabbed my wrist as I was about to give ten dollars to a valet for a tip?

Or Ellen when she refused to eat food, even though her weight dropped to 82 pounds?

The answer would appear to be that they weren't thinking at all, that their power of reason was overwhelmed by emotional drives and feelings, headquartered in a metaphorical part of the brain labeled by Ted Croft's advertising agency as the *Inner Dummy*.

Ever since most of us can remember, we've been told by our parents and others who influence our lives that we must learn to manage our emotional feelings and drives. By the time we became adults, most of us had our emotional drives under some kind of control. While in our thoughts or fantasies, we might want to injure or have injured others who demean us, we'll fight the urge and give ourselves time for the feeling to pass. Or we'll fight the urge to steal things that aren't ours, or make sexual advances to a good friend's spouse, to whom we are intensely attracted. Keeping our temptations under control, we are told, is the mark of a mature adult.

We have been aware since the start of recorded history, at the least, that there are drives within our minds that may cause us to think or act irrationally. But we've been content to attribute them to such causes as the evil or demons within us, or to our dark side or simply to human nature or human frailties, to name a few, all of which have remained mystery-laden explanations, which we don't seem to question beyond Jay Leno's lament of "What were they thinking?"

And yet in the combined worlds of psychology and neural science we appear to have within our grasp a comprehensible explanation that all of us can sink our teeth into, academics and the common person alike. That explanation centers on the limbic system, the anatomical shorthand for those brain organs that control our emotional drives and feelings and that thrive on settings developed for that evolutionary period when we were living primitive lives in caves and on the savannahs, and that apparently haven't been modulated significantly for a modern civilization filled with the wonders of technology, scholarship, music, art, literature, invention, the law, and so forth. Our cerebral cortex, the napkin-sized brain section that apparently is the heart of our power of reason and creativity, appears to have grown right over the limbic brain, which we share with the primates.

Thus, for all intents and purposes, we have two basic mental operating systems in our brains, our power of reason or ego system and our limbic system, the latter of which appears to have its own agenda and can be impervious to reason.

The term *Inner Dummy* seems appropriate for this system of limbic brain organs because whether they reward us with feelings of joy, love, and happiness or punish us with feelings of depression, jealousy, and hate is more or less out of our rational control. Once that signaling device, which Daniel Goleman in his book *Emotional Intelligence*[1] called the *emotional sentinel*, communicates directly to the appropriate limbic organs what traumatic events are happening in front of us—a potential spouse standing there to whom we are becoming romantically attached, the final score showing we have won the championship, someone who is telling us our father just died, a boss telling us we are fired, an elevator accident in which we are involved, and so forth—our emotional response is practically automatic. *Autonomic* is the word used by neural scientists: "occurring involuntarily, relating to the autonomic nervous system."

Many of us aren't happy to hear this. We pride ourselves on being in control of our lives. But being in control of our emotional drives and feelings means for most of us not that we are capable of controlling them, but of masking them. They might be churning in our heads, driving us to lash out or be dejected, or whatever, but we manage to look calm and organized.

I recall reading the work of the Eastern philosopher J. Krishnamurti more than twenty years ago, discussing with my good friend Ronald Rattner, whose Hindu name, as I pointed out earlier, is Roseek, what Krishnamurti meant when he talked about the importance of the "observer" and the "observed" within our minds. Roseek and I would discuss our thoughts about what within our minds was the "observer" and what was the "observed," and I can't even remember what my opinion was.

It is obvious to me now, however, that the "observer" is the rational or ego side of minds that left uninhibited would allow us to think or act simply through the power of reason offered to us by the cerebral cortex that forms the outer layer of our brain. And that the "observed" is our id, our limbic system, our Inner Dummy that needs to be constantly observed if we are to manage it and keep it under control so that we can be judged to be within the wide parameters offered by the definition of normalcy. Our careers, for one thing, will not go very far if we are judged to be a "wacko," an "office nut," unless someone left us a lot of money or we have stupendous skills.

The important thing appears to be giving a label to these limbic brain organs so that we can separate them from the rest of the brain sections that operate our minds. If we mistakenly step on a sprinkler head hidden by high grass on our lawn and tear the ligaments in our knee, we go to a medical doctor who treats us and then prescribes hours of therapy for that knee.

There is nothing personally impugning about this experience. We readily tell our family and friends about the accident and the ongoing therapy. But this is not the case with another form of injury; for example, a traumatic failure to get a promotion we wanted intensely that went to one of our peers instead and which throws us into a clinical depression in which the experience of any pleasure can no longer be sensed. We may then consult a clinical psychiatrist or psychologist, but chances are we'll keep it a secret because most of the people in the world consider a clinical problem with their mind (for example, a depression) a weakness. Dr. Freud's concept of the id or Dr. LeDoux's concept of limbic organs that react separately from our power of reason haven't been well communicated to the public at large. So this system of limbic organs that may be vulnerable to specific traumas and that may act autonomously when they occur, creating an "injury" that is as biological as sprained knee ligaments, are not blamed for the problem. Rather our minds as a whole are and we are ridiculed for not having the strength of will to prevent the traumas from affecting us in the first place.

Some of us recall the 1972 presidential elections when Sen. Thomas F. Eagleton was selected as a running mate by George McGovern, the democratic candidate. When, during the campaign, it was discovered that Senator Eagleton was at one time treated for manic depression, he was dropped from the ticket in midcampaign in favor of R. Sargent Shriver Jr. The fact that Senator Eagleton claimed his treatment was successful and that he had an excellent record as a senator was brushed aside. Public perception appears to have improved only slightly since then.

But if Senator Eagleton could have communicated to a *more aware general public* the fact that doctors had confirmed some years ago that certain of his limbic organs and their biological connections were not functioning properly, causing manic and depressive periods, but that through therapy and medication the "injury" was treated successfully, there is the possibility that he might have been able to remain on the ticket.

I don't think he could have done as well if he said his Inner Dummy was injured, but has now been fixed. This term is for those among us who take a lighter view of the world.

Most of us have been aware for years that we have this Inner Dummy within us. When I would tell people that the title for the book I was completing was *Battling the Inner Dummy*, they would think for an instant and nod or in other ways signal their recognition of the concept. There is probably no one on the face of the earth who hasn't battled what we've called "our personal demons" from time to time. We've all had strange thoughts and fantasies, but fortunately most of us are capable of keeping them under control, of course with significant support from police forces, armies, and systems of justice.

We also have observed that some of us are "power hungry," or "control freaks," or "sex maniacs," or "possessive," or "fearless," or "sensitive," or "messianic," or "anal," or the opposite on the continuum of what those expressions describe—"meek," "insensitive," "paranoid," "ambivalent," "asexual," and so forth. But again, these characteristics have been ascribed to the outlooks of the mind as a whole, not to a section of it, an id, a limbic system or Inner Dummy, where attention can be focused and something can be done to change the intensity of the drives that appear to create those characteristics or to ameliorate the punishments they are capable of meting out if we are up for it.

We have also been aware of the lasting effects of intense traumas, and we know how difficult, if not impossible, it is to talk ourselves or others out of many of them. We know how important it is to rush counselors to a high school where killings have taken place. We have talked about the "scarring" of the mind, we understand the process in general, but again we don't attribute the effects to a specific section of our mind, but to a broad, amorphous concept of it.

Some cultures of the world have taken greater notice of the fact that some of us have ids or Inner Dummies that are much more sensitive or vulnerable to "scarring" than others. In some remote aboriginal tribes I've read about that have been studied during the past fifty years, there is no such thing as hazing of children, nor are there cliques allowed among the children, which is nothing more than a manifestation of the limbic drive for power or status. Nor are there caste systems. Nor is there such a passion for winning every contest, under the flawed concept that "winning is everything," another manifestation of the drive for power or status, which in the United States has taken on a life of its own. Nor are there many examples of continuing hatreds, with conflicts being mediated quickly by the chieftains and so children grow up without the urge to hate and kill, which in Oscar Hammerstein's lyric in the musical *South Pacific*, he wrote that "we have to be carefully taught." On the other hand, according to Jared Diamond in his book *The Third Chimpanzee*, there are tribes in New Guinea that will injure you or worse if you travel up a river they consider within their territory without asking permission.[2] So there are probably no perfect worlds.

An entire book or possibly a series of books could be written or adapted from existing works about how to behave ourselves so that the drives of our

Inner Dummy or those of others are not unduly provoked. How to enforce this behavior, once we are agreed on the causes, is another thing altogether. How do we reach the mothers and fathers who have been captured by their Inner Dummies to the point that they abuse their children, but are otherwise normal enough not to be thought dysfunctional? Or how do we keep potential leaders of governments like Joseph Stalin, Adolf Hitler, or Slobodan Milosevic out of power, when their limbic characteristics are such that they are undaunted in their drive to achieve power and killing others along the way up, sometimes in the millions, doesn't ruin a night's sleep? These are the big questions. But any start toward resolving them must begin with the recognition that we all carry around in our heads this primitive id, this limbic system, this Inner Dummy, that causes us most of our problems and troubles. It has long been said that to solve any problem, the recognition must come first. We can only hope that in the next hundred years or so, we will have it figured out and with any luck, a lot sooner.

And now my Inner Dummy is signaling me that it's time to stop writing.

NOTES

1. Daniel Goleman, *Emotional Intelligence* (New York: Bantam, 1995), p. 17.

2. Jared Diamond, *The Third Chimpanzee: The Evolution and Future of the Human Animal* (New York: HarperPerennial, 1992), p. 228.

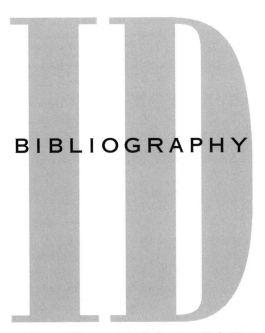

BIBLIOGRAPHY

Ackerman, Diane. *A Natural History of the Senses*. New York: Vintage Books, 1991.

Andreasen, Nancy C. *The Broken Brain: The Biological Revolution in Psychiatry*. New York: Harper & Row, 1984.

Ardrey, Robert. *The Territorial Imperative: A Personal Inquiry into the Animal Origins of Property and Nations*. New York: Kodansha International, 1996.

Barkow, Jerome H., Leda Cosmides, and John Tooby, eds. *The Adapted Mind: Evolutionary Psychology and the Generation of Culture*. Oxford: Oxford University Press, 1992.

Barret, Karen C. "A Functionalist Approach to Shame and Guilt." In *Self-Conscious Emotions*, ed. June P. Tangney and Kurt W. Fischer. New York: Guilford Press, 1995.

Beck, Aaron T., and Gary Emery with Ruth L. Greenberg. *Anxiety Disorders and Phobias: A Cognitive Perspective*. New York: BasicBooks, 1985.

Beck, Aaron T., et al. *Cognitive Therapy of Personality Disorders*. New York: Guilford Press, 1990.

Beck, Aaron T., and A. John Rush, with Brian F. Shaw and Gary Emery. *Cognitive Therapy of Depression*. New York: Guilford Press, 1979.

Beck, Judith S. *Cognitive Therapy: Basics and Beyond*. New York: Guilford Press, 1995.

Bednar, Richard L. *Self-Esteem: Paradoxes and Innovations in Clinical Theory and Practice*. Washington, D.C.: American Psychological Association, 1995.

Bemis, Judith, and Amr Barrada. *Embracing the Fear: Learning to Manage Anxiety and Panic Attacks.* Center City, Minn.: Hazelden, 1994.

Berger, Diane, and Lisa Berger. *We Heard the Angels of Madness: A Family Guide to Coping with Manic Depression.* New York: William Morrow and Company, 1991.

Bergin, Allen E., and Sol L. Garfield, eds. *Handbook of Psychotherapy and Behavior Change.* New York: Wiley, 1994.

Berkowitz, Leonard. "Frustration-Aggression Hypothesis: Examination and Reformulation." *Psychological Bulletin* 106, no. 1 (1989): 59–73.

Berne, Eric. *Games People Play: The Basic Handbook of Transactional Analysis.* New York: Ballantine, 1992.

———. *A Layman's Guide to Psychiatry and Psychoanalysis.* Middlesex, England: Penguin, 1968.

Blumenfeld, Larry, ed. *The Big Book of Relaxation.* Roslyn, N.Y.: Relaxation Co., 1994.

Bowlby, John. *Attachment.* New York: BasicBooks, 1982.

———. *Loss: Sadness and Depression.* New York: BasicBooks, 1980.

Brandan, Nathaniel. *The Art of Living Consciously: The Power of Awareness to Transform Everyday Life.* New York: Simon & Schuster, 1997.

Brodsky, Gary. *The Art of Getting Even.* Edison, N.J.: Castle Books, 1990.

Brooke, James. "Sect Disappears, Awaiting the Millennium." *New York Times,* November 22, 1998, sec. 1, p. 17.

Bruno, Frank J. *The Family Mental Health Encyclopedia.* New York: Wiley, 1991.

Buss, David M. "Evolutionary Personality Psychology." *Annual Review of Psychology.* (1991): 459–91.

Butler, Gillian, and Tony Hope. *Managing Your Mind: The Mental Fitness Guide.* Oxford: Oxford University Press, 1995.

Caplan, Paula J. *They Say You're Crazy: How the World's Most Powerful Psychiatrists Decide Who's Normal.* Reading, Mass.: Addison-Wesley, 1995.

Carter, Bill. *Letterman, Leno, and the Network Battle for the Night.* New York: Hyperion, 1994.

Catalono, Ellen M., and Nina Sonenberg. *Consuming Passions: Help for Compulsive Shoppers.* Oakland, Calif.: New Harbinger Publications, 1993.

Chang, Iris. *The Rape of Nanking: The Forgotten Holocaust of World War II.* New York: BasicBooks, 1997.

Changeux, Jean-Pierre. *Neuronal Man: The Biology of Man.* New York: Pantheon Books, 1995.

Chapman, A. H., and Miriam Chapman-Santana. *The Handbook of Problem-Oriented Psychotherapy.* Northvale, N.J.: Jason Aronson, Inc., 1997.

Chodorow, Joan. *Dance Therapy and Depth Psychology: The Moving Imagination.* New York: Rutledge, 1991.

Chopra, Deepak. *Ageless Body, Timeless Mind.* New York: Harmony Books, 1993.

Christie, Richard, and Florence L. Geis. *Studies in Machiavellianism.* New York: Academic Press, 1970.

Christopher, James. *SOS Sobriety: The Proven Alternative to 12-Step Programs.* Amherst, N.Y.: Prometheus Books, 1992.

Clarkson, Petruska, and Michael Pokorny, eds. *The Handbook of Psychotherapy.* London: Routledge, 1994.

Collins, Nancy L., and Stephen J. Read. "Adult Attachment, Working Models, and Relationship Quality in Dating Couples." *Journal of Personality and Social Psychology* 58, no. 4 (1990): 644–63.

Colwell, Shelley M. "Aromatherapy: Waiting to Inhale." *Soap/Cosmetics/Chemical Specialties* (December 1996): 35–39.

Cooper, Jack R., Floyd E. Bloom, and Robert H. Roth. *The Biochemical Basis of Neuropharmacology.* Oxford: Oxford University Press, 1991.

Corey, Gerald. *Theory and Practice of Counseling and Psychotherapy.* Pacific Grove, Calif.: Brooks/Cole Publishing Company, 1996.

Crenshaw, Theresa L. *The Alchemy of Love and Lust: Discovering Our Sex Hormones and How They Determine Who We Love, When We Love, and How Often We Love.* New York: G. P. Putman's Sons, 1996.

Crick, Francis H. C. *The Astonishing Hypothesis: The Scientific Search for the Soul.* New York: Macmillian, 1994.

Csikszentmihalyi, Mihaly. *Flow: The Psychology of Optimal Experience.* New York: HarperPerennial, 1990.

Cunningham, J. Barton. *The Stress Management Sourcebook.* Los Angeles: Lowell House, 1997.

Davis, Joel. *Mapping the Mind: The Secrets of the Human Brain and How It Works.* Secaucus, N.J.: Carol Publishing Group, 1997.

Davis, Kathy Diamond. *Therapy Dogs: Training Your Dog to Reach Others.* New York: Macmillan, 1992.

Dawkins, Richard. *The Selfish Gene.* Oxford: Oxford University Press, 1989.

Daws, Gavan. *Prisoners of the Japanese: POWs of World War II in the Pacific.* New York: William Morrow, 1994.

de Camp, Sprague L. *The Apeman Within.* Amherst, N.Y.: Prometheus Books, 1995.

de Waal, Frans. *Chimpanzee Politics: Power and Sex among Apes.* Baltimore, Md.: Johns Hopkins University Press, 1989.

Dennett, Daniel C. *Consciousness Explained.* Boston: Little Brown and Company, 1991.

Deutsch, Helene. *Neuroses and Character Types.* New York: International Universities Press, 1965.

Diamond, Jared. *The Third Chimpanzee: The Evolution and Future of the Human Animal.* New York: HarperPerennial, 1992.

Doctor, Ronald M., and Ada P. Kahn. *The Encyclopedia of Phobias, Fears, and Anxieties.* New York: Facts On File, 1989.

Durden-Smith, Jo, and Diane Desimone. *Sex and the Brain.* New York: Arbor House, 1983.

Dyson-Hudson, Rada, and Eric A. Smith. "Human Territoriality: An Ecological Reassessment." *American Anthropologist* (March 1978): 21–41.

Eagle, Morris N. *Recent Developments in Psychoanalysis: A Critical Evaluation.* Cambridge, Mass.: Harvard University Press, 1984.

Early, Emmett. *The Raven's Return: The Influence of Psychological Trauma on Individuals and Culture.* Wilmette, Ill.: Chiron Publications, 1993.

Ekman, Paul. "An Argument for Basic Emotions." *Cognition and Emotion* (March 1992): 169–200.

Elin, Nan, ed. *Architecture of Fear.* New York: Princeton Architectural Press, 1997.

Ellis, Albert, and Raymond C. Tafrate. *How to Control Your Anger Before It Controls You.* Secaucus, N.J.: Birch Lane Press, 1997.

Eysenck, Michael, ed. *Psychology: An Integrated Approach.* Essex, England: Addison-Wesley Longman, 1998.

Farley, Frank. "The Big T in Personality." *Psychology Today* (May 1986): 44–52.

Fenichel, Otto. *The Psychoanalytic Theory of Neurosis.* New York: Norton, 1972.

Ferris, Craig F., and Thomas Grisso, eds. *Understanding Aggressive Behavior in Children.* New York: New York Academy of Sciences, 1996.

Ferris, Paul. *Dr. Freud, A Life.* Washington, D.C.: Counterpoint, 1997.

Fogel, Alan, and Gail F. Melson, eds. *Origins of Nurturance.* Hillsdale, N.J.: Lawrence Erlbaum Associates, Inc., 1986.

Fortey, Richard. *Life: A Natural History of the First Four Billion Years of Life on Earth.* New York: Knopf, 1997.

Forward, Susan. *Emotional Blackmail: When the People in Your Life Use Fear, Obligation, and Guilt to Manipulate You.* New York: HarperCollins, 1997.

Fossey, Dian. *Gorillas in the Mist.* Boston: Houghton Mifflin, 1983.

Frances, Allen. *Diagnostic and Statistical Manual of Mental Disorders: DSM-IV.* Washington, D.C.: American Psychiatric Association, 1994.

Freedland, Michael. *Jolson: The Story of Al Jolson.* London: Virgin Books, 1995.

Freud, Sigmund. *Introductory Lectures on Psycho-Analysis.* New York: Norton, 1935.

———. *The Problem of Anxiety.* New York: Norton, 1936.

———. "Instincts and Their Vicissitudes." In *Sigmund Freud, Collected Papers,* vol. 4. Edited by Ernest Jones. New York: BasicBooks, 1959.

———. "Repression." Ernest Jones, ed. In *Sigmund Freud, Collected Papers,* vol. 4. Edited by Ernest Jones. New York: BasicBooks, 1959.

———. "On Narcissm: An Introduction." In *Sigmund Freud, Collected Papers,* vol. 4. Edited by Ernest Jones. New York: BasicBooks, 1959.

———. *The Ego and the Id.* New York: Norton, 1960.

———. *Jokes and Their Relation to the Unconscious.* New York: Norton, 1960.

———. *The Psychopathology of Everyday Life.* New York: Norton, 1985.

Fulker, David W., and Sybil B. G. Eysenck. "A Genetic and Environmental Analysis of Sensation Seeking." *Journal of Research in Personality* 14 (1980): 261–81.

Furedi, Frank. *Culture of Fear: Risk-Taking and the Morality of Low Expectation.* London: Wellington House, 1997.

Gay, Peter, ed. *The Freud Reader.* New York: Norton, 1989.

Glick, Robert A., and Stanley Bone, eds. *Pleasure Beyond the Pleasure Principle: The Role of Affect in Motivation, Development, and Adaptation.* New Haven, Conn.: Yale University Press, 1990.

Goldfried, Melvin R., and Gerald C. Davison. *Clinical Behavior Therapy.* New York: Wiley, 1994.

Goleman, Daniel. *Emotional Intelligence.* New York: Bantam, 1995.

Goodall, Jane. *In the Shadow of Man.* Boston: Houghton Mifflin, 1988.

————. *Through a Window: My Thirty Years with the Chimpanzees of Gombe.* Boston: Houghton Mifflin, 1990.

Greenfield, Susan A. *The Human Brain.* New York: BasicBooks, 1997.

Gregory, Richard L., ed. *The Oxford Companion to the Mind.* Oxford: Oxford University Press, 1987.

Griffiths, Paul E. *What Emotions Really Are: The Problem of Psychological Categories.* Chicago: University of Chicago Press, 1997.

Hall, Doug, with David Wecker. *Making the Courage Connection: Finding the Courage to Journey from Fear to Freedom.* New York: Simon & Schuster, 1997.

Hamer, Dean, and Peter Copeland. *Living with Our Genes: Why They Matter More Than You Think.* New York: Doubleday, 1998.

Harris, Judith R. *The Nurture Assumption: Why Children Turn Out the Way They Do.* New York: Simon & Schuster, 1998.

Hawking, Stephen W. *A Brief History of Time: From the Big Bang to Black Holes.* New York: Bantam, 1988.

Hawton, Keith, et al., eds. *Cognitive Behaviour Therapy for Psychiatric Problems: A Practical Guide.* Oxford: Oxford University Press, 1989.

Hayduke, George. *Make 'Em Pay.* Secaucus, N.J.: Carol Publishing Group, 1986.

Hazan, Cindy, and Phillip Shaver. "Romantic Love Conceptualized as an Attachment Process." *Journal of Personality and Social Psychology* 52, no. 3 (1987): 511–24.

Hellman, Hal. *Great Feuds in Science: Ten of the Liveliest Disputes Ever.* New York: Wiley, 1988.

Herman, Judith L. *Trauma and Recovery: The Aftermath of Violence from Domestic Abuse to Political Terror.* New York: BasicBooks, 1992.

Herrnstein, Richard J., and Charles Murray. *The Bell Curve: Intelligence and Class Structure in American Life.* New York: Simon & Schuster, 1994.

Hicks, Robert M. *Trauma: The Pain That Stays.* Grand Rapids, Mich.: Baker Book House, 1993.

Holmes, David S. *Abnormal Psychology.* New York: Longman, 1997.

Holmes, Jeremy. *John Bowlby and Attachment Theory.* London: Routledge, 1993.

Holy, Ladislav. *Anthropological Perspectives on Kinship.* London: Pluto Press, 1996.

Horgan, John. "Can Science Explain Consciousness?" *Scientific American* (July 1994): 88–98.

Horney, Karen. *Our Inner Conflicts: A Constructive Theory of Neurosis*. New York: W. W. Norton, 1945.

———. *Neurosis and Human Growth: The Struggle Toward Self-Realization*. New York: Norton, 1950.

———. *The Neurotic Personality of Our Time*. New York: Norton, 1937.

Hunt, Morton. *The Story of Psychology*. New York: Doubleday, 1993.

Hymowitz, Carol. "High Anxiety: In the Name of Freud, Why Are Psychiatrists Complaining So Much?" *Wall Street Journal*, December 21, 1995, p. A1.

Izard, Carroll E., Jerome Kagan, and Robert B. Zajonc. *Emotions, Cognition, and Behavior*. Cambridge: Cambridge University Press, 1984.

James, John W., and Frank Cherry. *The Grief Recovery Handbook: A Step-by-Step Program for Moving Beyond Loss*. New York: HarperPerennial, 1988.

Janda, Louis. *The Psychologist's Book of Self-Tests*. New York: Perigree, 1996.

Kalschel, Donald. *The Inner World of Trauma: Archetypal Defenses of the Personal Spirit*. London: Routledge, 1996.

Kanfer, Frederick H., and Arnold P. Goldstein, eds. *Helping People Change: A Textbook of Methods*. New York: Pergamon Press, 1991.

Kaplan, Harold I., and Benjamin J. Sadock. *Comprehensive Textbook of Psychiatry/IV*. Baltimore, Md.: Williams & Wilkins, 1985.

Kaplan, Helen S. *The Sexual Desire Disorders: Dysfunctional Regulation of Sexual Motivation*. Bristol, Pa.: Brunner/Mazel, 1995.

Katselas, Milton. *Dreams into Action: Getting What You Want*. Beverly Hills, Calif.: Dove Books, 1996.

Kennerly, Helen. *Overcoming Anxiety: A Self-Help Guiding Using Cognitive Behavioral Techniques*. Washington Square, N.Y.: New York University Press, 1997.

Keyes, Ken, Jr. *Handbook to Higher Consciousness*. Coos Bay, Ore.: Love Line Books, 1975.

Kingdon, David C., and Douglas Turkington. *Cognitive-Behavioral Therapy of Schizophrenia*. New York: Guilford Press, 1994.

Klaus, Marshall H., John H. Kennell, and Phyllis H. Klaus. *Bonding: Building the Foundations of Secure Attachment and Independence*. Reading, Mass.: Addison-Wesley, 1995.

Kolb, Bryan, and Ian Q. Whishaw. *Fundamentals of Human Neuropsychology*. New York: W. H. Freeman and Company, 1996.

Koopmans, Judith R., et al. "A Multivariate Genetic Analysis of Sensation Seeking." *Behavior Genetics* 25, no. 4 (1995): 349–56.

Kotulak, Ronald. *Inside the Brain: Revolutionary Discoveries of How the Mind Works*. Kansas City, Mo.: Andrews and McMeel, 1996.

Kroll, Jerome. *The Challenge of the Borderline Patient: Competency in Diagnosis and Treatment*. New York: Norton, 1988.

Lane, David A., and Andrew Miller, eds. *Child and Adolescent Therapy: A Handbook.* Buckingham, England: Open University Press, 1992.

Larson, Ruth. "New Hope for Mentally Ill." *Insight on the News* (September 7, 1998): 43.

LeDoux, Joseph E. *The Emotional Brain: The Mysterious Underpinnings of Emotional Life.* New York: Simon & Schuster, 1996.

Lee, Thomas F. *The Human Genome Project: Cracking the Genetic Code of Life.* New York: Plenum Press, 1991.

Levinson, Harold N., with Steven Carter. *Phobia Free.* New York: M. Evans and Company, 1986.

Levy, Steven. "Dr. Edelman's Brain." *The New Yorker*, (May 2, 1994): 62–73.

Lewis, Dorothy O. *Guilty by Reason of Insanity: A Psychiatrist Explores the Minds of Killers.* New York: Ballantine, 1998.

Lewis, Michael, and Jeanette M. Haviland, eds. *Handbook of Emotions.* New York: Guilford Press, 1993.

Lichtenberg, Ronna, with Gene Stone. *Work Would Be Great If It Weren't for the People: Ronna and Her Evil Twin's Guide to Making Office Politics Work for You.* New York: Hyperion, 1998.

Lickey, Marvin E., and Barbara Gordon. *Medicine and Mental Illness.* New York: Freeman, 1991.

Linehan, Marsha M. *Cognitive-Behavioral Treatment of Borderline Personality Disorder.* New York: Guilford Press, 1993.

Lingerman, Hal A. *The Healing Energies of Music.* Wheaton, Ill.: Quest Books, 1995.

Luft, Lorna. *Me and My Shadows.* New York: Pocket Books, 1998.

Luria, A. R. *The Working Brain: An Introduction to Neuropsychology.* New York: BasicBooks, 1973.

MacLean, Paul. *A Triune Concepts of the Brain and Behavior.* Toronto: University of Toronto Press, 1973.

Madden, John, with Dave Anderson. *One Size Doesn't Fit All.* New York: Jove Books, 1988.

Makover, Richard B. *Treatment Planning for Psychotherapists.* Washington, D.C.: American Psychiatric Press, 1996.

Malchiodi, Cathy A. *The Art Therapy Sourcebook: Art Making for Personal Growth.* Lincolnwood, Ill.: Lowell House, 1998.

Manderson, Lenore, and Margaret Jolly. *Sites of Desire, Economies of Pleasure: Sexualities in Asia and the Pacific.* Chicago: University of Chicago Press, 1997.

Maples, William R., with Michael Browning. *Dead Men Do Tell Tales: The Strange and Fascinating Cases of a Forensic Anthropologist.* Pittstown, N.J.: Main Street Books, 1995.

Marris, Peter. *The Politics of Uncertainty: Attachment in Private and Public Life.* London: Routledge, 1996.

Maslow, Abraham, with Heil Gary and Deborah C. Stephens. *Maslow on Management.* New York: Wiley, 1998.

Masson, Jeffrey M. *Dogs Never Lie About Love: Reflections on the Emotional World of Dogs.* New York: Crown Publishers, 1997.

Masters, John C., et al. *Behavior Therapy: Techniques and Empirical Findings.* New York: Harcourt Brace Jovanovich College Publishers, 1987.

McMullin, Rian E. *Handbook of Cognitive Therapy Techniques.* New York: Norton, 1986.

Meloy, J. Reid. *Violent Attachments.* Northvale, N.J.: Jason Aronson, Inc., 1997.

Miller, Michael W. "Creating a Buzz: With Remedy in Hand, Drug Firms Get Ready to Popularize an Illness." *Wall Street Journal,* April 25, 1994, p. A1.

Miller, William I. *The Anatomy of Disgust.* Cambridge, Mass.: Harvard University Press, 1997.

Montgomery, Sy. *Walking with the Great Apes: Jane Goodall, Dian Fossey, Biruté Galdikas.* Boston: Houghton Mifflin, 1991.

Mooney, Al J., Arlene Eisenberg, and Howard Eisenberg. *The Recovery Book.* New York: Workman Publishing, 1992.

Morris, Desmond. *The Human Zoo: A Zoologist's Classic Study of the Urban Animal.* New York: Kodansha International, 1996.

Morrison, James. *DSM-IV Made Easy: The Clinician's Guide to Diagnosis.* New York: Guilford Press, 1995.

Musson, Paul H., John J. Gonger, and Jerome Kagen. *Child Development and Personality.* New York: Harper & Row, 1974.

Nakken, Craig. *The Addictive Personality: Understanding the Addictive Process and Compulsive Behavior.* Center City, Minn.: Hazelden Publishing, 1988.

Nesse, Randolph M. "Evolutionary Explanations of Emotions." *Human Nature* 1, no. 3 (1990): 261–89.

Nicholson, Nigel. "How Hardwired Is Human Behavior?" *Harvard Business Review* (July–August 1998): 135–47.

O'Donohue, William, and Leonard Krasner, eds. *Theories of Behavior Therapy: Exploring Behavior Change.* Washington, D.C.: American Psychological Association, 1995.

Ortony, Andrew, and Terence J. Turner. "What's Basic about Basic Emotions?" *Psychological Review* 97, no. 3 (1990): 315–31.

Osborn, Ian. *Tormenting Thoughts and Secret Rituals: The Hidden Epidemic of Obsessive-Compulsive Disorder.* New York: Pantheon Books, 1998.

Othmer, Ekkehard, and Sieglinde C. Othmer. *The Clinical Interview Using DSM-IV.* Vol. 2. *The Difficult Patient.* Washington, D.C.: American Psychiatric Press, 1994.

Pardeck, John T. *Using Bibliotherapy in Clinical Practice: A Guide to Self-help Books.* Westport, Conn.: Greenwood Press, 1993.

Peale, Norman V. *The Power of Positive Thinking.* New York: Fawcett Crest, 1956.

Pearce, John Ed. *Days of Darkness: The Feuds of Eastern Kentucky.* Lexington: University of Kentucky Press, 1994.

Penrose, Roger. *Shadows of the Mind: A Search for the Missing Science of Consciousness.* Oxford: Oxford University Press, 1994.

Pert, Candice B. *Molecules of Emotion: Why You Feel The Way You Feel.* New York: Scribner, 1997.

Pervin, Lawrence A., ed. *Handbook of Personality Theory and Research.* New York: Guilford Press, 1990.

―――. *Overcoming Anxiety: From Short-term Fixes to Long-term Recovery.* New York: Holt, 1997.

Peurifoy, Reneau Z. *Anxiety, Phobias, and Panic: A Step-by-Step Program for Regaining Control of Your Life.* New York: Warner Books, 1995.

Piercy, Fred P., et al. *Family Therapy Sourcebook.* New York: Guilford Press, 1996.

Pinker, Steven. *How the Mind Works.* New York: Norton, 1997.

Plaud, Joseph J., and George H. Eifert, eds. *From Behavior Theory to Behavior Therapy.* Boston: Allyn and Bacon, 1998.

Plomin, Robert. *Nature and Nurture: An Introduction to Behavioral Genetics.* Belmont, Calif.: Brooks/Cole, 1990.

Plomin, Robert, et al. *Behavioral Genetics.* New York: W. H. Freeman, 1997.

Pollock, Ellen J. "Side Effects: Managed Care's Focus on Psychiatric Drugs Alarms Many Doctors." *Wall Street Journal,* December 1, 1995, p. A1.

Polster, Erving, and Miriam Polster. *Gestalt Therapy Integrated.* New York: Vintage Books, 1978.

Ponton, Lynn E. *The Romance of Risk: Why Teenagers Do the Things They Do.* New York: BasicBooks, 1997.

Pratto, Felicia, et al. "Social Dominance Orientation: A Personality Variable Predicting Social and Political Attitudes." *Journal of Personality and Social Psychology* 67, no. 4 (1994): 741–63.

Pressman, Steven. *Outrageous Betrayal: The Dark Journey of Werner Erhard from EST to Exile.* New York: St. Martin's Press, 1993.

Rachman, S., ed. *The Best of Behavior Research and Therapy.* Tarrytown, N.Y.: Pergamon, 1997.

Ramachandran, V. S., and Sandra Blakeslee. *Phantoms in the Brain: Probing the Mysteries of the Human Mind.* New York: Morrow, 1998.

Randall, Peter. *Adult Bullying: Perpetrators and Victims.* London: Routledge, 1997.

Restak, Richard M. *The Brain the Last Frontier.* New York: Warner Books, 1979.

―――. *The Mind.* New York: Bantam Books, 1988.

―――. *Receptors.* New York: Bantam Books, 1993.

―――. *The Modular Brain.* New York: Scribner, 1994.

Retzinger, Suzanne M. *Violent Emotions: Shame and Rage in Marital Quarrels.* Newbury Park, Calif.: Sage Publications, 1991.

Ridley, Matt. *The Origins of Virtue: Human Instincts and the Evolution of Cooperation.* New York: Penguin, 1997.

Robbins, Anthony. *Awaken the Giant Within: How to Take Immediate Control of Your Mental, Emotional, Physical, and Financial Destiny.* New York: Fireside, 1991.

Roberts, Francine M. *The Therapy Sourcebook.* Los Angeles: Lowell House, 1998.

Roberts, Monty. *The Man Who Listens to Horses.* New York: Random House, 1996.

Roose, Steven P., and Robert A. Glick, eds. *Anxiety as Symptom Signal.* Hillsdale, N.J.: Analytic Press, 1995.

Rosenbaum, Joshua. "Talk Therapy: Ready for the Trash Heap?" *American Health* 13, no. 8, Pages 60–65.

Ross, Jerilyn. *Triumph Over Fear.* New York: Bantam, 1994.

Ruback, Barry R., and Daniel Juieng. "Territorial Defense in Parking Lots: Retaliation Against Waiting Drivers." *Journal of Applied Social Psychology* 27, no. 9 (1997): 821–34.

Russell, Peter. *The Brain Book.* New York: Penguin, 1979.

Sabini, John. *Social Psychology.* New York: Norton, 1995.

Sagan, Carl, and Ann Druyan. *Shadows of Forgotten Ancestors.* New York: Ballantine, 1992.

Samerow, Stanton. *Inside the Criminal Mind.* New York: Times Books, 1984.

Sanday, Peggy R. *Female Power and Male Dominance: On the Origins of Sexual Inequality.* Cambridge: Cambridge University Press, 1981.

Selye, Hans. *The Stress of Life.* New York: McGraw-Hill, 1956.

Service, Elman R. *Profiles in Ethnology.* New York: HarperCollins, 1998.

Shane, Morton, Estelle Shane, and Mary Gales. *Intimate Attachments: Toward a New Self-Psychology.* New York: Guilford Press, 1997.

Sheffield, Anne. *How You Can Survive When They're Depressed: Living and Coping with Depression Fallout.* New York: Harmony, 1998.

Shorter, Edward. "How Prozac Slew Freud." *American Heritage* (September 1998): 42–48.

Shubentsov, Yefim, and Barbara Gordon. *Cure Your Cravings.* New York: Putnam, 1998.

Siever, Larry J., with William Frucht. *The New View of Self: How Genes and Neurotransmitters Shape Your Mind, Personality, and Your Mental Health.* New York: Macmillan, 1997.

Simmons, Steve M., and John C. Simmons Jr. *Measuring Emotional Intelligence.* Arlington, Tex.: Summit Publishing Group, 1997.

Simpson, Jeffry A., and W. Steven Rholes, eds. *Attachment Theory and Close Relationships.* New York: Guilford Press, 1998.

Snitow, Ann, Christein Stansell, and Sharon Thompson. *Powers of Desire: The Politics of Sexuality.* New York: Monthly Review Press, 1983.

Somers, Suzanne. *After the Fall.* New York: Crown Publishers, 1998.

Sperling, Michael B., and William H. Berman, eds. *Attachment in Adults: Clinical and Developmental Perspectives*. New York: Guilford Press, 1994.

Spitzer, Robert L., et al. *DSM-IV Case Book: A Learning Companion to the Diagnostic and Statistical Manual of Mental Disorders*. Washington, D.C.: American Psychiatric Press, Inc., 1994.

Springer, Sally L., and George Deutsch. *Left Brain, Right Brain: Perspectives from Cognitive Neuroscience*. New York: W. H. Freeman, 1998.

Stafford-Clark, David. *What Freud Really Said*. New York: Schocken Books, 1965.

Stanley, Jacqueline D. *Reading to Heal: How to Use Bibliotherapy to Improve Your Life*. New York: Element, 1999.

Stark, Martha. *Working with Resistance*. Northvale, N.J.: Jason Aronson, 1994.

Steen, R. Grant. *DNA and Destiny: Nature and Nurture in Human Behavior*. New York: Plenum Press, 1996.

Stevens, Anthony, and John Price. *Evolutionary Psychiatry: A New Beginning*. London: Routledge, 1996.

Stosny, Steven. *Treating Attachment Abuse: A Compassionate Approach*. New York: Springer, 1995.

Strum, Shirley C. *Almost Human: A Journey into the World of Baboons*. New York: Norton, 1987.

Sutcliffe, Jenny. *The Complete Book of Relaxation Techniques*. Allentown, Pa.: Quarto, 1991.

Szasz, Thomas S. *Pain and Pleasure: A Study of Bodily Feelings*. Syracuse, N.Y.: Syracuse University Press, 1988.

Talbot, Michael. *The Holligraphic Universe*. New York: HarperPerennial, 1991.

Taylor, Ralph B., and Joseph C. Lanni. "Territorial Dominance: The Influence of the Resident Advantage in Traduce Decision Making." *Journal of Personality and Social Psychology* 41, no. 5 (1981): 909–15.

Tedeschi, Richard G., and Lawrence G. Calhoun. *Trauma and Transformation: Growing in the Aftermath of Suffering*. Thousand Oaks, Calif.: Sage Publications, 1985.

Temple, Christine. *The Brain: An Introduction to the Psychology of the Human Brain and Behavior*. New York: Penguin, 1993.

Terr, Lenore. *Unchained Memories: True Stories of Traumatic Memories, Lost and Found*. New York: BasicBooks, 1994.

Thorpe, Geoffrey L., and Sheryl L. Olson. *Behavior Therapy: Concepts, Procedures, and Applications*. Boston: Allyn and Bacon, 1997.

Twerski, Abraham J. *Addictive Thinking: Understanding Self-Deception*. Center City, Minn.: Hazelden Publishing, 1997.

Tye, Larry. *The Father of Spin: Edward L. Bernays and the Birth of Public Relations*. New York: Random House, 1998.

Valenstein, Elliot S. *Blaming the Brain: The Truth about Drugs and Mental Health*. New York: Free Press, 1998.

Verma, Santosh K., and Shekhar Rao. "Recent Trends in Clinical Psychological Intervention (Methods Based on Other Than Behavior Therapy)." *Nimhans Journal* 14, no. 4 (1996): 307–14.

Wachtel, Paul L., and Stanley B. Messer, eds. *Theories of Psychotherapy: Origins and Evolution.* Washington, D.C.: American Psychological Association, 1997.

Wachtler, Sol. *After the Madness: A Judge's Own Prison Memoir.* New York: Random House, 1997.

Wade, Nicholas. "To Err Really Is Human, DNA Analysis Shows." *New York Times,* January 28, 1999, p. A22.

Weiner, David L. *Brain Tricks: How to Cope with the Dark Side of Your Brain and Win the Ultimate Mind Game.* Amherst, N.Y.: Prometheus Books, 1993.

Wenning, Kenneth. *Winning Cooperation from Your Child: A Comprehensive Method to Stop Defiant and Aggressive Behavior in Children.* Northvale, N.J.: Jason Aronson, Inc., 1996.

Whybrow, Peter C. *A Mood Apart: The Thinker's Guide to Emotion and Its Disorders.* New York: HarperPerennial, 1997.

Wilson, Edward O. *On Human Nature.* Cambridge, Mass.: Harvard University Press, 1978.

———. *Sociobiology.* Cambridge, Mass.: Belknap Press of Harvard University Press, 1980.

———. *Consilience: The Unity of Knowledge.* New York: Knopf, 1998.

Wright, Lawrence. *Twins: And What They Tell Us About Who We Are.* New York: Wiley, 1997.

Wright, Robert. *The Moral Animal: The New Science of Evolutionary Psychology.* New York: Pantheon, 1994.

Wright, William. *Born That Way: Genes, Behavior, Personality.* New York: Knopf, 1998.

Yalom, Irvin D. *Existential Psychotherapy.* New York: BasicBooks, 1980.

Yunker, Teresa. "Yard Rage: Protecting Your Turf Is a Basic Instinct, but It's Best to Try Friendly Persuasion when Tempers Flare over Real or Imagined Space Violations." *Los Angeles Times,* March 1, 1998, Part K, p. 1.

Zimbardo, Philip G. *Shyness: What It Is, What to Do About It.* Reading, Mass.: Addison-Wesley Publishing, 1977.

Zuckerman, Marvin, Monte S. Buchsbaum, and Dennis L. Murphy. "Sensation Seeking and Its Biological Correlates." *Psychological Bulletin* 88, no. 1 (1980): 187–214.

INDEX

David L. Weiner (left) is a "late blooming" (as he puts it) popular psychology writer. His previous book was *Brain Tricks: Coping with Your Defective Brain* (Prometheus Books). He has also been a top business consultant for four decades, dealing with business personnel at all levels, including CEOs, who have wrestled with their Inner Dummies.

Gilbert M. Hefter, M.D. (right), is Associate Professor of Clinical Psychiatry at Northwestern University Medical School. He is on the medical staff and is a former Director of Clinical Services of the Department of Psychiatry at Northwestern Memorial Hospital in Chicago. He is a practicing clinical psychiatrist.